THE REVOLUTIONARY PHILOSOPHY OF MARXISM

Selected Writings on Dialectical Materialism

NEW YORK

THE REVOLUTIONARY PHILOSOPHY OF MARXISM
Selected Writings on Dialectical Materialism

WR Books, 2018
Second Printing, 2021
Copyright © WR Books. All rights reserved.

Edited by John Peterson
Introduction by Alan Woods
Proofread by Steve Iverson
Layout by Antonio Balmer
Cover design by Mark Rahman and Laura Brown

United States distribution:
WR Books
PO Box 1575
New York, NY 10013

Email: sales@marxistbooks.com
marxistbooks.com

United Kingdom distribution:
Wellred Books
PO Box 50525
London
E14 6WG

Email: contact@socialist.net
wellredbooks.net

ISBN 978 1 900007 97 9

Πάντα ῥεῖ
[Everything flows]

δὶς ἐς τὸν αὐτὸν ποταμὸν οὐκ ἂν ἐμβαίης
[You cannot step in the same river twice]

—Heraclitus
c. 535–c. 475 BCE

सब्बे संखारा अनिच्चा
[All phenomena are impermanent]

—Siddhārtha Gautama,
c. 563/480–c. 483/400 BCE

Marx and I were pretty well the only people to rescue conscious dialectics from German idealist philosophy and apply it in the materialist conception of nature and history.

—Friedrich Engels, *Anti-Dühring*, 1877

Without revolutionary theory, there can be no revolutionary movement. This idea cannot be insisted upon too strongly at a time when the fashionable preaching of opportunism goes hand in hand with an infatuation for the narrowest forms of practical activity.

—V.I. Lenin, *What Is to Be Done?* 1902

For forty-three years of my conscious life I have remained a revolutionist; for forty-two of them I have fought under the banner of Marxism. If I had to begin all over again I would of course try and avoid this or that mistake, but the main course of my life would remain unchanged. I shall die a proletarian revolutionist, a Marxist, a dialectical materialist, and, consequently, an irreconcilable atheist. My faith in the communist future of mankind is not less ardent, indeed it is firmer today, than it was in the days of my youth.

Natasha has just come up to the window from the courtyard and opened it wider so that the air may enter more freely into my room. I can see the bright green strip of grass beneath the wall, and the clear blue sky above the wall, and sunlight everywhere. Life is beautiful. Let the future generations cleanse it of all evil, oppression, and violence and enjoy it to the full.

—Leon Trotsky's Testament, February 27, 1940

CONTENTS

EDITOR'S FOREWORD

O N THE BICENTENNIAL OF HIS BIRTH, Karl Marx's ideas are more relevant than ever. While he is perhaps best known for his writings on economics and history, his philosophical method runs like Ariadne's thread through all of his work. Anyone who wishes to have a fully rounded understanding of Marxism must strive to master his dialectical materialist method, which itself developed out of an assiduous study and critique of Hegelian dialectics.

Marxist theory represents the synthesized experience, historical memory, and guide to action of the working class in its struggle against capitalist exploitation and oppression. Without revolutionary theory, Marxists would be as helpless as sailors without a compass on a tempestuous sea. Without the "magnetic North" of theory to keep us on course, it is all too easy to drift into opportunist reformism or ultraleft isolation from the masses—or to sink altogether.

At every decisive turning point in history, scientific socialists must go back to basics. Without the fundamentals, it would be impossible to make sense of the chaotic political, economic, and social currents swirling around us. New combinations of contradictions emerge on a daily basis as capitalism teeters on the brink. But at root, the basic functioning of the system is the same as when Marx, Engels, Lenin, Luxemburg, and Trotsky were alive. A deep dive into their writings is the surest way to stay oriented. It is not an exaggeration to say that all the methodological tools we need to understand today's world can be found in the writings of these great fighters for the working class. However, one will not find "answers" in their words, in the way one can "Google" this or that fact. The task of today's Marxists is to study and absorb their *method* and to apply it to the living struggles of today.

After the fall of the Soviet Union, socialism and Marxism were written off and the "end of history" declared. But the "mole of history," burrowing beneath the surface, has not yet finished with capitalism, and the contradictions of the system have led inevitably to a resurgence of mass struggle—and renewed interest in socialism. The 2008 crisis—which in turn led to the meteoric rise of Sanders and Trump's election—was a key turning point. After the events of the last ten years, millions of Americans now self-identify as socialists. But there is socialism and socialism. The liberals and reformists seek to limit it to small, gradual reforms within capitalist limits. They have no confidence in the working class and believe that capitalism cannot be overthrown. Therefore, they argue, socialist revolution in our lifetime is a pipe dream.

But for Marxists, genuine socialism is not an unrealizable impossibility, it is an objectively attainable historical necessity if humanity is to survive into the next century. For us, socialism is the transitional phase between capitalism and communism, the period after the working class wins political and economic power and proceeds to dismantle capitalism's state apparatus and exploitative relations of production. This is the perspective that inspired Marx and which inspires us today.

Willingness to sacrifice and enthusiasm to throw oneself into the thick of the class struggle are essential. But the desire to "do something" in the abstract is not enough to defeat our class enemy. We need to think carefully about what it is we need to do, maximize the use of our finite energy and resources, and connect our short-term efforts with our long-term goals. To achieve this, the working class needs a mass revolutionary party, and that party must be armed with Marxist ideas. To build such a party, we must first build a revolutionary cadre organization with the understanding that, under the right conditions, an organization of a few hundred can grow into hundreds of thousands virtually overnight. As Hegel and Marx would have put it, we must be confident that quality can be transformed into quantity. And our confidence flows from the fact that nature and history provide countless examples of precisely this.

If we are to take on and defeat the centralized power of the capitalists and their state, we need the clear ideas, bold perspectives, and democratic, yet disciplined organizational methods that flow from Marxist theory. Likewise, if we are to tackle the reactionary postmodernist ideology of the bourgeois and petty bourgeois, who seek to derail us into the swamp of class collaboration, confusion, and reformism, we need Marxist theory.

And Marxist theory starts with the philosophy of Marxism: dialectical materialism.

Dialectical materialism is not a philosophical invention, but a mode of thinking that approximates—as closely as possible, given the limitations of our sense organs—the real, objective, and infinite process of movement, change, and development in the world around us, which exists whether or not we are there to observe it. It does not suffice merely to be a materialist or to be a dialectician. Some of the greatest thinkers of the past were materialists, and others were dialecticians. However, Marx was the first to understand the essential unity of both of these aspects of reality, which, as Trotsky explained, "gives to concepts, by means of closer approximations, corrections, concretizations, a richness of content and flexibility; I would even say a succulence which to a certain extent brings them close to living phenomena."

By embracing contradiction, polarization, and change instead of rejecting or attempting to write them out of reality, dialectical materialism allows us to approach processes as they are, not as we would like them to be. It allows us to understand, draw out, and explain the essential class interests in any situation. Without this, it would be impossible to get the right balance on questions such as the permanent revolution, imperialism, the national question, oppression, fascism, the dynamics of revolution and counterrevolution, and much more.

As Alan Woods explains in his exemplary and easy-to-understand introduction to this volume, one must make a concerted effort to learn to think dialectically. Although "nature is the proof of dialectics," as Engels explained, dialectical thinking does not come naturally. This is particularly true in the United States, where "practical common sense," "git 'er done!" pragmatic empiricism, and religious-spiritual superstition have penetrated deeply into the psychology of the masses. These pressures and prejudices—which surround us from the cradle to the grave—must be consciously combatted.

Trotsky understood this feature of the American psyche as well. Before his death, he had great hopes for the Socialist Workers Party. Here was a growing section of the Fourth International in a country of millions in the throes of the Great Depression with a second world war on the horizon. Colossal class battles were being waged in the US with city-wide general strikes, factory occupations, and the rise of the Congress of Industrial Organizations. The US section had a decisive role to play in the worldwide struggle against Stalinism and fascism and Trotsky was anxious to ensure its comrades had a firm grounding in Marxist theory. SWP member George Novack recounted his first discussion with Trotsky upon his arrival in Mexico on January 10, 1937, in his book, *Understanding History*:

> Our conversation was animated; there was so much to tell, especially about developments around the Moscow trials. (This was in the interval between the first and second of Stalin's stage-managed judicial frame-ups.) At one point Trotsky asked about the philosopher John Dewey, who had joined the American committee set up to obtain asylum for him and hear his case.
>
> From there, our discussion glided into the subject of philosophy, in which, he was informed, I had a special interest. We talked about the best ways of studying dialectical materialism, about Lenin's *Materialism and Empiriocriticism*, and about the theoretical backwardness of American radicalism. Trotsky brought forward the name of Max Eastman, who in various works had polemicized against dialectics as a worthless idealist hangover from the Hegelian heritage of Marxism.
>
> He became tense, agitated. "Upon going back to the States," he urged, "you comrades must at once take up the struggle against [Max] Eastman's distortion and repudiation of dialectical materialism. There is nothing more important than this. Pragmatism, empiricism, is the greatest curse of American thought. You must inoculate younger comrades against its infection."
>
> I was somewhat surprised at the vehemence of his argumentation on this matter at such a moment. As the principal defendant in absentia in the Moscow trials, and because of the dramatic circumstances of his voyage in exile, Trotsky then stood in the center of international attention. He was fighting for his reputation, liberty, and life against the powerful government of Stalin, bent on his defamation and death. After having been imprisoned and gagged for months by the Norwegian authorities, he had been kept incommunicado for weeks aboard their tanker.
>
> Yet on the first day after reunion with his cothinkers, he spent more than an hour explaining how important it was for a Marxist movement to have a correct philosophical method and to defend dialectical materialism against its opponents!

Unfortunately, the leaders of the SWP did not take Trotsky's exhortations seriously, and they made a whole series of political mistakes in the years after his death—which can ultimately be traced to their lack of a dialectical analysis and understanding. As always, mistakes in theory lead to mistakes in practice, and the failure of the Fourth International to develop into a truly mass force for socialist change led to many lost revolutionary opportunities in the postwar period. As a result, humanity has had to endure many more decades of capitalist immiseration and brutality. Such is the vital importance of revolutionary theory to the workers' movement!

The International Marxist Tendency stands apart from other left tendencies in that we have always put theory at the center of our work. Following Trotsky's advice, we view it, not as something secondary, supplemental, or elective, but as an absolute necessity if the working class is to succeed in forging a mass revolutionary force capable of ending capitalism. To that end, we have produced dozens of books, booklets, and articles on theoretical topics, including modern classics such as *Reason in Revolt: Marxist Philosophy and Modern Science*. We have also republished Engels's *Anti-Dühring* and *Dialectics of Nature*, and Trotsky's *In Defense of Marxism*. And we are proud of the fact that our articles and reading guides on Marxist philosophy are among the most read on the *In Defence of Marxism* website (Marxist.com). Given the growing popularity and enormous importance of these ideas, we decided it was high time we produced a collection of works on Marxist philosophy, conveniently available in a single volume.

Choosing the contents for a book of this type was no simple task, primarily because there is so much that deserves to be included. For reasons of space, we did not include material from Marx's *Poverty of Philosophy*, Engels's *Socialism: Utopian and Scientific*, Lenin's *What Is To Be Done?* or Marx's *Capital*, that masterpiece of applied dialectics. As Lenin said: "In *Capital*, Marx applied to a single science logic, dialectics, and the theory of knowledge of materialism [three words are not needed: it is one and the same thing] which has taken everything valuable in Hegel and developed it further." We hope the reader will forgive these and other omissions, as well as any errors that may have crept in, and will be inspired to read these works separately, armed with the deeper understanding of Marxist philosophy that this volume aims to provide.

We decided to present the selections roughly thematically, with the material organized more or less chronologically in each section. The first section focuses on the origins and genesis of dialectical materialism, its emergence out of Hegel, through the Young Hegelians and Feuerbach, and finally onto the world stage as scientific socialism. We then provide a range of articles and excerpts examining dialectics, including some little-known material not available until relatively recently. Following that, we take a closer look at the question of materialism, and we end with several articles that examine the dialectics of the class struggle, party building, and the socialist transition from capitalism to communism.

In the interest of readability and uniformity of formatting for this collection, the original punctuation, markings, notations, etc., have not necessarily been preserved, and quotations and citations have been cleaned up. This is especially true in the case of the excerpts from notebooks and marginal notes that are included, which were never intended for publication by their authors, but which provide important insights into their thinking. Those who wish to study these works in their full historical context should have no problem finding reference copies at the library.

In most instances, foreign language publication titles and terms have been translated directly to English. Only footnotes that add important context and additional depth have been retained; most of these are from the Soviet editions of these works or the Marxists Internet Archive. Wherever editorial comments have been inserted, these have been framed by [brackets] or otherwise indicated. Where only excerpts from a work are included, this is indicated in the title of the selection. And where it seemed useful to provide additional context, explanatory notes have been included at the beginning of the selection.

We would like to thank Alan Woods for writing an all-new introduction on short notice; Jon Lange and Leroy James for their much-appreciated help with proofreading; Steve Iverson, for the countless hours spent proofreading and poring over the final proofs; Antonio Balmer for the long hours needed to ensure a polished and professional layout; and Mark Rahman and Laura Brown for their striking cover design. We also extend our gratitude to the comrades of Wellred UK for their technical advice and inspiration. Last but not least, we thank Marxists.org for all their work over the years in making these and other Marxist works available to the general public.

Producing this book has truly been a labor of love, and we hope the new generation of revolutionary Marxists will enjoy reading as much as we enjoyed producing it.

John Peterson

October 12, 2018
Brooklyn, NY

INTRODUCTION

Alan Woods
October 8, 2018

I was delighted to learn of the plan of the comrades of the US section of the IMT to publish an anthology of basic writings on Marxist philosophy. Every specialized branch of human activity presupposes a certain level of understanding and study. This applies as much to carpentry as to brain surgery. The idea that we can get along without some degree of learning is in flat contradiction to everyday experience.

If I go to the dentist and he says to me, "I have never studied dentistry and know nothing about it, but open your mouth and I will have a go," I think I would make a hasty exit. If I'm experiencing problems with my central heating and a man comes to my house, pulls a hammer out of his bag and says: "I know nothing about plumbing, but show me your central heating system and I will learn by trial and error," I would certainly show him where the exit is.

Most people would not dream of expressing an informed opinion about brain surgery or quantum mechanics without specialized knowledge of these fields, but matters seem to be quite different when it comes to Marxism. It seems that anyone can express an opinion about Marxism without having read a single line of what Marx and Engels actually wrote. This statement applies just as much—in fact, far more—to the so-called academic experts who write books attacking Marxism, which clearly show that they have not read Marx, or if they have read a little, they have not understood a single word of it.

This situation is sufficiently lamentable, but even more unfortunate is the fact that many people who call themselves Marxists are equally ignorant of the writings of Marx and Engels. In my experience, even many people who consider themselves to be Marxist cadres rarely bother to plumb the depths of Marxist theory in all its richness and variety. All too often they merely skate over the surface, repeating thoughtlessly a few slogans and quotes taken out of context which they have learned by rote, the genuine content of which remains a closed book for them.

Many people think they know what Marxism is. Over time they have become familiar with some of the basic ideas. But what is familiar is not understood—*precisely because it is familiar*. A long time ago I read something that Hegel wrote that made a deep impression on me. I cannot remember where I read it and I am writing from memory: "*Aber was* **bekannt** *ist, ist darum noch nicht* **erkannt**" (But what is *known* is not on that account *understood*).

Nowhere is this affirmation clearer than in the very important area of philosophy. It is too often forgotten that Marxism began as a philosophy, and the philosophical method of Marxism is of fundamental importance in understanding the ideas of Marx and Engels.

Here, however, we are confronted with a difficulty. The most systematic account of dialectics is contained in the writings of Hegel, in particular his massive work *The Science of Logic*. But the reader can soon be disheartened by the highly inaccessible way in which Hegel sets forth his ideas—"abstract and abstruse"—Engels called it, while Lenin commented that reading *The Science of Logic* was the best way of getting a headache.

Marx intended to write a work on dialectical materialism in order to make available to the general reader the rational kernel of Hegel's thought. Unfortunately, he died before he could do so. Marx's indefatigable comrade, Friedrich Engels, wrote a number of brilliant studies on dialectical philosophy including *Ludwig Feuerbach and the End of German Classical Philosophy*, *Anti-Dühring*, and *The Dialectics of Nature*.

The last-named work was intended to be the basis for a longer work on Marxist philosophy, but unfortunately, Engels was prevented from completing it by the immense work of finishing the second and third volumes of *Capital*, which Marx left unfinished at his death. It is true that, scattered throughout the works of Marx, Engels, Lenin, Trotsky, and Plekhanov, one can find a very large amount of material on this subject, but it would take a very long time to extract all this information.

Over 20 years ago, in collaboration with my comrade and teacher, Ted Grant, I wrote a book called *Reason in Revolt*. To the best of my knowledge, this was the first attempt to apply the method of dialectical materialism to the results of modern science since Engels wrote *The Dialectics of Nature*. But the task of putting together a more or less systematic exposition of Marxist philosophy still remains to be done.

For some time, I have been planning to write a work of Marxist philosophy that will hopefully present the ideas of Hegel in a way that will be more accessible to the general reader. Unfortunately, this work has been delayed by other tasks, mainly the production of the complete version of Trotsky's *Stalin*. I hope to complete this task in the not too distant future. In the meantime, the present anthology will prove of invaluable assistance to the student of scientific socialism who wishes to acquire a better grasp of Marxist philosophy, and I welcome its publication with every possible enthusiasm.

The decay of modern philosophy

The attitude of most people these days regarding philosophy is usually one of indifference or even contempt. As far as modern philosophy is concerned this is quite understandable. The fiddling and fussing about meaning and semantics strikingly resembles the rarefied atmosphere and convoluted debates of the medieval Schoolmen who argued endlessly over the sex of angels and how many angels could dance on the head of the needle.

For the past one-and-a-half centuries, the realm of philosophy has resembled an arid desert with only the occasional trace of life. One will search in vain in this wasteland for any source of illumination. It is hard to say what is worse: the intolerable pretensions of so-called postmodernism, or the obvious emptiness of its content. The treasure trove of the past, with its ancient glories and flashes of illumination seems utterly extinguished.

With the latest craze for so-called postmodernism, bourgeois philosophy has reached its nadir. The meager content of this trend has not prevented its adherents from assuming the most absurd airs and graces, accompanied by an arrogant contempt for the great philosophers of the past. When we examine the cesspit of modern philosophy, the words of Hegel in the *Preface to the Phenomenology of Mind* immediately spring to mind: "*By the little which can thus satisfy the needs of the human spirit we can measure the extent of its loss.*"

The contempt for philosophy, or rather, the complete indifference that most people display towards it is richly deserved. But it is unfortunate that in turning aside from the present-day philosophical swamp, people neglect the great thinkers of the past who, in contrast to the modern charlatans, were giants of human thought. One can learn a great deal from the Greeks, Spinoza, and Hegel, who were pioneers, who prepared the way for the brilliant achievements of Marxist philosophy and can rightly be considered as an important part of our revolutionary heritage.

Empiricism versus dialectics

The Anglo-Saxon world in general has proved remarkably impervious to philosophy. Insofar as they possess any philosophy, the Americans and their English cousins have limited the scope of their thought to the narrow boundaries of empiricism and its soulmate, pragmatism. Broad generalizations of a more theoretical character have always been regarded with something akin to suspicion.

Philosophy is abstract thought, but philosophical generalizations are alien to the Anglo-Saxon tradition. The empiricist tradition is impatient with generalizations. It constantly demands the concrete, the facts, but in confining itself to this narrow approach, it constantly misses the forest for the trees.

In its day, empiricism played a most progressive, and even revolutionary role in the development of human thought and science. However, empiricism is helpful only within certain limits. In the late 16th and early 17th centuries, the empirical school of thought associated with the name of Sir Francis Bacon exercised a contradictory influence upon subsequent developments.

On the one hand, by stressing the need for observation and experiment, it gave a stimulus to scientific investigation. On the other hand, it gave rise to the narrow empiricist outlook that has had a negative effect on the development of philosophical thought, above all, in Britain and the United States. That peculiarly Anglo-Saxon aversion to theory, the tendency towards narrow empiricism, the slavish worship of the "facts," and a stubborn refusal to accept generalizations, has dominated educated thought in Britain and, by extension, the United States, for so long that it has acquired the character of a rooted prejudice.

For the empirical thinker, nothing exists except in its outward manifestation. This thought always examines things in their singleness, stillness, and isolation, and ends up examining the idea of a thing, and not the thing itself. Sense perception is thought on a very low and basic level. For everyday purposes, such forms of thought may suffice, but for more complex processes, the narrowness of empiricism immediately becomes an obstacle to a mind that aspires to attain the truth.

By the truth we mean human knowledge that correctly reflects the objective world, its laws, and properties. In this sense it does not depend on a subject, as imagined by Bishop Berkeley, Hume, and the other early representatives of English empiricism, who inevitably fell into the swamp of subjective idealism.

The demand for "the facts"

Many people only feel secure when they can refer to the *facts*. Yet the "facts" do not select themselves. A definite method is required that will help us to look beyond the immediately given and lay bare the processes that lie beyond the "facts." Despite claims made to the contrary, it is impossible to proceed from the "facts" without any preconceptions. Such supposed objectivity has never existed and will never exist.

In approaching the facts, we bring our own conceptions and categories with us. These can either be conscious or unconscious, but they are always present. Those who imagine that they can get along quite happily without a philosophy—as is the case with many scientists—merely repeat unconsciously the existing "official" philosophy of the day and the current prejudices of the society in which they live. It is therefore indispensable that scientists, and thinking people in general, should strive to work out a consistent way of looking at the world, a coherent philosophy which can serve as an adequate tool for analyzing things and processes.

The conclusions drawn from sense perception are hypothetical, demanding further proof. Over a long period of observation, combined with practical activity which enables us to test the correctness or otherwise of our ideas, we discover a series of essential connections between phenomena, which show that they possess common features, and belong to a particular genus or species.

The process of human cognition proceeds from the particular to the universal, but also from the universal to the particular. It is therefore incorrect and one-sided to counterpose one to the other. Dialectical materialism does not regard induction and deduction as mutually incompatible, but as different aspects of the dialectical process of cognition, which are inseparably connected, and condition one another.

Inductive reasoning, in the last analysis, is the basis of all knowledge, since all we know is ultimately derived from observation of the objective world and experience. However, on closer examination, the limitations of a strictly inductive method become clear. No matter how many facts are examined, it only takes a single exception to undermine whatever general conclusion we have drawn from them. If we have seen a thousand white swans and draw the conclusion that all swans are white, and then see a black swan, our conclusion no longer holds good.

In *The Dialectics of Nature*, Engels pointed out the paradox of the empirical school, which imagined that it had disposed of metaphysics once and for all, but actually ended up accepting all kinds of mystical ideas.

> [This trend] which, exalting mere experience, treats thought with sovereign disdain . . . really has gone to the furthest extreme in emptiness of thought.

In the *Introduction to The Philosophy of History*, Hegel rightly ridicules those historians—all too common in Britain—who pretend to limit themselves to the facts, presenting a spurious façade of "academic objectivity," while giving free reign to their prejudices:

> We must proceed historically—empirically. Among other precautions we must take care not to be misled by professed historians who . . . are chargeable with the very procedure of which they accuse the philosopher—introducing *a priori* inventions of their own into the records of the past . . . We might then announce it as the first condition to be observed, that we should faithfully adopt all that is historical. But in such general expressions themselves, as "faithfully" and "adopt," lies the ambiguity. Even the ordinary, the "impartial" historiographer, who believes and professes that he maintains a simply receptive attitude; surrendering himself only to the data supplied him—is by no means passive as regard the exercise of his thinking powers. He brings his categories with him, and sees the phenomena presented to his mental vision, exclusively through these media. And, especially in all that pretends to the name of science, it is indispensable that Reason should not sleep—that reflection should be in full play. To him who looks upon the world rationally, the world in its turn presents a rational aspect. The relation is mutual. But the various exercises of reflection—the different points of view—the modes of deciding the simple question of the relative importance of events (the first category that occupies the attention of the historian), do not belong to this place.

Bertrand Russell, whose views are diametrically opposed to dialectical materialism, nevertheless makes a valid criticism of the limitations of empiricism, which follows in the same line as Hegel's remarks:

> As a rule, the framing of hypotheses is the most difficult part of scientific work, and the part where great ability is indispensable. So far, no method has been found which would make it possible to invent hypotheses by rule. Usually some hypothesis is a necessary preliminary to the collection of facts, since the selection of facts demands some way of determining relevance. Without something of this kind, the mere multiplicity of facts is baffling (*The History of Western Philosophy*).

Dialectics

The term "dialectics" comes from the Greek *dialektike*, derived from *dialegomai*, to converse, or discuss. Originally, it signified the art of discussion, which may be seen in its highest form in the Socratic dialogues of Plato.

Setting out from a particular idea or opinion, usually derived from the concrete experiences and problems of life of the person involved, Socrates would, step by step, by a rigorous process of argument, bring to light the inner contradictions contained in the original proposition, show its limitations, and take the discussion to a higher level, involving an entirely different proposition.

An initial argument—thesis—is advanced. This is answered by a contrary argument—antithesis. Finally, after examining the question thoroughly, dissecting it to reveal its inner contradictions, we arrive at a conclusion on a higher level—synthesis. This may or may not mean that the two sides reach agreement, but in the very process of developing the discussion itself, the understanding of both sides is deepened, and the discussion proceeds from a lower to a higher level. This is the dialectic of discussion in its classical form.

Dialectics is a dynamic view of nature that frees human thought from the *rigor mortis* of formal logic. The first real exponent of dialectics was a remarkable man, the Greek philosopher Heraclitus (c. 544–484 BCE). His work survives today as a series of brief but profound aphorisms, such as the following:

> Fire lives the death of air, and air lives the death of fire;

> Water lives the death of earth, and earth lives the death of water.

It is the same thing in us that is living and dead, asleep and awake, young and old; each changes place and becomes the other.

We step and we do not step into the same stream; we are and are not.

These utterances seemed so difficult to understand, because they contradict what is known as the "common sense" view of the world. So obscure and paradoxical did they appear to his contemporaries that they earned him the nickname of "Heraclitus the Dark." They did not understand what he was saying, but he was entirely indifferent to their incomprehension and treated it with scorn:

Though this word is true ever more, yet men are as unable to understand it when they hear it for the first time as before they have heard it at all . . . But other men know not what they are doing when awake, even as they forget what they do in sleep.

Fools, although they hear, are like the deaf; to them the adage applies that when present they are absent.

Heraclitus was able to see what others, who based themselves purely on the empirical evidence of the senses, could not. In a devastating criticism of empiricism, he wrote:

Eyes and ears are bad witnesses for men if they have souls that understand not their language.

Of course, all our knowledge is ultimately derived from our senses, but sense perception can only tell us part of the story, and not necessarily the most important part. It is sufficient to remember that our senses tell us that the Earth is flat. Hegel, who had a very high opinion of Heraclitus as a philosopher, wrote in his *History of Philosophy*: "Here we see land. There is no proposition of Heraclitus which I have not adopted in my *Logic*."

The psychologist Carl Jung wrote: "Old Heraclitus, who was indeed a very great sage, discovered the most marvelous of all psychological laws: the regulative function of opposites . . . A running contrariwise, by which he meant that sooner or later, everything runs into its opposite" (*Two essays on Analytical Psychology*).

In *Anti-Dühring* Engels gives the following appraisal of Heraclitus's dialectical world outlook:

When we reflect on nature or the history of mankind or our own intellectual activity, at first we see the picture of an endless maze of connections and interactions, in which nothing remains what, where, and as it was, but everything moves, changes, comes into being, and passes away. At first, therefore, we see the picture as a whole, with its individual parts still more or less kept in the background; we observe the movements, transitions, connections, rather than the things that move, change, and are connected. This primitive, naïve, but intrinsically correct conception of the world is that of Greek philosophy, and was first clearly formulated by Heraclitus: everything is and is not, for everything is in flux, is constantly changing, constantly coming into being and passing away.

> . . . Motion is the mode of existence of matter. Never anywhere has there been matter without motion, or motion without matter, nor can there be.

In his *Dialectics of Nature* Engels writes:

> Change of form of motion is always a process that takes place between at least two bodies, of which one loses a definite quantity of motion of one quality (e.g., heat), while the other gains a corresponding quantity of motion of another quality (mechanical motion, electricity, chemical decomposition).

> Dialectics, so-called *objective* [materialist] dialectics, prevails throughout nature, and so-called subjective dialectics, dialectical thought, is only the reflection of the motion through opposites which asserts itself everywhere in nature, and which by the continual conflict of the opposites and their final passage into one another, or into higher forms, determines the life of nature.

In *Socialism: Utopian and Scientific*, Engels wrote: "the whole world, natural, historical, intellectual, is represented as a process—i.e., as in constant motion, change, transformation, development—and the attempt is made to trace out the internal connection that makes a continuous whole of all this movement and development."

The Hegelian dialectic

The dialectical method appears in the writings of Heraclitus in an embryonic, undeveloped form. It was developed to its highest degree by Hegel. However, it appears here in a mystical, idealist form. It was rescued by the theoretical labors of Marx and Engels, who for the first time showed the rational kernel in Hegel's thought. In its scientific—materialist—form, the dialectical method provides us with an indispensable tool for understanding the workings of nature, society and human thought.

Hegel's great dialectical masterpiece was *The Science of Logic*, the structure of which, he claimed, was an abstraction from the history of philosophy. It resembles the process the mind of a child undergoes when it first starts to receive external perceptions, beginning with the category of "being," and from it, moving to more abstract—Hegel would have said concrete—ideas.

But the basic problem with *The Science of Logic* lies in the structure of the work itself. As an idealist, Hegel tried to create a philosophical system that, proceeding step by step through all the processes of conscious thought, would lead ultimately to the Absolute Idea, which Feuerbach, correctly, saw as just another name for God. That was also Lenin's opinion. He wrote in his *Philosophical Notebooks*: "Hegel's *Logic* cannot be applied in its given form, it cannot be taken as given. One must separate out from it the logical (epistemological) nuances, after purifying them from the mysticism of ideas: that is still a big job."

The artificial character of Hegel's philosophical system is commented on by Engels in a Nov. 1, 1891 letter to Conrad Schmidt. He remarked that the structure of Hegel's *Logic* is artificial, and that the transition from one category to the other is often made in a forced way. He did this by means of a pun: as in "*zugrunde gehen*" in order to get to the category of "*Grund*," reason, ground.

As for the Absolute Idea, Engels commented ironically, the problem with this is that Hegel tells us absolutely nothing about it. The attempt to force what was undoubtedly a masterpiece of dialectical thinking into the straitjacket of idealism meant that the work frequently had a forced and arbitrary character. It was, to quote Engels yet again, "a colossal miscarriage."

Nevertheless, for the patient reader, Hegel's *Logic* offers a vast number of profound and rewarding ideas. Despite its idealist, and often quite obscure, character, it is possible to discern, as if through a distorting mirror, the reflection of material reality—not merely the history of philosophy—but the history of society and the laws and processes of nature in general. For this, it is necessary to read Hegel from a critical and materialist standpoint, which was what Lenin did in his *Philosophical Notebooks*.

The law of identity

The inclusion in the present anthology of Trotsky's brilliant little article *The ABC of Materialist Dialectics* was an absolutely correct decision. Here, in a few words, the essence of dialectics is explained with impressive clarity. It is hardly surprising that this article has driven the critics of dialectics into paroxysmal rage. It challenges the very basis of the logical conceptions that have dominated philosophy for hundreds of years: the law of identity.

The generalizations arrived at over a lengthy period of human development, some of which are considered as axioms, play an important role in the development of thought and cannot be so easily dispensed with. The thought forms of traditional logic play an essential role, establishing elementary rules for avoiding absurd contradictions and following an internally consistent line of argument, but this formalistic way of thinking remains true only within certain limits.

The law of identity ($a = a$) is the basic, dogmatic assumption of all formal logic, and has been for over 2,000 years. It is typical of formal thinking: empty, rigid, and abstract. Dialectical thinking, on the contrary, is concrete, dynamic, and complex in its multiple determinations: it is movement expressed in its most general form.

In his book *The Metaphysics*, Aristotle worked out the principle of non-contradiction: "It is impossible that one and the same attribute should belong and not belong to the same subject, considered at the same time and in the same relation." An extension of the same idea is the principle of the excluded middle: "If that which is false is only the negation of what is true, then it will be impossible for all to be false: one of the two sides of the contradiction must be true."

However, in another of his works, the *Organon*, Aristotle worked out the basic laws of dialectics. Unfortunately, the ideas of Aristotle have mainly come down to us in the lifeless and scholastic form in which they were "preserved" by the Church in the Middle Ages—like a corpse preserved in formaldehyde. The Aristotle of formal logic and the syllogism was preserved in a one-sided way, but the Aristotle of the *Organon* was consigned to oblivion.

Since then, logical formalism has generally been utilized as a kind of scholastic device—or "artifice," as Kant correctly observed—to avoid reality and, following in the footsteps of the medieval Schoolmen, as a kind of "opium" to burrow deep into the supposed "profundities" of the linguistic vacuum, where they dispute endlessly the meaning of words, just as the Schoolmen entertained themselves with endless debates on the sex of angels.

Logical Positivism, which dominated Anglo-Saxon philosophy in the 20th century in different disguises, was a worthy inheritor of this bad tradition of medieval Scholasticism, with its obsession with form and linguistic hairsplitting. For these people, dialectics is a book sealed with seven seals. Their way of thinking is completely dogmatic and formalistic.

Whether we call it the law of identity or the principle of equivalence really makes no difference. In the end $a = a$, the same old formal dogma established by Aristotle. The forms may have been changed and expressed as symbols or anything you please, but the content remains what it always was: an empty shell, or as Hegel put it "the lifeless bones of a skeleton."

The law of identity very clearly states that a given thing is equal to itself (or self-identical, it does not really matter). But, as Trotsky points out, since things in the material world are in a constant state of change— they constantly flow, to use Heraclitus's wonderfully profound aphorism—they are never self-identical. Thus, the law of identity is, at best, only a rough approximation. It cannot lay hold of a constantly changing reality. This is precisely the Achilles heel of formal logic.

All attempts to eliminate contradiction from logic are the equivalent of attempting to remove contradiction from nature itself—but contradiction is at the basis of all movement, life, and development. The idea that "everything flows" has been brilliantly confirmed by the discoveries of modern science, especially physics.

In the space of the last 100 years or so, physics has furnished a vast amount of evidence to show that change and motion are fundamental qualities of matter. Engels asserted that motion is the mode of existence of matter—a brilliant prediction. But Einstein went much further than that. In 1905 he proved that matter and energy are—*the same.*

It is not possible to understand the dynamics of the world we live in, let alone be a conscious revolutionary—that is, someone who intervenes actively and consciously in the historical process—without the aid of dialectical thinking. The breakthrough in scientific thinking associated with chaos theory is ample proof of this assertion.

Cognition

The first law of dialectical materialism is absolute objectivity of consideration: not examples, not digressions, but the thing itself. The basis of all our knowledge is, of course, sensory experience. I experience the world through my senses, and can experience it in no other way. This is the essential content of empiricism.

The early empiricists—Bacon, Locke, and Hobbes—were materialists. Their battle cry was: *Nihil est in intellectu quod non sit prius in sensu* (Nothing is in the mind that was not first in the senses). Their insistence upon sensory perception as the basis of all knowledge represented in its day a gigantic leap forward with regard to the empty speculation of the medieval Schoolmen. It paved the way for the rapid expansion of science, based upon empirical investigation, observation, and experiment.

Yet, despite its tremendously revolutionary character, this form of materialism was one-sided, limited, and therefore incomplete. It tended to regard the facts as isolated and static. Taken to an extreme, as it was by the likes of Hume and Berkeley, it led to subjective idealism, which denied the existence of a material reality independent of the observer. As Bishop Berkeley put it: *Esse est percipi* (To be is to be perceived).

The statement "I interpret the world through my senses" is correct but one-sided. One must add that the world exists independent of my senses. Otherwise, we are left with the absurd proposition that if I close my eyes, the world ceases to exist. This argument was comprehensively demolished by Lenin in his philosophical masterpiece *Materialism and Empiriocriticism*.

In reality, empiricism presents cognition in a very superficial and one-sided manner. Hegel, whose objective idealism is in flat contradiction to subjective idealism, went to great lengths to show that cognition is a process that proceeds through different stages. Of these stages, sensory perception is the lowest, confining itself to the mere statement that "*it is.*"

But this elementary conception immediately comes into a series of contradictions, if what is being analyzed is considered, not as an isolated atom, but as a process of constant change, in which things can be transformed into their opposites.

The process of cognition has two essential elements: a thinking subject and an object of thought. In the *Phenomenology of Mind*, which Marx described as "Hegel's voyage of discovery," the great dialectician did not intend to analyze either the one side or the other, but to demonstrate their unity in the process of thought. It was thought itself that was to be examined.

However, Hegel's method had an inherent weakness. As an idealist, Hegel did not set out from real, concrete, sensuous human thought, but from an idealist abstraction. In reality, we do not think only with our mind but with all our senses—with our whole body in fact. What links humans with the external world (nature) is not abstract thought but human labor, which transforms nature, and at the same time transforms humankind itself.

The possibilities of sensory cognition are limited. The cognition of phenomena that are beyond the reach of sensation can only be arrived at through abstract thought, dialectical thought. The object of thought has an inherent being—in German, *an sich*. The purpose of thought is to turn this "being in itself" into "being for us", i.e., to proceed from ignorance to knowledge.

We do not get any closer to the truth by compiling a mass of facts. When we say "all animals" we do not assume that this amounts to zoology. In *Lectures on the Philosophy of History*, Hegel pointed out that, "It is, in fact, the wish for rational insight, not the ambition to amass a mere heap of requirements, that should be presupposed in every case as possessing the mind of the learner in the study of science."

The power of thought lies precisely in its capacity for abstraction, its ability to exclude particulars and arrive at generalizations that express the main and most essential aspects of a given phenomenon. The initial step is merely to obtain a sense of the being as an individual object. This, however, proves to be impossible and compels us to delve deeper into the subject, revealing inner contradictions that provide the impulse for movement and change, in which things turn into their opposite.

The unity of opposites

For Hegel, the division of the One and the knowledge of its contradictory parts constitutes the essence of dialectics. For the One is the whole consisting of two conflicting and opposite poles. It is only by identifying these contradictory tendencies that a correct knowledge of the object under consideration can be recognized in its true, dynamic reality.

Hegel's basic idea was that of *development through contradictions*. To give it another name, dialectics is *the logic of contradiction*. Whereas traditional (formal) logic attempts to banish contradiction, dialectics embraces it, accepts it as a normal and necessary element of all life and nature. Giordano Bruno, the 16th-century Italian philosopher, astronomer, and mathematician—whose theories anticipated modern science and whose reward by the Inquisition was to be burned at the stake—gave us a charming definition of dialectics when he described it as *la divina arte degli opposti* ("the divine art of opposites").

Hegel refers to the "restless unity," that underlying tension which is the basis of all matter. The unity—coincidence, identity, and resultant dynamic interplay—of opposites is conditional, temporary, transitory, and relative. The mutually exclusive relationship of opposites is *absolute*, and it is the basis of all movement, change, and evolution.

In *Moralizing Criticism and Critical Morality* Marx wrote: "It is characteristic of the whole *grobianism* of 'sound common sense,' which feeds upon the 'fullness of life' and does not stunt its *natural* faculties with any philosophical or other studies, that where it succeeds in seeing *differences*, it does not see *unity*, and that where it sees *unity*, it does not see *differences*. If it propounds *differentiated determinants*, they at once become fossilized in its hands, and it can see only the most reprehensible sophistry when these wooden concepts are knocked together so that they take fire."

In the *Science of Logic*, Hegel begins with the category of Being, with the bare assertion "it is." But this statement, despite its apparently commonsensical and concrete character—we have established the basic fact of existence—does not get us very far, and in fact leads us to a false conclusion. Pure Being, as Hegel points out, is *the same as pure nothing*. It is being stripped of all its concreteness and actuality. What appeared to be concrete turns out to be an empty abstraction.

Being and nothing are generally considered to be mutually exclusive opposites. But in reality, there can be no being without nothing, and no nothing without being. The unity of being and not being, as Hegel points out, is *becoming*: the constant movement of change that means that at any given moment, we are, and are not.

Life and death are considered to be mutually exclusive opposites. But *in fact, death is an integral part of life*. Life is not conceivable without death. We begin to die the moment we are born, for in fact, it is only the death of trillions of cells and their replacement by trillions of new cells, that constitutes life and human development.

Without death there could be no life, no growth, no change, no development. Thus, the attempt to banish death from life—as if the two things could be separated—is to arrive at a state of absolute immutability, changeless, static equilibrium, but this is just another name for—death. For there can be no life without change and movement.

I have before me a photograph of a baby, taken many years ago. That baby was me, but no longer exists. A vast number of changes have occurred since that photograph was taken, so that I am no longer what I was. And yet it is possible for me to say to somebody looking at the photograph: "oh, that's me," and I would not be telling a lie. This dialectical process was described most beautifully by Hegel in the *Preface to The Phenomenology of Mind*:

> The bud disappears when the blossom breaks through, and we might say that the former is refuted by the latter; in the same way when the fruit comes, the blossom may be explained to be a false form of the plant's existence, for the fruit appears as its true nature in place of the blossom. These stages are not merely differentiated; they supplant one another as being incompatible with one another. But the ceaseless activity of their own inherent nature makes them at the same time moments of an organic unity, where they not merely do not contradict one another, but where one is as necessary as the other; and this equal necessity of all moments constitutes alone and thereby the life of the whole.

Love and hate are opposites. Yet it is common knowledge that love and hate are very closely identified, and can easily be transformed from one to the other. It is the same with pleasure and pain. One cannot exist without the other. From a medical point of view, pain has an important function. It is not just an evil, but a warning from the body that all is not well. Pain is part of the human condition. Not only that: pain and pleasure are dialectically related.

Without the existence of pain, pleasure could not exist. Don Quixote explained to Sancho Panza that the best sauce was hunger. Likewise, we rest far better after a period of vigorous exertion. And in Shakespeare's *Henry IV*, Prince Hal says:

> *If all the year were playing holidays, To sport would be as tedious as to work; But when they seldom come, they wish'd for come.*

A world in which everything was white would actually be the same as a world in which everything was black, as polar explorers discovered when they suffered from snow blindness.

Quantity and quality

In the *Science of Logic*, particularly the section on measurement, Hegel elaborates his theory of *the nodal line of development*, in which a series of small, apparently insignificant changes eventually reach a critical point in which there is a qualitative leap. Chaos theory and its derivatives are clearly a form of dialectical thinking. In particular, the idea of the transformation from quantity to quality is central to it—one of the basic laws of dialectics.

In his book *Anti-Dühring*, Engels pointed out that in the last analysis, nature works dialectically. The advances of science over the last hundred years have completely borne out this assertion. American scientists have been at the forefront of some of the most important developments in modern science. I am thinking in particular of the work of R.C. Lewontin in the field of genetics, and above all, the writings of the evolutionary biologist, Stephen J. Gould.

Let us cite one easily understood example.

When water at normal atmospheric pressure is heated or cooled, there is a leap from one state of aggregation to another: at 0 degrees Celsius it is a solid (ice), and at 100 degrees it changes to a gaseous state (steam). If we increase the temperature still further, to 550 degrees, it becomes *plasma*, an entirely different state of matter, where the dissociation of atoms and molecules occurs. The leaps between each of these states are known as *phase transitions*. The study of phase transitions constitutes a very important branch of modern physics. Similar changes can be observed in the history of society, where the equivalent of a phase transition is a revolution.

Nucleation is the first step in the formation of either a new thermodynamic phase or a new structure by means of self-organization. It is the process that determines how much time is required before a new phase or self-organized structure appears. This phenomenon is seen in thermodynamic phase transitions of every type. From a saturated solution to a crystal, from the evaporation of a liquid to a gas, or in the transition from water to ice.

It is possible to actually reach a position of supersaturation of a solution, where, for example, water under normal conditions can be heated or cooled above 100°C or below 0°C without becoming steam or a solid. What is required in many circumstances for the phase transition to occur is either an external shock or the presence of some impurity. Water, when heated, does not form bubbles of steam at any random point, but they all begin ascending from a scratch or imperfection on the surface of the saucepan. This is a nucleation point forming around a catalyst.

In thermodynamic terms, a supersaturated solution will have reached a level of concentration—or temperature or whatever other quantitative element is involved—where the alternative phase represents a lower entropy, but there is an entropy cost in forming the first "nucleus." Sometimes this nucleation point forms randomly over a period of time and, as is also the case with radioactive decay, there is an increasing probability over time of it forming. However, its formation is aided by the presence of some catalyst on whose surface the entropy leap is lowered.

We can visualize this process when we think of the crystallization of a pearl in a clam. Indeed, we often talk about the "crystallization" of anger within a factory or society and the analogy is an apt one. In the case of the formation of a pearl, *all* of the conditions for its formation can exist except one: some impurity around which it can take shape. That "impurity" is often a worm that has burrowed through the shell of a clam and died. Here the imagery is quite striking: a beautiful pearl forming a sarcophagus around a rather ugly piece of dead biological matter.

We will return to this analogy later.

We often see the apparent repetition of stages of development that have long since been overcome. We see the same thing in the study of embryos, which apparently go through the stages of evolution. A human embryo starts as a single cell, then divides and acquires more complex forms. At one stage it has gills like a fish, later it has a tail like a monkey. The similarity between human embryos and those of other animals, including fish and reptiles, is striking, and was already noted by the ancient Greeks. Over two thousand years before Darwin, Anaximander (c. 611–546 BCE) deduced that man had evolved from a fish.

The genetic difference between humans and chimpanzees is less than two percent and we share a large percentage of our genes with fruit flies and even more primitive organisms. The last desperate counterattack of the Creationists—hiding behind the banner of "intelligent design"—was shattered against the remarkable results of the Human Genome Project. However, the two percent difference that separates us from the other primates is a qualitative leap that carries humankind to an entirely different and higher level.

The process of evolution has gone on uninterruptedly from the first primitive life forms that emerged, as we now know, at a surprisingly early period in the Earth's history. The first primitive organisms probably emerged on the bed of the primeval oceans, deriving energy, not from the sun, but from volcanic vents, generating heat from below the earth's crust. The earliest protozoa developed into *chordata*, through to the earliest land-dwelling amphibians, to reptiles, and later to mammals and humans.

History and nature know both evolution—slow, gradual development—and revolution—a qualitative leap, where the process of evolution is enormously accelerated. Evolution prepares the way for revolution, which in turn prepares the way for a new period of evolution on a higher level.

The unity of opposites can be clearly observed at all levels of matter. Conflicting tendencies are found at all levels in nature, from the largest galaxies to the smallest subatomic particles. The identity of opposites is the recognition—or discovery—of the mutually exclusive tendencies that exist in all the phenomena and processes of nature. This is what Engels meant when he defined dialectics as the most general laws of nature, society, and human thought.

Criticality

It is an elementary truth of chemistry that opposite charges attract, while like charges repel. But here we have an apparent paradox. The nuclei of all atoms except hydrogen contain more than one proton, and each proton carries a positive charge. The protons must feel a repulsive force from the other protons. So why would the nuclei of these atoms stay together? What holds the nucleus together?

The unity of opposites pulling together and tearing apart the atom are the strong nuclear force and the electrostatic force respectively. Neutrons and protons bind to each other through the strong nuclear force, however, this force only operates over a very short range. Positively charged protons, however, are constantly repelling each other through electrostatic repulsion. This force operates over much larger distances.

The strong nuclear force holds most ordinary matter together. In addition, the strong force binds neutrons and protons to create atomic nuclei. Just as centrifugal forces attempt to tear galaxies apart while gravity holds them together, electromagnetism is the force that would theoretically rip a nucleus apart, while the nuclear force—130 times stronger than electromagnetism—holds it together.

The nucleus holds together, but only within certain limits. If the number of protons or neutrons exceeds these limits, the nucleus becomes unstable due to radioactive decay. If the nucleus becomes *very* large it can undergo an even more dramatic transformation.

As the nucleus increases in size, the repulsive electrostatic force eventually overcomes the attractive nuclear force and the nucleus becomes unstable. All that is then required is to fire a single neutron at the nucleus and—quantity transforms into quality—the nucleus splits in two, emitting a large amount of energy and often emitting more neutrons in the process. This is what physicists refer to as nuclear fission.

If a certain amount of fissionable material is present, it will ensure that neutrons released by fission will strike another nucleus, thus producing a chain reaction. The more fissionable material is present, the greater the odds that such an event will occur. Critical mass is defined as the amount of material at which a neutron produced by a fission process will, on average, create another fission event.

In the transition from a controlled to an uncontrolled nuclear reaction there is a qualitative leap—a transition from quantity into quality. If you insert material—a control rod—into the fissile material to absorb more neutrons than are being emitted by the fission reaction, the reaction remains under control. However, remove the control rod an inch too far and you have a cascade of neutrons and quantity transforms into quality—producing a nuclear meltdown.

The same processes can be observed at all levels of nature. In his book *Ubiquity*, the American physicist and author, Mark Buchanan, points out that phenomena as diverse as heart attacks, avalanches, forest fires, the rise and fall of animal populations, stock exchange crises, the movement of traffic, and even revolutions in art and fashion are all governed by the same basic law, which can be expressed as a mathematical equation known as a power law. This is yet another striking conformation of the dialectical law of the transformation of quantity into quality.

The dialectics of *Capital*

In his marvelously profound *Philosophical Notebooks*, written during the period of his Swiss exile in the years of World War I, Lenin wrote: "It is impossible completely to understand Marx's *Capital*, and especially its first chapter, without having thoroughly studied and understood the *whole* of Hegel's *Logic*. Consequently, half a century later none of the Marxists understood Marx!"

Even allowing for an element of exaggeration—these were, after all, rough notes written for self-clarification, not intended for publication—the fundamental idea expressed by Lenin is correct. *Capital* itself is a masterful application of the dialectical method refined by Hegel and perfected by Marx and Engels. The first chapter of the first volume is purely philosophical in character and is precisely based on Hegel, as Marx himself pointed out.

For that very reason, this chapter is generally considered one of the most difficult in the entire work. It is not about economics but about philosophy. It is rooted in the method of Hegel's dialectical masterpiece *The Science of Logic*. Yet it is fundamental to an understanding of Marx's analysis of the capitalist economy.

In the first volume of *Capital*, Marx derives all the laws of capitalist society from an analysis of its basic "cell"—the commodity. Marx analyzes the commodity and explains that it has two aspects, which are really contradictory tendencies. At first sight, the commodity appears to be something very simple and concrete: an object of use. Whether this use is really necessary or is the product of caprice is indifferent to this consideration. But on closer examination, we see the commodity is not simple at all. It is not just a use value, but also an exchange value—something entirely different.

Humankind has produced use values from the earliest period, but under capitalism, the nature of commodities undergoes a fundamental change. The capitalist does not produce objects for human use but objects for sale in order to obtain a profit.

The use value of a commodity is confined to its concrete attributes; but in exchange value there is not a single atom of matter. The price of an individual commodity is determined by a vast number of transactions that take place daily in the world economy. Prices fluctuate according to the laws of supply and demand, but these fluctuations take place around a given point, which is the real value of a commodity. This value, as even economists prior to Marx explained, is the product of human labor.

Particular and universal

In his *Philosophical Notebooks*, Lenin writes:

> In his *Capital*, Marx first analyzes the simplest, most ordinary and fundamental, most common and everyday *relation* of bourgeois (commodity) society, a relation encountered billions of times, viz., the exchange of commodities. In this very simple phenomenon, in this "cell" of bourgeois society, analysis reveals *all* the contradictions (or the germs of *all* contradictions) of modern society. The subsequent exposition shows us the development (*both* growth *and* movement) of these contradictions and of this society in the sum of its individual parts. From its beginning to its end.
>
> Such must also be the method of exposition (or study) of dialectics in general—for with Marx the dialectics of bourgeois society is only a particular case of dialectics. To begin with what is the simplest, most ordinary, common, etc., with *any proposition*: the leaves of a tree are green; John is a man; Fido is a dog, etc. Here already we have *dialectics* (as Hegel's genius recognized): the *individual* is the *universal*.
>
> The medieval scholastics cracked their brains over the question as to whether universals (abstractions) actually exist. Hegel solved this problem brilliantly by pointing out that the particular and the universal *are in fact the same*: every particular is, in one way or another, a universal. Every individual belongs to a genus or species that defines its true nature, however, genesis and species are made up of individual creatures. The limit of these categories in biology is determined by the ability to reproduce.
>
> Consequently, the opposites—the particular as opposed to the universal—are identical: the individual exists only in the connection that leads to the universal. The universal exists only in the individual and through the individual. Every individual is—in one way or another—a universal. Every universal is a fragment, or an aspect, or the essence of an individual. Every universal only approximately embraces all the individual objects. Every individual enters incompletely into the universal, etc., etc. Every individual is connected by thousands of transitions with other kinds of individuals—things, phenomena, processes, etc. As Aristotle pointed out: "But of course, there cannot be a house in general, apart from individual houses" (*Metaphysics*).
>
> . . . This apparently contradictory assertion can be shown from even the simplest sentence. It is impossible to express the nature of any particular without immediately turning it into a universal. Such is the nature of any definition, for example when we say John is a man, Fido is a dog, this is a leaf of a tree, etc., we disregard a number of attributes as contingent; we separate the essence from the appearance, and counterpose the one to the other.

Hegel pointed out that, in ordinary language, statements do not take the form of "*a = a*" (John is John, a house is a house, etc.) but "*a = b*" (John is a man, a house is a building), which implies the unity of identity and difference. And Lenin comments:

> *Here already* we have the elements, the germs, the concepts of *necessity*, of objective connection in nature, etc. Here already we have the contingent and the necessary, the phenomenon and the essence. . .

> . . . Thus in any proposition we can—and must—disclose as in a "nucleus" ("cell") the germs of *all* the elements of dialectics, and thereby show that dialectics is a property of all human knowledge in general. And natural science shows us—and here again it must be demonstrated in *any* simple instance—objective nature with the same qualities, the transformation of the individual into the universal, of the contingent into the necessary, transitions, modulations, and the reciprocal connection of opposites. Dialectics *is* the theory of knowledge of (Hegel and) Marxism. This is the "aspect" of the matter—it is not "an aspect" but the *essence* of the matter—to which Plekhanov, not to speak of other Marxists, paid no attention.

Can human society be understood?

Even the most superficial observation proves that human society has passed through a number of definite stages and that certain processes are repeated at regular intervals. Just as in nature we see the transformation of quantity into quality, so in history we see that long periods of slow, almost imperceptible change are interrupted by periods in which the process is accelerated to produce a qualitative leap.

In nature, the long periods of slow change—stasis—can last for millions of years. They are interrupted by catastrophic events, which are invariably accompanied by the extinction of animal species that were previously dominant, and the rise of other species that previously were insignificant but were better adapted to take advantage of the new circumstances. In human society, wars and revolutions play such a significant role that we are accustomed to using them as milestones that separate one historical period from another.

It was Marx and Engels who discovered that the real driving force of history is the development of the productive forces. This does not mean, as the enemies of Marxism frequently assert, that Marx reduced everything to economics. There are many other factors that enter into the development of society: religion, morality, philosophy, politics, patriotism, tribal alliances, etc. All these enter into a complex web of social interrelations that create a rich and confusing mosaic of phenomena and processes.

At first sight it seems impossible to make sense of this. But the same thing could be said of nature, yet the complexity of the universe does not deter scientists from attempting to separate the different elements, to analyze and categorize them. By what right do men and women imagine that they are above nature, and that they alone in the entire universe cannot be understood by science? The very idea is preposterous and a manifestation of that burning desire of humans to be some kind of special creation, entirely separate from all other animals and with a special relation to the rest of the universe determined by God. But science has mercilessly stripped away these egocentric illusions.

Marx and Engels, for the first time, gave communism a scientific character. They explained that the real emancipation of the masses depends on the level of development of the productive forces—industry, agriculture, science and technology—which will create the necessary conditions for a general reduction of the working day and access to culture for all, as the only way of transforming the way people think and behave towards each other.

Historical materialism

Marx gives an excellent though little-quoted definition of historical materialism in the third volume of *Capital*:

> The specific economic form in which unpaid labor is pumped out of the direct producers determines the relationship of domination and servitude, as this grows directly out of production itself and reacts back on it in turn as a determinant.
>
> On this is based the entire configuration of the economic community arising from the actual relations of production, and hence also its specific political form. It is in each case the direct relationship of the owners of the conditions of production to the immediate producers— a relationship whose particular form naturally corresponds always to a certain level of development of the type and manner of labor, and hence to its social productive power—in which we find the innermost secret, the hidden basis of the entire social edifice, and hence also the political form of the relationship of sovereignty and dependence, in short, the specific form of state in each case.

> This does not prevent the same economic basis—the same in its major conditions—from displaying endless variations and gradations in its appearance, as the result of innumerable different empirical circumstances, natural conditions, racial relations, historical influences acting from outside, etc., and these can only be understood by analyzing these empirically given conditions.

The essential *content* of social development is the development of the productive forces. But on the basis of the productive forces there arise property relations and a complex superstructure of legal, religious, and ideological relations. The latter constitute the *forms* through which the former express themselves. Content and form can come into contradiction, but in the last analysis, the content will always determine the form.

The content changes faster than the forms, creating contradictions that must be resolved. The obsolete superstructure impedes the development of the productive forces. Thus, at the present time, the development of the productive forces, which has attained levels undreamed of in previous history, is in open conflict with private ownership and the nation-state. The old forms are strangling the development of the productive forces. They must be burst asunder in order to resolve the contradiction. The obsolete forms are burst apart and replaced by new forms that are in consonance with the needs of the productive forces.

Every successive socioeconomic formation opens up the possibility for a greater development of the productive forces and therefore increases humanity's power over nature. In this way, the material basis is prepared for what Engels described as humanity's leap from the realm of necessity to the realm of freedom.

Class society

The species *Homo sapiens* emerged about 100,000 to 250,000 years ago, perhaps even as long as 400,000 years ago. What we call civilization, which arose on the basis of the division of society into classes, is roughly five thousand years old. Thus, during at least 95% of its history, humanity was denied the blessings of private property, class struggle, the police and the army, the monogamous family, and the antagonism between town and country—all those institutions that are accepted as given and eternal by mainstream social scientists.

Class society itself has seen a succession of fundamental changes, or revolutions, in the course of its development. Broadly speaking, as Marx explained, the economic development of society has been marked by a succession of stages or "epochs." At a certain level of development of the productive forces, socioeconomic systems based on communal land ownership, slavery, serfdom, and wage labor have arisen, each with their own political and cultural "superstructure" and their own laws of motion.

It is therefore pointless to try to discover the laws of political economy "in general," equally applicable to, say, ancient Egypt, medieval Europe, and the modern world economy. It is necessary to discover the particular laws that govern each system, "to appropriate the material in detail, to analyze its different forms of development, *to trace out their inner connection*," to use Marx's expression.

Today, the anarchy of production cannot contain the demands of modern industry, technology, and science. The only way to solve the contradictions of capitalism that are the cause of starvation, poverty, wars, and terrorism is through the socialist transformation of society.

It is important to note how the process of human development has undergone a constant acceleration. The fall of the Roman Empire, which represented slavery in its most developed form, caused, first a collapse of civilization in Europe, then a slow revival under the feudal system that lasted just over a thousand years. Feudalism lasted for a shorter time than slavery, and capitalism has existed for only two or three centuries.

It must be noted that the pace of development of the productive forces under capitalism has been far more rapid than in any previous society. There have been more inventions in this period than in all previous history. But this feverish development of industry, science, and technique has come into conflict with the narrow limits of private property and the nation-state.

Capitalism in its period of senile decay is no longer capable of developing the productive forces as it did in the past. This is the fundamental cause of the present crisis, which is beginning to threaten the very existence of humanity.

Contradictions in society

The dialectical laws are not confined to nature, but also apply to society, history, and economics. To this list of phase transitions described in books such as *Ubiquity*, we can also add revolutions, which are an expression of war between the classes.

We have already dealt with the phenomenon of criticality in relation to phenomena such as the atom, showing that the internal contradictions are contained by specific forces within certain limits, but that when these limits are exceeded, criticality results with explosive consequences. A similar process can be observed in society.

The *Communist Manifesto* explains that the history of all hitherto existing society—excluding pre-class societies—is the history of class struggle. The existence of class antagonisms threatens to tear society apart. In order to regulate and control the class struggle, a power emerges that stands above society and is increasingly alienated from it. This power is the state.

The role of the state power is to guarantee the maintenance of the status quo, maintain order and ensure that the forces that threaten to tear society apart are kept within acceptable limits. In the last analysis, the state consists of armed bodies: the police, the army, the prisons, courts, and judiciary. Ultimately, the ruling class, which is a minority, must rely upon violence, or the threat of violence, to maintain its domination over the masses.

However, the appeal to violence is only a last resort. The ruling class has in its hands a whole battery of instruments for keeping control. Not only does it possess a monopoly of armed force, it also has a monopoly of culture. The schools and universities, the press and mass media, and all the other paraphernalia of culture are the privileged preserve of the ruling class, which it uses and abuses in its own interests.

The philosophy departments in universities, like all the rest, have a very useful function from the standpoint of the ruling class: to combat Marxism and any other "subversive" tendencies, and to inculcate in the youth ideas that tend to serve the interests of the ruling class and the status quo. It is sufficient to quote the avalanche of antirevolutionary propaganda that flooded the bookshops and television screens during the 100th anniversary of the Russian Revolution to underline this point.

One of the most powerful weapons in the hands of the ruling class is religion. The utilitarian—or rather, cynical—view was expressed long ago by the Roman philosopher Seneca when he said: "Religion is regarded by the common people as true, by the wise as false, and by rulers as useful." There is some truth in this view, particularly when it is used to explain the role of organized religion.

Napoleon saw the Church as a very useful way of controlling the masses and bolstering his own power, although he himself did not believe a word of it. Probably the same was true of the emperor Constantine, who adopted Christianity as the state religion of the Roman Empire, although there is no real proof that he himself was ever baptized.

But this cannot explain the deep roots of religion in the popular psyche, or the powerful hold it has on the minds of the masses. To understand that, one must go deeper into the nature of class society and the role of alienation. In that sense, Marx had a far more profound understanding than the Left Hegelians such as Strauss.

In capitalist society, men and women are alienated from each other and subordinated to alien forces beyond their control or understanding. The real God of capitalism is neither Jehovah nor Muhammad, but Mammon, the god of wealth. Its real temples are not the churches, mosques, or synagogues, but the stock exchanges that determine the fate of millions of people.

In the first volume of *Capital* there is a famous chapter on the fetishism of commodities. This explains in very graphic terms the power of money in bourgeois society. All human relations are mediated by this power, which distorts and warps them into something inhuman, ugly, and oppressive. Human psychology is powerfully conditioned by this alien force, by which human beings are judged, not on the basis of their natural abilities, physical strength, beauty, or intellect, but purely by the amount of money they possess.

This produces a monstrous situation in which all natural human relations stand on their head. If we judge the level of civilized conduct by the standards of treatment of women, children, and old people, our modern "civilization" stands condemned from every point of view.

The ghastly record of wife and child abuse, orphans, and prostitution under capitalism compares most unfavorably with the communal child rearing practiced by humanity during most of its history—that is, before the advent of that strange social arrangement that men are fond of calling civilization. We recall the words of a Native American to a missionary:

> You white people love your own children only. We love the children of the clan. They belong to all the people, and we care for them. They are bone of our bone, and flesh of our flesh. We are all father and mother to them. White people are savages; they do not love their children. If children are orphaned, people have to be paid to look after them. We know nothing of such barbarous ideas (M. F. Ashley Montagu, ed., *Marriage: Past and Present: A Debate Between Robert Briffault and Bronislaw Malinowski*).

The tipping point

Just as within the nucleus there are forces that prevent it from flying apart, so in society there are a whole series of mechanisms that serve a similar purpose. But by far the most powerful of these is a force within the heads of the people themselves. Tradition, habit, and routine constitute an extremely powerful force of inertia in society.

Most people do not like change. They fear any disturbance in the existing order as a terrifying leap into the unknown. Most people will cling to ideas, prejudices, religious beliefs, well-known political parties, and leaders with extraordinary tenacity. This is the most powerful glue that serves to preserve the existing order. But like everything else in nature, this powerful force of inertia can hold things together only up to a definite point.

Beneath the surface of apparent tranquillity in which "nothing happens here," there is a seething discontent, and accumulation of anger, bitterness, and frustration that is striving to find a conscious expression. Sooner or later, the point is reached where quantity becomes transformed into quality.

We can see the same process in every strike, where people become transformed. Workers who were always apathetic and inactive in the past suddenly become energized and move into action in a way that surprises those who liked to consider themselves as more advanced. In the words of the Bible: "for the first shall be last and the last shall be first." That is a very dialectical affirmation!

The emergence of a critical state was expressed in very poetic and striking language by Hegel in his *Phenomenology of Mind*:

> For the rest it is not difficult to see that our epoch is a birth time, and a period of transition. The spirit of man has broken with the old order of things hitherto prevailing, and with the old ways of thinking, and is in the mind to let them all sink into the depths of the past and to set about its own transformation. It is indeed never at rest, but carried along the stream of progress ever onward. But it is here as in the case of the birth of a child; after a long period of nutrition in silence, the continuity of the gradual growth in size, of quantitative change, is suddenly cut short by the first breath drawn—there is a break in the process, a qualitative change and the child is born. In like manner the spirit of the time, growing slowly and quietly ripe for the new form it is to assume, disintegrates one fragment after another of the structure of its previous world. That it is tottering to its fall is indicated only by symptoms

here and there. Frivolity and again ennui, which are spreading in the established order of things, the undefined foreboding of something unknown—all these betoken that there is something else approaching. This gradual crumbling to pieces, which did not alter the general look and aspect of the whole, is interrupted by the sunrise, which, in a flash and at a single stroke, brings to view the form and structure of the new world.

The contradictions within society—the class struggle—continues unabated in one form or another, and to a greater or lesser degree of intensity, until the critical point is reached. At this point, certain symptoms emerge that demonstrate the impossibility of continuing as before: the ruling class splits and is unable to rule in the old way; the masses move into action to challenge the existing order; the middle layers of society vacillate between revolution and reaction. All these symptoms indicate the imminence of a drastic change.

The process by which society finally splits apart on class lines was best expressed by the great Russian revolutionary Leon Trotsky. In the chapter on dual power in his *History of Russian Revolution*, he writes the following:

> Antagonistic classes exist in society everywhere, and a class deprived of power inevitably strives to some extent to swerve the governmental course in its favor. This does not as yet mean, however, that two or more powers are ruling in society. The character of a political structure is directly determined by the relation of the oppressed classes to the ruling class. A single government, the necessary condition of stability in any régime, is preserved so long as the ruling class succeeds in putting over its economic and political forms upon the whole of society as the only forms possible . . .
>
> This double sovereignty does not presuppose—generally speaking, indeed, it excludes—the possibility of a division of the power into two equal halves, or indeed any formal equilibrium of forces whatever. It is not a constitutional, but a revolutionary fact. It implies that a destruction of the social equilibrium has already split the state superstructure. It arises where the hostile classes are already each relying upon essentially incompatible governmental organizations—the one outlived, the other in process of formation—which jostle against each other at every step in the sphere of government. The amount of power which falls to each of these struggling classes in such a situation is determined by the correlation of forces in the course of the struggle.

The role of the individual

On October 13, 1806, an excited Hegel wrote in a letter to his friend Niethammer: "I saw the Emperor—this World-Spirit—riding out of the city on reconnaissance. It is indeed a wonderful sensation to see such an individual, who, concentrated here at a single point, astride a horse, reaches out over the world and masters it."

Like Beethoven and many of the most progressive intellectuals of his time, the young Hegel was a fervent admirer of the French Revolution. In the person of Napoleon, he thought he saw the spirit of that revolution riding on horseback. Of course, his appraisal of the nature and role of Napoleon was mistaken. Nevertheless, in his vision of the French Revolution as the essential spirit of the times, he was not mistaken at all. Marxism does not deny the role of the individual in history, as Engels explains:

> Men make their history themselves, but not as yet with a collective will or according to a collective plan or even in a definitely defined, given society. Their efforts clash, and for that very reason all such societies are governed by *necessity*, which is supplemented by and appears under the forms of *accident*. The necessity which here asserts itself amidst all accident is again ultimately economic necessity. This is where the so-called great men come in for treatment. That such and such a man and precisely that man arises at that particular time in that given country is of course pure accident. But cut him out and there will be a demand for a substitute, and this substitute will be found, good or bad, but in the long run he will be found. That Napoleon, just that particular Corsican, should have been the military dictator whom the French Republic, exhausted by its own war, had rendered necessary, was an accident; but that, if a Napoleon had been lacking, another would have filled the place, is proved by the fact that the man has always been found as soon as he became necessary: Caesar, Augustus, Cromwell, etc. While Marx discovered the materialist conception of history, Thierry, Mignet, Guizot, and other historians writing before 1850 are the proof that it was being striven for. Lewis Morgan's investigations into early society also proves that the time was ripe for it and that it *had* to be discovered.
>
> So with all the other accidents, and apparent accidents, of history. The further the particular sphere which we are investigating is removed from the economic sphere and approaches that of pure abstract ideology, the more shall we find it exhibiting accidents in its development, the more will its curve run in a zigzag. So also you will find that the axis of this curve will approach more and more nearly parallel to the axis of the curve of economic development the longer the period considered and the wider the field dealt with (Engels, *Letter to Borgius*, January 25, 1894).

We have already mentioned the process of nucleation, that critical point where a given phenomenon is hovering on the brink of a fundamental change. The transformation of quantity into quality is brought about either by an external shock or the presence of a catalyst. We see just the same process in a revolution.

All the objective factors necessary for a revolution may be present, but in order for the potential to become actual, something else is needed. The role of a catalyst in the prerevolutionary situation is played by the revolutionary party and its leadership. It is this that provides the as yet undeveloped, shapeless, and confused movement of the masses with the necessary coherence, structure, aims, and organization that are needed to overthrow the existing order, which, even when it is tottering for a fall, still represents a formidable force of resistance that must be consciously overcome.

Every revolutionary party in history always begins as a small minority. In the beginning it does not apparently present a serious challenge to the existing order. It starts, like every other living organism, as an embryo. But an embryo, providing it includes all the necessary genetic information to form a healthy human being, can grow and develop.

Although it seems to be a paradox, the determinism of the early Calvinists, far from leading to pessimism and a paralysis of the will, had exactly the opposite effect. The Puritans were convinced that they were fighting on the side of a force that had all the power of inevitability behind it. It was their religious duty to "fight the good fight" and assist God's Kingdom to come into existence as soon as possible. Their absolute conviction of its ultimate success spurred them on to action.

Likewise, Marxists believe in the inevitability of socialism, in the sense that capitalism has exhausted its potential for developing society and advancing the cause of culture and civilization. By developing the forces of production to their present level, it has prepared the way for the next logical stage, which will be the socialization of the means of production, which are in revolt against the suffocating restrictions of private ownership and the nation-state.

This process can be accelerated or delayed by a series of factors, not least of which is the subjective factor. There will be many opportunities for the working class to take power into its hands, but the mere existence of a possibility does not necessarily mean that the potential will be realized. That depends on the actions of human beings, their willingness to fight, and the quality of their leaders.

Capitalism is in a state of self-evident decay. The senile decadence of capitalism poses a deadly threat to civilization and to the human species itself. To prolong the agony signifies a deepening of the crisis, with all the attendant evils of economic and social collapse, poverty, suffering, wars, death, and destruction on a massive scale.

It is, therefore, the duty of Marxists to fight to lessen the sufferings of the human race by doing everything possible to accelerate the process of revolution, which alone can put an end to the death agony of a superannuated, rotten, and thoroughly decayed system. In that sense, conscious revolutionaries are agents of historical necessity, in the same way as Oliver Cromwell's Ironsides, the French Jacobins, and the Russian Bolsheviks were the agents of a necessary social transformation in an earlier period.

Dialectics—the scientific basis of revolutionary practice

The equivalent of genetic information in the revolutionary party is Marxist theory. The party, even when it is small, must contain the necessary quality in order to grow. If it conducts its work correctly and has the necessary opportunities at its disposal, it can grow and develop. Quality becomes transformed into quantity, but quantity in turn at a certain point becomes quality. A mass party becomes a factor in the situation, and its actions can now influence large numbers of people. It will be in a position to lead the masses to victory.

The history of the Bolshevik Party is highly instructive in this respect. No other party in history has ever achieved such striking success in such a relatively short space of time, transforming what were originally tiny and isolated groups of Marxist cadres into a mass party capable of carrying out the greatest social revolution in history.

What is most important to note is the colossal importance that Lenin and Trotsky always gave to theory, and the serious working out of perspectives, tactics, and strategy. This, in the last analysis, was the secret of their success. From the very beginning Lenin always insisted on the key importance of theory. In *What Is to Be Done* he wrote: "Without revolutionary theory there can be no revolutionary movement. This idea cannot be insisted upon too strongly at a time when the fashionable preaching of opportunism goes hand in hand with an infatuation for the narrowest forms of practical activity."

The fundamental importance of the dialectical method as the scientific basis for all revolutionary practice was explained in a brilliant way in Trotsky's autobiography, *My Life*:

> Later, the feeling of the supremacy of the general over the particular became an integral part of my literary and political work. The dull empiricism, the unashamed, cringing worship of the fact which is so often only imaginary, and falsely interpreted at that, were odious to me. Beyond the facts, I looked for laws. Naturally, this led me more than once into hasty and incorrect generalizations, especially in my younger years when my knowledge, book-acquired, and my experience in life were still inadequate. But in every sphere, barring none, I felt that I could move and act only when I held in my hand the thread of the general. The social-revolutionary radicalism which has become the permanent pivot for my whole inner life grew out of this intellectual enmity toward the striving for petty ends, toward out-and-out pragmatism, and toward all that is ideologically without form and theoretically ungeneralized.

This "dull empiricism, the unashamed, cringing worship of the fact," as Trotsky points out, is the philosophical basis of reformism, of that cowardly surrender to what is called "the facts of life," of politics conceived as "the art of the possible," in which all serious challenges to the status quo are regarded as something impossible, a utopian dream or dangerous adventurism. Marxism, on the contrary, presents us with a scientific analysis of the status quo, penetrating beneath the surface of the "facts" to reveal the hidden contradictions that will eventually lead what appears to be stable, solid, and unchangeable into its opposite.

Marx and Engels said that there were two alternatives before humanity: socialism or barbarism. The elements of barbarism already exist, not only in the so-called developing world, where millions of people are forced to live in nightmare conditions of poverty, hunger, disease, and war, but also in the so-called advanced capitalist countries.

The aim of Marxists is to fight for the socialist transformation of society on a national and international scale. We believe that the capitalist system has long ago outlived its historical usefulness and has converted itself into a monstrously oppressive, unjust, and inhuman system. The ending of exploitation and the creation of a harmonious socialist world order, based on a rational and democratically run plan of production, will be the first step in the creation of a new and higher form of society in which men and women will relate to themselves as genuinely free human beings.

The role of philosophy in the modern epoch must be the noble task of facilitating the work of the socialist revolution, combating false ideas, and providing a rational explanation of the most important manifestations of our age, thus clearing the ground for a fundamental change in society. In the celebrated words of Karl Marx:

> The philosophers have only interpreted the world, in various ways; *the point is to change it.*

I

GENESIS AND ORIGINS

THESES ON FEUERBACH

Karl Marx
1845

I

The chief defect of all hitherto existing materialism—that of Feuerbach included—is that the thing, reality, sensuousness, is conceived only in the form of the object or of contemplation, but not as sensuous human activity, practice, not subjectively. Hence, in contradistinction to materialism, the active side was developed abstractly by idealism—which, of course, does not know real, sensuous activity as such. Feuerbach wants sensuous objects, really distinct from the thought objects, but he does not conceive human activity itself as objective activity. Hence, in *The Essence of Christianity*, he regards the theoretical attitude as the only genuinely human attitude, while practice is conceived and fixed only in its dirty-judaical manifestation. Hence he does not grasp the significance of "revolutionary," of "practical-critical," activity.

II

The question whether objective truth can be attributed to human thinking is not a question of theory but is a practical question. Man must prove the truth—i.e., the reality and power, the this-sidedness of his thinking in practice. The dispute over the reality or non-reality of thinking that is isolated from practice is a purely scholastic question.

III

The materialist doctrine concerning the changing of circumstances and upbringing forgets that circumstances are changed by men and that it is essential to educate the educator himself. This doctrine must, therefore, divide society into two parts, one of which is superior to society. The coincidence of the changing of circumstances and of human activity or self-changing can be conceived and rationally understood only as revolutionary practice.

IV

Feuerbach starts out from the fact of religious self-alienation, of the duplication of the world into a religious world and a secular one. His work consists in resolving the religious world into its secular basis.

But that the secular basis detaches itself from itself and establishes itself as an independent realm in the clouds can only be explained by the cleavages and self-contradictions within this secular basis. The latter must, therefore, in itself be both understood in its contradiction and revolutionized in practice. Thus, for instance, after the earthly family is discovered to be the secret of the holy family, the former must then itself be destroyed in theory and in practice.

V

Feuerbach, not satisfied with abstract thinking, wants contemplation; but he does not conceive sensuousness as practical, human-sensuous activity.

VI

Feuerbach resolves the religious essence into the human essence. But the human essence is no abstraction inherent in each single individual.

In its reality it is the ensemble of the social relations. Feuerbach, who does not enter upon a criticism of this real essence, is consequently compelled:

1. To abstract from the historical process and to fix the religious sentiment as something by itself and to presuppose an abstract—isolated—human individual.

2. Essence, therefore, can be comprehended only as "genus," as an internal, dumb generality which naturally unites the many individuals.

VII

Feuerbach, consequently, does not see that the "religious sentiment" is itself a social product, and that the abstract individual whom he analyzes belongs to a particular form of society.

VIII

All social life is essentially practical. All mysteries which lead theory to mysticism find their rational solution in human practice and in the comprehension of this practice.

IX

The highest point reached by contemplative materialism, that is, materialism which does not comprehend sensuousness as practical activity, is contemplation of single individuals and of civil society.

X

The standpoint of the old materialism is civil society; the standpoint of the new is human society, or social humanity.

XI

The philosophers have only interpreted the world, in various ways; the point is to change it.

MARX'S REVOLUTION IN PHILOSOPHY: REFLECTIONS ON THE THESES ON FEUERBACH

Alan Woods
London, May 17, 2013

Feuerbach is the only one who has a serious, critical attitude to the Hegelian dialectic and who has made genuine discoveries in this field. He is in fact the true conqueror of the old philosophy.—Marx, 1844

The problem of knowledge has occupied a central place in philosophy for centuries. But this so-called problem only arises when human knowledge is regarded

    a) as something separate from a physical body;
    b) as something separate from the material world.

What we have here is a one-sided view of consciousness, which is presented as a *barrier* that is supposed to shut us off from the "external" world. In fact, we are part of this world, not separate from it, and consciousness does not separate us but *connects us to it.* The relationship of humans to the physical world from the very beginning was *not contemplative but active.*

We do not only think with our brain, but with our whole body. Thinking must be seen, not as an isolated activity ("the ghost in the machine") *but as part of the whole human experience, of human sensuous activity and interaction with the world and with other people.* It must be seen as part of this complex process of permanent interaction, not as an isolated activity that is mechanically juxtaposed to it.

Materialism rejects the notion that mind, consciousness, soul, etc. is something separate from matter. Thought is merely the mode of existence of the brain, which, like life itself, is only matter organized in a certain way. Mind is what we call the sum total of the activity of the brain and the nervous system. *However, dialectically, the whole is greater than the sum of its parts.*

This materialist view corresponds closely to the conclusions of science, which is gradually uncovering the workings of the brain and revealing its secrets. By contrast, the idealists persist in presenting consciousness as a "mystery," something that we cannot comprehend. At this point our old friend the Soul reemerges triumphantly, accompanied by the Holy of Holies, angels, the Devil, and all the rest of the mystical paraphernalia that science ought to have consigned to a museum long ago.

Descartes and dualism

Hiding behind the respectable façade of philosophical idealism is religion and superstition. Idealism is always, in the final analysis, religion. The Immaculate and Eternal Soul was supposed to be locked up inside the grubby, imperfect, and short-lived material body, longing for release at the moment of death, when we "give up the ghost" and float up to Paradise (if we are lucky).

In this way, matter was thought of as a second-class citizen, a scruffy peasant, destined to give way before His Majesty the Immortal Soul. This idea is at least as old as Plato and Pythagoras, who saw the physical world as a poor imitation of the perfect Idea (Form), which existed before the world was thought of.

The idea that the soul exists independently of the body was carried into modern times by the famous French philosopher Descartes (1596–1650). He confused the issue then and it has been confused ever since. He introduced the notion of dualism, which says that thought (consciousness) is something separate from matter. Here mind is regarded as something that is present inside the body, but is quite different to it. The insurmountable difficulty with dualism is this: if the mind is entirely different to the physical body, *how can they interact?*

The mistake is to treat consciousness as a "thing," an independent entity, separate and apart from human sensuous activity.

Modern science has forever banished the notion of consciousness as an independent "thing." We now know what Descartes did not know about the workings of nature, the world of molecules, atoms, and sub-atomic particles, of the electric impulses that govern the workings of the brain. In place of a mysterious soul, we are beginning to acquire a scientific understanding of how the human body and brain function.

The action of nerve cells is both electrical and chemical. At the ends of each nerve cell there are specialized regions, the *synaptic terminals*, which contain large numbers of tiny membranous sacs that hold neurotransmitter chemicals. These chemicals transmit nerve impulses from one nerve cell to another. After an electrical nerve impulse has traveled along a neuron, it reaches the terminal and stimulates the release of neurotransmitters from their sacs.

The neurotransmitters travel across the synapse (the junction between the neighboring neurons) and stimulate the production of an electrical charge, which carries the nerve impulse forward. This process is repeated over and over again until a muscle is moved or relaxed or a sensory impression is noted by the brain. These electrochemical events can be considered the "language" of the nervous system, by which information is transmitted from one part of the body to another. This scientific explanation immediately does away with the mystical-idealist view of thought and consciousness as something mysterious and inexplicable, something divorced from the normal workings of nature and other bodily functions.

Hand and brain

The idealist view of consciousness and language is abstract and arbitrary and at odds with the facts of human evolution. It is also unhistorical. The relationship of early humans (and protohumans) to the physical environment was determined by the need to find food and escape from predators. The erect stance—brought about by the changes to the environment due to climate change—freed the hands, which could then be used for manual labor.

Consciousness arises from the evolution of the brain and the central nervous system. This evolution is in turn intimately related to human practical activity, that is, work. Humans transform their environment through physical labor, and in doing so, also transform themselves. This process has taken place over millions of years, and has its roots in earlier stages of evolution, in particular, the transition from invertebrates to vertebrates, which leads to the development of a central nervous system and eventually a brain.

The connection between hand and brain is well documented. Increased manual dexterity and the development of a multiplicity of manual activities led to a rapid growth of the brain and increased capacity for thinking. As a matter of fact, there is a dialectical relationship between the large size of the brain, the erect posture, and the development of the hand for specific operations. What a marvelous production of evolution is the human hand! The opposition of the thumb to the rest of the hand is the first adaptation that permits gripping and manipulation. This is the prior condition for all subsequent development.

The apes used their hands to swing in the trees. They also used them for grasping sticks, which in some cases were even used as primitive tools for quite sophisticated operations like digging for termites. Once our distant ancestors adopted the upright stance, the hands were free to experiment with many other operations. With constant practice, the hands became ever more skilled and able to perform finer and more complex operations, particularly the manipulation of natural objects as tools.

It was the hand that developed the brain, not vice versa. This can be seen also in lower animals. They also do not contemplate the world—*they eat it.* In the same way, a human baby "knows" the world by putting it in its mouth. Likewise, language is not a "tool," like a hammer or a shovel that is manufactured and manipulated at will. In fact, language evolves together with consciousness, as a product of social intercourse and collective production. It is not "made" but arises spontaneously from collective human activity and social life over a long period of time.

The regular use of tools and collective labor must have necessitated some kind of language, triggering a whole series of interdependent factors. All bodily and mental functions are closely connected. Dialectically, cause becomes effect and effect becomes cause. The human hand is closely linked to the eye and the brain, and the coordination needed to create even the most rudimentary stone tool is considerable. All humans make and use tools and the correlation of hand, eye, and brain required for tool making is what drove the development of the brain over millions of years.

> Use of tools appears to have predated major growth of the brain in mankind and is associated with fossil men of the *Australopithecus* type (H.J. Fleure and M. Davies, *A Natural History of Man in Britain*).

The conscious manufacture of elementary stone tools was clearly the driving force of the formation of elementary concepts and the development of thinking. This undoubtedly had an effect on the inner structure of the brain, which was manifested in a growth in its size. These transformations, taken in their totality, represented the qualitative leap that separated humanity from all other forms of living matter. Our species was, therefore, not fashioned by God as a special act of creation, but was the product of evolution, in which the decisive element was manual labor. Thus, as Engels explained over a hundred years ago—it was not the brain that developed our humanity, but the hand that developed the brain.

Marx's philosophical revolution

In the third of his *Theses on Feuerbach*, Marx wrote:

> The materialist doctrine concerning the changing of circumstances and upbringing forgets that circumstances are changed by men and that it is essential to educate the educator himself. This doctrine must, there-fore, divide society into two parts, one of which is superior to society. The coincidence of the changing of circumstances and of human activ-ity or self-changing can be conceived and rationally understood only as revolutionary practice.

In these few concentrated sentences is contained a philosophical revolu-tion. The great German philosopher Hegel came close to discovering the truth, but despite his colossal genius he failed to make the decisive leap from theory to practice, blinded as he was by his idealist preconceptions. In Hegel, the dialectic remained obscured, its profound truths hidden in a mass of abstract and abstruse reasoning. It required the genius of a Marx to discover the rational kernel that lay hidden in the pages of Hegel's *Logic* and to apply it to the real, material world.

With Marx, philosophy finally emerges out of the dark and airless cellar to which it was confined for centuries by scholastic thought and dragged out, blinking, into the light of day. Here at last thought is united with activ-ity—not the one-sided purely intellectual activity of the scholar but real, sensuous human activity. The great German poet Goethe, answering the biblical assertion, "in the beginning was the Word," countered: "In the be-ginning was the Deed."

But real human activity (labor) is not the activity of isolated atoms. It is necessarily collective in essence. It is the combination of the individual efforts, strivings, and creativity of men and women that gives rise to all the wonders of civilization. It is the concrete realization of what old Hegel called the "unity of the Particular and the Universal." Yet this necessary unity has been stubbornly denied. The thoughts and actions of human-kind are presented, not as a collective activity, but as the work of isolated individuals.

This false idea is at once a reflection of bourgeois prejudice and an attempt to justify the structures, morals, and values of bourgeois society, a society in which the Ego (the "individual") is said to rule supreme. In reality, the individuality of the great majority is crushed and enslaved to the individuality of a tiny handful that own and control the means of production and thus the key to life itself. And to tell the whole truth, even this minority is subject to forces that they do not and cannot control.

Alienation and bourgeois society

The late, unlamented Margaret Thatcher once famously remarked: "There is no such thing as society." But when Aristotle said man is a po-litical animal, he meant that *man is a social animal*. The key to all human development—including thought and speech—is social activity and this has its roots in collective labor. Hegel said that the richness of a person's character is the richness of their connections. A person who is marooned on a desert island or held for many years in solitary confinement would find their ability to think and communicate gravely impaired.

Capitalism tends to isolate, atomize, and alienate people, who are taught to see themselves as "individuals," that is, as isolated atoms. This reflects the social reality of the bourgeoisie and petty bourgeoisie, who are constantly competing against each other. This finds its reflection in politics, religion, and philosophy. The bourgeoisie waged its first great battles against feudalism in the wars of religion of the 16th and 17th centuries when the Protestants claimed the right of every individual to worship God in his own way.

Bourgeois individualism was a progressive force in the period of capi-talist ascent, when the bourgeoisie was still capable of developing the productive forces and pushing forward the horizons of human civiliza-tion and culture. But that has receded into mists of history. In the epoch of capitalist decay, individualism has become mere egotism, selfishness, and inhumanity. It breeds indifference towards the sufferings of others and foments barbaric attitudes and behaviors which threaten to under-mine the very basis of culture and civilization.

We all like to think that we are "free" to do what we like. But this is not the case. As the German philosopher Leibniz once observed, if a magnetic needle could think, it would doubtless imagine that it pointed north due to its own free will. In the 19th century, Darwin fought to show that human beings were not the special creation of the Almighty but had evolved from the animal world. In the 20th century, Freud demonstrated that many of our actions are unconscious and that "free will" is really an illusion.

At every stage, however, men and women have tried to deny these facts and sought to assert a special, privileged status for human beings in the great order of things. The very notion that we are not free agents and that our actions are determined by forces we cannot understand and control is profoundly repugnant to us. Yet, as Hegel explained, true freedom is not the *denial* of necessity but the *understanding* of necessity.

Consciousness is determined by the physical environment. If Albert Einstein had been born in a peasant's hut in an Indian village, his native intelligence might have made him an expert in planting rice, but does anyone believe that he would have discovered the theory of relativity? Trotsky once asked, "How many Aristotles are herding swine, and how many swineherds are sitting on thrones?"

The whole outlook of the bourgeoisie is egotistical. But with the working class things are very different. Marx explains that without organization the working class is only raw material for exploitation. The workers are obliged to cooperate in collective labor, on the production line, where production is social, not individual. An individual peasant can say: "I grew that cabbage." But no individual worker in a Ford plant can say: "I made that car."

The consciousness of the worker, therefore, naturally tends to be collective. The weapons of working-class struggle are collective in character: the strike, the general strike, the mass meeting, and mass demonstrations. Individualism is the hallmark of strikebreakers, who place their own egotistical interests above those of their workmates. That is why the capitalist press always praises the "courage" of the scab, who is allegedly standing up for "the freedom of the individual."

Men and women make their own history by fighting to change and mold the circumstances that surround them. However, in changing social conditions, we also change ourselves. The idea that there is an eternal and fixed thing called "human nature" is a deeply ingrained prejudice, but has no basis in fact. So-called human nature has been transformed many times in history, is still changing, and will change even more in the future.

We live in an alienated, irrational world, which people cannot understand. In such a world, rational thought is unfashionable. In such a world it is better not to think at all. The emptiness of modern bourgeois philosophy reflects this idea perfectly, as in the vacuous platitudes of postmodernism. Men and women feel that they have lost control of their lives, that they are being displaced by strange and incomprehensible forces that are beyond their control. Human life is stripped of all its value and humanity and plunged into savagery and violence that destroys the foundation of a civilized and rational existence. "Reason becomes Unreason," as Hegel put it.

The alienation that is an all-pervasive feature of life in modern bourgeois society is even expressed in popular culture. How can one explain the strange modern fascination with disaster movies and robots that escape from human control and who take over the world, as in the *Terminator* movies? Such works of science fiction tell us little or nothing about the nature of consciousness, whether in humans or robots, but speak volumes about the alienated world that humans inhabit in the first decades of the 21st century.

In the nightmare world of *Terminator*, "things"—machines, robots— have taken over the world and are enslaving people. But this nightmare is already a reality. In our times, people are reduced to the level of things, and things—especially money—are elevated above the level of people. In ancient times pagan priests sacrificed babies to Moloch. Today millions of babies are sacrificed every year at the altar of Capital.

The only way to abolish this sense of alienation is to abolish its material base. The only way to abolish irrational thought is to abolish the irrational relations between human beings in capitalist society. The only way to eliminate the feeling that we have lost control of our lives and destinies is to overthrow the contradictory relations of production and establish a rational planned economy, where all the decisions are taken democratically by genuinely free men and women.

In a rational society, that is to say, a socialist planned society, the domination of people by things will be replaced by the administration of things by free men and women. Instead of being slaves to the machines, the latter will be our obedient slaves. Under capitalism, every advance of technology only serves to lengthen the working day and increase the servitude of the workers. Under socialism, instead of toiling longer to produce ever greater amounts of surplus value, people will work less and live life more.

The stunning advances of science and technology over the past century have placed in our hands all that is necessary to transform the planet. What science has revealed about the workings of the universe is far more fascinating, exciting, and beautiful than all the supposed "revealed truths" of religion. By revolutionizing its conditions of life, humanity will prepare the way for transforming itself, putting an end to the prehistory of our species, so that human beings will live, act, and think as humans, not animals, as free men and women, not slaves.

Which brings us back to Marx's third thesis on Feuerbach:

> The coincidence of the changing of circumstances and of human activity or self-changing [*Selbstveränderung*] can be conceived and rationally understood only as revolutionary practice.

In other words, *to revolutionize thought it is necessary to revolutionize society*.

THE THREE SOURCES AND THREE COMPONENT PARTS OF MARXISM (EXCERPT)

V.I. Lenin
March 1913

In this classic work, published on the 30th anniversary of Marx's death, Lenin explains how Marxism represents a new, higher-level synthesis of the most profound thinking previously developed by humanity. "The Marxist doctrine is omnipotent because it is true. It is comprehensive and harmonious and provides men with an integral world outlook irreconcilable with any form of superstition, reaction, or defense of bourgeois oppression. It is the legitimate successor to the best that man produced in the nineteenth century, as represented by German philosophy, English political economy, and French socialism." We present here the section on Marxist philosophy and encourage readers to read this short work in full, as it is an outstanding primer on the basics of the Marxist method.

The philosophy of Marxism is *materialism*. Throughout the modern history of Europe, and especially at the end of the eighteenth century in France, where a resolute struggle was conducted against every kind of medieval rubbish, against serfdom in institutions and ideas, materialism has proved to be the only philosophy that is consistent, true to all the teachings of natural science and hostile to superstition, cant and so forth. The enemies of democracy have, therefore, always exerted all their efforts to "refute," undermine, and defame materialism, and have advocated various forms of philosophical idealism, which always, in one way or another, amounts to the defense or support of religion.

Marx and Engels defended philosophical materialism in the most determined manner and repeatedly explained how profoundly erroneous is every deviation from this basis. Their views are most clearly and fully expounded in the works of Engels, *Ludwig Feuerbach* and *Anti-Dühring*, which, like the *Communist Manifesto*, are handbooks for every class-conscious worker.

But Marx did not stop at eighteenth-century materialism: he developed philosophy to a higher level, he enriched it with the achievements of German classical philosophy, especially of Hegel's system, which in its turn had led to the materialism of Feuerbach. The main achievement was *dialectics*, i.e., the doctrine of development in its fullest, deepest, and most comprehensive form, the doctrine of the relativity of human knowledge that provides us with a reflection of eternally developing matter. The latest discoveries of natural science—radium, electrons, the transmutation of elements—have been a remarkable confirmation of Marx's dialectical materialism despite the teachings of the bourgeois philosophers with their "new" reversions to old and decadent idealism.

Marx deepened and developed philosophical materialism to the full, and extended the cognition of nature to include the cognition of *human society*. His *historical materialism* was a great achievement in scientific thinking. The chaos and arbitrariness that had previously reigned in views on history and politics were replaced by a strikingly integral and harmonious scientific theory, which shows how, in consequence of the growth of the productive forces, out of one system of social life another and higher system develops—how capitalism, for instance, grows out of feudalism.

Just as man's knowledge reflects nature (i.e., developing matter), which exists independently of him, so man's *social knowledge* (i.e., his various views and doctrines—philosophical, religious, political, and so forth) reflects the *economic system* of society. Political institutions are a superstructure on the economic foundation. We see, for example, that the various political forms of the modern European states serve to strengthen the domination of the bourgeoisie over the proletariat.

Marx's philosophy is a consummate philosophical materialism which has provided mankind, and especially the working class, with powerful instruments of knowledge.

LUDWIG FEUERBACH AND THE END OF CLASSICAL GERMAN PHILOSOPHY

Friedrich Engels
London, February 21, 1888

After Marx's death, his lifelong collaborator Engels made it his life mission to complete his friend's major unfinished works and to defend and disseminate the ideas they had jointly developed over the previous decades. Written five years after Marx's passing, this work was intended to arm the German working-class movement with the Marxist method. It was a final "settling of accounts" with Hegel, the Young Hegelians, and Feuerbach, summarizing their ideas and place in the pantheon of human thought, and asserting Marx's position at its pinnacle. Concise yet thorough, it is a marvelous introduction to this essential period of the history of philosophy and the basic ideas of dialectics and materialism.

Foreword

In the preface to *A Contribution to the Critique of Political Economy*, published in Berlin, 1859, Karl Marx relates how the two of us in Brussels in the year 1845 set about "to work out in common the opposition of our view"—the materialist conception of history which was elaborated mainly by Marx—to the ideological view of German philosophy, in fact, to settle accounts with our erstwhile philosophical conscience. The resolve was carried out in the form of a criticism of post-Hegelian philosophy. The manuscript, two large octavo volumes, had long reached its place of publication in Westphalia when we received the news that altered circumstances did not allow of its being printed. We abandoned the manuscript to the gnawing criticism of the mice all the more willingly as we had achieved our main purpose—self-clarification!

Since then more than 40 years have elapsed and Marx died without either of us having had an opportunity of returning to the subject. We have expressed ourselves in various places regarding our relation to Hegel, but nowhere in a comprehensive, connected account. To Feuerbach, who after all in many respects forms an intermediate link between Hegelian philosophy and our conception, we never returned.

In the meantime, the Marxist world outlook has found representatives far beyond the boundaries of Germany and Europe and in all the literary languages of the world. On the other hand, classical German philosophy is experiencing a kind of rebirth abroad, especially in England and Scandinavia, and even in Germany itself people appear to be getting tired of the pauper's broth of eclecticism which is ladled out in the universities there under the name of philosophy.

In these circumstances, a short, coherent account of our relation to the Hegelian philosophy, of how we proceeded, as well as of how we separated, from it, appeared to me to be required more and more. Equally, a full acknowledgement of the influence which Feuerbach, more than any other post-Hegelian philosopher, had upon us during our period of storm and stress, appeared to me to be an undischarged debt of honor. I therefore willingly seized the opportunity when the editors of *Neue Zeit* asked me for a critical review of Starcke's book on Feuerbach. My contribution was published in that journal in the fourth and fifth numbers of 1886 and appears here in revised form as a separate publication.

Before sending these lines to press, I have once again ferreted out and looked over the old manuscript of 1845–46 [*The German Ideology*].

The section dealing with Feuerbach is not completed. The finished portion consists of an exposition of the materialist conception of history which proves only how incomplete our knowledge of economic history still was at that time. It contains no criticism of Feuerbach's doctrine itself; for the present purposes, therefore, it was unusable. On the other hand, in an old notebook of Marx's I have found the 11 *Theses on Feuerbach* ...

These are notes hurriedly scribbled down for later elaboration, absolutely not intended for publication, but invaluable as the first document in which is deposited the brilliant germ of the new world outlook.

Part 1: Hegel

The volume before us carries us back to a period which, although in time no more than a generation behind us, has become as foreign to the present generation in Germany as if it were already a hundred years old. Yet it was the period of Germany's preparation for the Revolution of 1848, and all that has happened since then in our country has been merely a continuation of 1848, merely the execution of the last will and testament of the revolution.

Just as in France in the 18th century, so in Germany in the 19th, a philosophical revolution ushered in the political collapse. But how different the two looked! The French were in open combat against all official science, against the church and often also against the state; their writings were printed across the frontier, in Holland or England, while they themselves were often in jeopardy of imprisonment in the Bastille. On the other hand, the Germans were professors, state-appointed instructors of youth; their writings were recognized textbooks, and the termination system of the whole development—the Hegelian system—was even raised, as it were, to the rank of a royal Prussian philosophy of state! Was it possible that a revolution could hide behind these professors, behind their obscure, pedantic phrases, their ponderous, wearisome sentences? Were not precisely these people who were then regarded as the representatives of the revolution, the liberals, the bitterest opponents of this brain-confusing philosophy? But what neither the government nor the liberals saw was seen at least by one man as early as 1833, and this man was indeed none other than Heinrich Heine.

Let us take an example. No philosophical proposition has earned more gratitude from narrow-minded governments and wrath from equally narrow-minded liberals than Hegel's famous statement: "All that is real is rational, and all that is rational is real." That was tangibly a sanctification of things that be, a philosophical benediction bestowed upon despotism, police government, Star Chamber proceedings, and censorship. That is how Frederick William III and how his subjects understood it. But according to Hegel certainly not everything that exists is also real, without further qualification. For Hegel the attribute of reality belongs only to that which at the same time is necessary: "In the course of its development reality proves to be necessity." A particular governmental measure—Hegel himself cites the example of "a certain tax regulation"—is therefore for him by no means real without qualification. That which is necessary, however, proves itself in the last resort to be also rational, and, applied to the Prussian state of that time, the Hegelian proposition, therefore, merely means: this state is rational, corresponds to reason, insofar as it is necessary, and if it nevertheless appears to us to be evil, but still, in spite of its evil character, continues to exist, then the evil character of the government is justified and explained by the corresponding evil character of its subjects. The Prussians of that day had the government that they deserved.

Now, according to Hegel, reality is, however, in no way an attribute predictable of any given state of affairs, social or political, in all circumstances and at all times. On the contrary. The Roman Republic was real, but so was the Roman Empire, which superseded it. In 1789, the French monarchy had become so unreal, that is to say, so robbed of all necessity, so irrational, that it had to be destroyed by the Great Revolution, of which Hegel always speaks with the greatest enthusiasm. In this case, therefore, the monarchy was the unreal and the revolution the real. And so, in the course of development, all that was previously real becomes unreal, loses its necessity, its right of existence, its rationality. And in the place of moribund reality comes a new, viable reality—peacefully if the old has enough intelligence to go to its death without a struggle; forcibly if it resists this necessity. Thus the Hegelian proposition turns into its opposite through Hegelian dialectics itself: All that is real in the sphere of human history, becomes irrational in the process of time, is therefore irrational by its very destination, is tainted beforehand with irrationality, and everything which is rational in the minds of men is destined to become real, however much it may contradict existing apparent reality. In accordance with all the rules of the Hegelian method of thought, the proposition of the rationality of everything which is real resolves itself into the other proposition: All that exists deserves to perish.

But precisely therein lay the true significance and the revolutionary character of the Hegelian philosophy (to which, as the close of the whole movement since Kant, we must here confine ourselves), that it once and for all dealt the death blow to the finality of all products of human thought and action. Truth, the cognition of which is the business of philosophy, was in the hands of Hegel no longer an aggregate of finished dogmatic statements, which, once discovered, had merely to be learned by heart. Truth lay now in the process of cognition itself, in the long historical development of science, which mounts from lower to ever higher levels of knowledge without ever reaching, by discovering so-called absolute truth, a point at which it can proceed no further, where it would have nothing more to do than to fold its hands and gaze with wonder at the absolute truth to which it had attained. And what holds good for the realm of philosophical knowledge holds good also for that of every other kind of knowledge and also for practical action. Just as knowledge is unable to reach a complete conclusion in a perfect, ideal condition of humanity, so is history unable to do so; a perfect society, a perfect "state," are things which can only exist in imagination. On the contrary, all successive historical systems are only transitory stages in the endless course of development of human society from the lower to the higher. Each stage is necessary, and therefore justified for the time and conditions to which it owes its origin. But in the face of new, higher conditions which gradually develop in its own womb, it loses vitality and justification. It must give way to a higher stage which will also in its turn decay and perish. Just as the bourgeoisie by large-scale industry, competition, and the world market dissolves in practice all stable time-honored institutions, so this dialectical philosophy dissolves all conceptions of final, absolute truth and of absolute states of humanity corresponding to it. For it [dialectical philosophy], nothing is final, absolute, sacred. It reveals the transitory character of everything and in everything; nothing can endure before it except the uninterrupted process of becoming and of passing away, of endless ascendancy from the lower to the higher. And dialectical philosophy itself is nothing more than the mere reflection of this process in the thinking brain. It has, of course, also a conservative side; it recognizes that definite stages of knowledge and society are justified for their time and circumstances but only so far. The conservatism of this mode of outlook is relative; its revolutionary character is absolute—the only absolute dialectical philosophy admits.

It is not necessary, here, to go into the question of whether this mode of outlook is thoroughly in accord with the present state of natural science, which predicts a possible end even for the Earth, and for its habitability a fairly certain one; which therefore recognizes that for the history of mankind, too, there is not only an ascending but also a descending branch. At any rate, we still find ourselves a considerable distance from the turning-point at which the historical course of society becomes one of descent, and we cannot expect Hegelian philosophy to be concerned with a subject which natural science, in its time, had not at all placed upon the agenda as yet.

But what must, in fact, be said here is this: that in Hegel the views developed above are not so sharply delineated. They are a necessary conclusion from his method, but one which he himself never drew with such explicitness. And this, indeed, for the simple reason that he was compelled to make a system and, in accordance with traditional requirements, a system of philosophy must conclude with some sort of absolute truth. Therefore, however much Hegel, especially in his *Logic*, emphasized that this eternal truth is nothing but the logical, or the historical, process itself; he nevertheless finds himself compelled to supply this process with an end, just because he has to bring his system to a termination at some point or other. In his *Logic*, he can make this end a beginning again, since here the point of the conclusion, the absolute idea—which is only absolute insofar as he has absolutely nothing to say about it— "alienates," that is, transforms, itself into nature and comes to itself again later in the mind, that is, in thought and in history. But at the end of the whole philosophy, a similar return to the beginning is possible only in one way. Namely, by conceiving of the end of history as follows: mankind arrives at the cognition of the selfsame absolute idea, and declares that this cognition of the absolute idea is reached in Hegelian philosophy. In this way, however, the whole dogmatic content of the Hegelian system is declared to be absolute truth, in contradiction to his dialectical method, which dissolves all dogmatism. Thus the revolutionary side is smothered beneath the overgrowth of the conservative side. And what applies to philosophical cognition applies also to historical practice. Mankind, which, in the person of Hegel, has reached the point of working out the absolute idea, must also in practice have gotten so far that it can carry out this absolute idea in reality. Hence the practical political demands of the absolute idea on contemporaries may not be stretched too far. And so we find at the conclusion of the *Philosophy of Right* that the absolute idea is to be realized in that monarchy based on social estates which Frederick William III so persistently but vainly promised to his subjects, that is, in a limited, moderate, indirect rule of the possessing classes suited to the petty-bourgeois German conditions of that time, and, moreover, the necessity of the nobility is demonstrated to us in a speculative fashion.

The inner necessities of the system are, therefore, of themselves sufficient to explain why a thoroughly revolutionary method of thinking produced an extremely tame political conclusion. As a matter of fact, the specific form of this conclusion springs from this, that Hegel was a German, and like his contemporary Goethe had a bit of the philistine's queue dangling behind. Each of them was an Olympian Zeus in his own sphere, yet neither of them ever quite freed himself from German philistinism.

But all this did not prevent the Hegelian system from covering an incomparably greater domain than any earlier system, nor from developing in this domain a wealth of thought, which is astounding even today. The phenomenology of mind (which one may call a parallel of the embryology and paleontology of the mind, a development of individual consciousness through its different stages, set in the form of an abbreviated reproduction of the stages through which the consciousness of man has passed in the course of history), logic, natural philosophy, philosophy of mind, and the latter worked out in its separate, historical subdivisions: philosophy of history, of right, of religion, history of philosophy, esthetics, etc.—in all these different historical fields Hegel labored to discover and demonstrate the pervading thread of development. And as he was not only a creative genius but also a man of encyclopedic erudition, he played an epoch-making role in every sphere. It is self-evident that owing to the needs of the "system" he very often had to resort to those forced constructions about which his pigmy opponents make such a terrible fuss even today. But these constructions are only the frame and scaffolding of his work. If one does not loiter here needlessly, but presses on farther into the immense building, one finds innumerable treasures which today still possess undiminished value. With all philosophers it is precisely the "system" which is perishable, and for the simple reason that it springs from an imperishable desire of the human mind—the desire to overcome all contradictions. But if all contradictions are once and for all disposed of, we shall have arrived at so-called absolute truth—world history will be at an end. And yet it has to continue, although there is nothing left for it to do—hence, a new, insoluble contradiction. As soon as we have once realized—and in the long run no one has helped us to realize it more than Hegel himself—that the task of philosophy thus stated means nothing but the task that a single philosopher should accomplish that which can only be accomplished by the entire human race in its progressive development—as soon as we realize that, there is an end to all philosophy in the hitherto accepted sense of the word. One leaves alone "absolute truth," which is unattainable along this path or by any single individual;

instead, one pursues attainable relative truths along the path of the posi-tive sciences, and the summation of their results by means of dialectical thinking. At any rate, with Hegel philosophy comes to an end; on the one hand, because in his system he summed up its whole development in the most splendid fashion; and on the other hand, because, even though un-consciously, he showed us the way out of the labyrinth of systems to real positive knowledge of the world.

One can imagine what a tremendous effect this Hegelian system must have produced in the philosophy-tinged atmosphere of Germany. It was a triumphant procession which lasted for decades and which by no means came to a standstill on the death of Hegel. On the contrary, it was precise-ly from 1830 to 1840 that "Hegelianism" reigned most exclusively, and to a greater or lesser extent infected even its opponents. It was precisely in this period that Hegelian views, consciously or unconsciously, most extensively penetrated the most diversified sciences and leavened even popular literature and the daily press, from which the average "educated consciousness" derives its mental pabulum. But this victory along the whole front was only the prelude to an internal struggle.

As we have seen, the doctrine of Hegel, taken as a whole, left plenty of room for giving shelter to the most diverse practical party views. And in the theoretical Germany of that time, two things above all were practical: religion and politics. Whoever placed the chief emphasis on the Hegelian *system* could be fairly conservative in both spheres; whoever regarded the dialectical *method* as the main thing could belong to the most ex-treme opposition, both in politics and religion. Hegel himself, despite the fairly frequent outbursts of revolutionary wrath in his works, seemed on the whole to be more inclined to the conservative side. Indeed, his sys-tem had cost him much more "hard mental plugging" than his method. Towards the end of the thirties, the cleavage in the school became more and more apparent. The Left wing, the so-called Young Hegelians, in their fight with the pietist orthodox and the feudal reactionaries, abandoned bit by bit that philosophical-genteel reserve in regard to the burning questions of the day which up to that time had secured state toleration and even protection for their teachings. And when in 1840, orthodox pietism and absolutist feudal reaction ascended the throne with Fred-erick William IV, open partisanship became unavoidable. The fight was still carried on with philosophical weapons, but no longer for abstract philosophical aims. It turned directly on the destruction of traditional religion and of the existing state. And while in the *Deutsche Jahrbücher* the practical ends were still predominantly put forward in philosophical disguise, in the *Rheinische Zeitung* of 1842 the Young Hegelian school revealed itself directly as the philosophy of the aspiring radical bourgeoisie and used the meager cloak of philosophy only to deceive the censorship.

At that time, however, politics was a very thorny field, and hence the main fight came to be directed against religion; this fight, particularly since 1840, was indirectly also political. Strauss's *Life of Jesus*, published in 1835, had provided the first impulse. The theory therein developed of the formation of the gospel myths was combated later by Bruno Bauer with proof that a whole series of evangelical stories had been fabricated by the authors themselves. The controversy between these two was carried out in the philosophical disguise of a battle between "self-consciousness" and "substance." The question whether the miracle stories of the gospels came into being through unconscious-traditional myth-creation within the bosom of the community or whether they were fabricated by the evangelists themselves was magnified into the question whether, in world history, "substance" or "self-consciousness" was the decisive operative force. Finally came Stirner, the prophet of contemporary anarchism—Bakunin has taken a great deal from him—and capped the sovereign "self-consciousness" by his sovereign "ego."

We will not go further into this side of the decomposition process of the Hegelian school. More important for us is the following: the main body of the most determined Young Hegelians was, by the practical necessities of its fight against positive religion, driven back to Anglo-French materialism. This brought them into conflict with the system of their school. While materialism conceives nature as the sole reality, nature in the Hegelian system represents merely the "alienation" of the absolute idea, so to say, a degradation of the idea. At all events, thinking and its thought-product, the idea, is here the primary, nature the derivative, which only exists at all by the condescension of the idea. And in this contradiction they floundered as well or as ill as they could.

Then came Feuerbach's *Essence of Christianity*. With one blow, it pulverized the contradiction, in that without circumlocutions it placed materialism on the throne again. Nature exists independently of all philosophy. It is the foundation upon which we human beings, ourselves products of nature, have grown up. Nothing exists outside nature and man, and the higher beings our religious fantasies have created are only the fantastic reflection of our own essence. The spell was broken; the "system" was exploded and cast aside, and the contradiction, shown to exist only in our imagination, was dissolved. One must himself have experienced the liberating effect of this book to get an idea of it. Enthusiasm was general; we all became at once Feuerbachians. How enthusiastically Marx greeted the new conception and how much—in spite of all critical reservations—he was influenced by it, one may read in the *The Holy Family*.

Even the shortcomings of the book contributed to its immediate effect. Its literary, sometimes even high-flown, style secured for it a large public and was at any rate refreshing after long years of abstract and abstruse Hegelianizing. The same is true of its extravagant deification of love, which, coming after the now intolerable sovereign rule of "pure reason," had its excuse, if not justification. But what we must not forget is that it was precisely these two weaknesses of Feuerbach that "true Socialism," which had been spreading like a plague in educated Germany since 1844, took as its starting point, putting literary phrases in the place of scientific knowledge, the liberation of mankind by means of "love" in place of the emancipation of the proletariat through the economic transformation of production—in short, losing itself in the nauseous fine writing and ecstasies of love typified by Herr Karl Grün.

Another thing we must not forget is this: the Hegelian school disintegrated, but Hegelian philosophy was not overcome through criticism; Strauss and Bauer each took one of its sides and set it polemically against the other. Feuerbach smashed the system and simply discarded it. But a philosophy is not disposed of by the mere assertion that it is false. And so powerful a work as Hegelian philosophy, which had exercised so enormous an influence on the intellectual development of the nation, could not be disposed of by simply being ignored. It had to be "sublated" in its own sense, that is, in the sense that while its form had to be annihilated through criticism, the new content which had been won through it had to be saved. How this was brought about we shall see below.

But in the meantime, the Revolution of 1848 thrust the whole of philosophy aside as unceremoniously as Feuerbach had thrust aside Hegel. And in the process, Feuerbach himself was also pushed into the background.

Part 2: Materialism

The great basic question of all philosophy, especially of more recent philosophy, is that concerning the relation of thinking and being. From the very early times when men, still completely ignorant of the structure of their own bodies, under the stimulus of dream apparitions came to believe that their thinking and sensation were not activities of their bodies, but of a distinct soul which inhabits the body and leaves it at death—from this time men have been driven to reflect about the relation between this soul and the outside world. If, upon death, it took leave of the body and lived on, there was no occasion to invent yet another distinct death for it. Thus arose the idea of immortality, which at that stage of development appeared not at all as a consolation but as a fate against which it was no use fighting, and often enough, as among the Greeks, as a positive misfortune. The quandary arising from the common universal ignorance of what to do with this soul, once its existence had been accepted, after the death of the body, and not religious desire for consolation, led in a general way to the tedious notion of personal immortality. In an exactly similar manner, the first gods arose through the personification of natural forces. And these gods in the further development of religions assumed more and more extramundane form, until finally by a process of abstraction, I might almost say of distillation, occurring naturally in the course of man's intellectual development, out of the many more or less limited and mutually limiting gods there arose in the minds of men the idea of the one exclusive God of the monotheistic religions.

Thus the question of the relation of thinking to being, the relation of the spirit to nature—the paramount question of the whole of philosophy—has, no less than all religion, its roots in the narrow-minded and ignorant notions of savagery. But this question could for the first time be put forward in its whole acuteness, could achieve its full significance, only after humanity in Europe had awakened from the long hibernation of the Christian Middle Ages. The question of the position of thinking in relation to being, a question which, by the way, had played a great part also in the scholasticism of the Middle Ages, the question: which is primary, spirit or nature—that question, in relation to the church, was sharpened into this: Did God create the world or has the world been in existence eternally?

The answers which the philosophers gave to this question split them into two great camps. Those who asserted the primacy of spirit to nature and, therefore, in the last instance, assumed world creation in some form or other—and among the philosophers, Hegel, for example, this creation often becomes still more intricate and impossible than in Christianity—comprised the camp of idealism. The others, who regarded nature as primary, belong to the various schools of materialism.

These two expressions, idealism and materialism, originally signify nothing else but this, and here too they are not used in any other sense. What confusion arises when some other meaning is put to them will be seen below.

But the question of the relation of thinking and being had yet another side: in what relation do our thoughts about the world surrounding us stand to this world itself? Is our thinking capable of the cognition of the real world? Are we able in our ideas and notions of the real world to produce a correct reflection of reality? In philosophical language this question is called the question of identity of thinking and being, and the overwhelming majority of philosophers give an affirmative answer to this question. With Hegel, for example, its affirmation is self-evident; for what we cognize in the real world is precisely its thought-content—that which makes the world a gradual realization of the absolute idea, which absolute idea has existed somewhere from eternity, independent of the world and before the world. But it is manifest without further proof that thought can know a content which is from the outset a thought-content. It is equally manifest that what is to be proved here is already tacitly contained in the premises. But that in no way prevents Hegel from drawing the further conclusion from his proof of the identity of thinking and being that his philosophy, because it is correct for his thinking, is therefore the only correct one, and that the identity of thinking and being must prove its validity by mankind immediately translating his philosophy from theory into practice and transforming the whole world according to Hegelian principles. This is an illusion which he shares with well-nigh all philosophers.

In addition, there is yet a set of different philosophers—those who question the possibility of any cognition, or at least of an exhaustive cognition, of the world. To them, among the more modern ones, belong Hume and Kant, and they played a very important role in philosophical development. What is decisive in the refutation of this view has already been said by Hegel, insofar as this was possible from an idealist standpoint. The materialistic additions made by Feuerbach are more ingenious than profound. The most telling refutation of this as of all other philosophical crotchets is practice—namely, experiment and industry. If we are able to prove the correctness of our conception of a natural process by making it ourselves, bringing it into being out of its conditions and making it serve our own purposes into the bargain, then there is an end to the Kantian ungraspable "thing-in-itself." The chemical substances produced in the bodies of plants and animals remained just such "things-in-themselves" until organic chemistry began to produce them one after another, whereupon the "thing-in-itself" became a thing for us—as, for instance, alizarin, the coloring matter of the madder, which we no longer trouble to grow in the madder roots in the field, but produce much more cheaply and simply from coal tar. For 300 years, the Copernican solar system was a hypothesis with 100, 1,000, 10,000 to 1 chances in its favor, but still always a hypothesis. But then Leverrier, by means of the data provided by this system, not only deduced the necessity of the existence of an unknown planet, but also calculated the position in the heavens which this planet must necessarily occupy, and when [Johann] Galle really found this planet [Neptune, discovered 1846, at the Berlin Observatory], the Copernican system was proved. If, nevertheless, the neo-Kantians are attempting to resurrect the Kantian conception in Germany, and the agnostics that of Hume in England—where in fact it never became extinct—this is, in view of their theoretical and practical refutation accomplished long ago, scientifically a regression and practically merely a shamefaced way of surreptitiously accepting materialism, while denying it before the world.

But during this long period from Descartes to Hegel and from Hobbes to Feuerbach, these philosophers were by no means impelled, as they thought they were, solely by the force of pure reason. On the contrary, what really pushed them forward most was the powerful and ever more rapidly onrushing progress of natural science and industry. Among the materialists this was plain on the surface, but the idealist systems also filled themselves more and more with a materialist content and attempted pantheistically to reconcile the antithesis between mind and matter. Thus, ultimately, the Hegelian system represents merely a materialism idealistically turned upside down in method and content.

It is, therefore, comprehensible that Starcke in his characterization of Feuerbach first of all investigates the latter's position in regard to this fundamental question of the relation of thinking and being. After a short introduction, in which the views of the preceding philosophers, particularly since Kant, are described in unnecessarily ponderous philosophical language, and in which Hegel, by an all too formalistic adherence to certain passages of his works, gets far less his due, there follows a detailed description of the course of development of Feuerbach's "metaphysics" itself, as this course was successively reflected in those writings of this philosopher which have a bearing here. This description is industriously and lucidly elaborated; only, like the whole book, it is loaded with a ballast of philosophical phraseology by no means everywhere unavoidable, which is the more disturbing in its effect the less the author keeps to the manner of expression of one and the same school, or even of Feuerbach himself, and the more he interjects expressions of very different tendencies, especially of the tendencies now rampant and calling themselves philosophical.

The course of evolution of Feuerbach is that of a Hegelian—a never quite orthodox Hegelian, it is true—into a materialist; an evolution which at a definite stage necessitates a complete rupture with the idealist system of his predecessor. With irresistible force, Feuerbach is finally driven to the realization that the Hegelian premundane existence of the "absolute idea," the "pre-existence of the logical categories" before the world existed, is nothing more than the fantastic survival of the belief in the existence of an extramundane creator; that the material, sensuously perceptible world to which we ourselves belong is the only reality, and that our consciousness and thinking, however supra-sensuous they may seem, are the product of a material, bodily organ, the brain. Matter is not a product of mind, but mind itself is merely the highest product of matter. This is, of course, pure materialism. But, having got so far, Feuerbach stops short. He cannot overcome the customary philosophical prejudice, prejudice not against the thing but against the name materialism. He says:

> To me materialism is the foundation of the edifice of human essence and knowledge, but to me it is not what it is to the physiologist, to the natural scientists in the narrower sense, for example, to Moleschott, and necessarily is from their standpoint and profession, namely, the edifice itself. Backwards I fully agree with the materialists, but not forwards.

Here, Feuerbach lumps together the materialism that is a general world outlook resting upon a definite conception of the relation between matter and mind, and the special form in which this world outlook was expressed at a definite historical stage—namely, in the 18th century. More than that, he lumps it with the shallow, vulgarized form in which the materialism of the 18th century continues to exist today in the heads of naturalists and physicians, the form which was preached on their tours in the fifties by Büchner, Vogt, and Moleschott. But just as idealism underwent a series of stages of development, so also did materialism. With each epoch-making discovery even in the sphere of natural science, it has to change its form, and after history was also subjected to materialistic treatment, a new avenue of development has opened here, too.

The materialism of the last century was predominantly mechanical, because at that time, of all natural sciences, only mechanics, and indeed only the mechanics of solid bodies—celestial and terrestrial—in short, the mechanics of gravity, had come to any definite close. Chemistry at that time existed only in its infantile, phlogistic form. Biology still lay in swaddling clothes; vegetable and animal organisms had been only roughly examined and were explained by purely mechanical causes. What the animal was to Descartes, man was to the materialists of the 18th century—a machine. This exclusive application of the standards of mechanics to processes of a chemical and organic nature—in which processes the laws of mechanics are, indeed, also valid, but are pushed into the backgrounds by other, higher laws—constitutes the first specific but at that time inevitable limitations of classical French materialism.

The second specific limitation of this materialism lay in its inability to comprehend the universe as a process, as matter undergoing uninterrupted historical development. This was in accordance with the level of the natural science of that time, and with the metaphysical, that is, anti-dialectical manner of philosophizing connected with it. Nature, so much was known, was in eternal motion. But according to the ideas of that time, this motion turned, also eternally, in a circle and therefore never moved from the spot; it produced the same results over and over again. This conception was at that time inevitable. The Kantian theory of the origin of the Solar System [that the Sun and planets originated from incandescent rotating nebulous masses] had been put forward but recently and was still regarded merely as a curiosity. The history of the development of the Earth, geology, was still totally unknown, and the conception that the animate natural beings of today are the result of a long sequence of development from the simple to the complex could not at that time scientifically be put forward at all. The ahistorical view of nature was therefore inevitable. We have the less reason to reproach the philosophers of the 18th century on this account since the same thing is found in Hegel. According to him, nature, as a mere "alienation" of the idea, is incapable of development in time—capable only of extending its manifoldness in space, so that it displays simultaneously and alongside of one another all the stages of development comprised in it, and is condemned to an eternal repetition of the same processes. This absurdity of a development in space, but outside of time—the fundamental condition of all development—Hegel imposes upon nature just at the very time when geology, embryology, the physiology of plants and animals, and organic chemistry were being built up, and when everywhere on the basis of these new sciences brilliant foreshadowings of the later theory of evolution were appearing (for instance, Goethe and Lamarck). But the system demanded it; hence the method, for the sake of the system, had to become untrue to itself.

This same ahistorical conception prevailed also in the domain of history. Here the struggle against the remnants of the Middle Ages blurred the view. The Middle Ages were regarded as a mere interruption of history by a thousand years of universal barbarism. The great progress made in the Middle Ages—the extension of the area of European culture, the viable great nations taking form there next to each other, and finally the enormous technical progress of the 14th and 15th centuries—all this was not seen. Thus a rational insight into the great historical interconnectedness was made impossible, and history served at best as a collection of examples and illustrations for the use of philosophers.

The vulgarizing peddlers, who in Germany in the fifties dabbled in materialism, by no means overcame this limitation of their teachers. All the advances of natural science which had been made in the meantime served them only as new proofs against the existence of a creator of the world, and, indeed, they did not in the least make it their business to develop the theory any further. Though idealism was at the end of its tether and was dealt a death blow by the Revolution of 1848, it had the satisfaction of seeing that materialism had for the moment fallen lower still. Feuerbach was unquestionably right when he refused to take responsibility for this materialism; only he should not have confounded the doctrines of these itinerant preachers with materialism in general.

Here, however, there are two things to be pointed out. First, even during Feuerbach's lifetime, natural science was still in that process of violent fermentation which only during the last 15 years had reached a clarifying, relative conclusion. New scientific data were acquired to a hitherto unheard-of extent, but the establishing of interrelations, and thereby the bringing of order into this chaos of discoveries following closely upon each other's heels, has only quite recently become possible. It is true that Feuerbach had lived to see all three of the decisive discoveries—that of the cell, the transformation of energy, and the theory of evolution named after Darwin. But how could the lonely philosopher, living in rural solitude, be able sufficiently to follow scientific developments in order to appreciate at their full value discoveries which natural scientists themselves at that time either still contested or did not know how to make adequate use of? The blame for this falls solely upon the wretched conditions in Germany, in consequence of which cobweb-spinning eclectic flea-crackers had taken possession of the chairs of philosophy, while Feuerbach, who towered above them all, had to rusticate and grow sour in a little village. It is therefore not Feuerbach's fault that this historical conception of nature, which had now become possible and which removed all the one-sidedness of French materialism, remained inaccessible to him.

Secondly, Feuerbach is quite correct in asserting that exclusively natural-scientific materialism is indeed "the foundation of the edifice of human knowledge, but not the edifice itself." For we live not only in nature but also in human society, and this also no less than nature has its history of development and its science. It was therefore a question of bringing the science of society, that is, the sum total of the so-called historical and philosophical sciences, into harmony with the materialist foundation, and of reconstructing it thereupon. But it did not fall to Feuerbach's lot to do this. In spite of the "foundation," he remained here bound by the traditional idealist fetters, a fact which he recognizes in these words: "Backwards I agree with the materialists, but not forwards!"

But it was Feuerbach himself who did not go "forwards" here, in the social domain, who did not get beyond his standpoint of 1840 or 1844. And this was again chiefly due to this reclusion which compelled him, who, of all philosophers, was the most inclined to social intercourse, to produce thoughts out of his solitary head instead of in amicable and hostile encounters with other men of his caliber. Later, we shall see in detail how much he remained an idealist in this sphere.

It need only be added here that Starcke looks for Feuerbach's idealism in the wrong place.

Feuerbach is an idealist; he believes in the progress of mankind.

> The foundation, the substructure of the whole, remains nevertheless idealism. Realism for us is nothing more than a protection against aberrations, while we follow our ideal trends. Are not compassion, love, and enthusiasm for truth and justice ideal forces?

In the first place, idealism here means nothing, but the pursuit of ideal aims. But these necessarily have to do at the most with Kantian idealism and its "categorical imperative"; however, Kant himself called his philosophy "transcendental idealism" by no means because he dealt therein also with ethical ideals, but for quite other reasons, as Starcke will remember. The superstition that philosophical idealism is pivoted around a belief in ethical, that is, social, ideals, arose outside philosophy, among the German philistines, who learned by heart from Schiller's poems the few morsels of philosophical culture they needed. No one has criticized more severely the impotent "categorical imperative" of Kant—impotent because it demands the impossible, and therefore never attains to any reality—no one has more cruelly derided the philistine sentimental enthusiasm for unrealizable ideals purveyed by Schiller than precisely the complete idealist Hegel (see, for example, his *Phenomenology*).

In the second place, we simply cannot get away from the fact that everything that sets men acting must find its way through their brains—even eating and drinking, which begins as a consequence of the sensation of hunger or thirst transmitted through the brain, and ends as a result of the sensation of satisfaction likewise transmitted through the brain. The influences of the external world upon man express themselves in his brain, are reflected therein as feelings, impulses, volitions—in short, as "ideal tendencies," and in this form become "ideal powers." If, then, a man is to be deemed an idealist because he follows "ideal tendencies" and admits that "ideal powers" have an influence over him, then every person who is at all normally developed is a born idealist and how, in that case, can there still be any materialists?

In the third place, the conviction that humanity, at least at the present moment, moves on the whole in a progressive direction has absolutely nothing to do with the antagonism between materialism and idealism. The French materialists no less than the deists, Voltaire and Rousseau, held this conviction to an almost fanatical degree and often enough made the greatest personal sacrifices for it. If ever anybody dedicated his whole life to the "enthusiasm for truth and justice"—using this phrase in the good sense—it was Diderot, for instance. If, therefore, Starcke declares all this to be idealism, this merely proves that the word materialism, and the whole antagonism between the two trends, has lost all meaning for him here.

The fact is that Starcke, although perhaps unconsciously, in this makes an unpardonable concession to the traditional philistine prejudice against the word materialism resulting from its long-continued defamation by the priests. By the word materialism, the philistine understands gluttony, drunkenness, lust of the eye, lust of the flesh, arrogance, cupidity, avarice, covetousness, profit hunting, and stock exchange swindling—in short, all the filthy vices in which he himself indulges in private. By the word idealism he understands the belief in virtue, universal philanthropy, and in a general way a "better world," of which he boasts before others but in which he himself at the utmost believes only so long as he is having the blues or is going through the bankruptcy consequent upon his customary "materialist" excesses. It is then that he sings his favorite song: What is man? Half beast, half angel.

For the rest, Starcke takes great pains to defend Feuerbach against the attacks and doctrines of the vociferous assistant professors who today go by the name of philosophers in Germany. For people who are interested in this afterbirth of classical German philosophy this is, of course, a matter of importance; for Starcke himself it may have appeared necessary. We, however, will spare the reader this.

Part 3: Feuerbach

The real idealism of Feuerbach becomes evident as soon as we come to his philosophy of religion and ethics. He by no means wishes to abolish religion; he wants to perfect it. Philosophy itself must be absorbed in religion.

> The periods of humanity are distinguished only by religious changes. A historical movement is fundamental only when it is rooted in the hearts of men. The heart is not a form of religion, so that the latter should exist also in the heart; the heart is the essence of religion (Quoted by Starcke).

According to Feuerbach, religion is the relation between human beings based on the affections, the relation based on the heart, which relation until now has sought its truth in a fantastic mirror image of reality—in the mediation of one or many gods, the fantastic mirror images of human qualities—but now finds it directly and without any mediation in the love between "*I*" and "*Thou.*" Thus, finally, with Feuerbach sexual love becomes one of the highest forms, if not the highest form, of the practice of his new religion.

Now relations between human beings, based on affection, and especially between the two sexes, have existed as long as mankind has. Sexual love in particular has undergone a development and won a place during the last 800 years which has made it a compulsory pivotal point of all poetry during this period. The existing positive religions have limited themselves to the bestowal of a higher consecration upon state-regulated sexual love—that is, upon the marriage laws—and they could all disappear tomorrow without changing in the slightest the practice of love and friendship. Thus the Christian religion in France, as a matter of fact, so completely disappeared in the year 1793–95 that even Napoleon could not reintroduce it without opposition and difficulty, and this without any need for a substitute in Feuerbach's sense, making itself in the interval.

Feuerbach's idealism consists here in this: he does not simply accept mutual relations based on reciprocal inclination between human beings, such as sexual love, friendship, compassion, self-sacrifice, etc., as what they are in themselves—without associating them with any particular religion which to him, too, belongs to the past, but instead he asserts that they will attain their full value only when consecrated by the name of religion. The chief thing for him is not that these purely human relations exist, but that they shall be conceived of as the new, true, religion. They are to have full value only after they have been marked with a religious stamp. Religion is derived from *religare* ["to bind"] and meant, originally, a bond. Therefore, every bond between two people is a religion. Such etymological tricks are the last resort of idealist philosophy. Not what the word means according to the historical development of its actual use, but what it ought to mean according to its derivation is what counts. And so sexual love, and the intercourse between the sexes, is apotheosized to a *religion*, merely in order that the word religion, which is so dear to idealistic memories, may not disappear from the language. The Parisian reformers of the Louis Blanc trend used to speak in precisely the same way in the forties. They, likewise, could conceive of a man without religion only as a monster and used to say to us: "Well, then atheism is your religion!" If Feuerbach wishes to establish a true religion upon the basis of an essentially materialist conception of nature, that is the same as regarding modern chemistry as true alchemy. If religion can exist without its god, alchemy can exist without its philosopher's stone. By the way, there exists a very close connection between alchemy and religion. The philosopher's stone has many godlike properties, and the Egyptian-Greek alchemists of the first two centuries of our era had a hand in the development of Christian doctrines, as the data given by Kopp and Bertholet have proved.

Feuerbach's assertion that "the periods of humanity are distinguished only by religious changes" is decidedly false. Great historical turning-points have been *accompanied* by religious changes only so far as the three world religions which have existed up to the present—Buddhism, Christianity, and Islam—are concerned. The old tribal and national religions, which arose spontaneously, did not proselytize and lost all their power of resistance as soon as the independence of the tribe or people was lost. For the Germans, it was sufficient to have simple contact with the decaying Roman world empire and with its newly adopted Christian world religion which fitted its economic, political, and ideological conditions. Only with these world religions, arisen more or less artificially, particularly Christianity and Islam, do we find that the more general historical movements acquire a religious imprint. Even in regard to Christianity, the religious stamp in revolutions of really universal significance is restricted to the first stages of the bourgeoisie's struggle for emancipation—from the 13th to the 17th century—and is to be accounted for, not as Feuerbach thinks by the hearts of men and their religious needs, but by the entire previous history of the Middle Ages, which knew no other form of ideology than religion and theology. But when the bourgeoisie of the 18th century was strengthened enough likewise to possess an ideology of its own, suited to its own class standpoint, it made its great and conclusive revolution—the French—appealing exclusively to juristic and political ideas, and troubling itself with religion only in so far as it stood in its way. But it never occurred to it to put a new religion in place of the old. Everyone knows how Robespierre failed in his attempt.

The possibility of purely human sentiments in our intercourse with other human beings has nowadays been sufficiently curtailed by the society in which we must live, which is based upon class antagonism and class rule. We have no reason to curtail it still more by exalting these sentiments to a religion. And similarly the understanding of the great historical class struggles has already been sufficiently obscured by current historiography, particularly in Germany, so that there is also no need for us to make such an understanding totally impossible by transforming the history of these struggles into a mere appendix of ecclesiastical history. Already here it becomes evident how far today we have moved beyond Feuerbach. His "finest" passages in glorification of his new religion of love are totally unreadable today.

The only religion which Feuerbach examines seriously is Christianity, the world religion of the Occident, based upon monotheism. He proves that the Christian god is only a fantastic reflection, a mirror image, of man. Now, this god is, however, himself the product of a tedious process of abstraction, the concentrated quintessence of the numerous earlier tribal and national gods. And man, whose image this god is, is therefore also not a real man, but likewise the quintessence of the numerous real men, man in the abstract, therefore himself again a mental image. Feuerbach, who on every page preaches sensuousness, absorption in the concrete, in actuality, becomes thoroughly abstract as soon as he begins to talk of any other than mere sexual relations between human beings.

Of these relations, only one aspect appeals to him: morality. And here we are again struck by Feuerbach's astonishing poverty when compared to Hegel. The latter's ethics, or doctrine of moral conduct, is the philosophy of right, and embraces: 1) abstract right, 2) morality, 3) social ethics, under which are comprised: the family, civil society, and the state.

Here the content is as realistic as the form is idealistic. Besides morality, the whole sphere of law, economy, politics is here included. With Feuerbach, it is just the reverse. In the form he is realistic since he takes his start from man, but there is absolutely no mention of the world in which this man lives; hence, this man remains always the same abstract man who occupied the field in the philosophy of religion. For this man is not born of woman; he issues, as from a chrysalis, from the god of monotheistic religions. He therefore does not live in a real world historically come into being and historically determined. True, he has intercourse with other men; however, each one of them is just as much an abstraction as he himself. In his philosophy of religion we still had men and women, but in his ethics even this last distinction disappears. Feuerbach, to be sure, at long intervals makes such statements as: "Man thinks differently in a palace and in a hut." "If because of hunger, of misery, you have no stuff in your body, you likewise have no stuff for morality in your head, in your mind, or heart." "Politics must become our religion," etc.

But Feuerbach is absolutely incapable of achieving anything with these maxims. They remain mere phrases, and even Starcke has to admit that for Feuerbach politics constituted an impassable frontier and the "science of society, sociology, was *terra incognita* to him."

He appears just as shallow, in comparison with Hegel, in his treatment of the antithesis of good and evil.

"One believes one is saying something great," Hegel remarks, "if one says that 'man is naturally good.' But one forgets that one says something far greater when one says 'man is naturally evil.'"

With Hegel, evil is the form in which the motive force of historical development presents itself. This contains the twofold meaning that, on the one hand, each new advance necessarily appears as a sacrilege against things hallowed, as a rebellion against condition, though old and moribund, yet sanctified by custom, and that, on the other hand, it is precisely the wicked passions of man—greed and lust for power—which, since the emergence of class antagonisms, serve as levers of historical development—a fact of which the history of feudalism and of the bourgeoisie, for example, constitutes a single continuous proof. But it does not occur to Feuerbach to investigate the historical role of moral evil. To him, history is altogether an uncanny domain in which he feels ill at ease. Even his dictum: "Man as he sprang originally from nature was only a mere creature of nature, not a man. Man is a product of man, of culture, of history"—with him, even this dictum remains absolutely sterile.

What Feuerbach has to tell us about morals can, therefore, only be extremely meager. The urge towards happiness is innate in man, and must therefore form the basis of all morality. But the urge towards happiness is subject to a double correction. First, by the natural consequences of our actions: after the debauch comes the "blues," and habitual excess is followed by illness. Secondly, by its social consequences: if we do not respect the similar urge of other people towards happiness they will defend themselves, and so interfere with our own urge toward happiness. Consequently, in order to satisfy our urge, we must be in a position to appreciate rightly the results of our conduct and must likewise allow others an equal right to seek happiness. Rational self-restraint with regard to ourselves, and love—again and again love!—in our intercourse with others—these are the basic laws of Feuerbach's morality; from them all others are derived. And neither the most spirited utterances of Feuerbach nor the strongest eulogies of Starcke can hide the tenuity and banality of these few propositions.

Only very exceptionally, and by no means to his and other people's profit, can an individual satisfy his urge towards happiness by preoccupation with himself. Rather, it requires preoccupation with the outside world, with means to satisfy his needs—that is to say, food, an individual of the opposite sex, books, conversation, argument, activities, objects for use and working up. Feuerbach's morality either presupposes that these means and objects of satisfaction are given to every individual as a matter of course, or else it offers only inapplicable good advice and is, therefore, not worth a brass farthing to people who are without these means. And Feuerbach himself states this in plain terms:

> Man thinks differently in a palace and in a hut. If because of hunger, of misery, you have no stuff in your body, you likewise have no stuff for morality in your head, in your mind, or heart.

Do matters fare any better in regard to the equal right of others to satisfy their urge towards happiness? Feuerbach posed this claim as absolute, as holding good for all times and circumstances. But since when has it been valid? Was there ever in antiquity between slaves and masters, or in the Middle Ages between serfs and barons, any talk about an equal right to the urge towards happiness? Was not the urge towards happiness of the oppressed class sacrificed ruthlessly and "by the right of law" to that of the ruling class? Yes, that was indeed immoral; nowadays, however, equality of rights is recognized. Recognized in words ever since and inasmuch as the bourgeoisie, in its fight against feudalism and in the development of capitalist production, was compelled to abolish all privileges of estate, that is, personal privileges, and to introduce the equality of all individuals before law, first in the sphere in private law, then gradually also in the sphere of public law. But the urge towards happiness thrives only to a trivial extent on ideal rights. To the greatest extent of all it thrives on material means, and capitalist production takes care to ensure that the great majority of those equal rights shall get only what is essential for bare existence. Capitalist production has, therefore, little more respect, if indeed any more, for the equal right to the urge towards happiness of the majority than had slavery or serfdom. And are we better off in regard to the mental means of happiness, the educational means? Is not even "the schoolmaster of Sadowa" a mythical person?

More. According to Feuerbach's theory of morals, the Stock Exchange is the highest temple of moral conduct, provided only that one always speculates right. If my urge towards happiness leads me to the Stock Exchange, and if there I correctly gauge the consequences of my actions so that only agreeable results and no disadvantages ensue—that is, I always win—then I am fulfilling Feuerbach's precept. Moreover, I do not thereby interfere with the equal right of another person to pursue his happiness; for that other man went to the Exchange just as voluntarily as I did and in concluding the speculative transaction with me he has followed his urge towards happiness as I have followed mine. If he loses his money, his action is *ipso facto* proved to have been unethical, because of his bad reckoning, and since I have given him the punishment he deserves, I can even slap my chest proudly, like a modern Rhadamanthus. Love, too, rules on the Stock Exchange, in so far as it is not simply a sentimental figure of speech, for each finds in others the satisfaction of his own urge towards happiness, which is just what love ought to achieve and how it acts in practice. And if I gamble with correct prevision of the consequences of my operations, and therefore with success, I fulfill all the strictest injunctions of Feuerbachian morality—and become a rich man into the bargain. In other words, Feuerbach's morality is cut exactly to the pattern of modern capitalist society, little as Feuerbach himself might desire or imagine it.

But love!—yes, with Feuerbach, love is everywhere and at all times the wonder-working god who should help to surmount all difficulties of practical life—and at that in a society which is split into classes with diametrically opposite interests. At this point, the last relic of the revolutionary character disappears from his philosophy, leaving only the old cant: Love one another—fall into each other's arms regardless of distinctions of sex or estate—a universal orgy of reconciliation!

In short, the Feuerbachian theory of morals fares like all its predecessors. It is designed to suit all periods, all peoples, and all conditions, and precisely for that reason it is never and nowhere applicable. It remains, as regards the real world, as powerless as Kant's categorical imperative. In reality every class, even every profession, has its own morality, and even this it violates whenever it can do so with impunity. And love, which is to unite all, manifests itself in wars, altercations, lawsuits, domestic broils, divorces, and every possible exploitation of one by another.

Now how was it possible that the powerful impetus given by Feuerbach turned out to be so unfruitful for himself? For the simple reason that Feuerbach himself never contrives to escape from the realm of abstraction—for which he has a deadly hatred—into that of living reality. He clings fiercely to nature and man, but nature and man remain mere words with him. He is incapable of telling us anything definite either about real nature or real men. But from the abstract man of Feuerbach, one arrives at real living men only when one considers them as participants in history. And that is what Feuerbach resisted, and therefore the year 1848, which he did not understand, meant to him merely the final break with the real world, retirement into solitude. The blame for this again falls chiefly on the conditions then obtaining in Germany, which condemned him to rot away miserably.

But the step which Feuerbach did not take nevertheless had to be taken. The cult of abstract man, which formed the kernel of Feuerbach's new religion, had to be replaced by the science of real men and of their historical development. This further development of Feuerbach's standpoint beyond Feuerbach was inaugurated by Marx in 1845 in *The Holy Family*.

Part 4: Marx

Strauss, Bauer, Stirner, Feuerbach—these were the offshoots of Hegelian philosophy, in so far as they did not abandon the field of philosophy. Strauss, after his *Life of Jesus* and *Dogmatics*, produced only literary studies in philosophy and ecclesiastical history after the fashion of Renan. Bauer only achieved something in the field of the history of the origin of Christianity, though what he did here was important. Stirner remained a curiosity, even after Bakunin blended him with Proudhon and labelled the blend "anarchism." Feuerbach alone was of significance as a philosopher. But not only did philosophy—claimed to soar above all special sciences and to be the science of sciences connecting them—remain to him an impassable barrier, an inviolable holy thing, but as a philosopher, too, he stopped halfway, he was a materialist below and an idealist above. He was incapable of disposing of Hegel through criticism; he simply threw him aside as useless, while he himself, compared with the encyclopedic wealth of the Hegelian system, achieved nothing positive beyond a turgid religion of love and a meager, impotent morality.

Out of the dissolution of the Hegelian school, however, there developed still another tendency, the only one which has borne real fruit. And this tendency is essentially connected with the name of Marx.[1]

The separation from Hegelian philosophy was here also the result of a return to the materialist standpoint. That means it was resolved to comprehend the real world—nature and history—just as it presents itself to everyone who approaches it free from preconceived idealist crotchets. It was decided mercilessly to sacrifice every idealist fancy which could not be brought into harmony with the facts conceived in their own and not in a fantastic interconnection. And materialism means nothing more than this. But here the materialistic world outlook was taken really seriously for the first time and was carried through consistently—at least in its basic features—in all domains of knowledge concerned.

Hegel was not simply put aside. On the contrary, a start was made from his revolutionary side, described above, from the dialectical method. But in its Hegelian form, this method was unusable. According to Hegel, dialectics is the self-development of the concept. The absolute concept does not only exist—unknown where—from eternity; it is also the actual living soul of the whole existing world. It develops into itself through all the preliminary stages which are treated at length in the *Logic* and which are all included in it. Then it "alienates" itself by changing into nature, where, unconscious of itself, disguised as a natural necessity, it goes

---

1   Here I may be permitted to make a personal explanation. Lately repeated reference has been made to my share in this theory, and so I can hardly avoid saying a few words here to settle this point. I cannot deny that both before and during my 40 years' collaboration with Marx I had a certain independent share in laying the foundation of the theory, and more particularly in its elaboration. But the greater part of its leading basic principles, especially in the realm of economics and history, and, above all, their final trenchant formulation, belong to Marx. What I contributed—at any rate with the exception of my work in a few special fields—Marx could very well have done without me. What Marx accomplished I would not have achieved. Marx stood higher, saw further, and took a wider and quicker view than all the rest of us. Marx was a genius; we others were at best talented. Without him the theory would not be by far what it is today. It therefore rightly bears his name.

through a new development and finally returns as man's consciousness of himself. This self-consciousness then elaborates itself again in history in the crude form until finally the absolute concept again comes to itself completely in the Hegelian philosophy. According to Hegel, therefore, the dialectical development apparent in nature and history—that is, the causal interconnection of the progressive movement from the lower to the higher, which asserts itself through all zigzag movements and temporary retrogression—is only a *copy* of the self-movement of the concept going on from eternity, no one knows where, but at all events independently of any thinking human brain. This ideological perversion had to be done away with. We again took a materialistic view of the thoughts in our heads, regarding them as *images* of real things instead of regarding real things as images of this or that stage of the absolute concept. Thus dialectics reduced itself to the science of the general laws of motion, both of the external world and of human thought—two sets of laws which are identical in substance, but differ in their expression in so far as the human mind can apply them consciously, while in nature and also up to now for the most part in human history, these laws assert themselves unconsciously, in the form of external necessity, in the midst of an endless series of seeming accidents. Thereby the dialectic of concepts itself became merely the conscious reflex of the dialectical motion of the real world and thus the dialectic of Hegel was turned over; or rather, turned off its head, on which it was standing, and placed upon its feet. And this materialist dialectic, which for years has been our best working tool and our sharpest weapon, was, remarkably enough, discovered not only by us but also, independently of us and even of Hegel, by a German worker, Joseph Dietzgen.

In this way, however, the revolutionary side of Hegelian philosophy was again taken up and at the same time freed from the idealist trimmings which with Hegel had prevented its consistent execution. The great basic thought that the world is not to be comprehended as a complex of ready-made *things*, but as a complex of *processes*, in which the things apparently stable no less than their mind images in our heads, the concepts, go through an uninterrupted change of coming into being and passing away, in which, in spite of all seeming accidentally and of all temporary retrogression, a progressive development asserts itself in the end—this great fundamental thought has, especially since the time of Hegel, so thoroughly permeated ordinary consciousness that in this generality it is now scarcely ever contradicted. But to acknowledge this fundamental thought in words and to apply it in reality in detail to each domain of investigation are two different things. If, however, investigation always proceeds from this standpoint, the demand for final solutions and eternal truths ceases once for all; one is always conscious of the necessary limitation of all acquired knowledge, of the fact that it is conditioned by the circumstances in which it was acquired. On the other hand, one no longer permits oneself to be imposed upon by the antithesis, insuperable for the still common old metaphysics, between true and false, good and bad, identical and different, necessary and accidental. One knows that these antitheses have only a relative validity; that that which is recognized now as true has also its latent false side which will later manifest itself, just as that which is now regarded as false has also its true side by virtue of which it could previously be regarded as true. One knows that what is maintained to be necessary is composed of sheer accidents and that the so-called accidental is the form behind which necessity hides itself—and so on.

The old method of investigation and thought which Hegel calls "metaphysical," which preferred to investigate *things* as given, as fixed and stable, a method the relics of which still strongly haunt people's minds, had a great deal of historical justification in its day. It was necessary first to examine things before it was possible to examine processes. One had first to know what a particular thing was before one could observe the changes it was undergoing. And such was the case with natural science. The old metaphysics, which accepted things as finished objects, arose from a natural science which investigated dead and living things as finished objects. But when this investigation had progressed so far that it became possible to take the decisive step forward, that is, to pass on the systematic investigation of the changes which these things undergo in nature itself, then the last hour of the old metaphysics struck in the realm of philosophy also. And in fact, while natural science up to the end of the last century was predominantly a *collecting* science, a science of finished things, in our century it is essentially a *systematizing* science, a science of the processes, of the origin and development of these things and of the interconnection which binds all these natural processes into one great whole. Physiology, which investigates the processes occurring in plant and animal organisms; embryology, which deals with the development of individual organisms from germs to maturity; geology, which investigates the gradual formation of the Earth's surface—all these are the offspring of our century.

But, above all, there are three great discoveries which have enabled our knowledge of the interconnection of natural processes to advance by leaps and bounds:

First, the discovery of the cell as the unit from whose multiplication and differentiation the whole plant and animal body develops. Not only is the development and growth of all higher organisms recognized to proceed according to a single general law, but the capacity of the cell to change indicates the way by which organisms can change their species and thus go through a more than individual development.

Second, the transformation of energy, which has demonstrated to us that all the so-called forces operative in the first instance in inorganic nature—mechanical force and its complement, so-called potential energy, heat, radiation (light or radiant heat), electricity, magnetism, and chemical energy—are different forms of manifestation of universal motion, which pass into one another in definite proportions so that in place of a certain quantity of the one which disappears, a certain quantity of another makes its appearance, and thus the whole motion of nature is reduced to this incessant process of transformation from one form into another.

Finally, the proof which Darwin first developed in connected form that the stock of organic products of nature environing us today, including man, is the result of a long process of evolution from a few originally unicellular germs, and that these again have arisen from protoplasm or albumen, which came into existence by chemical means.

Thanks to these three great discoveries, and the other immense advances in natural science, we have now arrived at the point where we can demonstrate the interconnection between the processes in nature not only in particular spheres but also the interconnection of these particular spheres on the whole, and so can present in an approximately systematic form a comprehensive view of the interconnection in nature by means of the facts provided by an empirical science itself. To furnish this comprehensive view was formerly the task of so-called natural philosophy. It could do this only by putting in place of the real but as yet unknown interconnections ideal, fancied ones, filling in the missing facts by figments of the mind and bridging the actual gaps merely in imagination. In the course of this procedure it conceived many brilliant ideas and foreshadowed many later discoveries, but it also produced a considerable amount of nonsense, which indeed could not have been otherwise. Today, when one needs to comprehend the results of natural scientific investigation only dialectically, that is, in the sense of their own interconnection, in order to arrive at a "system of nature" sufficient for our time; when the dialectical character of this interconnection is forcing itself against their will even into the metaphysically trained minds of the natural scientists, today natural philosophy is finally disposed of. Every attempt at resurrecting it would be not only superfluous but a *step backwards*.

But what is true of nature, which is hereby recognized also as a historical process of development, is likewise true of the history of society in all its branches and of the totality of all sciences which occupy themselves with things human—and divine. Here, too, the philosophy of history, of right, of religion, etc., has consisted in the substitution of an interconnection fabricated in the mind of the philosopher for the real interconnection to be demonstrated in the events; has consisted in the comprehension of history as a whole as well as in its separate parts, as the gradual realization of ideas—and naturally always only the pet ideas of the philosopher himself. According to this, history worked unconsciously but of necessity towards a certain ideal goal set in advance—as, for example, in Hegel, towards the realization of his absolute idea—and the unalterable trend towards this absolute idea formed the inner interconnection in the events of history. A new mysterious providence—unconscious or gradually coming into consciousness—was thus put in the place of the real, still unknown interconnection. Here, therefore, just as in the realm of nature, it was necessary to do away with these fabricated, artificial interconnections by the discovery of the real ones—a task which ultimately amounts to the discovery of the general laws of motion which assert themselves as the ruling ones in the history of human society.

In one point, however, the history of the development of society proves to be essentially different from that of nature. In nature—insofar as we ignore man's reaction upon nature—there are only blind, unconscious agencies acting upon one another, out of whose interplay the general law comes into operation. Nothing of all that happens—whether in the innumerable apparent accidents observable upon the surface, or in the ultimate results which confirm the regularity inherent in these accidents—happens as a consciously desired aim. In the history of society, on the contrary, the actors are all endowed with consciousness, are men acting with deliberation or passion, working towards definite goals; nothing happens without a conscious purpose, without an intended aim. But this distinction, important as it is for historical investigation, particularly of single epochs and events, cannot alter the fact that the course of history is governed by inner general laws. For here, also, on the whole, in spite of the consciously desired aims of all individuals, accident apparently reigns on the surface. That which is willed happens but rarely; in the majority of instances the numerous desired ends cross and conflict with one another, or these ends themselves are from the outset incapable of realization, or the means of attaining them are insufficient. Thus the conflicts of innumerable individual wills and individual actions in the domain of history produce a state of affairs entirely analogous to that prevailing in the realm of unconscious nature. The ends of the actions are intended, but the results which actually follow from these actions are not intended, or when they do seem to correspond to the end intended, they ultimately have consequences quite other than those intended. Historical events thus appear on the whole to be likewise governed by chance. But where on the surface accident holds sway, there actually it is always governed by inner, hidden laws, and it is only a matter of discovering these laws.

Men make their own history, whatever its outcome may be, in that each person follows his own consciously desired end, and it is precisely the resultant of these many wills operating in different directions, and of their manifold effects upon the outer world, that constitutes history. Thus it is also a question of what the many individuals desire. The will is determined by passion or deliberation. But the levers which immediately determine passion or deliberation are of very different kinds. Partly they may be external objects, partly ideal motives, ambition, "enthusiasm for truth and justice," personal hatred, or even purely individual whims of all kinds. But, on the one hand, we have seen that the many individual wills active in history for the most part produce results quite other than those intended—often quite the opposite; that their motives, therefore, in relation to the total result are likewise of only secondary importance. On the other hand, the further question arises: What driving forces in turn stand behind these motives? What are the historical forces which transform themselves into these motives in the brains of the actors?

The old materialism never put this question to itself. Its conception of history, insofar as it has one at all, is therefore essentially pragmatic; it divides men who act in history into noble and ignoble and then finds that as a rule the noble are defrauded and the ignoble are victorious. Hence, it follows for the old materialism that nothing very edifying is to be got from the study of history, and for us that in the realm of history the old materialism becomes untrue to itself because it takes the ideal driving forces which operate there as ultimate causes, instead of investigating what is behind them, what are the driving forces of these driving forces. This inconsistency does not lie in the fact that *ideal* driving forces are recognized, but in the investigation not being carried further back behind these into their motive causes. On the other hand, the philosophy of history, particularly as represented by Hegel, recognizes that the ostensible and also the really operating motives of men who act in history are by no means the ultimate causes of historical events; that behind these motives are other motive powers, which have to be discovered. But it does not seek these powers in history itself, it imports them rather from outside, from philosophical ideology, into history. Hegel, for example, instead of explaining the history of ancient Greece out of its own inner interconnections, simply maintains that it is nothing more than the working out of "forms of beautiful individuality," the realization of a "work of art" as such. He says much in this connection about the old Greeks that is fine and profound, but that does not prevent us today from refusing to be put off with such an explanation, which is a mere manner of speech.

When, therefore, it is a question of investigating the driving powers which—consciously or unconsciously, and indeed very often unconsciously—lie behind the motives of men who act in history and which constitute the real ultimate driving forces of history, then it is not a question so much of the motives of single individuals, however eminent, as of those motives which set in motion great masses, whole people, and again whole classes of the people in each people, and this, too, not merely for an instant, like the transient flaring up of a straw fire which quickly dies down, but as a lasting action resulting in a great historical transformation. To ascertain the driving causes which here in the minds of acting masses and their leaders—the so-called great men—are reflected as conscious motives, clearly or unclearly, directly or in an ideological, even glorified, form—is the only path which can put us on the track of the laws holding sway both in history as a whole and at particular periods and in particular lands. Everything which sets men in motion must go through their minds, but what form it will take in the mind will depend very much

upon the circumstances. The workers have by no means become reconciled to capitalist machine industry, even though they no longer simply
break the machines to pieces, as they still did in 1848 on the Rhine.

But while in all earlier periods the investigation of these driving causes
of history was almost impossible—on account of the complicated and
concealed interconnections between them and their effects—our present period has so far simplified these interconnections that the riddle
could be solved. Since the establishment of large-scale industry—that is,
at least since the European peace of 1815—it has been no longer a secret
to any man in England that the whole political struggle there pivoted on
the claims to supremacy of two classes: the landed aristocracy and the
bourgeoisie (middle class). In France, with the return of the Bourbons,
the same fact was perceived, the historians of the Restoration period,
from Thierry to Guisot, Mignet, and Thiers, speak of it everywhere as
the key to the understanding of all French history since the Middle Ages.
And since 1830, the working class, the proletariat, has been recognized
in both countries as a third competitor for power. Conditions had become
so simplified that one would have had to close one's eyes deliberately not
to see in the light of these three great classes and in the conflict of their
interests the driving force of modern history—at least in the two most
advanced countries.

But how did these classes come into existence? If it was possible at
first glance still to ascribe the origin of the great, formerly feudal landed
property—at least in the first instance—to political causes, to taking possession by force, this could not be done in regard to the bourgeoisie and
the proletariat. Here, the origin and development of two great classes
was seen to lie clearly and palpably in purely economic causes. And it
was just as clear that in the struggle between landed property and the
bourgeoisie, no less than in the struggle between the bourgeoisie and
the proletariat, it was a question, first and foremost, of economic interests, to the furtherance of which political power was intended to serve
merely as a means. Bourgeoisie and proletariat both arose in consequences of a transformation of the economic conditions, more precisely,
of the mode of production. The transition, first from guild handicrafts
to manufacture, and then from manufacture to large-scale industry, with
steam and mechanical power, had caused the development of these two
classes. At a certain stage, the new productive forces set in motion by the
bourgeoisie—in the first place the division of labor and the combination

of many detail laborers in one general manufactory—and the conditions and requirements of exchange, developed through these productive forces, became incompatible with the existing order of production handed down by history and sanctified by law—that is to say, incompatible with the privileges of the guild and the numerous other personal and local privileges (which were only so many fetters to the unprivileged estates) of the feudal order to society. The productive forces represented by the bourgeoisie rebelled against the order of production represented by the feudal landlords and the guild-masters. The result is known, the feudal fetters were smashed, gradually in England, at one blow in France. In Germany, the process is not yet finished. But just as, at a definite stage of its development, manufacture came into conflict with the feudal order of production, so now large-scale industry has already come into conflict with the bourgeois order of production established in its place. Tied down by this order, by the narrow limits of the capitalist mode of production, this industry produces, on the one hand, an ever-increasing proletarianization of the great mass of the people, and on the other hand, an ever greater mass of unsalable products. Overproduction and mass misery, each the cause of the other—that is the absurd contradiction which is its outcome, and which of necessity calls for the liberation of the productive forces by means of a change in the mode of production.

In modern history at least it is, therefore, proved that all political struggles are class struggles, and all class struggles for emancipation, despite their necessarily political form—for every class struggle is a political struggle—turn ultimately on the question of *economic* emancipation. Therefore, here at least, the state—the political order—is the subordination, and civil society—the realm of economic relations—the decisive element. The traditional conception, to which Hegel, too, pays homage, saw in the state the determining element and in civil society the element determined by it. Appearances correspond to this. As all the driving forces of the actions of any individual person must pass through his brain and transform themselves into motives of his will in order to set him into action, so also all the needs of civil society—no matter which class happens to be the ruling one—must pass through the will of the state in order to secure general validity in the form of laws. That is the formal aspect of the matter—the one which is self-evident. The question arises, however, what is the content of this merely formal will—of the individual as well as of the state—and whence is this content derived?

Why is just this willed and not something else? If we enquire into this, we discover that in modern history the will of the state is, on the whole, determined by the changing needs of civil society, by the supremacy of this or that class, in the last resort, by the development of the productive forces and relations of exchange.

But if even in our modern era, with its gigantic means of production and communication, the state is not an independent domain with an independent development, but one whose existence as well as development is to be explained in the last resort by the economic conditions of life of society, then this must be still more true of all earlier times when the production of the material life of man was not yet carried on with these abundant auxiliary means, and when, therefore, the necessity of such production must have exercised a still greater mastery over men. If the state even today, in the era of big industry and of railways, is on the whole only a reflection, in concentrated form, of the economic needs of the class controlling production, then this must have been much more so in an epoch when each generation of men was forced to spend a far greater part of its aggregate lifetime in satisfying material needs, and was therefore much more dependent on them than we are today. An examination of the history of earlier periods, as soon as it is seriously undertaken from this angle, most abundantly confirms this. But, of course, this cannot be gone into here.

If the state and public law are determined by economic relations, so, too, of course, is private law, which indeed in essence only sanctions the existing economic relations between individuals which are normal in the given circumstances. The form in which this happens can, however, vary considerably. It is possible, as happened in England, in harmony with the whole national development, to retain in the main the forms of the old feudal laws while giving them a bourgeois content; in fact, directly reading a bourgeois meaning into the feudal name. But also, as happened in Western continental Europe, Roman law, the first world law of a commodity-producing society, with its unsurpassably fine elaboration of all the essential legal relations of simple commodity owners—of buyers and sellers, debtors and creditors, contracts, obligations, etc.—can be taken as the foundation. In which case, for the benefit of a still petty-bourgeois and semifeudal society, it can either be reduced to the level of such a society simply through judicial practice (common law), or with the help of allegedly enlightened, moralizing jurists, it can be worked into a special code of law to correspond with such social level—a code which in these circumstances will be a bad one also from the legal standpoint (for instance, Prussian *Landrecht*). But after a great bourgeois revolution it is, however, also possible for such a classic law code of bourgeois society as the French *Code Civile* to be worked out upon the basis of this same Roman law. If, therefore, bourgeois legal rules merely express the economic life conditions of society in legal form, then they can do so well or ill according to circumstances.

The state presents itself to us as the first ideological power over man. Society creates for itself an organ for the safeguarding of its common interests against internal and external attacks. This organ is the state power. Hardly come into being, this organ makes itself independent vis-à-vis society, and, indeed, the more so, the more it becomes the organ of a particular class, the more it directly enforces the supremacy of that class. The fight of the oppressed class against the ruling class becomes necessarily a political fight, a fight first of all against the political dominance of this class. The consciousness of the interconnection between this political struggle and its economic basis becomes dulled and can be lost altogether. While this is not wholly the case with the participants, it almost always happens with the historians. Of the ancient sources on the struggles within the Roman Republic, only Appian tells us clearly and distinctly what was at issue in the last resort—namely, landed property.

But once the state has become an independent power vis-à-vis society, it produces forthwith a further ideology. It is indeed among professional politicians, theorists of public law, and jurists of private law, that the connection with economic facts gets lost for fair. Since in each particular case, the economic facts must assume the form of juristic motives in order to receive legal sanction, and since, in so doing, consideration of course has to be given to the whole legal system already in operation, the juristic form is, in consequence, made everything and the economic content nothing. Public law and private law are treated as independent spheres, each being capable of and needing a systematic presentation by the consistent elimination of all inner contradictions.

Still higher ideologies, that is, such as are still further removed from the material, economic basis, take the form of philosophy and religion. Here the interconnection between conceptions and their material conditions of existence becomes more and more complicated, more and more obscured by intermediate links. But the interconnection exists. Just as the whole Renaissance period, from the middle of the 15th century, was an essential product of the towns and, therefore, of the burghers, so also was the subsequently newly awakened philosophy. Its content was in essence only the philosophical expression of the thoughts corresponding to the development of the small and middle burghers into a big bourgeoisie. Among last century's Englishmen and Frenchmen who in many cases were just as much political economists as philosophers, this is clearly evident, and we have proved it above in regard to the Hegelian school.

We will now in addition deal only briefly with religion, since the latter stands further away from material life and seems to be most alien to it. Religion arose in very primitive times from erroneous, primitive conceptions of men about their own nature and external nature surrounding them. Every ideology, however, once it has arisen, develops in connection with the given concept material, and develops this material further; otherwise, it would not be an ideology, that is, occupation with thoughts as with independent entities, developing independently and subject only to their own laws. In the last analysis, the material life conditions of the persons inside whose heads this thought process goes on determine the course of the process, which of necessity remains unknown to these persons, for otherwise there would be an end to all ideology. These original religious notions, therefore, which in the main are common to each group of kindred peoples, develop, after the group separates, in a manner peculiar to each people, according to the conditions of life falling to their lot. For a number of groups of peoples, and particularly for the Aryans (so-called Indo-Europeans) this process has been shown in detail by comparative mythology. The gods thus fashioned within each people were national gods, whose domain extended no farther than the national territory which they were to protect; on the other side of its boundaries, other gods held undisputed sway. They could continue to exist, in imagination, only as long as the nation existed; they fell with its fall. The Roman world empire, the economic conditions of whose origin we do not need to examine here, brought about this downfall of the old nationalities. The old national gods decayed, even those of the Romans, which also were patterned to suit only the narrow confines of the city of Rome. The need to complement the world empire by means of a world religion was clearly revealed in the attempts made to recognize all foreign gods that were the least bit respectable and provide altars for them in Rome alongside the native gods. But a new world religion is not to be made in this fashion, by imperial decree. The new world religion, Christianity, had already quietly come into being, out of a mixture of generalized Oriental, particularly Jewish, theology, and vulgarized Greek, particularly Stoic, philosophy. What it originally looked like has to be first laboriously discovered, since its official form, as it has been handed down to us, is merely that in which it became the state religion to which purpose it was adapted by the Council of Nicaea. The fact that already after 250 years it became the state religion suffices to show that it was the religion in correspondence with the conditions of the time. In the Middle Ages, in the same measure as feudalism developed, Christianity grew into the religious counterpart to it, with a corresponding feudal hierarchy. And when the burghers began to thrive, there developed, in opposition to feudal Catholicism, the Protestant heresy, which first appeared in Southern France among the Albigenses, at the time the cities there reached the highest point of their fluorescence. The Middle Ages had attached to theology all the other forms of ideology—philosophy, politics, jurisprudence—and made them subdivisions of theology. It thereby constrained every social and political movement to take on a theological form. The sentiments of the masses were fed with religion to the exclusion of all else; it was therefore necessary to put forward their own interests in a religious guise in order to produce a great tempest. And just as the burghers from the beginning brought into being an appendage of propertyless urban plebeians, day laborers, and servants of all kinds, belonging to no recognized social estate, precursors of the later proletariat, so likewise heresy soon became divided into a burgher-moderate heresy and a plebeian-revolutionary one, the latter an abomination to the burgher heretics themselves.

The ineradicability of the Protestant heresy corresponded to the invincibility of the rising burghers. When these burghers had become sufficiently strengthened, their struggle against the feudal nobility, which till then had been predominantly local, began to assume national dimensions. The first great action occurred in Germany—the so-called Reformation. The burghers were neither powerful enough nor sufficiently developed to be able to unite under their banner the remaining rebellious estates—the plebeians of the towns, the lower nobility, and the peasants on the land. At first, the nobles were defeated; the peasants rose in a revolt which formed the peak of the whole revolutionary struggle; the cities left them in the lurch, and thus the revolution succumbed to the armies of the secular princes who reaped the whole profit. Thenceforward, Germany disappears for three centuries from the ranks of countries playing an independent active part in history. But, beside the German Luther appeared the Frenchman Calvin. With true French acuity, he put the bourgeois character of the Reformation in the forefront, republicanized and democratized the Church. While the Lutheran Reformation in Germany degenerated and reduced the country to rack and ruin, the Calvinist Reformation served as a banner for the republicans in Geneva, in Holland, and in Scotland, freed Holland from Spain and from the German Empire, and provided the ideological costume for the second act of the bourgeois revolution, which was taking place in England. Here, Calvinism justified itself as the true religious disguise of the interests of the bourgeoisie of that time, and on this account did not attain full recognition when the revolution ended in 1689 in a compromise between one part of the nobility and the bourgeoisie. The English state Church was reestablished, but not in its earlier form of a Catholicism which had the king for its pope, being, instead, strongly Calvinized. The old state Church had celebrated the merry Catholic Sunday and had fought against the dull Calvinist one. The new, bourgeoisified Church introduced the latter, which adorns England to this day.

In France, the Calvinist minority was suppressed in 1685 and either Catholicized or driven out of the country. But what was the good? Already at that time the freethinker Pierre Bayle was at the height of his activity, and in 1694 Voltaire was born. The forcible measures of Louis XIV only made it easier for the French bourgeoisie to carry through its revolution in the irreligious, exclusively political form which alone was suited to a developed bourgeoisie. Instead of Protestants, freethinkers took their seats in the national assemblies. Thereby Christianity entered into its final stage. It was incapable of doing any future service to any progressive class as the ideological garb of its aspirations. It became more and more the exclusive possession of the ruling classes; they apply it as a mere means of government, to keep the lower classes within bounds. Moreover, each of the different classes uses its own appropriate religion: the landed nobility—Catholic Jesuitism or Protestant orthodoxy; the liberal and radical bourgeoisie—rationalism; and it makes little difference whether these gentlemen themselves believe in their respective religions or not.

We see, therefore: religion, once formed, always contains traditional material, just as in all ideological domains tradition forms a great conservative force. But the transformations which this material undergoes spring from class relations—that is to say, out of the economic relations of the people who execute these transformations. And here that is sufficient.

In the above, it could only be a question of giving a general sketch of the Marxist conception of history, at most with a few illustrations, as well. The proof must be derived from history itself, and, in this regard, it may be permitted to say that is has been sufficiently furnished in other writings. This conception, however, puts an end to philosophy in the realm of history, just as the dialectical conception of nature makes all natural philosophy both unnecessary and impossible. It is no longer a question anywhere of inventing interconnections from out of our brains but of discovering them in the facts. For philosophy, which has been expelled from nature and history, there remains only the realm of pure thought, so far as it is left: the theory of the laws of the thought process itself, logic and dialectics.

With the Revolution of 1848, "educated" Germany said farewell to theory and went over to the field of practice. Small production and manufacture, based upon manual labor, were superseded by real large-scale industry. Germany again appeared on the world market. The new little German Empire abolished at least the most crying of the abuses with which this development had been obstructed by the system of petty states, the relics of feudalism, and bureaucratic management. But to the same degree that speculation abandoned the philosopher's study in order to set up its temple in the Stock Exchange, educated Germany lost the great aptitude for theory which had been the glory of Germany in the days of its deepest political humiliation—the aptitude for purely scientific investigation, irrespective of whether the result obtained was practically applicable or not, whether likely to offend the police authorities or not. Official German natural science, it is true, maintained its position in the front rank, particularly in the field of specialized research. But even the American journal *Science* rightly remarks that the decisive advances in the sphere of the comprehensive correlation of particular facts and their generalization into laws are now being made much more in England, instead of, as formerly, in Germany. And in the sphere of the historical sciences, philosophy included, the old fearless zeal for theory has now disappeared completely, along with classical philosophy. Inane eclecticism and an anxious concern for career and income, descending to the most vulgar job hunting, occupy its place. The official representatives of these sciences have become the undisguised ideologists of the bourgeoisie and the existing state—but at a time when both stand in open antagonism to the working class.

Only among the working class does the German aptitude for theory remain unimpaired. Here, it cannot be exterminated. Here, there is no concern for careers, for profit making, or for gracious patronage from above. On the contrary, the more ruthlessly and disinterestedly science proceeds the more it finds itself in harmony with the interest and aspirations of the workers. The new tendency, which recognized that the key to the understanding of the whole history of society lies in the history of the development of labor, from the outset addressed itself by preference to the working class and here found the response which it neither sought nor expected from officially recognized science. The German working-class movement is the inheritor of German classical philosophy.

FUNDAMENTAL PROBLEMS OF MARXISM (EXCERPTS)

Georgi Plekhanov
1907

In his last major work, the "Father of Russian Marxism" elaborates on the origins, genesis, and explanatory power of dialectical and historical materialism. Written for the 25th anniversary of Marx's death, it was published as a pamphlet in 1908. As most readers will know, Plekhanov subsequently moved to the right and joined the reaction against the Bolshevik Revolution. Nonetheless, his earlier defense and explanation of Marx and Engels's intellectual and philosophical development remains of great interest to this day.

Marxism is an integral world outlook. Expressed in a nutshell, it is contemporary materialism, at present the highest stage in the development of that view upon the world whose foundations were laid down in ancient Greece by Democritus, and in part by the Ionian thinkers who preceded that philosopher. What was known as hylozoism was nothing but a naïve materialism. It is to Karl Marx and his friend, Friedrich Engels, that the main credit for the development of present-day materialism must no doubt go. The historical and economic aspects of this world outlook, that is, what is known as *historical materialism*, and the closely related sum of views on the tasks, method, and categories of political economy, and on the economic development of society, especially capitalist society, are in their fundamentals almost entirely the work of Marx and Engels. That which was introduced into these fields by their precursors should be regarded merely as the preparatory work of amassing material, often copious and valuable, but not as yet systematized or illuminated by a single fundamental idea, and therefore not appraised or utilized in its real significance.

What Marx and Engels's followers in Europe and America have done in these fields is merely a more or less successful elaboration of specific problems, sometimes, it is true, of the utmost importance. That is why the term "Marxism" is often used to signify only these two aspects of the present-day materialist world outlook not only among the "general public," which has not yet achieved a deep understanding of philosophical theories, but even among people, both in Russia and the entire civilized world, who consider themselves faithful followers of Marx and Engels. In such cases these two aspects are looked upon as something independent of "philosophical materialism," and at times as something almost opposed to it. And since these two aspects cannot but hang in midair when arbitrarily they are torn out of the general context of cognate views constituting their theoretical foundation, those who perform that tearing-out operation naturally feel an urge to "substantiate Marxism" anew by joining it—again quite arbitrarily and most frequently under the influence of philosophical moods prevalent at the time among ideologists of the bourgeoisie—with some philosopher or another: with Kant, Mach, Avenarius, or Ostwald, and of late with Joseph Dietzgen. True, the philosophical views of J. Dietzgen have arisen quite independently of bourgeois influences and are in considerable measure related to the philosophical views of Marx and Engels. The latter views, however, possess an incomparably more consistent and rich content, and for that reason alone cannot be supplemented by Dietzgen's teachings but can only be popularized by them. No attempts have yet been made to "supplement Marx" with Thomas Aquinas. It is, however, quite feasible that, despite the Pope's recent encyclical against the Modernists, the Catholic world will at some time produce from its midst a thinker capable of performing this feat in the sphere of theory.

I. Philosophical Writings of Marx and Engels

Attempts to show that Marxism must be "supplemented" by one philosopher or another are usually backed up with reference to the fact that Marx and Engels did not anywhere set forth their philosophical views. This reasoning is hardly convincing, however, apart from the consideration that, even if these views were indeed not set forth anywhere, that could provide no logical reason to have them replaced by the views of any random thinker who, in the main, holds an entirely different point of view. It should be remembered that we have sufficient literary material at our disposal to form a correct idea of the philosophical views of Marx and Engels.

In their *final* shape, these views were fairly fully set forth, although in a polemical form, in the first part of Engels's book *Herr Eugen Dühring's Revolution in Science [Anti-Dühring]* (of which there are several Russian translations). Then there is a splendid booklet by the same author, *Ludwig Feuerbach and the End of Classical German Philosophy* (which I have translated into Russian and supplied with a preface and explanatory notes), in which the views constituting the philosophical foundation of Marxism are expounded in a positive form. A brief but vivid account of the same views, related to agnosticism, was given by Engels in his preface to the English translation of the pamphlet *The Development of Scientific Socialism*. As for Marx, I will mention as important for an understanding of the philosophical aspect of his teachings, in the first place, the characterization of the materialist dialectic—as distinct from Hegel's idealist dialectic—given in the preface to Volume I of *Capital*, and, secondly, the numerous remarks made *en passant* in the same volume. Also significant in certain respects are some of the pages in *The Poverty of Philosophy* (which has been translated into Russian). Finally, the process of the development of Marx and Engels's philosophical views is revealed with sufficient clarity in their early writings, republished by Franz Mehring under the title of *From the Literary Remains of Karl Marx* (Stuttgart, 1902).

In his doctoral dissertation "The Difference Between the Democritean and Epicurean Philosophy of Nature," as well as in several articles republished by Mehring in Volume I of the publication just mentioned, the young Marx appears before us as an idealist *pur sang* [of pure blood] of the Hegelian school. However, in the articles which have now been included in the same volume, and which first appeared in the *Deutsch-Französische Jahrbüchern [Franco-German Annals]*, Marx—like Engels, who also collaborated in the *Annals*—was a firm adherent of Feuerbachian "*humanism.*"[1]

---

1 Note to the German edition of 1910: Of considerable importance for a characterization of the evolution of Marx's philosophical views is his letter of October 20, 1843 to Feuerbach. Inviting Feuerbach to come out against Schelling, Marx wrote the following: "You are just the man for this because you are *Schelling in reverse*. The *sincere thought*—we may believe the best of our opponent—of the *young* Schelling for the realization of which however

The Holy Family, or Critique of Critical Criticism, which appeared in 1845 and has been republished in Volume II of the Mehring publication, shows us our two authors, that is, both Marx and Engels, as having made several important steps in the further development of Feuerbach's philosophy. The direction they gave to this elaboration can be seen from the eleven "Theses on Feuerbach" written by Marx in the spring of 1845, and published by Engels as an appendix to the aforementioned pamphlet, *Ludwig Feuerbach*. In short, there is no lack of material here; the only thing needed is the ability to make use of it, that is, the need to have the proper training for its understanding. Present-day readers, however, do not have the training required for that understanding, and consequently do not know how to make use of it.

Why is that so? For a variety of reasons. One of the principal reasons is that nowadays there is, in the first place, little knowledge of Hegelian philosophy, without which it is difficult to learn Marx's method, and, in the second place, little knowledge of the history of materialism, the absence of which does not permit present-day readers to form a clear idea of the doctrine of Feuerbach, who was Marx's immediate precursor in the field of philosophy, and who in considerable measure worked out the philosophical foundation of what can be called the world outlook of Marx and Engels.

---

he did not possess the necessary qualities except imagination, he had no energy but vanity, no driving force but opium, no organ but the irritability of a feminine perceptivity, this sincere thought of his youth, which in his case remained a fantastic youthful dream, has become truth, reality, manly seriousness in your case. Schelling is therefore an *anticipated caricature* of you, and as soon as reality confronts the caricature, the latter must dissolve into thin air. I therefore regard you as the necessary, natural—that is, nominated by Their Majesties Nature and History—opponent of Schelling. Your struggle with him is the struggle of the imagination of philosophy with philosophy itself" (Marx and Engels, Letter of October 3, 1843). This seems to show that Marx understood "Schelling's youthful thought" in the meaning of a materialist monism. Feuerbach, however, did not share this opinion of Marx's, as will be seen from his reply to the latter. He considered that already in his first works Schelling "merely converts the idealism of *thought* into the idealism of the *imagination*, and attributes just as little reality to things as to the *Ich*, with the only difference that it had a different appearance, and that he replaced the determinate '*Ich*' by the indefinite Absolute, and gave idealism a pantheistic coloring" (K. Grün, *Ludwig Feuerbach: His Correspondence and Literary Remains*).

Nowadays Feuerbach's "humanism" is usually described as something very vague and indefinite. F.A. Lange, who has done so much to spread, both among the "general public" and in the learned world, an absolutely false view of the essence of materialism and of its history, refused to recognize Feuerbach's "humanism" as a materialist teaching. Lange's example is being followed, in this respect, by almost all who have written on Feuerbach in Russia and other countries. P.A. Berlin, too, seems to have been affected by this influence, since he depicts Feuerbach's "humanism" as a kind of materialism that is not quite "pure." I must admit that I do not know for certain how this question is regarded by Franz Mehring, whose knowledge of philosophy is the best, and probably unique, among German Social Democrats. But it is perfectly clear to me that it was the materialist that Marx and Engels saw in Feuerbach. True, Engels speaks of Feuerbach's inconsistency, but that does not in the least prevent him from recognizing the fundamental propositions of his philosophy as purely materialist.[2] But then these propositions cannot be viewed otherwise by anybody who has gone to the trouble of making a study of them.

II. Feuerbach and Marx

I am well aware that in saying all this I risk surprising very many of my readers. I am not afraid to do so; the ancient thinker was right in saying that astonishment is the mother of philosophy. For the reader not to remain at the stage, so to say, of astonishment, I shall first of all recommend that he ask himself what Feuerbach meant when, while giving a terse but vivid outline of his philosophical *curriculum vitae*, he wrote, "God was my

---

2 Note to the German edition of 1910: F. Engels wrote: "The course of evolution of Feuerbach is that of a Hegelian—a never quite orthodox Hegelian, it is true—into a materialist; an evolution which at a definite stage necessitates a complete rupture with the idealist system of his predecessor. With irresistible force Feuerbach is finally driven to the realization that the Hegelian premundane existence of the 'absolute idea,' the 'pre-existence of the logical categories' before the world existed, is nothing more than the fantastic survival of the belief in the existence of an extramundane creator; that the material, sensuously perceptible world to which we ourselves belong is the only reality; and that our consciousness and thinking, however suprasensuous they may seem, are the product of a material, bodily organ, the brain. Matter is not a product of mind, but mind itself is merely the highest product of matter. This is, of course, pure materialism."

first thought, Reason the second, and Man the third and last thought." I contend that this question is conclusively answered in the following meaningful words of Feuerbach himself:

> In the controversy between materialism and spiritualism . . . the human head is under discussion . . . once we have learned what kind of matter the brain is made up of, we shall soon arrive at a clear view upon all other matter as well, matter in general.

Elsewhere he says that his "anthropology," that is, his "humanism," merely means that man takes for God that which is his own essence, his own spirit. He goes on to say that Descartes did not eschew this "anthropological" point of view. How is all this to be understood? It means that Feuerbach made "Man" the point of departure of his philosophical reasoning only because it was from that point of departure that he hoped the sooner to achieve his aim—to bring forth a correct view upon matter in general and its relation to the "spirit." Consequently, what we have here is a methodological device, whose value was conditioned by circumstances of time and place, that is, by the thinking habits of the learned, or simply educated, Germans of the time,[3] and not by any specificity of world outlook.[4]

The above quotation from Feuerbach regarding the "human head" shows that when he wrote these words the problem of "the kind of matter the brain is made up of" was solved by him in a "purely" materialistic sense. This solution was also accepted by Marx and Engels. It provided the foundation of their own philosophy, as can be seen with the utmost clarity from Engels's works, so often quoted here—*Ludwig Feuerbach* and *Anti-Dühring*. That is why we must make a closer study of this solution; in doing so, we shall at the same time be studying the philosophical aspect of Marxism.

In an article entitled "Provisional Theses for the Reform of Philosophy," which came out in 1842 and, judging by the facts, had a strong influence

---

3   Feuerbach himself has very well said that the *beginnings* of any philosophy are determined by the prior state of philosophical thought

4   Note to the German edition of 1910: F. Lange states: "A genuine materialist will always be prone to turn his glance to the totality of external Nature and consider Man merely as a wavelet in the ocean of the eternal movement of matter. To the materialist, Man's nature is merely a particular instance of general physiology, just as thinking is a special instance in the chain of physical processes of life." (*History of Materialism*)

on Marx, Feuerbach said that "the real relation of thinking to being is only as follows: being is the *subject*; thinking, the *predicate*. Thinking is conditioned by being, and not being by thinking. Being is conditioned by itself . . . has its foundation in itself."

This view on the relation of being to thinking, which Marx and Engels made the foundation of the materialistic explanation of history, is a most important outcome of the criticism of Hegel's idealism already completed in its main features by Feuerbach, a criticism whose conclusions can be set forth in a few words.

Feuerbach considered that Hegel's philosophy had removed the contradiction between being and thinking, a contradiction that had expressed itself in striking relief in Kant. However, as Feuerbach thought, it removed that contradiction, while continuing to remain within the latter, that is, within one of its elements, namely, thinking. With Hegel, *thinking is being*: "Thinking is the subject; being, the predicate." It follows that Hegel, and idealism in general, eliminated the contradiction only by removing one of its component elements, that is, being, matter, nature. However, removing one of the component elements in a contradiction does not at all mean doing away with that contradiction. "Hegel's doctrine that reality is 'postulated' by the Idea is merely a translation into rationalistic terms of the theological doctrine that Nature was created by God—and reality, matter, by an abstract, nonmaterial being." This applies not only to Hegel's absolute idealism. Kant's transcendental idealism, according to which the external world receives its laws from Reason instead of Reason receiving them from the external world, is closely akin to the theological concept that the world's laws were dictated to it by the divine Reason. Idealism does not establish the unity of being and thinking, nor can it do so; it tears that unity asunder.

Idealistic philosophy's point of departure—the "*I*" as the fundamental philosophical principle—is totally erroneous. It is not the "*I*" that must be the starting point of genuine philosophy, but the "*I*" and the "*you*." It is such a point of departure that makes it possible to arrive at a proper understanding of the relation between thinking and being, between the subject and the object. I am "*I*" to myself, and at the same time I am "*you*" to others. The "I" is the *subject*, and at the same time the *object*. It must at the same time be noted that I am not the abstract being idealistic philosophy operates with. I am an *actual* being; my *body* belongs to my *essence*; moreover, my body, as a whole, is my *I*, my genuine essence. It is not an abstract being that thinks, but this actual being, this body. Thus, contrary to what the idealists assert, an actual and material being proves to be the subject; and thinking, the predicate. Herein lies the only possible solution of the contradiction between being and thinking, a contradiction that idealism sought so vainly to resolve. None of the elements in the contradiction is removed; both are preserved, revealing their real unity. "That which to me, or subjectively, is a purely spiritual, nonmaterial and nonsensuous act is in itself an objective, material, and sensuous act."

Note that in saying this, Feuerbach stands close to Spinoza, whose philosophy he was already setting forth with great sympathy at the time his own breakaway from idealism was taking shape, that is, when he was writing his history of modern philosophy.[5] In 1843 he made the subtle observation, in his *Principles of the Philosophy of the Future*, that pantheism is a theological materialism, a negation of theology but as yet on a theological standpoint. This confusion of materialism and theology constituted Spinoza's inconsistency, which, however, did not prevent him from providing a "correct—at least for his time—philosophical expression for the materialist trend of modern times." That was why Feuerbach called Spinoza "the Moses of the modern free-thinkers and materialists." In 1847 Feuerbach asked: "What then, under careful examination, is that which Spinoza calls *Substance*, in terms of logics or metaphysics, and *God* in terms of theology?" To this question he replied categorically, "Nothing else but Nature." He saw Spinozism's main shortcoming in the fact that "in it the sensible, antitheological essence of Nature assumes the aspect of an abstract, metaphysical being." Spinoza eliminated the dualism of God and Nature, since he declared that the acts of Nature were those of God. However, it was just because he regarded the acts of Nature to be those of God, that the latter remained, with Spinoza, a being distinct from Nature, but forming its foundation. He regarded God as the subject and Nature as the predicate. A philosophy that has completely liberated itself from theological traditions must remove this important shortcoming

---

5 Note to the German edition of 1910: By that time Feuerbach had already written the following noteworthy lines: "Despite all the oppositeness of practical realism in the so-called sensualism and materialism of the English and the French—a realism that denies any speculation—and the spirit of *all* of Spinoza, they nevertheless have their *ultimate* foundation in the viewpoint on *matter* expressed by Spinoza, as a metaphysician, in the celebrated proposition: 'Matter is an Attribute of God'" (K Grün, *L. Feuerbach*).

in Spinoza's philosophy, which in its essence is sound. "Away with this contradiction!" Feuerbach exclaimed. "Not *Deus sive Natura* [God or Nature] but *aut Deus aut Natura* [either God or Nature] is the watchword of Truth."

Thus, Feuerbach's "humanism" proved to be nothing else but Spinozism disencumbered of its theological pendant. And it was the viewpoint of this kind of Spinozism, which Feuerbach had freed of its theological pendant, that Marx and Engels adopted when they broke with idealism.

However, disencumbering Spinozism of its theological setting meant revealing its true and *materialist* content. Consequently, the Spinozism of Marx and Engels was indeed materialism brought up to date.

Further: Thinking is not the *cause* of being, but its *effect*, or rather its *property*. Feuerbach says: *Folge und Eigenschaft*, I feel and think, not as a subject counterposed to an object, but as a *subject-object*, as an actual and material being. "For us the object is not merely the thing sensed, but also the basis, the indispensable condition of my sensation." The objective world is not only without me but also within me, inside my own skin.[6] Man is only a part of Nature, a part of being; there is, therefore, no room for any contradiction between his thinking and his being. Space and time exist not only as forms of thinking. They are also forms of being, forms of my contemplation. They are such, solely because I myself am a creature that lives in time and space, and because I sense and feel as such a creature. In general, the laws of being are at the same time laws of thinking.

That is what Feuerbach said. And the same thing, though in a different wording, was said by Engels in his polemic with Dühring.[7] This already

---

6 Note to the German edition of 1910: "How do we cognize the external world? How do we cognize the *inner* world? For ourselves we have no other means than we have for others! Do I know anything about myself without the medium of my senses? Do I exist if I do not exist outside myself, that is, outside my conception? But how do I know that I exist? How do I know that I exist, not in my *conception*, but in my sensations, in actual fact, unless I perceive myself through my senses?" (K Grün, *L. Feuerbach*).

7 Note to the German edition of 1910: I particularly recommend to the reader's attention the thought expressed by Engels in *Anti-Dühring*, that the laws of external Nature and the laws governing man's bodily and mental existence are "two classes of laws which we can separate from each other at most only in thought but not in reality." This is the selfsame *doctrine of the unity of being and thinking, of object and subject.* Regarding space and

shows what an important part of Feuerbach's philosophy became an integral part of the philosophy of Marx and Engels.

If Marx began to elaborate his materialist explanation of history by criticizing Hegel's philosophy of Right, he could do so only because Feuerbach had completed his criticism of Hegel's speculative philosophy.

Even when criticizing Feuerbach in his Theses, Marx often develops and augments the former's ideas. Here is an instance from the sphere of "epistemology." Before thinking of an object, man, according to Feuerbach, experiences its action on himself, contemplates and senses it.

It was this thought that Marx had in mind when he wrote:

> The chief defect of all previous materialism (that of Feuerbach included) is that the object, reality, sensuousness, is conceived only in the form of the *object*, or of *contemplation*, but not as *human sensuous activity*, *practice*, not subjectively.

This shortcoming in materialism, Marx goes on to say, accounts for the circumstance that, in his *Essence of Christianity*, Feuerbach regards theoretical activity as the only genuine human activity. Expressed in other words, this means that, according to Feuerbach, our *I* cognizes the object by coming under its action. Marx, however, objects by saying: our *I* cognizes the object, *while at the same time acting upon that object*. Marx's thought is a perfectly correct one: as Faust already said, "In the beginning was the deed."

It may of course be objected, in defense of Feuerbach, that, in the process of our acting upon objects, we cognize their properties only in the measure in which they, for their part, act upon us. In both cases *sensation* precedes *thinking*; in both cases we first *sense* their properties, and only then *think* of them. But that is something that Marx did not deny. For him the gist of the matter was not the indisputable fact that sensation precedes thinking, but the fact that man is induced to think chiefly by the sensations he experiences in the process of his acting upon the outer world. Since this action on the outer world is prescribed to man by the struggle for existence, the theory of knowledge is closely linked up by Marx with his materialist view of the history of human civilization. It was not for nothing that the thinker who directed against Feuerbach the

---

time, see Chapter 5 of Part I of the work just mentioned. This chapter shows that to Engels, just as to Feuerbach, space and time are not only forms of contemplation, but also forms of being.

thesis we are here discussing wrote in Volume 1 of *Capital*: "By thus acting on the external world and changing it, he [man] at the same time changes his own nature." This proposition fully reveals its profound meaning only in the light of Marx's theory of knowledge. We shall see how well this theory is confirmed by the history of cultural development and, incidentally, even by the science of language. It must, however, be admitted that Marx's epistemology stems directly from that of Feuerbach, or, if you will, it is, properly speaking, the epistemology of Feuerbach, only rendered more profound by the masterly correction brought into it by Marx.

I shall add, in passing, that this masterly correction was prompted by the "spirit of the times." The striving to examine the interaction between object and subject precisely from the point of view in which the subject appears in an *active* role, derived from the public mood of the period in which the world outlook of Marx and Engels was taking shape. The revolution of 1848 was in the offing.

III. Thinking and Being in Feuerbach

The doctrine of the unity of subject and object, thinking and being, which was shared in equal measure by Feuerbach and by Marx and Engels, was also held by the most outstanding materialists of the seventeenth and eighteenth centuries.

Elsewhere I have shown that La Mettrie and Diderot—each after his own fashion—arrived at a world outlook that was a "brand of Spinozism," that is, a Spinozism without the theological setting that distorted its true content. It would also be easy to show that, inasmuch as we are speaking of the unity of subject and object, Hobbes too stood very close to Spinoza. That, however, would be taking us too far afield, and, besides, there is no immediate need for that. Probably of greater interest to the reader is the fact that today every naturalist who has delved even a little into the problem of the relation of thinking to being arrives at that doctrine of their unity which we have met in Feuerbach.

When Huxley wrote the following words: "Surely no one who is cognizant of the facts of the case, nowadays, doubts that the roots of psychology lie in the physiology of the nervous system," and went on to say that the operations of the mind "are functions of the brain," he was expressing just what Feuerbach had said—only with these words he connected concepts that were far less clear. It was precisely because the concepts connected with these words were far less clear than with Feuerbach that he attempted to link up the view just quoted with Hume's philosophical skepticism.

In just the same way, Haeckel's "monism," which created such a stir, is nothing else but a purely materialist doctrine—in essence close to that of Feuerbach—of the unity of subject and object. Haeckel, however, is poorly versed in the history of materialism, which is why he considers it necessary to struggle against its "one-sidedness"; he should have gone to the trouble of making a study of its theory of knowledge in the form it took with Feuerbach and Marx, which would have preserved him from the many lapses and one-sided assumptions that have made it easier for his opponents to wage a struggle against him on philosophical grounds.

A very close approach to the most modern materialism—that of Feuerbach, Marx, and Engels—has been made by August Forel in various of his writings, for instance in the paper *Brain and Soul*, which he read to the Sixty-Sixth Congress of German Naturalists and Physicians held in Vienna in 1894. In places Forel not only expresses ideas resembling Feuerbach's but—and this is amazing—marshals his arguments just as Feuerbach did his. According to Forel, each new day brings us convincing proofs that the psychology and the physiology of the brain are merely two ways of looking at "one and the same thing." The reader will not have forgotten Feuerbach's identical view, which I have quoted above and which pertains to the same problem. This view can be supplemented here with the following statement: "I am the psychological object to myself," Feuerbach says, "but a physiological object to others." In the final analysis, Forel's main idea boils down to the proposition that consciousness is the "inner reflex of cerebral activity." This view is already materialist.

Objecting to the materialists, the idealists and Kantians of all kinds and varieties claim that what we apprehend is only the *mental* aspect of the phenomena that Forel and Feuerbach deal with. This objection was excellently formulated by Schelling, who said that "the Spirit will always be an island which one cannot reach from the sphere of matter, otherwise than by a leap." Forel is well aware of this, but he provides convincing proof that science would be an impossibility if we made up our minds in earnest not to leave the bounds of that island. "Every man," he says, "would have only the psychology of his own subjectivism . . . and would positively be obliged to doubt the existence of the external world and of other people." Such doubt is absurd, however.[8]

> Conclusions arrived at by analogy, natural-scientific induction, a comparison of the evidence provided by our five senses, prove to us the existence of the external world, of other people, and the psychology of the latter. Likewise they prove to us that comparative psychology, animal psychology and, finally, our own psychology would be incomprehensible and full of contradictions if we considered it apart from the activities of our brain; first and foremost, it would seem a contradiction of the law of the conservation of energy.

Feuerbach not only reveals the contradictions that inevitably beset those who reject the materialist standpoint, but also shows how the idealists reach their "island."

"I am *I* to myself," he says, "and *you* to another. But I am such an *I* only as a sensible [that is, material] being. The abstract intellect isolates this being-for-oneself as Substance, the atom, ego, God; that is why, to it, the connection between being-for-oneself and being-for-another is arbitrary. That which I think of as extra-sensuous, I think of as without and outside any connection."

This most significant consideration is accompanied by an analysis of that process of abstraction which led to the appearance of Hegelian logic as an *ontological* doctrine.

Had Feuerbach possessed the information provided by present-day ethnology, he would have been able to add that philosophical idealism descends, in the historical sense, from the animism of primitive peoples. This was already pointed out by Edward B. Tylor, and certain historians of philosophy are beginning to take it, in part, into consideration, though for the time being more as a curiosity than a fact from the history of culture, and of tremendous theoretical and cognitive significance.

----

8 Note to the German edition of 1910: Moreover, on his return from exile, Chernyshevsky published an article, "The Character of Human Knowledge," in which he proves, very wittily, that a person who doubts the existence of the external world should also doubt the fact of his own existence. Chernyshevsky was always a faithful adherent of Feuerbach. The fundamental idea of his article can be expressed in the following words of Feuerbach: "I am not different from things and creatures without me, because I distinguish myself from them; I distinguish myself because I am different from them physically, organically, and in fact. Consciousness presupposes being, is merely conscious being, that-which-is as realized and presented in the mind" (K Grün, *L. Feuerbach*).

These ideas and arguments of Feuerbach's were not only well known to Marx and Engels and given careful thought by them, but indubitably and in considerable measure helped in the evolution of their own world outlook. If Engels later had the greatest contempt for post-Feuerbachian German philosophy, it was because that philosophy, in his opinion, merely resuscitated the old philosophical errors already revealed by Feuerbach. That, indeed, was the case. Not one of the latest critics of materialism has brought forward a single argument that was not refuted either by Feuerbach himself or, before him, by the French materialists. But to the "critics of Marx"—to E. Bernstein, C. Schmidt, B. Croce, and the like—"the pauper's broth of eclecticism" of the most up-to-date, German, so-called philosophy seems a perfectly new dish; they have fed on it, and, seeing that Engels did not see fit to address himself to it, they imagined that he was "evading" any analysis of an argumentation he had long ago considered and found absolutely worthless. That is an old story, but one that is always new. Rats will never stop thinking that the cat is far stronger than the lion.

In recognizing the striking similarity—and, in part, also the identity—in the views of Feuerbach and A. Forel, we shall, however, note that while the latter is far better informed in natural science, Feuerbach had the advantage of a thorough knowledge of philosophy. That is why Forel makes mistakes we do not find in Feuerbach. Forel calls his theory the *psychophysiological theory of identity*. To this no objection of any significance can be raised, because all terminology is conventional. However, since the theory of identity once formed the foundation of an absolutely definite idealist philosophy, Forel would have done well to have straightforwardly, boldly, and simply declared his theory to be materialist. He seems to have preserved certain prejudices against materialism, and therefore chose another name. That is why I think it necessary to note that identity in the Forelian sense has nothing in common with identity in the idealist sense.

The "critics of Marx" do not know even this. In his polemic with me, C. Schmidt ascribed to the materialists precisely the idealist doctrine of identity. In actual fact, materialism recognizes the *unity* of subject and object, not their identity. This was well shown by the selfsame Feuerbach.

According to Feuerbach, the unity of subject and object, of thinking and being, makes sense only when man is taken as the basis of that unity. This has a special kind of "humanist" sound to it, and most students of

Feuerbach have not found it necessary to give deeper thought to *how* man serves as the basis of the unity of the opposites just mentioned. In actual fact, this is how Feuerbach understood the matter: "It is only when thinking is not a *subject for itself*, but the predicate of a real [that is, material] being that thought is not something separated from being." The question now is: Where, in which philosophical systems, is thinking a "subject for itself," that is to say, something independent of the bodily existence of a thinking individual? The answer is clear: in systems that are *idealist*. The idealists first convert thinking into a self-contained essence, independent of man ("the subject for itself"), and then assert that it is in that essence that the contradiction between being and thinking is resolved, for the very reason that separate and independent being is a property of that independent-of-matter essence.[9] Indeed, the contradiction is resolved in that essence. In that case, what is that essence? It is *thinking*, and this thinking exists—is—independently of anything else. Such a resolution of the contradiction is a purely formal one, which, as we have already pointed out, is achieved only by eliminating one of its elements, namely, being, as something independent of thinking. Being proves to be a simple property of thinking, so that when we say that a given object exists, we mean that it exists only in our thinking. That is how the matter was understood by Schelling, for example. To him, thinking was the absolute principle from which the real world, that is, Nature and the "finite" spirit, followed of necessity. But *how* did it follow? What was meant by the existence of the real world? Nothing but existence in thinking. To Schelling, the Universe was merely the self-contemplation of the Absolute Spirit. We see the same thing in Hegel. Feuerbach, however, was not satisfied with such a purely formal resolving of the contradiction between thinking and being. He pointed out that there is no—there can be no—*thinking independent of man*, that is, of an actual and material creature. Thinking is activity of the brain. To quote Feuerbach: "But the brain is the organ of thinking only as long as it is connected with the human head and body."

---

9 Note to the German edition of 1910: Ernst Mach and his followers act in exactly the same way. First they transform *sensation* into an independent essence, noncontingent upon the sensing *body*—an essence which they call an element. Then they declare that this essence contains the resolution of the contradiction between being and thinking, subject and object. This reveals the grossness of the error committed by those who assert that Mach is close to Marx.

We now see in what sense Feuerbach considers man the basis of the unity of being and thinking. Man is that basis in the sense that he is nothing but a material being that possesses the ability to think. If he is such a being, then it is clear that none of the elements of the contradiction is eliminated—neither being nor thinking, "matter" or "spirit," subject or object. They are all combined in him as the subject-object. "I exist, and I think . . . only as a subject-object," Feuerbach says.

To be does not mean to exist in thought. In this respect, Feuerbach's philosophy is far clearer than that of J. Dietzgen. As Feuerbach put it: "To prove that something exists means to prove that it is not something that exists only in thought." This is perfectly true, but it means that the unity of thinking and being does not and cannot in any way mean their identity.

This is one of the most important features distinguishing materialism from idealism.

IV. Emergence of Historical Materialism

When people say that, for a certain period, Marx and Engels were followers of Feuerbach, it is often inferred that, when that period ended, Marx and Engels's world outlook changed considerably, and became quite different from Feuerbach's. That is how the matter is viewed by Karl Diehl, who finds that Feuerbach's influence on Marx is usually highly exaggerated. This is a gross mistake. When they ceased being followers of Feuerbach, Marx and Engels continued to share a very considerable part of his philosophical views. The best proof of this is the Theses which Marx wrote in criticism of Feuerbach. The Theses in no way eliminate the fundamental propositions in Feuerbach's philosophy, but only correct them, and—what is most important—call for a more consistent (than Feuerbach's) application in explaining the reality that surrounds man, and in particular his own activity. It is not thinking that determines being, but being that determines thinking. That is the fundamental thought in all of Feuerbach's philosophy. Marx and Engels made that thought the foundation of the materialist explanation of history. The materialism of Marx and Engels is a far more developed doctrine than Feuerbach's. The materialist views of Marx and Engels, however, developed in the direction indicated by the inner logic of Feuerbach's philosophy. That is why these views will not always be fully clear—especially in their philosophical aspect—to those who will not go to the trouble of finding out just which part of the Feuerbachian philosophy became incorporated in the world outlook of the founders of scientific socialism. And if the reader meets anyone who is much taken up with the problem of finding "philosophical substantiation" for historical materialism, he can be certain that this wise mortal is very much deficient in the respect I have just mentioned.

But let us return to the subject. Already in his Third Thesis on Feuerbach, Marx tackled the most difficult of all the problems he was to resolve in the sphere of social man's historical "practice," with the aid of the correct concept of the unity of subject and object, which Feuerbach had developed. The Thesis reads: "The materialist doctrine that men are products of circumstances and upbringing ... forgets that circumstances are changed precisely by men, and that the educator must himself be educated." Once this problem is solved, the "secret" of the materialist explanation of history has been uncovered. But Feuerbach was unable to solve it. In history—like the French eighteenth-century materialists with whom he had so much in common—remained an *idealist*.[10] Here Marx and Engels had to start from scratch, making use of the theoretical material that had been accumulated by social science, chiefly by the French historians of the Restoration period. But even here, Feuerbach's philosophy provided them with some valuable pointers. "Art, religion, philosophy, and science," Feuerbach says, "are but the manifestation or revelation of genuine human essence." Hence it follows that the "human essence" contains the explanation of all ideologies, that is, that the development of the latter is conditioned by the development of the "human essence." What is that essence? "Man's essence," Feuerbach replies, "is only in community, in Man's unity with Man." This is very vague, and here we see a border line that Feuerbach did not cross.[11] However, it is beyond

---

10 Note to the German edition of 1910: This accounts for the reservations always made by Feuerbach when speaking of materialism. For instance, "When I go backward from this point, I am in complete agreement with the materialists; when I go forward, I differ from them" (K Grün, *L. Feuerbach*).

11 Note to the German edition of 1910: Incidentally, Feuerbach too thinks that the "human being" is created by history. Thus he says: "I think only as a subject educated by history, generalized, united with the whole, with the genus, the spirit of world history. My thoughts do not have their beginning and basis directly in my particular subjectivity, but are the outcome; their beginning and their basis are those of world history itself" (K Grün). Thus we see in Feuerbach the embryo of a materialist understanding of history. In this respect, however, he does not go further than Hegel, and even lags behind

that border line that the region of the materialist explanation of history, a region discovered by Marx and Engels, begins; that explanation indicates the causes which in the course of history determine the "community, Man's unity with Man," that is, the mutual relations that men enter into. This border line not only *separates* Marx from Feuerbach, but testifies as well to his *closeness* to the latter.

The sixth Thesis on Feuerbach says that *the human essence is the ensemble of the social relations*. This is far more definite than what Feuerbach himself said, and the close genetic link between Marx's world outlook and Feuerbach's philosophy is here revealed with probably greater clarity than anywhere else.

When Marx wrote this Thesis he already knew, not only the direction in which the solution of the problem should be sought, but the solution itself. In his *Critique of Hegel's Philosophy of Right* he showed that the mutual relations of people in society,

> . . . legal relations as well as forms of state are to be grasped neither from themselves nor from the so-called general development of the human mind, but rather have their roots in the material conditions of life, the totality of which Hegel, following the example of English and French thinkers of the eighteenth century, combines under the name of "civil society". . . however, the anatomy of civil society is to be sought in political economy.

It now remained only to explain the origin and development of the economy to obtain a full solution of a problem that materialism had been unable to cope with for centuries on end. That explanation was provided by Marx and Engels.

It stands to reason that, when I speak of the full solution of that great problem, I am referring only to its general or algebraic solution, which

---

him. Together with Hegel, he stresses the significance of what the great German idealist called the geographic basis of world history. "The course of the history of mankind," he says, "is certainly prescribed to it, since man follows the course of Nature, the course taken by streams. Men go wherever they find room, and the kind of place that suits them best. Men settle in a particular locality, and are conditioned by the place they live in. The essence of India is the essence of the Hindu. What he is, what he has become, is merely the product of the East-Indian sun, the East-Indian air, the East-Indian water, the East-Indian animals and plants. How could man originally appear if not out of Nature? Men, who become acclimatized to any kind of nature, have sprung from Nature, which tolerates no extremes" (K Grün).

materialism could not find in the course of centuries. It stands to reason that, when I speak of a full solution, I am referring, not to the arithmetic of social development, but to its algebra; not to the causes of individual phenomena, but to how the discovery of those causes should be approached. And that means that the materialist explanation of history was primarily of a *methodological significance*. Engels was fully aware of this when he wrote: "What we need is not so much crude results as studies; results are meaningless if they are taken apart from the development that leads up to them." This, however, is sometimes not understood either by "critics" of Marx—whom, as they say, may God forgive!—or by some of his "followers," which is much worse. Michelangelo once said of himself, "My knowledge will engender a multitude of ignoramuses." These words have regrettably proved prophetic. Today Marx's knowledge is engendering ignoramuses. The fault lies, not with Marx, but with those who talk rubbish while invoking his name. For such rubbish to be avoided, an understanding of the methodological significance of historical materialism is necessary.

V. The Materialist Dialectic as Method

In general, one of the greatest services rendered to materialism by Marx and Engels lies in their elaboration of a *correct method*. Feuerbach, who concentrated his efforts on the struggle against the *speculative* element in Hegel's philosophy, had little appreciation of its *dialectical* element, and made little use of it. "The true dialectic," he said, "is no monologue by a solitary thinker with himself; it is a dialogue between the *ego* [*I*] and the *tu* [*thou*]." In the first place, however, with Hegel dialectics did not signify a "monologue by a solitary thinker with himself"; and, secondly, Feuerbach's remark gives a correct definition of the starting point of philosophy, but not of its method. This gap was filled by Marx and Engels, who understood that in waging a struggle against Hegel's speculative philosophy, it would be mistaken to ignore his dialectic. Some critics have declared that, during the years immediately following his break with idealism, Marx was highly indifferent to dialectic also. Though this opinion may seem to have some semblance of plausibility, it is controverted by the aforementioned fact that, in the *Franco-German Annals*, Engels was already speaking of the method as the soul of the new system of views.

In any case, the second part of *The Poverty of Philosophy* leaves no room for doubt that, at the time of his polemic with Proudhon, Marx was very well aware of the significance of the dialectical method and knew how to make good use of it. Marx's victory in this controversy was that of a man able to think dialectically, over one who had never been able to understand the nature of dialectics, but was trying to apply its method to an analysis of capitalist society. This same second part of *The Poverty of Philosophy* shows that dialectics, which with Hegel was of a purely idealist character and had remained so with Proudhon (so far as he had assimilated it), was placed on a *materialist foundation* by Marx.[12]

"To Hegel," Marx wrote subsequently, describing his own materialist dialectic, "the life process of the human brain, that is, the process of thinking, which, under the name of 'the Idea,' he even transforms into an independent subject, is the demiurgos of the real world, and the real world is only the external, phenomenal form of 'the Idea.' With me, on the contrary, the ideal is nothing else than the material world reflected by the human mind, and translated into forms of thought."

This description implies full agreement with Feuerbach, first in the attitude towards Hegel's "Idea," and, second, in the relation of thinking to being. The Hegelian dialectic could be "turned right side up" only by one who was convinced of the soundness of the basic principle of Feuerbach's philosophy, viz., that it is not thinking that determines being, but being that determines thinking.

Many people confuse dialectics with the doctrine of development; dialectics is, in fact, such a doctrine. However, it differs substantially from the vulgar "theory of evolution," which is completely based on the principle that neither Nature nor history proceeds in leaps and that all changes in the world take place by degrees. Hegel had already shown that, understood in such a way, the doctrine of development was untenable and ridiculous.

---

12 Addendum to the German edition of 1910: It should however be noted that Feuerbach too criticized Hegelian dialectic from the materialist viewpoint. "What kind of dialectic is it," he asked, "that contradicts natural origin and development? How do matters stand with its 'necessity'? Where is the 'objectivity' of a psychology, of a philosophy in general, which abstracts itself from the only categorical and imperative, fundamental and solid objectivity, that of physical Nature, a philosophy which considers that its ultimate aim, absolute truth, and fulfillment of the spirit lie in a full departure from that Nature, and in an absolute subjectiveness, unrestricted by any Fichtean non-ego, or Kantian thing-in-itself."

"When people want to understand the rise or disappearance of any-thing," he says in Volume I of his *Science of Logic*, "they usually imagine that they achieve comprehension through the medium of a conception of the *gradual character* of that rise or disappearance. However, changes in being take place, not only by a transition of one quantity into another, but also by a transition of qualitative differences into quantitative, and, on the contrary, by a transition that *interrupts gradualness*, and substitutes one phenomenon for another."

And every time gradualness is interrupted, a *leap* takes place. Hegel goes on to show by a number of examples how often leaps take place both in Nature and in history, and he exposes the ridiculous logical error underlying the vulgar "theory of evolution."

"Underlying the doctrine of gradualness," he remarks, "is the concep-tion that what is arising already exists in reality, and remains unobserved only because of its small dimensions. In like manner, when they speak of gradual destruction, people imagine that the nonexistence of the phe-nomenon in question, or the phenomenon that is to take its place, is an accomplished fact, although it is as yet imperceptible . . . But this can only suppress any notion of arising and destruction . . . To explain appearance or disappearance by the gradualness of the change means reducing the whole matter to absurd tautology and to imagining in an already com-plete state [that is, as already arisen or already destroyed] that which is in the course of appearing or being destroyed.

This dialectical view of Hegel's as to the inevitability of leaps in the process of development was adopted in full by Marx and Engels. It was developed in detail by Engels in his polemic with Dühring, and here he "turned it right side up," that is to say, he put it on a *materialist foundation*.

Thus he indicated that the transition from one form of energy to another cannot take place otherwise than by means of a *leap*. Thus he sought, in modern chemistry, a confirmation of the dialectical theorem of the transformation of quantity into quality. Generally speaking, he found that the laws of dialectical thinking are confirmed by the dialectical prop-erties of being. Here, too, being conditions thinking.

Without undertaking a more detailed characterization of materialist dialectic (its relation to what, by a parallel with elementary mathemat-ics, may be called elementary logic—see my preface to my translation of *Ludwig Feuerbach*), I shall remind the reader that, during the last two decades, the theory that sees only gradual changes in the process of development has begun to lose ground even in biology, where it used to be recognized almost universally. In this respect, the work of Armand Gautier and that of Hugo de Vries seem to show promise of epoch-making importance. Suffice it to say that de Vries's theory of mutations is a doctrine that the development of species takes place by leaps.

In the opinion of this outstanding naturalist, the weak point in Darwin's theory of the origin of species is that this origin can be explained by gradual changes. Also of interest, and most apt, is de Vries's remark that the dominance of the theory of gradual changes in the doctrine of the origin of species has had an unfavorable influence on the experimental study of relevant problems.

I may add that, in present-day natural science, and especially among the neo-Lamarckians, there has been a fairly rapid spread of the theory of the so-called animism of matter, that is, that matter in general, and especially any organized matter, possesses a certain degree of sensibility. This theory, which many regard as being diametrically opposed to materialism, is in fact, when properly understood, only a translation, into the language of present-day natural science, of Feuerbach's materialist doctrine of the unity of being and thinking, of object and subject. It may be confidently stated that Marx and Engels, who had assimilated this doctrine, would have been keenly interested in this trend in natural science, although far too little elaborated as yet.

Herzen was right in saying that Hegel's philosophy, which many considered conservative in the main, was a genuine algebra of revolution. With Hegel, however, this algebra remained wholly unapplied to the burning problems of practical life. Of necessity, the speculative element brought a spirit of conservatism into the philosophy of this great absolute idealist. It is quite different with Marx's materialist philosophy, in which revolutionary "algebra" manifests itself with all the irresistible force of its dialectical method.

"In its mystified form, Marx says, "dialectic became the fashion in Germany, because it seemed to transfigure and to glorify the existing state of things. In its rational form it is a scandal and abomination to bourgeoisdom and its doctrinaire professors, because it includes in its comprehension and affirmative recognition of the existing state of things, at the same time also, the recognition of the negation of that state, of its inevitable breaking up; because it regards every historically developed social form as in fluid movement, and therefore takes into account its transient nature not less than its momentary existence; because it lets nothing impose upon it, and is in its essence critical and revolutionary."

If we regard the materialist dialectic from the viewpoint of the history of Russian literature, we may say that this dialectic was the first to supply a method necessary and competent to solve the problem of the rational causes of all that exists, a problem that so greatly troubled our brilliant thinker Belinsky. It was only Marx's dialectical method, as applied to the study of Russian life, that has shown us how much *reality* and how much *semblance* of reality there was in it . . .

XIV. Class Struggle and Ideas

. . . The obstacles met by present-day materialism as a harmonious and consistent theory are incomparably greater than those that Newton's theory came up against, on its appearance. Against it are directly and decisively ranged the interests of the class now in power, to whose influence most scholars subordinate themselves of necessity. The materialist dialectic, "which regards every historically developed social form as in fluid movement, and . . . lets nothing impose upon it," cannot have the sympathy of the conservative class that the Western bourgeoisie today is. It stands in such contradiction to that class's frame of mind that its ideologists naturally tend to look upon it as something impermissible, improper, and unworthy of the attention both of "respectable" people in general, and of "esteemed" men of learning in particular. It is not surprising that each of these pundits considers himself morally obliged to avoid any suspicion of sympathy with materialism. Often enough such pundits denounce materialism the more emphatically, the more insistently they adhere to a materialist viewpoint in their special research. The result is a kind of semi-subconscious "conventional lie," which, of course, can have only a most injurious effect on theoretical thinking.

XV. Necessity and Freedom

. . . Marx very truly said that the greater the development of the contradiction between the growing productive forces and the existing social order, the more does the ideology of the master class become imbued with hypocrisy. The more the falseness of this ideology is revealed by life, the more elevated and virtuous does the language of that class become . . .

Incidentally, so immensely great are the advantages provided to the researcher by the Marxist method that even those who have willingly submitted to the "conventional lies" of our time are beginning to recognize them publicly. Among such people, for instance, is the American Edwin Seligman, author of a book published in 1902 under the title of *The Economic Interpretation of History*. Seligman frankly admits that scholars have shied away from the theory of historical materialism because of the socialist conclusions drawn from it by Marx. However, he thinks that you can eat your cake and have it too: "one can be an economic materialist" and yet remain hostile to socialism. As he puts it, "The fact that Marx's economics may be defective has no bearing on the truth or falsity of his philosophy of history." In actual fact, Marx's economic views were intimately bound up with his historical views. A proper understanding of *Capital* absolutely implies the *necessity* of previous and careful thought on the celebrated preface to *Critique of Political Economy*. However, we are unable here either to set forth Marx's economic views or to demonstrate the incontrovertible fact that they form merely an indispensable component of the doctrine known as historical materialism.[13] I shall add only that Seligman is sufficiently a "pundit" also to be scared of materialism. This economic "materialist" thinks it is going to intolerable extremes "to make religion depend on economic forces" or to "seek the explanation of Christianity itself in economic facts alone." All this goes to show clearly how deep are the roots of those prejudices—and consequently of the obstacles—that Marxist theory has to fight against. Yet the very fact of the appearance of Seligman's book, and even the very nature of the reservations he makes, give some reason to hope that historical materialism—even in a truncated or "purified" form—will in the end achieve recognition by those ideologists of the bourgeoisie who have not given up the idea of bringing order into their historical views.[14]

13 A few incidental words in explanation of what has been said. According to Marx, "economic categories are only the theoretical expressions, the abstractions of the social relations of production" (*The Poverty of Philosophy*). This means that Marx regards the categories of political economy likewise from the viewpoint of the mutual relations among men in the social process of production, relations whose development provides him with the basic explanation of mankind's historical movement.

14 The following parallel is highly instructive. Marx says that materialist dialectic, while explaining that which exists, at the same time explains its inevitable destruction. In this he saw its value, its progressive significance.

But the struggle against socialism, materialism, and other unpleasant extremes presupposes possession of a "spiritual weapon." What is known as subjective political economy, and more or less adroitly falsified statistics, at present constitute the spiritual weapon mainly used in the struggle against socialism. All possible brands of Kantianism form the main bulwark in the struggle against materialism. In the field of social science, Kantianism is utilized for this purpose as a dualist doctrine which tears asunder the tie between being and thinking. Since consideration of economic questions does not come within the province of this book, I shall confine myself to an appraisal of the philosophical spiritual weapon employed by bourgeois reaction in the ideological sphere.

Concluding his booklet, *Socialism: Utopian and Scientific*, Engels remarks that when the mighty means of production created by the capitalist epoch have become the property of society, and when production is organized in conformity with social needs, men will at last become masters of their social relations, and hence lords over nature, and their own masters. Only then will they begin consciously to make their own history; only then will the social causes they bring into play produce, in ever greater measure, effects that are desirable to them. "It is the ascent of man from the kingdom of necessity to the kingdom of freedom."

These words of Engels's have evoked objections from those who, unable in general to stomach the idea of "leaps," have been either unable or unwilling to understand any such "leap" from the kingdom of necessity into the kingdom of freedom. Such a "leap" seemed to them to contradict that view on freedom which Engels himself voiced in the first part of his *Anti-Dühring*. Therefore, if we would see our way through the confusion in the minds of such people, we must recall exactly what Engels said in the book mentioned above.

And here is what he said. Explaining Hegel's words that "Necessity is blind only insofar as it is not understood," Engels stated that freedom

---

But here is what Seligman says: "Socialism is a theory of what ought to be; historical materialism is a theory of what has been." For that reason alone, he considers it possible for himself to defend historical materialism. This means, in other words, that this materialism may be ignored when it comes to explaining the inevitable destruction of that which is and may be used to explain that which has been in the past. This is one of the numerous instances of the use of a double standard in the field of ideology, a phenomenon also engendered by economic causes.

consists in exercising "control over ourselves and over external nature, a control founded on knowledge of natural necessity." This idea is set forth by Engels with a clarity quite sufficient for people familiar with the Hegelian doctrine referred to. The trouble is that present-day Kantians only "criticise" Hegel, but do not study him. Since they have no knowledge of Hegel, they have been unable to understand Engels. To the author of *Anti-Dühring* they have made the objection that where there is submission to necessity, there is no freedom. This is quite consistent on the part of people whose philosophical views are imbued with a dualism that is incapable of uniting thinking with being. From the viewpoint of this dualism, the "leap" from necessity to freedom remains absolutely incomprehensible. But Marx's philosophy, like that of Feuerbach, proclaims the unity of being and thinking. Although, as we have already seen above, in the section on Feuerbach, Marxist philosophy understands that unity quite differently from the sense in which it is understood by absolute idealism, it (Marxist philosophy) does not at all disagree with Hegelian doctrine in the question we are concerned with, viz., the relation of freedom to necessity.

The gist of the whole matter is: precisely what should be understood by *necessity*? Aristotle already pointed out that the concept of necessity contains many shades of meaning: medicine is necessary for a cure to be effected; breathing is necessary for life; a trip to Aegina is necessary for a debt to be collected. All these are, so to say, *conditional* necessities; we *must* breathe *if* we want to live; we *must* take medicine *if* we want to get rid of an illness, and so on. In the process of acting on the world about him, man has constantly to do with necessity of this kind—he must of *necessity* sow *if* he would reap, shoot an arrow *if* he would kill game, stock fuel *if* he would get a steam engine operating, and so on. From the viewpoint of the neo-Kantian "criticism of Marx," it has to be admitted that there is an element of submission in this conditional necessity. Man would be freer if he were able to satisfy his wants without expending any labor at all. He always submits to nature, even when he forces her to serve him. This submission, however, is a condition of his becoming free; by submitting to nature, he thereby increases his power over her, that is, his freedom. It would be the same under the planned organization of social production. By submitting to certain demands of technical and economic necessity, men would put an end to that preposterous order of things under which they are dominated by the products of their own activities, that is to say, they would increase their freedom to a tremendous degree. Here, too, their submission would become a source of liberation to them.

Nor is that all. "Critics" of Marx, who have become used to considering that a gulf separates thinking and being, know of only one shade of necessity; to use Aristotle's wording, they imagine necessity only as a force that prevents us from acting according to our desires, and compels us to do that which is contrary to them. Necessity of this kind is indeed the opposite of freedom, and cannot but be irksome in greater or lesser degree. But we must not forget that a force seen by man as external coercion which is in conflict with his wishes may, in other circumstances, be seen by him in an entirely different light. As an illustration, let us take the agrarian question in Russia today. To the intelligent landowner who is a Constitutional-Democrat, the "forcible alienation of the land" may seem more or less a sad historical necessity—sad, that is to say, in reverse proportion to the size of the "fair compensation" given. But to the peasant who yearns for land, the reverse is true: the "fair compensation" will present itself as a more or less sad necessity, while "forcible alienation" is bound to be seen as an expression of his own unfettered will, and the most precious security of his freedom.

In saying this, I am touching upon what is perhaps the most important point in the doctrine of freedom—a point not mentioned by Engels only, of course, for its being self-evident to one who has gone through the Hegelian school.

In his philosophy of religion Hegel says, "Freedom lies in willing nothing but oneself." This observation sheds a strong light on the entire question of freedom, insofar as that question bears upon social psychology. The peasant who demands that the landowner's land should be transferred to him wants "nothing but himself"; the Constitutional-Democratic landowner who agrees to give him land no longer wants "himself" but that which history compels him to want. The former is free, while the latter wisely submits to necessity.

As with the peasant, it would be the same for the proletariat, which converts the means of production into social property and organizes social production on a new foundation. It would wish nothing "but itself," and would feel quite free. As for the capitalists, they would, of course, at best feel that they were in the position of the landowner who has accepted the Constitutional-Democratic agrarian program; they could not but think that freedom is one thing, and historical necessity, another.

As it seems to me, those "critics" who have objected to Engels's stand have failed to understand him, because while they are able to imagine themselves in the position of the capitalist, they are totally unable to imagine themselves in the proletarian's shoes. I hold the opinion that this, too, has its social—and ultimately economic—cause.

. . .

XVI. Necessity and Revolution

. . .

Highly noteworthy is the fact that theoreticians of Protestantism in the United States of America seem unable to understand the contraposition of freedom and necessity that has been exciting the minds of so many ideologists of the European bourgeoisie. H. Bargy says that "in America the most positive instructors in the field of energy are little prone to recognize freedom of the will." He ascribes this to their preference, as men of action, for "fatalist solutions." He is wrong, however, since fatalism has nothing to do with the matter. This is to be seen in his own remarks about the moralist Jonathan Edwards: 'Edwards's point of view . . . is that of any man of action. To anyone who has had an aim once in his lifetime freedom is the faculty of putting all his soul in the service of that aim." This is well put, and closely resembles Hegel's "willing nothing but oneself." But when a man "wills nothing but himself," he is in no way a fatalist; it is then that he is precisely a man of action.

Kantianism is not a philosophy of struggle, or a philosophy of men of action. It is a philosophy of half-hearted people, a philosophy of compromise.

The means of removing the existing social evil, Engels says, must be discovered in the existing material conditions of production, not invented by one social reformer or another. Stammler is in agreement with this, but accuses Engels of unclear thinking, since in Stammler's opinion the gist of the matter lies in ascertaining "the method with the aid of which this discovery must be made." This objection, which merely reveals Stammler's vague thinking, is eliminated by simply mentioning the fact that though the nature of the "method" is in such cases determined by a great variety of "factors," the latter can all be ultimately referred to the course of the economic development. The very fact of the appearance of

Marx's theory was determined by the development of the capitalist mode of production, whereas the predominance of utopianism in pre-Marxist socialism is quite understandable in a society suffering not only from the development of the aforementioned mode of production, but also—and in greater degree—from the insufficiency of that development.

It would be superfluous to dilate on the matter. The reader will perhaps not complain if, in concluding this article, I will draw his attention to the measure in which the tactical "method" of Marx and Engels is intimately bound up with the fundamental theses of their historical theory.

This theory tells us, as we already know, that mankind always sets itself only such tasks that it can solve, for "the problem itself arises only when the material conditions for its solution are already present or at least in the process of formation." Where these conditions already exist, the state of things is not quite the same as it is where they are still "in the process of formation." In the former instance the time for a "leap" has already arrived; in the latter instance the "leap" is, for the time being, a matter of the more or less distant future, "an ultimate aim" whose approach is prepared by a series of "gradual changes" in the mutual relations between social classes. What role should be played by innovators during the period in which a "leap" is still impossible? It evidently remains for them to contribute to the "gradual changes," that is, they must, in other words, try to bring about reforms. In this way, both the "ultimate aim" and reforms find their place, and the very contraposition of reform and "ultimate aim" loses all meaning, is relegated to the sphere of utopian legends. Those who would make such a contraposition—whether they are German "revisionists" like Eduard Bernstein, or Italian "revolutionary syndicalists" like those who took part in the latest syndicalist congress in Ferrara—will show themselves equally incapable of understanding the spirit and the method of modern scientific socialism. This is a good thing to remember at present, when reformism and syndicalism permit themselves to speak for Marx.

And what healthy optimism breathes in the words that mankind always sets itself only such tasks that it can solve! They do not, of course, mean that any solution of mankind's great problems, as suggested by the first utopian one meets, is a good one.

A utopian is one thing; mankind, or, more precisely, a social class representative of mankind's highest interests in a given period, is something else. As Marx has very well said, "With the thoroughness of the historical action, the size of the mass whose action it is will therefore increase." This is conclusive condemnation of a utopian attitude towards great historical problems. If Marx nevertheless thought that mankind never sets itself unachievable tasks, then his words are, from the viewpoint of theory, only a new way of expressing the idea of the unity of subject and object in its application to the process of historical development; from the viewpoint of practice they express that calm and courageous faith in the achievement of the "ultimate aim" which once prompted our unforgettable N.G. Chernyshevsky to exclaim fervently, "Come what may, we shall win."

II
DIALECTICS

ANTI-DÜHRING (EXCERPTS)

Friedrich Engels
1877

Originally published as Herr Eugen Dühring's Revolution in Science, Anti-Dühring *is yet another of Engels's classic defenses of the Marxist method intended to equip the working class with clear ideas. In it, he patiently but sharply took on Eugen Dühring's pompous and confusing philosophical system, which exemplified the growing pressure of alien class ideas on the German workers' movement. Although he had no desire to take on this polemic—which he likened to a "sour apple" and took two years of his valuable time to write—we can be most grateful that he did. Because* Anti-Dühring *is about as close as one can get to an expository "handbook" of the basics of Marxist philosophy, economics, and historical analysis, and deserves to be read in full by all class-conscious workers and youth. A selection from this work was later excerpted and published separately as* Socialism: Utopian and Scientific, *one of the most successful and essential pamphlets ever produced by the socialist movement. We present here selections focusing on the most fundamental laws of dialectics, which serve as an outstanding primer on the concepts of the transformation of quantity into quality (and vice versa) and the negation of the negation.*

1885 Preface

I had not expected that a new edition of this book would have to be published. The subject matter of its criticism is now practically forgotten; the work itself was not only available to many thousands of readers in the form of a series of articles published in the Leipzig *Vorwärts* in 1877 and 1878, but also appeared in its entirety as a separate book, of which a large edition was printed. How, then, can anyone still be interested in what I had to say about Herr Dühring years ago?

I think that I owe this, in the first place, to the fact that this book, as in general almost all my works that were still current at the time, was prohibited within the German Empire immediately after the Anti-Socialist Law was promulgated. To anyone whose brain has not been ossified by the hereditary bureaucratic prejudices of the countries of the Holy Alliance, the effect of this measure must have been self-evident: a doubled and trebled sale of the prohibited books, and the exposure of the impotence of the gentlemen in Berlin who issue prohibitions and are unable to enforce them. Indeed, the kindness of the Imperial Government has brought me more new editions of my minor works than I could really cope with; I have had no time to make a proper revision of the text, and, in most cases, have been obliged simply to allow it to be reprinted as it stood.

But there was also another factor. The "system" of Herr Dühring, which is criticized in this book, ranges over a very wide theoretical domain; and I was compelled to follow him wherever he went and to oppose my conceptions to his. As a result, my negative criticism became positive; the polemic was transformed into a more or less connected exposition of the dialectical method and of the communist world outlook championed by Marx and myself—an exposition covering a fairly comprehensive range of subjects. After its first presentation to the world in Marx's *The Poverty of Philosophy* and in *The Communist Manifesto*, this mode of outlook of ours, having passed through an incubation period of fully twenty years before the publication of *Capital*, has been more and more rapidly extending its influence among ever widening circles, and now finds recognition and support far beyond the boundaries of Europe, in every country which contains on the one hand proletarians and on the other undaunted scientific theoreticians. It seems, therefore, that there is a public whose interest in the subject is great enough for them to take into the bargain the polemic against the Dühring tenets merely for the sake of the positive conceptions developed alongside this polemic, in spite of the fact that the latter has now largely lost its point.

I must note in passing that inasmuch as the mode of outlook expounded in this book was founded and developed in far greater measure by Marx, and only to an insignificant degree by myself, it was self-understood between us that this exposition of mine should not be issued without his knowledge. I read the whole manuscript to him before it was printed, and the tenth chapter of the part on economics ("From *Critical History*") was written by Marx but unfortunately had to be shortened somewhat by me for purely external reasons. As a matter of fact, we had always been accustomed to helping each other out in special subjects.

. . .

It goes without saying that my recapitulation of mathematics and the natural sciences was undertaken in order to convince myself, also in detail, of what, in general, I was not in doubt—that in nature, amid the welter of innumerable changes, the same dialectical laws of motion force their way through as those which in history govern the apparent fortuitousness of events; the same laws which similarly form the thread running through the history of the development of human thought and gradually rise to consciousness in thinking man; the laws which Hegel first developed in all-embracing but mystic form, and which we made it one of our aims to strip of this mystic form and to bring clearly before the mind in their complete simplicity and universality. It goes without saying that the old philosophy of nature—in spite of its real value and the many fruitful seeds it contained—was unable to satisfy us.

As is more fully brought out in this book, natural philosophy, particularly in the Hegelian form, erred because it did not concede to nature any development in time, any "succession," but only "coexistence." This was on the one hand grounded in the Hegelian system itself, which ascribed historical evolution only to the "spirit," but on the other hand was also due to the whole state of the natural sciences in that period. In this, Hegel fell far behind Kant, whose nebular theory had already indicated the origin of the solar system, and whose discovery of the retardation of the earth's rotation by the tides also had proclaimed the doom of that system. And finally, to me there could be no question of building the laws of dialectics into nature, but of discovering them in it and evolving them from it.

But to do this systematically and in each separate department, is a gigantic task. Not only is the domain to be mastered almost boundless; natural science in this entire domain is itself undergoing such a mighty process of being revolutionized that even people who can devote the whole of their spare time to it can hardly keep pace. Since Karl Marx's death, however, my time has been requisitioned for more urgent duties, and I have therefore been compelled to lay aside my work. For the present, I must content myself with the indications given in this book, and must wait to find some later opportunity to put together and publish the results which I have arrived at, perhaps in conjunction with the extremely important mathematical manuscripts left by Marx.

Yet the advance of theoretical natural science may possibly make my work to a great extent or even altogether superfluous. For the revolution which is being forced on theoretical natural science by the mere need to set in order the purely empirical discoveries, great masses of which have been piled up, is of such a kind that it must bring the dialectical character of natural processes more and more to the consciousness even of those empiricists who are most opposed to it. The old rigid antagonisms, the sharp, impassable dividing lines are more and more disappearing. Since even the last "true" gases have been liquefied, and since it has been proved that a body can be brought into a condition in which the liquid and the gaseous forms are indistinguishable, the aggregate states have lost the last relics of their former absolute character. With the thesis of the kinetic theory of gases—that in perfect gases at equal temperatures the squares of the speeds with which the individual gas molecules move are in inverse ratio to their molecular weights—heat also takes its place directly among the forms of motion which can be immediately measured as such. Whereas only ten years ago the great basic law of motion, then recently discovered, was as yet conceived merely as a law of the *conservation* of energy, as the mere expression of the indestructibility and uncreatability of motion, that is, merely in its quantitative aspect, this narrow negative conception is being more and more supplanted by the positive idea of the *transformation* of energy, in which for the first time the qualitative content of the process comes into its own, and the last vestige of an extramundane creator is obliterated. That the quantity of motion (so-called energy) remains unaltered when it is transformed from kinetic energy (so-called mechanical force) into electricity, heat, potential energy, etc., and vice versa, no longer needs to be preached as something new; it serves as the already secured basis for the now much more pregnant investigation into the very process of transformation, the great basic process, knowledge of which comprises all knowledge of nature. And since biology has been pursued in the light of the theory of evolution, one rigid boundary line of classification after another has been swept away in the domain of organic nature. The almost unclassifiable intermediate links are growing daily more numerous, closer investigation throws organisms out of one class and into another, and distinguishing characteristics which almost became articles of faith are losing their absolute validity; we now have mammals that lay eggs, and, if the report is confirmed, also birds that walk on all fours. Years ago, Virchow was compelled, following the discovery of the cell, to dissolve the unity of the individual animal being into a federation of cell states—thus acting more progressively rather than scientifically and dialectically—and now the conception of animal (therefore also human) individuality is becoming far more complex owing to the discovery of the white blood corpuscles which creep about amoeba-like within the bodies of the higher animals. It is however precisely the polar antagonisms put forward as irreconcilable and insoluble, the forcibly fixed lines of demarcation and class distinctions, which have given modern theoretical natural science its restricted, metaphysical character. The recognition that these antagonisms and distinctions, though found in nature, are only of relative validity, and that on the other hand their imagined rigidity and absolute validity have been introduced into nature only by our reflective minds—this recognition is the kernel of the dialectical conception of nature. It is possible to arrive at this recognition because the accumulating facts of natural science compel us to do so; but one arrives at it more easily if one approaches the dialectical character of these facts equipped with an understanding of the laws of dialectical thought. In any case, natural science has now advanced so far that it can no longer escape dialectical generalization. However, it will make this process easier for itself if it does not lose sight of the fact that the results in which its experiences are summarized are concepts, that the art of working with concepts is not inborn and also is not given with ordinary everyday consciousness, but requires real thought, and that this thought similarly has a long empirical history, not more and not less than empirical natural science. Only by learning to assimilate the results of the development of philosophy during the past two and a half thousand years will it rid itself, on the one hand, of any natural philosophy standing apart from it, outside it, and above it, and, on the other hand, also of its own limited method of thought, which is its inheritance from English empiricism.

Part I: Philosophy
XII. Dialectics—Quantity and Quality

The first and most important principle of the basic logical properties of being refers to the *exclusion of contradiction*. Contradiction is a category which can only appertain to a combination of thoughts, but not to reality. There are no contradictions in things, or, to put it another way, contradiction accepted as reality is itself the apex of absurdity . . . The antagonism of forces measured against each other and moving in opposite directions is in fact the basic form of all actions in the life of the world and its creatures. But this opposition of the directions taken by the forces of elements and individuals does not in the slightest degree coincide with the idea of absurd contradictions . . . We can be content here with having cleared the fogs which generally rise from the supposed mysteries of logic by presenting a clear picture of the actual absurdity of contradictions in reality and with having shown the uselessness of the incense which has been burnt here and there in honor of the dialectics of contradiction—the very clumsily carved wooden doll which is substituted for the antagonistic world schematism.

This is practically all we are told about dialectics in [Dühring's] *Course of Philosophy*. In his *Critical History*, on the other hand, the dialectics of contradiction, and with it particularly Hegel, is treated quite differently.

Contradiction, according to the Hegelian logic, or rather Logos doctrine, is objectively present not in thought, which by its nature can only be conceived as subjective and conscious, but in things and processes themselves and can be met with in so to speak corporeal form, so that absurdity does not remain an impossible combination of thought but becomes an actual force. The reality of the absurd is the first article of faith in the Hegelian unity of the logical and the illogical . . . The more contradictory a thing the truer it is, or in other words, the more absurd the more credible it is. This maxim, which is not even newly invented but is borrowed from the theology of the Revelation and from mysticism, is the naked expression of the so-called dialectical principle.

The thought content of the two passages cited can be summed up in the statement that contradiction = absurdity, and therefore cannot occur in the real world. People who in other respects show a fair degree of common sense may regard this statement as having the same self-evident validity as the statement that a straight line cannot be a curve and a curve cannot be straight. But, regardless of all protests made by common sense, the differential calculus under certain circumstances nevertheless equates straight lines and curves, and thus obtains results which common sense, insisting on the absurdity of straight lines being identical with curves, can never attain. And in view of the important role which the so-called dialectics of contradiction has played in philosophy from the time of the ancient Greeks up to the present, even a stronger opponent

than Herr Dühring should have felt obliged to attack it with other arguments besides one assertion and a good many abusive epithets.

True, so long as we consider things as at rest and lifeless, each one
by itself, alongside and after each other, we do not run up against any
contradictions in them. We find certain qualities which are partly common to, partly different from, and even contradictory to each other, but
which in the last-mentioned case are distributed among different objects
and therefore contain no contradiction within. Inside the limits of this
sphere of observation we can get along on the basis of the usual, metaphysical mode of thought. But the position is quite different as soon as
we consider things in their motion, their change, their life, their reciprocal influence on one another. Then we immediately become involved in
contradictions. Motion itself is a contradiction: even simple mechanical
change of position can only come about through a body being at one and
the same moment of time both in one place and in another place, being in
one and the same place and also not in it. And the continuous origination
and simultaneous solution of this contradiction is precisely what motion
is.

Here, therefore, we have a contradiction which "is objectively present
in things and processes themselves and can be met with in so to speak
corporeal form." And what has Herr Dühring to say about it? He asserts
that up to the present there is absolutely "no bridge in rational mechanics from the strictly static to the dynamic."

The reader can now at last see what is hidden behind this favorite
phrase of Herr Dühring's—it is nothing but this: the mind which thinks
metaphysically is absolutely unable to pass from the idea of rest to the
idea of motion, because the contradiction pointed out above blocks its
path. To it, motion is simply incomprehensible because it is a contradiction. And in asserting the incomprehensibility of motion, it admits against
its will the existence of this contradiction, and thus admits the objective
presence, in things and processes themselves, of a contradiction which is
moreover an actual force.

If simple mechanical change of position contains a contradiction, this
is even more true of the higher forms of motion of matter, and especially
of organic life and its development. We saw above that life consists precisely and primarily in this—that a being is at each moment itself and yet
something else. Life is therefore also a contradiction which is present in
things and processes themselves, and which constantly originates and

resolves itself; and as soon as the contradiction ceases, life, too, comes to an end, and death steps in. We likewise saw that also in the sphere of thought we could not escape contradictions, and that for example the contradiction between man's inherently unlimited capacity for knowledge and its actual presence only in men who are externally limited and possess limited cognition finds its solution in what is—at least practically, for us—an endless succession of generations, in infinite progress.

We have already noted that one of the basic principles of higher mathematics is the contradiction that in certain circumstances straight lines and curves may be the same. It also establishes this other contradiction: that lines which intersect each other before our eyes nevertheless, only five or six centimeters from their point of intersection, can be shown to be parallel, that is, that they will never meet even if extended to infinity. And yet, working with these and with even far greater contradictions, it attains results which are not only correct but also quite unattainable for lower mathematics.

But even lower mathematics teems with contradictions. It is for example a contradiction that a root of A should be a power of A, and yet $A^{\frac{1}{2}}$ $=\sqrt{A}$. It is a contradiction that a negative quantity should be the square of anything, for every negative quantity multiplied by itself gives a positive square. The square root of minus one is therefore not only a contradiction, but even an absurd contradiction—a real absurdity. And yet $\sqrt{-1}$ is in many cases a necessary result of correct mathematical operations. Furthermore, where would mathematics—lower or higher—be, if it were prohibited from operation with $\sqrt{-1}$?

In its operations with variable quantities, mathematics itself enters the field of dialectics, and it is significant that it was a dialectical philosopher, Descartes, who introduced this advance. The relation between the mathematics of variable and the mathematics of constant quantities is in general the same as the relation of dialectical to metaphysical thought. But this does not prevent the great mass of mathematicians from recognizing dialectics only in the sphere of mathematics, and a good many of them from continuing to work in the old, limited, metaphysical way with methods that were obtained dialectically.

It would be possible to go more closely into Herr Dühring's antagonism of forces and his antagonistic world schematism only if he had given us something more on this theme than the mere *phrase*. After accomplishing this feat, this antagonism is not even once shown to us at work, either in his world schematism or in his natural philosophy—the most convincing admission that Herr Dühring can do absolutely nothing of a positive character with his "basic form of all actions in the life of the world and its creatures." When someone has in fact lowered Hegel's "Doctrine of Essence" to the platitude of forces moving in opposite directions but not in contradictions, certainly the best thing he can do is to avoid any application of this commonplace.

Marx's *Capital* furnishes Herr Dühring with another occasion for venting his anti-dialectical spleen.

> The absence of natural and intelligible logic which characterizes these dialectical frills and mazes and conceptual arabesques . . . Even to the part that has already appeared we must apply the principle that in a certain respect and also in general [!], according to a well-known philosophical preconception, all is to be sought in each and each in all, and that therefore, according to this mixed and misconceived idea, it all amounts to one and the same thing in the end.

This insight into the well-known philosophical preconception also enables Herr Dühring to prophesy with assurance what will be the "end" of Marx's economic philosophizing, that is, what the following volumes of *Capital* will contain, and this he does exactly seven lines after he has declared that "speaking in plain human language, it is really impossible to divine what is still to come in the two [final] volumes."

This, however, is not the first time that Herr Dühring's writings are revealed to us as belonging to the "things" in which "contradiction is objectively present and can be met with in so to speak corporeal form." But this does not prevent him from going on victoriously as follows:

> Yet sound logic will, in all probability, triumph over its caricature . . . This presence of superiority and this mysterious dialectical rubbish will tempt no one who has even a modicum of sound judgment left to have anything to do . . . with these deformities of thought and style. With the demise of the last relics of the dialectical follies this means of duping . . . will lose its deceptive influence, and no one will any longer believe that he has to torture himself in order to get behind some profound piece of wisdom where the husked kernel of the abstruse things reveals at best the features of ordinary theories if not of absolute commonplaces . . . It is quite impossible to reproduce the [Marxian] maze in accordance with the Logos doctrine without prostituting sound logic.

Marx's method, according to Herr Dühring, consists in "performing dialectical miracles for his faithful followers," and so on.

We are not in any way concerned here as yet with the correctness or incorrectness of the economic results of Marx's researches, but only with the dialectical method used by Marx. But this much is certain: most readers of *Capital* will have learned for the first time from Herr Dühring what it is, in fact, that they have read. And among them will also be Herr Dühring himself, who in the year 1867 was still able to provide what for a thinker of his caliber was a relatively rational review of the book; and he did this without first being obliged as he now declares is indispensable, to translate the Marxian argument into Dühringian language. And though even then he committed the blunder of identifying Marxian dialectics with the Hegelian, he had not quite lost the capacity to distinguish between the method and the results obtained by using it, and to understand that the latter are not refuted in detail by lampooning the former in general.

At any rate, the most astonishing piece of information given by Herr Dühring is the statement that from the Marxian standpoint "it all amounts to one and the same thing in the end," that therefore to Marx, for example, capitalists and wage workers, feudal, capitalist, and socialist modes of production are also "one and the same thing"—no doubt in the end even Marx and Herr Dühring are "one and the same thing." Such utter nonsense can only be explained if we suppose that the mere mention of the word dialectics throws Herr Dühring into such a state of mental irresponsibility that, as a result of a certain mixed and misconceived idea, what he says and does is "one and the same thing" in the end.

We have here a sample of what Herr Dühring calls

> *my* historical depiction in the grand style ... [or] ... the summary treatment which settles with genus and type, and does not condescend to honor what a Hume called the learned mob with an exposure in micrological detail; this treatment in a higher and nobler style is the only one compatible with the interests of complete truth and with one's duty to the public which is free from the bonds of the guilds.

Historical depiction in the grand style and the summary settlement with genus and type is indeed very convenient for Herr Dühring, inasmuch as this method enables him to neglect all known facts as micrological and equate them to zero, so that instead of proving anything, he need only use general phrases, make assertions and thunder his denunciations. The method has the further advantage that it offers no real foothold to an opponent, who is consequently left with almost no other possibility of reply than to make similar summary assertions in the grand style, to resort to general phrases and finally thunder back denunciations at Herr Dühring—in a word, as they say, engage in a clanging match, which is not to everyone's taste. We must therefore be grateful to Herr Dühring for occasionally, by way of exception, dropping the higher and nobler style, and giving us at least two examples of the unsound Marxian Logos doctrine.

> How comical is the reference to the confused, hazy Hegelian notion that quantity changes into quality, and that therefore an advance, when it reaches a certain size, becomes capital by this quantitative increase alone.

In this "expurgated" presentation by Herr Dühring, that statement certainly seems curious enough. Let us see how it looks in the original, in Marx . . . On the basis of his previous examination of constant and variable capital and surplus value, Marx draws the conclusion that "not every sum of money, or of value, is at pleasure transformable into capital. To effect this transformation, in fact, a certain minimum of money or of exchange value must be presupposed in the hands of the individual possessor of money or commodities." He takes as an example the case of a laborer in any branch of industry, who works daily eight hours for himself—that is, in producing the value of his wages—and the following four hours for the capitalist, in producing surplus value, which immediately flows into the pocket of the capitalist. In this case, one would have to have at his disposal a sum of values sufficient to enable one to provide two laborers with raw materials, instruments of labor and wages, in order to pocket enough surplus value every day to live on as well as one of his laborers. And as the aim of capitalist production is not mere subsistence but the increase of wealth, our man with his two laborers would still not be a capitalist. Now in order that he may live twice as well as an ordinary laborer, and turn half of the surplus value produced again into capital, he would have to be able to employ eight laborers, that is, he would have to possess four times the sum of values assumed above. And it is only after this, and in the course of still further explanations elucidating and substantiating the fact that not every petty sum of values is enough to be transformable into capital, but that in this respect each period of development and each branch of industry has its definite minimum sum, that Marx observes: "Here, as in natural science, *is shown* the correctness of the law discovered by Hegel in his *Logic*, that merely quantitative changes beyond a certain point pass into qualitative differences."

And now let the reader admire the higher and nobler style, by virtue of which Herr Dühring attributes to Marx the opposite of what he really said. Marx says: The fact that a sum of values can be transformed into capital only when it has reached a certain size, varying according to the circumstances, but in each case, a definite, minimum size—this fact is a *proof of the correctness* of the Hegelian law. Herr Dühring makes him say: *Because*, according to the Hegelian law, quantity changes into quality, "*therefore* an advance, when it reaches a certain size, becomes capital." That is to say, the very opposite.

In connection with Herr Dühring's examination of the Darwin case, we have already got to know his habit, "in the interests of complete truth" and because of his "duty to the public which is free from the bonds of the guilds," of quoting incorrectly. It becomes more and more evident that this habit is an inner necessity of the philosophy of reality, and it is certainly a very "summary treatment." Not to mention the fact that Herr Dühring further makes Marx speak of any kind of "advance" whatsoever, whereas Marx only refers to an advance made in the form of raw materials, instruments of labor, and wages; and that in doing this Herr Dühring succeeds in making Marx speak pure nonsense. And then he has the cheek to describe as *comic* the nonsense which he himself has fabricated. Just as he built up a Darwin of his own fantasy in order to try out his strength against him, so here he builds up a fantastic Marx. "Historical depiction in the grand style," indeed!

We have already seen earlier, in regard to world schematism, that in connection with this Hegelian nodal line of measurement relations—in which quantitative change suddenly passes at certain points into qualitative transformation—Herr Dühring had a little accident: in a weak moment he himself recognized and made use of this line. We gave there one of the best-known examples—that of the change of the aggregate states of water, which under normal atmospheric pressure changes at 0°C from the liquid into the solid state, and at 100°C from the liquid into the gaseous state, so that at both these turning points the merely quantitative change of temperature brings about a qualitative change in the condition of the water.

In proof of this law we might have cited hundreds of other similar facts from nature as well as from human society. Thus, for example, the whole of Part IV of Marx's *Capital*—production of relative surplus value—deals, in the field of cooperation, division of labor and manufacture, machinery and modern industry, with innumerable cases in which quantitative change alters the quality, and also qualitative change alters the quantity, of the things under consideration; in which therefore, to use the expression so hated by Herr Dühring, quantity is transformed into quality and *vice versa*. As for example the fact that the cooperation of a number of people, the fusion of many forces into one single force, to use Marx's phrase, creates a "new power," which is essentially different from the sum of its individual powers.

Over and above this, in the passage which, in the interests of complete truth, Herr Dühring perverted into its opposite, Marx had added a footnote: "The molecular theory of modern chemistry first scientifically worked out by Laurent and Gerhardt rests on no other law."

. . .

XIII. Dialectics—Negation of the Negation

This historical sketch [of the genesis of the so-called primitive accumulation of capital in England] is relatively the best part of Marx's book, and would be even better if it had not relied on dialectical crutches to help out its scholarly basis. The Hegelian negation of the negation, in default of anything better and clearer, has in fact to serve here as the midwife to deliver the future from the womb of the past. The abolition of "individual property," which since the sixteenth century has been effected in the way indicated above, is the first negation. It will be followed by a second, which bears the character of a negation of the negation and hence of a restoration of "individual property," but in a higher form, based on the common ownership of land and of the instruments of labor. Herr Marx calls this new "individual property" also "social property," and in this there appears the Hegelian higher unity, in which the contradiction is supposed to be sublated, that is to say, in the Hegelian verbal jugglery, both overcome and preserved . . . According to this, the expropriation of the expropriators is, as it were, the automatic result of historical reality in its materially external relations . . . It would be difficult to convince a sensible man of the necessity of the common ownership of land and capital, on the basis of credence in Hegelian word juggling such as the negation of the negation . . . The nebulous hybrids of Marx's conceptions will not however appear strange to anyone who realizes what nonsense can be concocted with Hegelian dialectics as the scientific basis, or rather what nonsense must necessarily spring from it. For the benefit of the reader who is not familiar with these artifices, it must be pointed out expressly that Hegel's first negation is the catechismal idea of the fall from grace and his second is that of a higher unity leading to redemption. The logic of facts can hardly be based on this nonsensical analogy borrowed from the religious sphere . . . Herr Marx remains cheerfully in the nebulous world of his property which is at once both individual and social and leaves it to his adepts to solve for themselves this profound dialectical enigma."

Thus far Herr Dühring.

So Marx has no other way of proving the necessity of the social revolution, of establishing the common ownership of land and of the means of production produced by labor, except by citing the Hegelian negation of the negation; and because he bases his socialist theory on these nonsensical analogies borrowed from religion, he arrives at the result that in the society of the future there will be dominant an ownership at once both individual and social, as Hegelian higher unity of the sublated contradiction.

But let the negation of the negation rest for the moment and let us have a look at the "ownership" which is "at once both individual and social." Herr Dühring characterizes this as a "nebulous world," and curiously enough he is really right on this point. Unfortunately, however, it is not Marx but again Herr Dühring himself who is in this nebulous world. Just as his dexterity in handling the Hegelian method of "delirious raving" enabled him without any difficulty to determine what the still unfinished volumes of *Capital* are sure to contain, so here, too, without any great effort he can put Marx right *à la* Hegel, by imputing to him the higher unity of a property, of which there is not a word in Marx. Marx says:

> It is the negation of negation. This reestablishes individual property, but on the basis of the acquisitions of the capitalist era, i.e., on cooperation of free workers and their common ownership of the land and of the means of production produced by labor itself. The transformation of scattered private property, arising from individual labor, into capitalist private property is, naturally, a process, incomparably more protracted, arduous, and difficult, than the transformation of capitalistic private property, already practically resting on socialized production, into socialized property." (Marx, *Capital*)

That is all. The state of things brought about by the expropriation of the expropriators is therefore characterized as the reestablishment of individual property, but *on the basis* of the social ownership of the land and of the means of production produced by labor itself. To anyone who understands plain talk this means that social ownership extends to the land and the other means of production, and individual ownership to the products, that is, the articles of consumption. And in order to make the matter comprehensible even to children of six, Marx assumes "a community of free individuals, carrying on their work with the means of production in common, in which the labor power of all the different individuals is consciously applied as the combined labor power of the community," that is, a society organized on a socialist basis; and he continues: "The total product of our community is a social product. One portion serves as fresh means of production and *remains social*. But another portion is consumed by the members as means of subsistence. *A distribution of this portion among them is consequently necessary.*" And surely that is clear enough even for Herr Dühring, in spite of his having Hegel on his brain.

The property which is at once both individual and social, this confusing hybrid, this nonsense which necessarily springs from Hegelian dialectics, this nebulous world, this profound dialectical enigma, which Marx leaves his adepts to solve for themselves—is yet another free creation and imagination on the part of Herr Dühring. Marx, as an alleged Hegelian, is obliged to produce a real higher unity, as the outcome of the negation of the negation, and as Marx does not do this to Herr Dühring's taste, the latter has to fall again into his higher and nobler style, and in the interests of complete truth impute to Marx things which are the products of Herr Dühring's own manufacture. A man who is totally incapable of quoting correctly, even by way of exception, may well become morally indignant at the "Chinese erudition" of other people, who always quote correctly, but precisely by doing this "inadequately conceal their lack of insight into the totality of ideas of the various writers from whom they quote." Herr Dühring is right. Long live historical depiction in the grand style!

Up to this point we have proceeded from the assumption that Herr Dühring's persistent habit of misquoting is done at least in good faith, and arises either from his total incapacity to understand things or from a habit of quoting from memory—a habit which seems to be peculiar to historical depiction in the grand style, but is usually described as slovenly. But we seem to have reached the point at which, even with Herr Dühring, quantity is transformed into quality. For we must take into consideration in the first place that the passage in Marx is in itself perfectly clear and is moreover amplified in the same book by a further passage which leaves no room whatever for misunderstanding; secondly, that Herr Dühring had discovered the monstrosity of "property which is at once both individual and social" neither in the critique of *Capital*, in the

Ergänzungsblätter, nor even in the critique contained in the first edition of his *Critical History*, but only in the second edition—that is, on his *third* reading of *Capital*; further, that in this second edition, which was rewritten in a socialist sense, it was deemed necessary by Herr Dühring to make Marx say the utmost possible nonsense about the future organization of society, in order to enable him, in contrast, to bring forward all the more triumphantly—as he in fact does—"the economic commune as described by *me* in economic and juridical outline in my *Course*"—when we take all this into consideration, we are almost forced to the conclusion that Herr Dühring has here deliberately made a "beneficent extension" of Marx's idea—beneficent for Herr Dühring.

But what role does the negation of the negation play in Marx? [In *Capital*] he sets out the final conclusions which he draws from the preceding fifty pages of economic and historical investigation into the so-called primitive accumulation of capital. Before the capitalist era, petty industry existed, at least in England, on the basis of the private property of the laborer in his means of production. The so-called primitive accumulation of capital consisted there in the expropriation of these immediate producers, that is, in the dissolution of private property based on the labor of its owner. This became possible because the petty industry referred to above is compatible only with narrow and primitive bounds of production and society, and at a certain stage brings forth the material agencies for its own annihilation. This annihilation, the transformation of the individual and scattered means of production into socially concentrated ones, forms the prehistory of capital. As soon as the laborers are turned into proletarians, their conditions of labor into capital, as soon as the capitalist mode of production stands on its own feet, the further socialization of labor and further transformation of the land and other means of production, and therefore the further expropriation of private proprietors, takes a new form.

> That which is now to be expropriated is no longer the laborer working for himself, but the capitalist exploiting many laborers. This expropriation is accomplished by the action of the immanent laws of capitalist production itself, by the concentration of capital. One capitalist always kills many. Hand in hand with this concentration, or this expropriation of many capitalists by a few, develop, on an ever growing scale, the cooperative form of the labor process, the conscious technical application of science, the methodical collective cultivation of the soil, the transformation of the instruments of labor into instruments of labor only

usable in common, and the economizing of all means of production by their use as the jointly owned means of production of combined, socialized labor. Along with the constantly diminishing number of the magnates of capital, who usurp and monopolize all advantages of this process of transformation, grows the mass of misery, oppression, slavery, degradation, and exploitation; but with this too grows the revolt of the working class, a class always increasing in numbers, and disciplined, united, and organized by the very mechanism of the process of capitalist production itself. Capital becomes a fetter upon the mode of production, which has sprung up and flourished along with, and under it. Concentration of the means of production and socialization of labor at last reach a point where they become incompatible with their capitalist integument. This integument is burst asunder. The knell of capitalist private property sounds. The expropriators are expropriated."

And now I ask the reader: where are the dialectical frills and mazes and conceptual arabesques; where the mixed and misconceived ideas according to which everything is all one and the same thing in the end; where the dialectical miracles for his faithful followers; where the mysterious dialectical rubbish and the maze in accordance with the Hegelian Logos doctrine, without which Marx, according to Herr Dühring, is unable to put his exposition into shape? Marx merely shows from history, and here states in a summarized form, that just as formerly petty industry by its very development necessarily created the conditions of its own annihilation, i.e., of the expropriation of the small proprietors, so now the capitalist mode of production has likewise itself created the material conditions from which it must perish. The process is a historical one, and if it is at the same time a dialectical process, this is not Marx's fault, however annoying it may be to Herr Dühring.

It is only at this point, after Marx has completed his proof on the basis of historical and economic facts, that he proceeds:

> The capitalist mode of production and appropriation, hence the capitalist private property, is the first negation of individual private property founded on the labor of the proprietor. Capitalist production begets, with the inexorability of a process of nature, its own negation. It is the negation of the negation.

Thus, by characterizing the process as the negation of the negation, Marx does not intend to prove that the process was historically necessary. On the contrary: only after he has proved from history that in fact the process has partially already occurred, and partially must occur in the future, he additionally characterizes it as a process which develops in accordance with a definite dialectical law. That is all. It is therefore once again a pure distortion of the facts by Herr Dühring when he declares that the negation of the negation has to serve here as the midwife to deliver the future from the womb of the past, or that Marx wants anyone to be convinced of the necessity of the common ownership of land and capital (which is itself a Dühringian contradiction in corporeal form) on the basis of credence in the negation of the negation.

Herr Dühring's total lack of understanding of the nature of dialectics is shown by the very fact that he regards it as a mere proof-producing instrument, as a limited mind might look upon formal logic or elementary mathematics. Even formal logic is primarily a method of arriving at new results, of advancing from the known to the unknown—and dialectics is the same, only much more eminently so; moreover, since it forces its way beyond the narrow horizon of formal logic, it contains the germ of a more comprehensive view of the world. The same correlation exists in mathematics. Elementary mathematics, the mathematics of constant quantities, moves within the confines of formal logic, at any rate taken as a whole; the mathematics of variable magnitudes, whose most important part is the infinitesimal calculus, is in essence nothing other than the application of dialectics to mathematical relations. In it, the simple question of proof is definitely pushed into the background, as compared with the manifold application of the method to new spheres of research. But almost all the proofs of higher mathematics, from the first—that of the differential calculus—on, are false, from the standpoint of elementary mathematics taken rigidly. And this is necessarily so, when, as happens in this case, an attempt is made to prove by formal logic results obtained in the field of dialectics. To attempt to prove anything by means of dialectics alone to a crass metaphysician like Herr Dühring would be as much a waste of time as was the attempt made by Leibniz and his pupils to prove the principles of the infinitesimal calculus to the mathematicians of their time. The differential gave them the same convulsions as Herr Dühring gets from the negation of the negation, in which, moreover, as we shall see, the differential also plays a certain role. Finally these gentlemen—or those of them who had not died in the interval—grudgingly gave way, not because they were convinced, but because it always came out right. Herr Dühring, as he himself tells us, is only in his forties, and if he attains old age, as we hope he may, perhaps his experience will be the same.

But what then is this fearful negation of the negation, which makes life so bitter for Herr Dühring and with him plays the same role of the unpardonable crime as the sin against the Holy Ghost does in Christianity? A very simple process which is taking place everywhere and every day, which any child can understand as soon as it is stripped of the veil of mystery in which it was enveloped by the old idealist philosophy and in which it is to the advantage of helpless metaphysicians of Herr Dühring's caliber to keep it enveloped.

Let us take a grain of barley. Billions of such grains of barley are milled, boiled, and brewed and then consumed. But if such a grain of barley meets with conditions which are normal for it, if it falls on suitable soil, then under the influence of heat and moisture it undergoes a specific change, it germinates; the grain as such ceases to exist, it is negated, and in its place appears the plant which has arisen from it, the negation of the grain. But what is the normal life process of this plant? It grows, flowers, is fertilized and finally once more produces grains of barley, and as soon as these have ripened the stalk dies, is in its turn negated. As a result of this negation of the negation we have once again the original grain of barley, but not as a single unit, but ten-, twenty- or thirtyfold. Species of grain change extremely slowly, and so the barley of today is almost the same as it was a century ago. But if we take a trainable ornamental plant, for example a dahlia or an orchid, and treat the seed and the plant which grows from it according to the gardener's art, we get as a result of this negation of the negation not only more seeds, but also qualitatively improved seeds, which produce more beautiful flowers, and each repetition of this process, each fresh negation of the negation, enhances this process of perfection.

With most insects, this process follows the same lines as in the case of the grain of barley. Butterflies, for example, spring from the egg by a negation of the egg, pass through certain transformations until they reach sexual maturity, pair and are in turn negated, dying as soon as the pairing process has been completed and the female has laid its numerous eggs. We are not concerned at the moment with the fact that with other plants and animals the process does not take such a simple form, that before they die they produce seeds, eggs, or offspring not once but many times; our purpose here is only to show that the negation of the negation *really does take place* in both kingdoms of the organic world.

Furthermore, the whole of geology is a series of negated negations, a series of successive chatterings of old and deposits of new rock formations. First the original earth crust brought into existence by the cooling of the liquid mass was broken up by oceanic, meteorological, and atmospheric chemical action, and these fragmented masses were stratified on the ocean bed. Local upheavals of the ocean bed above the surface of the sea subject portions of these first strata once more to the action of rain, the changing temperature of the seasons, and the oxygen and carbonic acid of the atmosphere. These same influences act on the molten masses of rock which issue from the interior of the earth, break through the strata, and subsequently cool off. In this way, in the course of millions of centuries, ever new strata are formed and in turn are for the most part destroyed, ever anew serving as material for the formation of new strata. But the result of this process has been a very positive one: the creation of a soil composed of the most varied chemical elements and mechanically fragmented, which makes possible the most abundant and diversified vegetation.

It is the same in mathematics. Let us take any arbitrary algebraic quantity: for example, a. If this is negated, we get $-a$ (minus a). If we negate that negation, by multiplying $-a$ by $-a$, we get $+a^2$, i.e., the original positive quantity, but at a higher degree, raised to its second power. In this case also it makes no difference that we can obtain the same a^2 by multiplying the positive a by itself, thus likewise getting a^2. For the negated negation is so securely entrenched in a^2 that the latter always has two square roots, namely, a and $-a$. And the fact that it is impossible to get rid of the negated negation, the negative root of the square, acquires very obvious significance as soon as we come to quadratic equations.

The negation of the negation is even more strikingly obvious in higher analysis, in those "summations of indefinitely small magnitudes" which Herr Dühring himself declares are the highest operations of mathematics, and in ordinary language are known as the differential and integral calculus. How are these forms of calculus used? In a given problem, for example, I have two variable magnitudes, x and y, neither of which can vary without the other also varying in a relation determined by the facts of the case. I differentiate x and y, i.e., I take x and y as so infinitely small that in comparison with any real quantity, however small, they disappear, so that nothing is left of x and y but their reciprocal relation without any, so to speak, material basis, a quantitative ratio in which there is no quantity. Therefore, dy/dx, the relation between the differentials of x and *y*, is equal to 0/0, but 0/0 taken as the expression of *y*/*x*. I only mention in passing that this relation between two magnitudes which have disappeared, caught at the moment of their disappearance, is a contradiction; but it cannot disturb us any more than it has disturbed the whole of mathematics for almost two hundred years. And yet, what have I done but negate *x* and *y*, though not in such a way that I need not bother about them any more, not in the way that metaphysics negates, but in the way that corresponds with the facts of the case? In place of *x* and *y*, therefore, I have their negation, *dx* and *dy*, in the formulas or equations before me. I continue then to operate with these formulas, treating *dx* and *dy* as quantities which are real, though subject to certain exceptional laws, and at a certain point I *negate the negation*, i.e., I integrate the differential formula, and in place of *dx* and *dy* again get the real quantities *x* and *y*, and am then not where I was at the beginning, but by using this method I have solved the problem on which ordinary geometry and algebra might perhaps have broken their teeth in vain.

It is the same in history, as well. All civilized peoples begin with the common ownership of the land. With all peoples who have passed a certain primitive stage, in the course of the development of agriculture this common ownership becomes a fetter on production. It is abolished—negated—and, after a longer or shorter series of intermediate stages, is transformed into private property. But at a higher stage of agricultural development, brought about by private property in land itself, private property conversely becomes a fetter on production, as is the case today both with small and large land ownership. The demand that it, too, should be negated, that it should once again be transformed into common property, necessarily arises. But this demand does not mean the restoration of the aboriginal common ownership, but the institution of a far higher and more developed form of possession in common which, far from being a hindrance to production, on the contrary for the first time will free production from all fetters and enable it to make full use of modern chemical discoveries and mechanical inventions.

Or let us take another example: The philosophy of antiquity was primitive, spontaneously evolved materialism. As such, it was incapable of clearing up the relation between mind and matter. But the need to get clarity on this question led to the doctrine of a soul separable from the body, then to the assertion of the immortality of this soul, and finally to monotheism. The old materialism was therefore negated by idealism. But in the course of the further development of philosophy, idealism, too, became untenable and was negated by modern materialism. This modern materialism, the negation of the negation, is not the mere reestablishment of the old, but adds to the permanent foundations of this old materialism the whole thought content of two thousand years of development of philosophy and natural science, as well as of the historical development of these two thousand years. It is in fact no longer a philosophy at all, but simply a world outlook which has to establish its validity and be applied not in a science of sciences standing apart, but in the real sciences. In this development, philosophy is therefore "sublated," that is, "both overcome and preserved"; overcome as regards its form, and preserved as regards its real content. Thus, where Herr Dühring sees only "verbal jugglery," closer inspection reveals an actual content.

Finally: Even the Rousseau doctrine of equality—of which Dühring's is only a feeble and distorted echo—could not have seen the light but for the midwife's services rendered by the Hegelian negation of the negation—though it was nearly twenty years before Hegel was born. And far from being ashamed of this, the doctrine in its first presentation bears almost ostentatiously the imprint of its dialectical origin. In the state of nature and savagery men were equal; and as Rousseau regards even language as a perversion of the state of nature, he is fully justified in extending the equality of animals within the limits of a single species also to the animal-men recently classified by Haeckel hypothetically as *Alali*: speechless. But these equal animal-men had one quality which gave them an advantage over the other animals: perfectibility, the capacity to develop further; and this became the cause of inequality. So Rousseau regards the rise of inequality as progress. But this progress contained an antagonism: it was at the same time retrogression.

> All further progress [beyond the original state] meant so many steps seemingly towards the *perfection of the individual man*, but in reality towards the *decay of the species* . . . Metallurgy and agriculture were the two arts the discovery of which produced this great revolution [the transformation of the primeval forest into cultivated land, but along with this the introduction of poverty and slavery through property]. For the poet it is gold and silver, but for the philosopher iron and corn, which have civilized *men* and ruined the human *race*. [Emphasis by Engels]

Each new advance of civilization is at the same time a new advance of inequality. All institutions set up by the society which has arisen with civilization change into the opposite of their original purpose.

> It is an incontestable fact, and the fundamental principle of all public law, that the peoples set up their chieftains to safeguard their liberty and not to enslave them.

And nevertheless the chiefs necessarily become the oppressors of the peoples, and intensify their oppression up to the point at which inequality, carried to the utmost extreme, again changes into its opposite, becomes the cause of equality: before the despot all are equal—equally ciphers.

> Here we have the extreme measure of inequality, *the final point which completes the circle and meets the point from which we set out*: here all private individuals become equal once more, just because they are ciphers, and the subjects have no other law but their master's will. [But the despot is only master so long as he is able to use force and therefore] when he is driven out [he cannot] complain of the use of force . . . Force alone maintained him in power, and force alone overthrows him; thus everything takes its natural course. [Emphasis by Engels]

And so inequality once more changes into equality; not, however, into the former naïve equality of speechless primitive men, but into the higher equality of the social contract. The oppressors are oppressed. It is the negation of the negation.

Already in Rousseau, therefore, we find not only a line of thought which corresponds exactly to the one developed in Marx's *Capital*, but also, in details, a whole series of the same dialectical turns of speech as Marx used: processes which in their nature are antagonistic, contain a contradiction; transformation of one extreme into its opposite; and finally, as the kernel of the whole thing, the negation of the negation. And though in 1754 Rousseau was not yet able to use the Hegelian jargon, he was certainly, sixteen years before Hegel was born, deeply bitten with the Hegelian pestilence, dialectics of contradiction, Logos doctrine, theology, and so forth. And when Herr Dühring, in his shallow version of Rousseau's theory of equality, begins to operate with his victorious two men, he himself is already on the slope down which he must slide helplessly into the arms of the negation of the negation. The state of things in which the equality of the two men flourished, which was also described as an ideal state, is characterized as the "primitive state." This primitive state, however, according to [another] page, was necessarily sublated by the "robber system"—the first negation. But now, thanks to the philosophy of reality, we have gone so far as to abolish the robber system and establish in its stead the economic commune based on equality which has been discovered by Herr Dühring—negation of the negation, equality on a higher plane. What a delightful spectacle, and how beneficently it extends our range of vision: Herr Dühring's eminent self committing the capital crime of the negation of the negation!

And so, what is the negation of the negation? An extremely general— and for this reason extremely comprehensive and important—law of development of nature, history, and thought; a law which, as we have seen, holds good in the animal and plant kingdoms, in geology, in mathematics, in history and in philosophy—a law which, in spite of all his stubborn resistance, even Herr Dühring, unwittingly and in his own way, has to follow. It is obvious that I do not say anything concerning the *particular* process of development of, for example, a grain of barley from germination to the death of the fruit-bearing plant, if I say it is a negation of the negation. For, as the integral calculus is also a negation of the negation, if I said anything of the sort I would only be making the nonsensical statement that the life-process of a barley plant was integral calculus or, for that matter, that it was socialism. That, however, is precisely what the metaphysicians are constantly imputing to dialectics. When I say that all these processes are a negation of the negation, I bring them all together under this one law of motion, and for this very reason I leave out of account the specific peculiarities of each individual process. Dialectics, however, is nothing more than the science of the general laws of motion and development of nature, human society and thought.

But someone may object: the negation that has taken place in this case is not a real negation: I negate a grain of barley also when I grind it, an insect when I crush it underfoot, or the positive magnitude a when I cancel it, and so on. Or I negate the sentence: the rose is a rose, when I say: the rose is not a rose; and what do I get if I then negate this negation and say: but after all the rose is a rose? These objections are in fact the chief arguments put forward by the metaphysicians against dialectics, and they are wholly worthy of the narrow-mindedness of this mode of thought. Negation in dialectics does not mean simply saying no, or declaring that something does not exist, or destroying it in any way one likes. Long ago Spinoza said: *omnis determinatio est negatio*—every limitation or determination is at the same time a negation. And further: the kind of negation is here determined, firstly, by the general and, secondly, by the particular nature of the process. I must not only negate, but also in turn sublate the negation. I must therefore arrange the first negation so that the second remains or becomes possible. How? This depends on the particular nature of each individual case. If I grind a grain of barley, or crush an insect, I have carried out the first part of the action, but have made the second part impossible. Every kind of thing therefore has a peculiar way of being negated in such manner that it gives rise to a development, and it is just the same with every kind of conception or idea. The infinitesimal calculus involves a form of negation which is different from that used in the formation of positive powers from negative roots. This has to be learned, like everything else. The bare knowledge that the barley plant and the infinitesimal calculus are both governed by negation of negation does not enable me either to grow barley successfully or to differentiate and integrate; just as little as the mere knowledge of the laws of the determination of sound by the thickness of strings enables me to play the violin.

But it is clear that from a negation of the negation which consists in the childish pastime of alternately writing and cancelling a, or in alternately declaring that a rose is a rose and that it is not a rose, nothing eventuates but the silliness of the person who adopts such a tedious procedure. And yet the metaphysicians try to make us believe that this is the right way to carry out a negation of the negation, if we ever should want to do such a thing.

Once again, therefore, it is no one but Herr Dühring who is mystifying us when he asserts that the negation of the negation is a stupid analogy invented by Hegel, borrowed from the sphere of religion and based on the story of the fall of man and his redemption. Men thought dialectically long before they knew what dialectics was, just as they spoke prose long before the term prose existed. [An allusion to Molière's comedy *Le Bourgeois Gentilhomme*] The law of negation of the negation, which is unconsciously operative in nature and history and, until it has been recognized, also in our heads, was only first clearly formulated by Hegel. And if Herr Dühring wants to operate with it himself on the quiet and it is only that he cannot stand the name, then let him find a better name. But if his aim is to banish the process itself from thought, we must ask him to be so good as first to banish it from nature and history and to invent a mathematical system in which $-a \times -a$ is not $+a^2$ and in which differentiation and integration are prohibited under severe penalties.

DIALECTICS OF NATURE (EXCERPTS)

Friedrich Engels
1883

Like many now-classic works, Dialectics of Nature *was not published until after the Russian Revolution, when the Soviet archivists of the Marx-Engels Institute scoured Europe for Marx and Engels's manuscripts, letters, and notes, and compiled what would become the* Collected Works, *an invaluable contribution to the working class's revolutionary heritage. Of particular interest for this volume are Engels's fragmentary notes, which are clearly the result of a careful reading and analysis of Hegel. It is reasonable to surmise that this was part of a plan for a comprehensive work on Marxist philosophy, and that* Dialectics of Nature *would have been the first volume. Regrettably, although Engels was incredibly efficient, his work on Marx's unfinished manuscripts and his correspondence with socialists around the world meant he had to put many of his personal projects aside. Some of the scientific data available to him may be considered dated, but his basic conclusions are remarkably advanced, even by today's standards. Nevertheless, the partial drafts and fragments that comprise* Dialectics of Nature *are an invaluable contribution to Marxism—and to science in general.*

For those who would like to delve more deeply into this topic, we highly recommend Reason in Revolt *by Ted Grant and Alan Woods. Written on the centenary of Engels's death, it draws on the colossal advances in science since that time, which conclusively prove that, as Engels wrote in* Socialism: Utopian and Scientific: *"Nature is the proof of dialectics, and it must be said for modern science that it has furnished this proof with very rich materials increasingly daily, and thus has shown that, in the last resort, Nature works dialectically and not metaphysically; that she does not move in the eternal oneness of a perpetually recurring circle, but goes through a real historical evolution. In this connection, Darwin must be named before all others. He dealt the metaphysical conception of Nature the heaviest blow by his proof that all organic beings, plants, animals, and man himself, are the products of a process of evolution going on through millions of years. But, the naturalists, who have learned to think dialectically, are few and far between, and this conflict of the results of discovery with preconceived modes of thinking, explains the endless confusion now reigning in theoretical natural science, the despair of teachers as well as learners, of authors and readers alike."*

II. Dialectics

The general nature of dialectics to be developed as the science of interconnections, in contrast to metaphysics.

It is, therefore, from the history of nature and human society that the laws of dialectics are abstracted. For they are nothing but the most general laws of these two aspects of historical development, as well as of thought itself. And indeed they can be reduced in the main to three:

- The law of the transformation of quantity into quality and vice versa;

- The law of the interpenetration of opposites;

- The law of the negation of the negation.

All three are developed by Hegel in his idealist fashion as mere laws of *thought*: the first, in the first part of his *Logic*, in the "Doctrine of Being"; the second fills the whole of the second and by far the most important part of his *Logic*, the "Doctrine of Essence"; finally, the third figures as the fundamental law for the construction of the whole system. The mistake lies in the fact that these laws are foisted on nature and history as laws of thought, and not deduced from them. This is the source of the whole forced and often outrageous treatment; the universe, willy-nilly, is made out to be arranged in accordance with a system of thought which itself is only the product of a definite stage of evolution of human thought. If we turn the thing round, then everything becomes simple, and the dialectical laws that look so extremely mysterious in idealist philosophy at once become simple and clear as noonday.

Moreover, anyone who is even only slightly acquainted with his Hegel will be aware that in hundreds of passages Hegel is capable of giving the most striking individual illustrations from nature and history of the dialectical laws.

We are not concerned here with writing a handbook of dialectics, but only with showing that the dialectical laws are really laws of development of nature, and therefore are valid also for theoretical natural science. Hence we cannot go into the inner interconnection of these laws with one another.

The law of the transformation of quantity into quality and vice versa. For our purpose, we could express this by saying that in nature, in a manner exactly fixed for each individual case, qualitative changes can only occur by the quantitative addition or subtraction of matter or motion (so-called energy).

All qualitative differences in nature rest on differences of chemical composition or on different quantities or forms of motion (energy) or, as is almost always the case, on both. Hence it is impossible to alter the quality of a body without addition or subtraction of matter or motion, i.e., without quantitative alteration of the body concerned. In this form, therefore, Hegel's mysterious principle appears not only quite rational but even rather obvious.

It is surely hardly necessary to point out that the various allotropic and aggregational states of bodies, because they depend on various groupings of the molecules, depend on greater or lesser quantities of motion communicated to the bodies.

But what is the position in regard to change of form of motion, or so-called energy? If we change heat into mechanical motion or vice versa, is not the quality altered while the quantity remains the same? Quite correct. But it is with change of form of motion as with Heine's vices; anyone can be virtuous by himself, for vices two are always necessary. Change of form of motion is always a process that takes place between at least two bodies, of which one loses a definite quantity of motion of one quality (e.g., heat), while the other gains a corresponding quantity of motion of another quality (mechanical motion, electricity, chemical decomposition). Here, therefore, quantity and quality mutually correspond to each other. So far it has not been found possible to convert motion from one form to another inside a single isolated body.

We are concerned here in the first place with nonliving bodies; the same law holds for living bodies, but it operates under very complex conditions, and at present, quantitative measurement is still often impossible for us.

If we imagine any nonliving body cut up into smaller and smaller portions, at first no qualitative change occurs. But this has a limit: if we succeed, as by evaporation, in obtaining the separate molecules in the free state, then it is true that we can usually divide these still further, yet only with a complete change of quality. The molecule is decomposed into its separate atoms, which have quite different properties from those of the molecule. In the case of molecules composed of various chemical elements, atoms or molecules of these elements themselves make their appearance in the place of the compound molecule; in the case of molecules of elements, the free atoms appear, which exert quite distinct qualitative effects: the free atoms of nascent oxygen are easily able to effect what the atoms of atmospheric oxygen, bound together in the molecule, can never achieve.

But the molecule is also qualitatively different from the mass of the body to which it belongs. It can carry out movements independently of this mass and while the latter remains apparently at rest, e.g., heat oscillations; by means of a change of position and of connection with neighboring molecules it can change the body into an allotrope or a different state of aggregation.

Thus, we see that the purely quantitative operation of division has a limit at which it becomes transformed into a qualitative difference: the mass consists solely of molecules, but it is something essentially different from the molecule, just as the latter is different from the atom. It is this difference that is the basis for the separation of mechanics, as the science of heavenly and terrestrial masses, from physics, as the mechanics of the molecule, and from chemistry, as the physics of the atom.

In mechanics, no qualities occur; at most, states such as equilibrium, motion, potential energy, which all depend on measurable transference of motion and are themselves capable of quantitative expression. Hence, insofar as qualitative change takes place here, it is determined by a corresponding quantitative change.

In physics, bodies are treated as chemically unalterable or indifferent; we have to do with changes of their molecular states and with the change of form of the motion, which in all cases, at least on one of the two sides, brings the molecule into play. Here, every change is a transformation of quantity into quality, a consequence of the quantitative change of the quantity of motion of one form or another that is inherent in the body or communicated to it.

> Thus, for instance, the temperature of water is first of all indifferent in relation to its state as a liquid; but by increasing or decreasing the temperature of liquid water a point is reached at which this state of cohesion alters and the water becomes transformed on the one side into steam and on the other into ice (Hegel, *Encyclopedia*).

Similarly, a definite minimum current strength is required to cause the platinum wire of an electric incandescent lamp to glow; and every metal has its temperature of incandescence and fusion, every liquid its definite freezing and boiling point at a given pressure—insofar as our means allow us to produce the temperature required; finally also every gas has its critical point at which it can be liquefied by pressure and cooling. In short, the so-called physical constants are for the most part nothing but designations of the nodal points at which quantitative addition or subtraction of motion produces qualitative alteration in the state of the body concerned, at which, therefore, quantity is transformed into quality.

The sphere, however, in which the law of nature discovered by Hegel celebrates its most important triumphs is that of chemistry. Chemistry can be termed the science of the qualitative changes of bodies as a result of changed quantitative composition. That was already known to Hegel himself (*Logic*). As in the case of oxygen: if three atoms unite into a molecule, instead of the usual two, we get ozone, a body which is very considerably different from ordinary oxygen in its odor and reactions. Again, one can take the various proportions in which oxygen combines with nitrogen or sulphur, each of which produces a substance qualitatively different from any of the others! How different laughing gas (nitrogen monoxide N_2O) is from nitric anhydride (nitrogen pentoxide, N_2O_5)! The first is a gas, the second, at ordinary temperatures, a solid, crystalline substance. And yet the whole difference in composition is that the second contains five times as much oxygen as the first, and between the two of them are three more oxides of nitrogen (NO, N_2O_3, NO_2), each of which is qualitatively different from the first two and from each other.

This is seen still more strikingly in the homologous series of carbon compounds, especially in the simpler hydrocarbons. Of the normal paraffins, the lowest is methane, CH_4; here the four linkages of the carbon atom are saturated by four atoms of hydrogen. The second, ethane, C_2H_6, has two atoms of carbon joined together and the six free linkages are saturated by six atoms of hydrogen. And so it goes on, with C_3H_8, C_4H_{10}, etc., according to the algebraic formula C_nH_{2n+2}, so that by each addition of CH_2 a body is formed that is qualitatively distinct from the preceding one. The three lowest members of the series are gases, the highest known, hexadecane, $C_{16}H_{34}$, is a solid body with a boiling point of $278°$ C. Exactly the same holds good for the series of primary alcohols with formula C_nH_{2n+2}, derived (theoretically) from the paraffins, and the series of monobasic fatty acids (formula $C_nH_{2n}O_2$). What qualitative difference can be caused by the quantitative addition of C_3H_6 is taught by experience if we consume ethyl alcohol, $C_2H_{12}O$, in any drinkable form without addition of other alcohols, and on another occasion take the same ethyl alcohol, but with a slight addition of amyl alcohol, $C_5H_{12}O$, which forms the main constituent of the notorious fusel oil. One's head will certainly be aware of it the next morning, much to its detriment; so that one could even say that the intoxication, and subsequent "morning after" feeling, is also quantity transformed into quality, on the one hand, of ethyl alcohol, and on the other hand, of this added C_3H_6.

In these series we encounter the Hegelian law in yet another form. The lower members permit only of a single mutual arrangement of the atoms. If, however, the number of atoms united into a molecule attains a size definitely fixed for each series, the grouping of the atoms in the molecule can take place in more than one way; so that two or more isomeric substances can be formed, having equal numbers of C, H, and O atoms in the molecule but nevertheless qualitatively distinct from one another. We can even calculate how many such isomers are possible for each member of the series. Thus, in the paraffin series, for C_4H_{10} there are two, for C_6H_{12} there are three; among the higher members the number of possible isomers mounts very rapidly. Hence, once again it is the quantitative number of atoms in the molecule that determines the possibility and, insofar as it has been proved, also the actual existence of such qualitatively distinct isomers.

Still more. From the analogy of the substances with which we are acquainted in each of these series, we can draw conclusions as to the physical properties of the still unknown members of the series and, at least for the members immediately following the known ones, predict their properties, boiling point, etc., with fair certainty.

Finally, the Hegelian law is valid not only for compound substances but also for the chemical elements themselves. We now know that "the chemical properties of the elements are a periodic function of their atomic weights" (Roscoe-Schorlemmer, *Complete Textbook of Chemistry*), and that, therefore, their quality is determined by the quantity of their atomic weight. And the test of this has been brilliantly carried out. Mendeleev proved that various gaps occur in the series of related elements arranged according to atomic weights, indicating that here new elements remain to be discovered. He described in advance the general chemical properties of one of these unknown elements, which he termed eka-aluminum, because it follows after aluminum in the series beginning with the latter, and he predicted its approximate specific and atomic weight as well as its atomic volume. A few years later, Lecoq de Boisbaudran actually discovered this element, and Mendeleev's predictions fitted with only very slight discrepancies. Eka-aluminum was realized in gallium. By means of the—unconscious—application of Hegel's law of the transformation of quantity into quality, Mendeleev achieved a scientific feat which it is not too bold to put on a par with that of Leverrier in calculating the orbit of the still unknown planet Neptune.

In biology, as in the history of human society, the same law holds good at every step, but we prefer to dwell here on examples from the exact sciences, since here the quantities are accurately measurable and traceable.

Probably the same gentlemen who up to now have decried the transformation of quantity into quality as mysticism and incomprehensible transcendentalism will now declare that it is indeed something quite self-evident, trivial, and commonplace, which they have long employed, and so they have been taught nothing new.

But to have formulated for the first time in its universally valid form a general law of development of nature, society, and thought, will always remain an act of historic importance. And if these gentlemen have for years caused quantity and quality to be transformed into one another, without knowing what they did, then they will have to console themselves with Molière's Monsieur Jourdain who had spoken prose all his life without having the slightest inkling of it.

Notes and Fragments on Dialectics

A. General questions on dialectics. The fundamental laws of dialectics

Dialectics, so-called *objective* [materialist] dialectics, prevails throughout nature, and so-called subjective dialectics, dialectical thought, is only the reflection of the motion through opposites which asserts itself everywhere in nature, and which by the continual conflict of the opposites and their final passage into one another, or into higher forms, determines the life of nature. Attraction and repulsion. Polarity begins with magnetism, it is exhibited in one and the same body; in the case of electricity, it distributes itself over two or more bodies which become oppositely charged. All chemical processes reduce themselves to processes of chemical attraction and repulsion. Finally, in organic life the formation of the cell nucleus is likewise to be regarded as a polarization of the living protein material, and from the simple cell onwards, the theory of evolution demonstrates how each advance up to the most complicated plant on the one side, and up to man on the other, is effected by the continual conflict between heredity and adaptation. In this connection it becomes evident how little applicable to such forms of evolution are categories like "positive" and "negative."

One can conceive of heredity as the positive, conservative side, adaptation as the negative side that continually destroys what has been inherited, but one can just as well take adaptation as the creative, active, positive activity, and heredity as the resisting, passive, negative activity. But just as in history progress makes its appearance as the negation of the existing state of things, so here also—on purely practical grounds—adaptation is better conceived as negative [negating] activity.

In history, motion through opposites is most markedly exhibited in all critical epochs of the foremost peoples. At such moments a people has only the choice between the two horns of a dilemma: "either-or!" and indeed the question is always put in a way quite different from that in which the philistines, who dabble in politics in every age, would have liked it put. Even the liberal German philistine of 1848 found himself in 1849 suddenly, unexpectedly, and against his will, confronted by the question: a return to the old reaction in an intensified form, or continuance of the revolution up to the republic, perhaps even the one and indivisible republic with a socialist background. He did not spend long in reflection and helped to create the Manteuffel reaction as the flower of German liberalism. Similarly, in 1851, the French bourgeois, when faced with a dilemma which he certainly did not expect: a caricature of the empire, praetorian rule, and the exploitation of France by a gang of scoundrels, or a social-democratic republic—and he bowed down before the gang of scoundrels so as to be able, under their protection, to go on exploiting the workers.

Hard and fast lines are incompatible with the theory of evolution. Even the borderline between vertebrates and invertebrates is now no longer rigid, just as little is that between fishes and amphibians, while that between birds and reptiles dwindles more and more every day. Between *Compsognathus* and *Archaeopteryx* only a few intermediate links are wanting, and birds' beaks with teeth crop up in both hemispheres. "Either-or" becomes more and more inadequate. Among lower animals the concept of the individual cannot be established at all sharply. Not only as to whether a particular animal is an individual or a colony, but also where in development one individual ceases and the other begins (nurses).

For a stage in the outlook on nature where all differences become merged in intermediate steps, and all opposites pass into one another through intermediate links, the old metaphysical method of thought no longer suffices. Dialectics, which likewise knows no hard and fast lines, no unconditional, universally valid "either-or," and which bridges the fixed metaphysical differences, and besides "either-or" recognizes also in the right place "both this-and that" and reconciles the opposites, is the sole method of thought appropriate in the highest degree to this stage. Of course, for everyday use, for the small change of science, the metaphysical categories retain their validity.

* * *

The transformation of quantity into quality = "mechanical" world outlook, quantitative change alters quality. The gentlemen never suspected that!

* * *

The character of mutual opposites belonging to the thought determinations of reason: *polarization*. Just as electricity, magnetism, etc., become polarized and move in opposites, so do thoughts. Just as in the former it is not possible to maintain any one-sidedness, and no natural scientist would think of doing so, so also in the latter.

* * *

The true nature of the determinations of "essence" is expressed by Hegel himself (*Encyclopedia*): "In essence everything is *relative*" (e.g., positive and negative, which have meaning only in their relation, not each for itself).

* * *

Part and whole, for instance, are already categories which become inadequate in organic nature. The ejection of seeds—the embryo—and the newborn animal are not to be conceived as a "part" that is separated from the "whole"; that would give a distorted treatment. It becomes a part only in a *dead body* (Hegel, *Encyclopedia*).[1]

* * *

Simple and compound. Categories which even in organic nature likewise lose their meaning and become inapplicable. An animal is expressed neither by its mechanical composition from bones, blood, gristle, muscles, tissues, etc., nor by its chemical composition from the elements. (*Encyclopedia*). The organism is *neither* simple *nor* compound, however complex it may be.

* * *

Abstract identity ($a = a$; and negatively, a cannot be simultaneously equal and unequal to a) is likewise inapplicable in organic nature. The plant, the animal, every cell is at every moment of its life identical with itself, and yet becoming distinct from itself, by absorption and excretion of

---

1 Hegel, *Encyclopedia of the Philosophical Sciences*, Addendum: "The limbs and organs, for instance, of an organic body are not merely parts of it: it is only in their unity that they are what they are, and they are unquestionably affected by that unity, as they also in turn affect it. These limbs and organs become mere parts, only when they pass under the hands of the anatomist, whose occupation, be it remembered, is not with the living body but with the corpse."

substances, by respiration, by cell formation and death of cells, by the process of circulation taking place, in short, by a sum of incessant molecular changes which make up life and the sum total of whose results is evident to our eyes in the phases of life—embryonic life, youth, sexual maturity, process of reproduction, old age, death.

The further physiology develops, the more important for it become these incessant, infinitely small changes, and hence the more important for it also the consideration of difference *within* identity, and the old abstract standpoint of formal identity, that an organic being is to be treated as something simply identical with itself, as something constant, becomes out of date. [In the margin of the manuscript occurs the remark: "Apart, moreover, from the evolution of species."] Nevertheless, the mode of thought based thereon, together with its categories, persists. But even in inorganic nature identity as such is in reality nonexistent. Everybody is continually exposed to mechanical, physical, and chemical influences, which are always changing it and modifying its identity. Abstract identity, with its opposition to difference, is in place only in mathematics— an abstract science which is concerned with creations of thought, even though they are reflections of reality—and even there it is continually being sublated (Hegel, *Encyclopedia*). The fact that identity contains difference within itself is expressed in *every sentence*, where the predicate is necessarily different from the subject; the *lily* is a *plant*; the *rose* is *red*; where, either in the subject or in the predicate, there is something that is not covered by the predicate or the subject (Hegel). That from the outset, *identity with itself* requires *difference from everything else* as its complement, is self-evident.

Identity. Continual change, i.e., sublation of abstract identity with itself, is also found in so-called inorganic nature. Geology is its history. On the surface, mechanical changes (denudation, frost), chemical changes (weathering); internally, mechanical changes (pressure), heat (volcanic), chemical (water, acids, binding substances); on a large scale—upheavals, earthquakes, etc. The slate of today is fundamentally different from the ooze from which it is formed, the chalk from the loose microscopic shells that compose it. Even more so limestone, which indeed, according to some, is of purely organic origin, and sandstone from the loose sea sand, which again is derived from disintegrated granite, etc., not to speak of coal.

* * *

The law of identity in the old metaphysical sense is the fundamental law of the old outlook: $a = a$. Each thing is equal to itself. Everything was permanent, the solar system, stars, organisms. This law has been refuted by natural science bit by bit in each separate case, but theoretically it still prevails and is still put forward by the supporters of the old in opposition to the new: a thing cannot simultaneously be itself and something else. And yet the fact that true, concrete identity includes difference, change, has recently been shown in detail by natural science (see above).

Abstract identity, like all metaphysical categories, suffices for *every-day* use, where small dimensions or brief periods of time are in question; the limits within which it is usable differ in almost every case and are determined by the nature of the object; for a planetary system, where in ordinary astronomical calculation the ellipse can be taken as the basic form for practical purposes without error, they are much wider than for an insect that completes its metamorphosis in a few weeks. (Give other examples, e.g., alteration of species, which is reckoned in periods of thousands of years.) For natural science in its comprehensive role, however, even in each single branch, abstract identity is totally inadequate, and although on the whole it has now been abolished in practice, theoretically it still dominates people's minds, and most natural scientists imagine that identity and difference are irreconcilable opposites, instead of one-sided poles which represent the truth only in their reciprocal action, in the inclusion of difference within identity.

*   *   *

Identity and difference—necessity and chance—cause and effect—the two main opposites which, treated separately, become transformed into one another.

*   *   *

Positive and negative. Can also be given the reverse names: in electricity, etc.; North and South, ditto. If one reverses this and alters the rest of the terminology accordingly, everything remains correct. We can call West East and East, West. The sun rises in the West, and planets revolve from East to West, etc., the names alone are changed. Indeed, in physics we call the real South pole of the magnet, which is attracted by the North pole, of the earth's magnetism, the *North pole*, and it does not matter.

***

That positive and negative are equivalent, irrespective of which side is positive and which negative, (holds good) not only in analytical geometry, but still more in physics.

***

Polarity. A magnet, on being cut through, polarizes the neutral middle portion, but in such a way that the old poles remain. On the other hand, a worm, on being cut into two, retains the receptive mouth at the positive pole and forms a new negative pole at the other end with excretory anus; but the old negative pole (the anus) now becomes positive, becoming a mouth, and a new anus or negative pole is formed at the cut end. *Voilà* transformation of positive into negative.

***

Chance and necessity

Another opposition in which metaphysics is entangled is that of chance and necessity. What can be more sharply contradictory than these two thought determinations? How is it possible that both are identical, that the accidental is necessary, and the necessary is also accidental? Common sense, and with it the majority of natural scientists, treats necessity and chance as determinations that exclude each other once for all. A thing, a circumstance, a process is either accidental or necessary, but not both. Hence both exist side by side in nature; nature contains all sorts of objects and processes, of which some are accidental, the others necessary, and it is only a matter of not confusing the two sorts with each other. Thus, for instance, one assumes the decisive specific characters to be necessary, other differences between individuals of the same species being termed accidental, and this holds good of crystals as it does for plants and animals. Then again, the lower group becomes accidental in relation to the higher, so that it is declared to be a matter of chance how many different species are included in the genus *felis* or *equus*, or how many genera and orders there are in a class, and how many individuals of each of these species exist, or how many different species of animals occur in a given region, or what in general the fauna and flora are like. And then it is declared that the necessary is the sole thing of scientific interest and that the accidental is a matter of indifference to science. That is to say: what can be brought under laws, hence, what one *knows*, is interesting; what cannot be brought under laws, and therefore, what one does not know, is a matter of indifference and can be ignored.

Thereby, all science comes to an end, for it has to investigate precisely that which we do not know. That is to say: what can be brought under general laws is regarded as necessary, and what cannot be so brought as accidental. Anyone can see that this is the same sort of science as that which proclaims natural what it can explain, and ascribes what it cannot explain to supernatural causes; whether I term the cause inexplicable chance, or whether I term it God, is a matter of complete indifference as far as the thing itself is concerned. Both are only equivalents for: I do not know, and therefore do not belong to science. The latter ceases where the requisite connection is wanting.

In opposition to this view there is determinism, which passed from French materialism into natural science, and which tries to dispose of chance by denying it altogether. According to this conception, only simple, direct necessity prevails in nature. That a particular peapod contains five peas and not four or six, that a particular dog's tail is five inches long and not a whit longer or shorter, that this year a particular clover flower was fertilized by a bee and another not, and indeed, by precisely one particular bee and at a particular time, that a particular windblown dandelion seed has sprouted and another not, that last night I was bitten by a flea at four o'clock in the morning, and not at three or five o'clock, and on the right shoulder and not on the left calf—these are all facts which have been produced by an irrevocable concatenation of cause and effect, by an unshatterable necessity of such a nature indeed that the gaseous sphere, from which the solar system was derived, was already so constituted that these events had to happen thus and not otherwise.

With this kind of necessity we likewise do not get away from the theological conception of nature. Whether with Augustine and Calvin we call it the eternal decree of God, or Kismet as the Turks do, or whether we call it necessity, is all pretty much the same for science. There is no question of tracing the chain of causation in any of these cases, so we are just as wise in one as in another; the so-called necessity remains an empty phrase, and with it—chance also remains—what it was before.

As long as we are not able to show on what the number of peas in the pod depends, it remains just a matter of chance, and the assertion that the case was foreseen already in the primordial constitution of the solar system does not get us a step further. Still more. A science which was to set about the task of following back the *casus* [cause] of this individual peapod in its causal concatenation would be no longer science but pure trifling; for this same peapod alone has in addition innumerable other individual, accidentally appearing qualities: shade of color, thickness and hardness of the pod, size of the peas, not to speak of the individual peculiarities revealed by the microscope. The *one* peapod, therefore, would already provide more causal connections for following up than all the botanists in the world could solve.

Hence, chance is not here explained by necessity, but rather necessity is degraded to the production of what is merely accidental. If the fact that a particular peapod contains six peas, and not five or seven, is of the same order as the law of motion of the solar system, or the law of the transformation of energy, then as a matter of fact, chance is not elevated into necessity, but rather, necessity degraded into chance. Furthermore, however much the diversity of the organic and inorganic species and individuals existing side by side in a given area may be asserted to be based on irrefragable necessity, for the separate species and individuals it remains what it was before—a matter of chance. For the individual animal it is a matter of chance, where it happens to be born, what environment it finds for living, what enemies and how many of them threaten it. For the mother plant it is a matter of chance whither the wind scatters its seeds, and, for the daughter plant, where the seed finds soil for germination; and to assure us that here also everything rests on irrefragable necessity is a poor consolation. The jumbling together of natural objects in a given region, still more in the whole world, for all the primordial determination from eternity, remains what it was before—a matter of chance.

In contrast to both conceptions, Hegel came forward with the hitherto quite unheard of propositions that the accidental has a cause because it is accidental, and just as much also has no cause because it is accidental; that the accidental is necessary, that necessity determines itself as chance, and, on the other hand, this chance is rather, absolute necessity (*Logic*). Natural science has simply ignored these propositions as paradoxical trifling, as self-contradictory nonsense, and, as regards theory, has persisted on the one hand, in the barrenness of thought of Wolffian metaphysics, according to which a thing is *either* accidental *or* necessary, but not both at once; or, on the other hand, in the hardly less thoughtless mechanical determinism, which in words denies chance in general, only to recognize it in practice in each particular case.

While natural science continued to *think* in this way, what did it *do* in the person of Darwin?

Darwin, in his epoch-making work, set out from the widest existing basis of chance. Precisely the infinite, accidental differences between individuals within a single species, differences which become accentuated until they break through the character of the species, and whose immediate causes even can be demonstrated only in extremely few cases, compelled him to question the previous basis of all regularity in biology, viz., the concept of species in its previous metaphysical rigidity and unchangeability. Without the concept of species, however, all science was nothing. All its branches needed the concept of species as basis: human anatomy and comparative anatomy—embryology, zoology, palaeontology, botany, etc.—what were they without the concept of species? All their results were not only put in question but directly set aside. Chance overthrows necessity, as conceived hitherto.

[*Note in the margin of the manuscript*: "The material on chance occurrences accumulated in the meantime has suppressed and shattered the old idea of necessity."]

The previous idea of necessity breaks down. To retain it means dictatorially to impose on nature as a law a human arbitrary determination that is in contradiction to itself and to reality, it means to deny thereby all inner necessity in living nature, it means generally to proclaim the chaotic kingdom of chance to be the sole law of living nature.

* * *

Fragments on Hegel's *Logic* and *Phenomenology*:

> Nothing that is opposed to something, the *nothing of any something*, is a *determinate nothing*.

> In view of the mutually determinant connection of the (world) whole, metaphysics could make the assertion (*which is really a tautology*) that if the least grain of dust were destroyed the whole universe must collapse.

Negation, main passage, "Introduction":

> that the self-contradictory resolves itself not into nullity, into abstract Nothingness, but essentially only *into the negation of its particular content* [etc.]

Negation of the negation. Bud, flower, fruit, etc.[2]

* * *

B) Dialectical Logic and the Theory of Knowledge.

On the "Limits of Knowledge"

Unity of nature and mind. To the Greeks it was self-evident that nature could not be unreasonable, but even today the stupidest empiricists prove by their reasoning (however wrong it may be) that they are convinced from the outset that nature cannot be unreasonable or reason contrary to nature.

* * *

The development of a concept, or of a conceptual relation (positive and negative, cause and effect, substance and accidency) in the history of thought, is related to its development in the mind of the individual dialectician, just as the evolution of an organism in paleontology is related to its development in embryology (or rather, in history and in the single embryo). That this is so was first discovered for concepts by Hegel. In historical development, chance plays its part, which in dialectical thinking, as in the development of the embryo, *is summed up in necessity.*

* * *

Abstract and concrete. The general law of the change of form of motion is much more concrete than any single "concrete" example of it.

---

2 The reference is to the following passage from Hegel's *Preface to Phenomenology of Mind*: "The bud disappears when the blossom breaks through, and we might say that the former is refuted by the latter; in the same way, when the fruit comes the blossom may be explained to be a false form of the plant's existence, for the fruit appears as its true nature in place of the blossom."

* * *

Understanding and reason. This Hegelian distinction, according to which only dialectical thinking is reasonable, has a definite meaning. We have in common with animals all activity of the understanding: *induction, deduction*, and hence also *abstraction* (Dido's generic concepts: quadrupeds and bipeds), *analysis* of unknown objects (even the cracking of a nut is a beginning of analysis), *synthesis* (in animal tricks), and, as the union of both, *experiment* (in the case of new obstacles and unfamiliar situations). In their nature all these modes of procedure—hence all means of scientific investigation that ordinary logic recognizes—are absolutely the same in men and higher animals. They differ only in degree (of development of the method in each case). The basic features of the method are the same and lead to the same results in man and animals, so long as both operate or make shift, merely with these elementary methods.

On the other hand, dialectical thought—precisely because it presupposes investigations of the nature of concepts themselves—is only possible for man, and for him only at a comparatively high stage of development (Buddhists and Greeks), and it attains its full development much later still through modern philosophy—and yet we have the colossal results already among the Greeks which by far anticipate investigation!

* * *

On the classification of judgments

Dialectical logic, in contrast to the old, merely formal logic, is not, like the latter, content with enumerating the forms of motion of thought, i.e., the various forms of judgment and conclusion, and placing them side by side without any connection. On the contrary, it derives these forms out of one another, it makes one subordinate to another instead of putting them on an equal level, it develops the higher forms out of the lower. Faithful to his division of the whole of logic, Hegel groups judgments as:

1. Judgment of inherence, the simplest form of judgment, in which a general property is affirmatively or negatively predicated of a single thing (positive judgment: the rose is red; negative judgment: the rose is not blue; infinite judgment: the rose is not a camel);

2. Judgment of subsumption, in which a relation determination is predicated on the subject (singular judgment: this man is mortal;

particular judgment: some, many men are mortal; universal judgment: all men are mortal, or, man is mortal);

3. Judgment of necessity, in which its substantial determination is predicated on the subject (categorical judgment: the rose is a plant; hypothetical judgment: when the sun rises it is daytime; disjunctive judgment: *Lepidosiren* is either a fish or an amphibian);

4. Judgment of the notion, in which is predicated on the subject how far it corresponds to its general nature, or, as Hegel says, to the notion of it (assertoric judgment: this house is bad; problematic judgment: if a house is constituted in such and such a way, it is good; apodictic judgment: the house that is constituted in such and such a way is good.

1. *Individual Judgment.* 2 and 3. *Special.* 4. *General.*

However dry this sounds here, and however arbitrary at first sight this classification of judgments may here and there appear, yet the inner truth and necessity of this grouping will become clear to anyone who studies the brilliant exposition in Hegel's larger *Logic*. To show how much this grouping is based not only on the laws of thought but also on the laws of nature, we should like to put forward here a very well-known example outside this connection.

That friction produces heat was already known practically to prehistoric man, who discovered the making of fire by friction perhaps more than 100,000 years ago, and who still earlier warmed cold parts of the body by rubbing. But from that to the discovery that friction is in general a source of heat, who knows how many thousands of years elapsed? Enough that the time came when the human brain was sufficiently developed to be able to formulate the judgment: *friction is a source of heat*, a judgment of inherence, and indeed a positive one.

Still further thousands of years passed until, in 1842, Mayer, Joule, and Colding investigated this special process in its relation to other processes of a similar kind that had been discovered in the meantime, i.e., as regards its immediate general conditions, and formulated the judgment: *all mechanical motion is capable of being converted into heat by means of friction.* So much time and an enormous amount of empirical knowledge were required before we could make the advance in knowledge of the object from the above positive judgment of inherence to this universal judgment of subsumption.

But from now on things went quickly. Only three years later, Mayer was able, at least in substance, to raise the judgment of subsumption to the level at which it now stands: *any form of motion, under conditions fixed for each case, is both able and compelled to undergo transformation, indirectly, into any other form of motion*—a judgment of the notion, and moreover an apodictic one, the highest form of judgment altogether.

What, therefore, in Hegel appears as a development of the thought-form of judgment as such, confronts us here as the development of our *empirically* based theoretical knowledge of the nature of motion in general. This shows, however, that laws of thought and laws of nature are necessarily in agreement with one another if only they are correctly known.

We can regard the first judgment as that of individuality; the isolated fact that friction produces heat is registered. The second judgment is that of particularity: a special form of motion, mechanical motion, exhibits the property, under special conditions (through friction), of passing into another special form of motion, viz., heat. The third judgment is that of universality: any form of motion proves able and compelled to undergo transformation into any other form of motion. In this form the law attains its final expression. By new discoveries we can give new illustrations of it, we can give it a new and richer content. But we cannot add anything to the law itself as here formulated. In its universality, equally universal in form and content, it is not susceptible of further extension: it is an absolute law of nature.

Unfortunately we are in a difficulty about the form of motion of protein, alias life, so long as we are not able to make protein.

* * *

Individuality, particularity, universality—these are the three determinations in which the whole "Doctrine of the Notion" moves. Under these heads, progression from the individual to the particular and from the particular to the universal takes place, not in one, but in many modalities, and this is often enough exemplified by Hegel as the progression: individual, species, genus. And now the Haeckels come forward with their induction and trumpet it as a great fact—against Hegel—that progression must be from the individual to the particular and then to the universal (!), from the individual to the species and then to the genus—and then permit *deductive* conclusions which are supposed to lead further. These people have got into such a deadlock over the opposition between induction and deduction that they reduce all logical forms of conclusion to these two, and in so doing do not notice that they 1) unconsciously employ quite different forms of conclusion under those names; 2) deprive themselves of the whole wealth of forms of conclusion insofar as it cannot be forced under these two; and 3) thereby convert both forms, induction and deduction, into sheer nonsense.

* * *

Haeckel's nonsense: induction against deduction. As if it were not the case that deduction = conclusion, and therefore, induction is also a deduction. This comes from polarization. Haeckel's *Genesis*. The conclusion polarized into induction and deduction!

* * *

By induction it was discovered 100 years ago that crayfish and spiders were insects and all lower animals were worms. By induction it has now been found that this is nonsense and there exist x classes. Wherein then lies the advantage of the so-called inductive conclusion, which can be just as false as the so-called deductive conclusion, the basis of which is nevertheless classification?

Induction can never prove that there will never be a mammal without lacteal glands. Formerly nipples were the mark of a mammal. But the platypus has none.

The whole swindle of induction [is derived] from the Englishmen; [William] Whewell, inductive sciences, comprising the purely mathematical [sciences], and so the antithesis to deduction invented. Logic, old or new, knows nothing of this. All forms of conclusion that start from the individual are experimental and based on experience, indeed the inductive conclusion even starts from UI–P [universal].

It is also characteristic of the thinking capacity of our natural scientists that Haeckel fanatically champions induction at the very moment when the *results* of induction—the classifications—are everywhere put in question (*Limulus* a spider, *Ascidia* a vertebrate or *chordate*, the *Dipnoi*, however, being fishes, in opposition to all original definitions of amphibia), and daily new facts are being discovered which overthrow the *entire* previous classification by induction. What a beautiful confirmation of Hegel's thesis that the inductive conclusion is essentially a problematic one! Indeed, owing to the theory of evolution, even the whole classification of organisms has been taken away from induction and brought back to "deduction," to descent—one species being literally *deduced* from another by descent—and it is impossible to prove the theory of evolution by induction alone, since it is quite anti-inductive. The concepts with which induction operates: species, genus, class, have been rendered fluid by the theory of evolution and so have become *relative*—but one cannot use relative concepts for induction.

* * *

To the Pan-Inductionists. [i.e., to those who regard induction as the only correct method.] With all the induction in the world we would never have got to the point of becoming clear about the *process* of induction. Only the *analysis* of this process could accomplish this. Induction and deduction belong together as necessarily as synthesis and analysis. [Note in the margin: "Chemistry, in which *analysis* is the predominant form of investigation, is nothing without its opposite—*synthesis*.] Instead of one-sidedly lauding one to the skies at the expense of the other, we should seek to apply each of them in its place, and that can only be done by bearing in mind that they belong together, that they supplement each other.

According to the inductionists, induction is an infallible method. It is so little so that its apparently surest results are every day overthrown by new discoveries. "Light corpuscles" and "caloric" were results of induction. Where are they now? Induction taught us that all vertebrates have a central nervous system differentiated into brain and spinal cord, and that the spinal cord is enclosed in cartilaginous or bony vertebrae—whence, indeed, the name is derived. Then *Amphioxus* was revealed as a vertebrate with an undifferentiated central nervous strand and *without* vertebrae. Induction established that fishes are those vertebrates which throughout life breathe exclusively by means of gills. Then animals come to light whose fish character is almost universally recognized, but which, besides gills, have also well-developed lungs, and it turns out that every fish carries a potential lung in the swim bladder. Only by audacious application of the theory of evolution did Haeckel rescue the inductionists, who were feeling quite comfortable in these contradictions.

If induction were really so infallible, whence come the rapid successive revolutions in classification of the organic world? They are the most characteristic product of induction, and yet they annihilate one another.

* * *

Induction and analysis. A striking example of how little induction can claim to be the sole or even the predominant form of scientific discovery occurs in thermodynamics: the steam engine provided the most striking proof that one can impart heat and obtain mechanical motion. 100,000 steam engines did not prove this more than *one*, but only more and more forced the physicists into the necessity of explaining it. Sadi Carnot was the first seriously to set about the task. But not by induction. He studied the steam engine, analyzed it, and found that in it the process which mattered does not appear in *pure form* but is concealed by all sorts of subsidiary processes. He did away with these subsidiary circumstances that have no bearing on the essential process, and an ideal steam engine (or gas engine), which it is true, is as little capable of being realized as, for instance, a geometrical line or surface, but in its way performs the same service as these mathematical abstractions: it presents the process in a pure, independent, and unadulterated form. And he came right up against the mechanical equivalent of heat (see the significance of his function C), which he only failed to discover and see because he believed in *caloric*. Here also proof of the damage done by false theories.

* * *

The empiricism of observation alone can never adequately prove necessity. *Post hoc* [after this] but not *propter hoc* [because of this] (Hegel, *Encyclopedia*). This is so very correct that it does not follow from the continual rising of the sun in the morning that it will rise again tomorrow, and in fact we know now that a time will come when one morning the sun will *not rise*. But the proof of necessity lies in human activity, in experiment, in work: if I am able to *make* the *post hoc*, it becomes identical with the *propter hoc*.

* * *

Causality. The first thing that strikes us in considering matter in motion is the interconnection of the individual motions of separate bodies, their *being determined by* one another. But not only do we find that a particular motion is followed by another, we find also that we can evoke a particular motion by setting up the conditions in which it takes place in nature, that we can even produce motions which do not occur at all in nature (industry), at least not in this way, and that we can give these motions a predetermined direction and extent. *In this way*, by the activity of human beings the idea of causality becomes established, the idea that one motion is the cause of another. True, the regular sequence of certain natural phenomena can by itself give rise to the idea of causality: the heat and light that come with the sun; but this affords no proof, and to that extent Hume's skepticism was correct in saying that a regular *post hoc* can never establish a *propter hoc*. But the activity of human beings *forms the test* of causality. If we bring the sun's rays to a focus by means of a concave mirror and make them act like the rays of an ordinary fire, we thereby prove that heat comes from the sun. If we bring together in a rifle the priming, the explosive charge, and the bullet, and then fire it, we count upon the effect known in advance from previous experience, because we can follow in all its details the whole process of ignition, combustion, explosion by the sudden conversion into gas and pressure of the gas on the bullet. And here the skeptic cannot even say that because of previous experience it does not follow that it will be the same next time. For, as a matter of fact, it does sometimes happen that it is not the same, that the priming or the gunpowder fails to work, that the barrel bursts, etc. But surely this *proves* causality instead of refuting it, because we can find out the cause of each such deviation from the rule by appropriate investigation: chemical decomposition of the priming, dampness, etc., of the gunpowder, defect in the barrel, etc., etc., so that here the test of causality is, so to say, a *double* one.

Natural science, like philosophy, has hitherto entirely neglected the influence of activity on their thought; both know only nature on the one hand and thought on the other. But it is precisely *the alteration of nature* by men, not solely nature as such, which is the most essential and immediate basis of human thought, and it is in the measure that man has learned to change nature that his intelligence has increased.

The naturalistic conception of history, as found, for instance, to a greater or lesser extent in Draper and other scientists, as if nature exclusively reacts on man, and natural conditions everywhere exclusively determined his historical development, is therefore one-sided and forgets that man also reacts on nature, changing it and creating new conditions of existence for himself. There is devilishly little left of "nature" as it was in Germany at the time when the Germanic peoples immigrated into it. The earth's surface, climate, vegetation, fauna, and the human beings themselves have infinitely changed, and all this owing to human activity, while the changes of nature in Germany which have occurred in this period of time without human interference are incalculably small.

* * *

Reciprocal action is the first thing that we encounter when we consider matter in motion as a whole from the standpoint of modern natural science. We see a series of forms of motion, mechanical motion, heat, light, electricity, magnetism, chemical union and decomposition, transitions of states of aggregation, organic life, all of which, if *at present* we *still* make an exception of organic life, pass into one another, mutually determine one another, are in one place cause and in another effect, the sum total of the motion in all its changing forms remaining the same (Spinoza: substance is *causa sui* [cause of itself] strikingly expresses the reciprocal action). Mechanical motion becomes transformed into heat, electricity, magnetism, light, etc., and vice versa. Thus, natural science confirms what Hegel has said (where?), that reciprocal action is the true *causa finalis* [final cause]of things. We cannot go back further than to knowledge of this reciprocal action, for the very reason that there is nothing behind to know. If we know the forms of motion of matter (for which it is true there is still very much lacking, in view of the short time that natural science has existed), then we know matter itself, and therewith our knowledge is complete. (Grove's whole misunderstanding about causality rests on the fact that he does not succeed in arriving at the category of reciprocal action; he has the thing, but not the abstract thought, and hence the confusion.) Only from this universal reciprocal action do we arrive at the real causal relation. In order to understand the separate phenomena, we have to tear them out of the general interconnection and consider them in isolation, and then the changing motions appear, one as cause and the other as effect.

* * *

For one who denies causality every natural law is a hypothesis, among others also the chemical analysis of heavenly bodies by means of the prismatic spectrum. What shallowness of thought to remain at such a viewpoint!

* * *

On [Carl] Nägeli's incapacity to know the infinite

Nägeli first of all says that we cannot know real qualitative differences, and immediately afterwards says that such "absolute differences" do not occur in nature!

Firstly, every quality has infinitely many quantitative gradations, e.g., shades of color, hardness and softness, length of life, etc., and these, although qualitatively distinct, are measurable and knowable.

Secondly, qualities do not exist, but only things *with* qualities, and indeed, with infinitely many qualities. Two different things always have certain qualities (properties of corporeality at least) in common, others differing in degree, while still others may be entirely absent in one of them. If we consider two such extremely different things—e.g., a meteorite and a man—in separation, we get very little out of it, at most that heaviness and other general properties of bodies are common to both. But an infinite series of other natural objects and natural processes can be put between the two things, permitting us to complete the series from meteorite to man and to allocate to each its place in the interconnection of nature and thus to *know* them. Nägeli himself admits this..

Thirdly, our various senses might give us impressions differing absolutely as regards quality. In that case, properties which we experience by means of sight, hearing, smell, taste, and touch would be absolutely different. But even here the differences disappear with the progress of investigation. Smell and taste have long ago been recognized as allied senses belonging together, which perceive conjoint if not identical properties. Sight and hearing both perceive wave oscillations. Touch and sight supplement each other to such an extent that from the appearance of an object we can often enough predict its tactile properties. And, finally, it is always the same "*I*" that receives and elaborates all these different sense impressions, that therefore comprehends them into a unity, and likewise these various impressions are provided by the same thing, appearing as its *common* properties, and therefore, helping us to know it.

To explain these different properties accessible only to different senses, to bring them into connection with one another, is precisely the task of science, which so far has not complained because we have not a general sense in place of the five special senses, or because we are not able to see or hear tastes and smells.

Wherever we look, nowhere in nature are there to be found such "qualitatively or absolutely distinct fields," which are alleged to be incomprehensible. The whole confusion springs from the confusion about quality and quantity. In accordance with the prevailing mechanical view, Nägeli regards all qualitative differences as explained only insofar as they can be reduced to quantitative differences (on which what is necessary is said elsewhere), or because quality and quantity are for him absolutely distinct categories. Metaphysics.

We can know *only the finite* [etc.]

This is quite correct insofar as only finite objects enter the sphere of our knowledge. But the proposition needs to be supplemented by this: "fundamentally we can know *only the infinite*." In fact all real, exhaustive knowledge consists solely in raising the individual thing in thought from individuality into particularity and from this into universality, in seeking and establishing the infinite in the finite, the eternal in the transitory. The form of universality, however, is the form of self-completeness, hence of infinity; it is the comprehension of the many finites in the infinite. We know that chlorine and hydrogen, within certain limits of temperature and pressure, and under the influence of light, combine with an explosion to form hydrochloric acid gas, and as soon as we know this, we know also, that this takes place *everywhere* and *at all times* where the above conditions are present, and it can be a matter of indifference, whether this occurs once or is repeated a million times, or on how many heavenly bodies. The form of universality in nature is *law*, and no one talks more of *the eternal character of the laws of nature* than the natural scientists. Hence when Nägeli says that the finite is made impossible to understand by not desiring to investigate merely this finite, but instead adding something eternal to it, then he denies either the possibility of knowing the laws of nature or their eternal character. All true knowledge of nature is knowledge of the eternal, the infinite, and hence essentially absolute.

But this absolute knowledge has an important drawback. Just as the infinity of knowable matter is composed of the purely finite things, so the infinity of the thought which knows the absolute is composed of an infinite number of finite human minds, working side by side and successively at this infinite knowledge, committing practical and theoretical blunders, setting out from erroneous, one-sided, and false premises, pursuing false, tortuous, and uncertain paths, and often not even finding what is right when they run their noses against it (Priestley). The cognition of the infinite is therefore beset with double difficulty and from its very nature can only take place in an infinite asymptotic progress. And that fully suffices us in order to be able to say: the infinite is just as much knowable as unknowable, and that is all that we need.

Curiously enough, Nägeli says the same thing:

> We can know only the finite, but we can know *all the finite* that comes into the sphere of our sensuous perception.

The finite that comes into the sphere, etc., constitutes in sum precisely the infinite, for *it is just from this that Nägeli has derived his idea of the infinite!* Without this finite, etc., he would have indeed no idea of the infinite!

* * *

Before this investigation of infinity comes the following:

1. The "insignificant sphere" in regard to space and time.

2. The "probably defective development of the sense organs."

3. That we "only know the finite, changing, transitory, only what is different in degree and relative, because we can only transfer mathematical concepts to natural objects and judge the latter only by measures obtained from them themselves. We have no notions for all that is infinite or eternal, for all that is permanent, for all absolute differences. We know exactly the meaning of an hour, a meter, a kilogram, but we do not know what time, space, force and matter, motion and rest, cause and effect are."

It is the old story. First of all, one makes sensuous things into abstractions, and then one wants to know them through the senses, to see time and smell space. The empiricist becomes so steeped in the habit of empirical experience, that he believes that he is still in the field of sensuous experience when he is operating with abstractions. We know what an hour is, or a meter, but not what time and space are! As if time was anything other than just hours, and space anything but just cubic meters!

The two forms of existence of matter are naturally nothing without matter, empty concepts, abstractions which exist only in our minds. But, of course, we are supposed not to know what matter and motion are! Of course not, for matter as such and motion as such have not yet been seen or otherwise experienced by anyone, only the various existing material things and forms of motions. Matter is nothing but the totality of material things from which this concept is abstracted, and motion as such, nothing but the totality of all sensuously perceptible forms of motion; words like matter and motion are nothing but *abbreviations* in which we comprehend many different sensuous perceptible things according to their common properties. Hence, matter and motion can be known in no other way than by investigation of the separate material things and forms of motion, and by knowing these, we also *pro tanto* [to that extent] know matter and motion *as such*. Consequently, in saying that we do not know what time, space, matter, motion, cause, and effect are, Nägeli merely says that first of all we make abstractions of the real world through our minds, and then cannot know these self-made abstractions because they are creations of thought and not sensuous objects, while all knowing is *sensuous measurement*! This is just like the difficulty mentioned by Hegel; we can eat cherries and plums, but not *fruit*, because no one has so far eaten fruit as such.[3]

* * *

When Nägeli asserts that there are probably a whole number of forms of motion in nature which we cannot perceive by our senses, that is a poor apology, equivalent to the suspension—at least *for our knowledge*—of the law of the uncreatability of motion. For they could certainly be *transformed into motion perceptible to us*! That would be an easy explanation of, for instance, contact electricity.

* * *

---

3 Cf. Hegel, *Encyclopedia of the Philosophical Sciences*, § 13, Note: "When the universal is made a mere form and coordinated with the particular, it sinks into a particular itself. Even common sense in everyday matters is above the absurdity of setting a universal beside the particulars. Would any one, who wished for fruit, reject cherries, pears, and grapes, on the ground that they were cherries, pears, or grapes, and not fruit?"

Ad vocem [the voice of] Nägeli. Impossibility of conceiving the infinite. When we say that matter and motion are not created and are indestructible, we are saying that the world exists as infinite progress, i.e., in the form of bad infinity, and thereby we have understood all of this process that is to be understood. At the most the question still arises whether this process is an eternal repetition—in great cycles—or whether the cycles have descending and ascending branches.

* * *

Bad infinity. True infinity was already correctly put by Hegel in *filled* space and time, in the process of nature and in history. The whole of nature also is now merged in history, and history is only differentiated from natural history as the evolutionary process of *self-conscious* organisms. This infinite complexity of nature and history has within it the infinity of space and time—bad infinity—only as a sublated factor, essential but not predominant. The extreme limit of our natural science until now has been our universe, and we do not need the infinitely numerous universes outside it to have knowledge of nature. Indeed, only a *single* sun among millions, with its solar system, forms the essential basis of our astronomical researches. For terrestrial mechanics, physics, and chemistry we are more or less restricted to our little earth, and for organic science entirely so. Yet this does not do any essential injury to the practically infinite diversity of phenomena and natural knowledge, any more than history is harmed by the similar, even greater limitation to a comparatively short period and small portion of the earth.

* * *

1. According to Hegel, infinite progress is a barren waste because it appears only as *eternal repetition of the same thing*: 1+1+1, etc.

2. In reality, however, it is no repetition, but a development, an advance or regression, and thereby it becomes a necessary form of motion. This, apart from the fact that it is not infinite: the end of the earth's lifetime can already be foreseen. But then, the earth is not the whole universe. In Hegel's system, any development was excluded from the temporal history of nature, otherwise nature would not be the being-beyond-self of spirit. But in human history infinite progress is recognized by Hegel as the sole true form of existence of "spirit," except

that fantastically this development is assumed to have an end—in the production of the Hegelian philosophy.

3. There is also infinite knowing (*Quantity.* Astronomy): *questo infinito che le cose non hanno in progresso, hanno in giro.* [this infinite, which things do not have in progress, they have in circling.] Thus the law of the change of form of motion is an infinite one, including itself in itself. Such infinities, however, are in their turn smitten with finiteness, and only occur piecemeal. So also $1/r^2$.

* * *

The eternal laws of nature also become transformed more and more into historical ones. That water is fluid from 0°–100°C is an eternal law of nature, but for it to be valid, there must be 1) water, 2) the given temperature, 3) normal [atmospheric] pressure. On the moon there is no water, in the sun only its elements, and the law does not exist for these two heavenly bodies.

The laws of meteorology are also eternal, but only for the earth, or for a body of the size, density, axial inclination, and temperature of the earth, and on condition that it has an atmosphere of the same mixture of oxygen and nitrogen and with the same amounts of water vapor being evaporated and precipitated. The moon has no atmosphere, the sun one of glowing metallic vapors; the former has no meteorology, that of the latter is quite different from ours.

Our whole official physics, chemistry, and biology are exclusively geocentric calculated only for the earth. We are still quite ignorant of the conditions of electric and magnetic tensions on the sun, fixed stars, and nebulae, even on the planets of a different density from ours. On the sun, owing to high temperature, the laws of chemical combination of the elements are suspended or only momentarily operative at the limits of the solar atmosphere, the compounds becoming dissociated again on approaching the sun. The chemistry of the sun is just in process of arising, and is necessarily quite different from that of the earth, not overthrowing the latter but standing outside it. In the nebulae, perhaps, there do not exist even those of the 65 elements which are possibly themselves of compound nature. Hence, if we wish to speak of general laws of nature that are uniformly applicable to *all* bodies—from the nebula to man—we are left only with gravity and perhaps the most general form of the theory of the transformation of energy, *vulgo*, the mechanical theory of heat. But, on its general, consistent application to all phenomena of nature, this theory itself becomes converted into a historical presentation of the successive changes occurring in a system of the universe from its origin to its passing away, hence into a history in which at each stage different laws, i.e., different phenomenal forms of the same universal motion, predominate, and so nothing remains as absolutely universally valid except—*motion*.

* * *

The *geocentric* standpoint in astronomy is prejudiced and has rightly been abolished. But as we go deeper in our investigations, it comes more and more into its own. The sun, etc., *serve* the earth (Hegel, *Philosophy of Nature*). (The whole huge sun exists merely for the sake of the little planets.) Anything other than geocentric physics, chemistry, biology, meteorology, etc., is impossible for us, and these sciences lose nothing by saying that they only hold good for the earth and are therefore only relative. If one takes that seriously and demands a centerless science, one puts a stop to *all* science. It suffices us to know that under the same conditions everywhere the same must take place, at a distance to the right or the left of us that is a trillion times as great as the distance from the earth to the sun.

* * *

Cognition. Ants have eyes different from ours, they can see chemical (?) light rays (*Nature*, June 8, 1882, Lubbock), but as regards knowledge of these rays that are invisible to, us, we are considerably more advanced than the ants, and the very fact that we are able to demonstrate *that* ants can see things invisible to us, and that this proof is based solely on perceptions made with *our* eyes, shows that the special construction of the human eye sets no absolute barrier to human cognition.

In addition to the eye, we have not only the other senses but also our thought activity. With regard to the latter, matters stand exactly as with the eye. To know what can be discovered by our thinking, it is no use, a hundred years after Kant, to try and find out the range of thought from the critique of reason or the investigation of the instrument of knowing. It is as little use as when Helmholtz uses the imperfection of our sight (indeed a necessary imperfection, for an eye that could see all rays would for that very reason see *nothing at all*), and the construction of our eye—which restricts sight to definite limits and even so does not give quite correct reproduction—as proof that the eye acquaints us incorrectly or unreliably with the nature of what is seen. What can be discovered by our thought is more evident from what it has already discovered and is every day still discovering. And that is already enough both as regards quantity and quality. On the other hand, the investigation of the *forms* of thought, the thought determinations, is very profitable and necessary, and since Aristotle this has been systematically undertaken only by Hegel.

In any case, we shall never find out *how* chemical rays appear to ants. Anyone who is distressed by this is simply beyond help.

* * *

The form of development of natural science, insofar as it thinks, is the *hypothesis*. A new fact is observed which makes impossible the previous method of explaining the facts belonging to the same group. From this moment onwards new methods of explanation are required—at first based on only a limited number of facts and observations. Further observational material weeds out these hypotheses, doing away with some and correcting others, until finally the law is established in a pure form. If one should wait until the material for a law was *in a pure form*, it would mean suspending the process of thought in investigation until then, and, if only for this reason, the law would never come into being.

The number and succession of hypotheses supplanting one another—given the lack of logical and dialectical education among natural scientists—easily gives rise to the idea that we cannot know the essence of things (Haller and Goethe). This is not peculiar to natural science, since all human knowledge develops in a much-twisted curve; and in the historical sciences also, including philosophy, theories displace one another, from which, however, nobody concludes that formal logic, for instance, is nonsense.

The last form of this outlook is the "thing-in-itself." In the first place, this assertion that we cannot know the thing-in-itself (Hegel, *Encyclopedia*) passes out of the realm of science into that of fantasy. Secondly, it does not add a word to our scientific knowledge, for if we cannot occupy ourselves with things, they do not exist for us. And, thirdly, it is a mere phrase and is never applied. Taken in the abstract it sounds quite sensible. But suppose one applies it. What would one think of a zoologist who said: "A dog *seems* to have four legs, but we do not know whether in reality it has four million legs or none at all"? Or of a mathematician who first of all defines a triangle as having three sides, and then declares that he does not know whether it might not have 25? That 2×2 *seems* to be 4? But scientists take care not to apply the phrase about the thing-in-itself in natural science, they permit themselves this only when passing into philosophy. This is the best proof of how little seriously they take it and what little value it has itself. If they did take it seriously, what would be the good of investigating anything?

Taken historically, the thing would have a certain meaning: we can only know under the conditions of our epoch and *as far as these allow*.

* * *

The thing-in-itself: Hegel, *Logic*, also later a whole section on it:

> Skepticism did not dare to affirm *it is*; modern idealism (i.e., Kant and Fichte) did not dare to regard cognition as a knowledge of the thing-in-itself . . . But at the same time, skepticism admitted manifold determinations of its show, or rather its show had for content all the manifold riches of the world. In the same manner the *appearance* of idealism (i.e., what idealism calls appearance) comprehends the whole range of these manifold determinatenesses . . . The content may then have no basis in any being nor in any thing nor thing-in-itself: *for itself it remains as it is; it has only been translated from being into show.*

Hegel, therefore, is here a much more resolute materialist than the modern natural scientists.

* * *

Valuable self-criticism of the Kantian *thing-in-itself*, which shows that Kant suffers shipwreck also on the thinking ego and likewise discovers in it an unknowable thing-in-itself (Hegel).

CRITIQUE OF HEGEL'S DIALECTIC AND PHILOSOPHY AS A WHOLE

(AN EXCERPT FROM THE THIRD OF MARX'S ECONOMIC AND PHILOSOPHIC MANUSCRIPTS OF 1844)

Karl Marx

Written between April and August of 1844, Marx's manuscripts were not published in the Soviet Union until 1932, and not in English until 1959. In these early notes—written some four years before the Communist Manifesto—*the outline of Marx's core ideas is already evident. Taking up everything from property relations to the alienation of labor, his critique of Hegel's philosophy represented a significant milestone in the emergence of scientific socialism, as Marx progressively extracted the "rational kernel" from Hegel's objective idealism and transformed it into dialectical materialism. These notes also serve as a useful introduction to Hegel's ideas for those who plan on diving directly into his dense but ultimately highly rewarding works.*

This is perhaps the place at which, by way of explanation and justification, we might offer some considerations in regard to the Hegelian dialectic generally and especially its exposition in the *Phenomenology* and *Logic* and also, lastly, the relation [to it] of the modern critical movement.

So powerful was modern German criticism's preoccupation with the past—so completely was its development entangled with the subject matter—that here prevailed a completely uncritical attitude to the method of criticizing, together with a complete lack of awareness about the *apparently formal*, but really vital question: how do we now stand as regards the Hegelian *dialectic*? This lack of awareness about the relationship of modern criticism to the Hegelian philosophy as a whole and especially to the Hegelian dialectic has been so great that critics like *Strauss* and *Bruno Bauer* still remain within the confines of the Hegelian logic; the former completely so and the latter at least implicitly so in his *Synoptiker*—where, in opposition to Strauss, he replaces the substance of "abstract nature" by the "self-consciousness" of abstract man—and even in *Christianity Exposed*. Thus, in *Christianity Exposed*, for example, you get:

> As though in positing the world, self-consciousness does not posit that which is different [from itself] and in what it is creating it does not create itself, since it in turn annuls the difference between what it has created and itself, since it itself has being only in creating and in the movement—as though its purpose were not this movement? [etc.; or again:] They [the French materialists] have not yet been able to see that it is only as the movement of self-consciousness that the movement of the universe has actually come to be for itself, and achieved unity with itself.

Such expressions do not even show any verbal divergence from the Hegelian approach, but on the contrary repeat it word for word.

How little consciousness there was in relation to the Hegelian dialectic during the act of criticism (Bauer, *The Synoptics*), and how little this consciousness came into being even after the act of material criticism, is proved by Bauer when, in his *The Good Cause of Freedom*, he dismisses the brash question put by Herr Gruppe—"What about logic now?"—by referring him to future critics.

But even now—now that *Feuerbach* both in his theses in the *Anekdota* and, in detail, in *Philosophy of the Future* has in principle overthrown the old dialectic and philosophy; now that that school of criticism, on the other hand, which was incapable of accomplishing this, has all the same seen it accomplished and has proclaimed itself pure, resolute, absolute criticism that has come into the clear with itself; now that this criticism, in its spiritual pride, has reduced the whole process of history to the relation between the rest of the world and itself—the rest of the world, in contrast to itself, falling under the category of "the masses"—and dissolved all dogmatic antitheses into the single dogmatic antithesis of its own cleverness and the stupidity of the world—the antithesis of the critical Christ and Mankind, the "*rabble*"; now that daily and hourly it has demonstrated its own excellence against the dullness of the masses; now, finally, that it has proclaimed the critical *Last Judgment* in the shape of an announcement that the day is approaching when the whole of decadent humanity will assemble before it and be sorted by it into groups, each particular mob receiving its *testimonium paupertatis* [proof of poverty]; now that it has made known in print its superiority to human feelings as well as its superiority to the world, over which it sits enthroned in sublime solitude, only letting fall from time to time from its sarcastic lips the ringing laughter of the Olympian Gods—even now, after all these delightful antics of idealism (i.e., of Young Hegelianism) expiring in the guise of criticism—even now it has not expressed the suspicion that the time was ripe for a critical settling of accounts with the mother of Young Hegelianism—the Hegelian dialectic—and even had nothing to say about its critical attitude towards the Feuerbachian dialectic. This shows a completely uncritical attitude to itself.

Feuerbach is the only one who has a *serious, critical* attitude to the Hegelian dialectic and who has made genuine discoveries in this field. He is in fact the true conqueror of the old philosophy. The extent of his achievement, and the unpretentious simplicity with which he, Feuerbach, gives it to the world, stand in striking contrast to the opposite attitude (of the others).

Feuerbach's great achievement is:

1. The proof that philosophy is nothing else but religion rendered into thought and expounded by thought, i.e., another form and manner of existence of the estrangement of the essence of man; hence equally to be condemned;
2. The establishment of *true materialism* and of *real science*, by making the social relationship of "man to man" the basic principle of the theory;
3. His opposing to the negation of the negation, which claims to be the absolute positive, the self-supporting positive, positively based on itself.

Feuerbach explains the Hegelian dialectic—and thereby justifies starting out from the positive facts which we know by the senses—as follows:

Hegel sets out from the estrangement of substance—in logic, from the infinite, abstractly universal—from the absolute and fixed abstraction; which means, put popularly, that he sets out from religion and theology.

Secondly, he annuls the infinite, and posits the actual, sensuous, real, finite, particular (philosophy, annulment of religion and theology).

Thirdly, he again annuls the positive and restores the abstraction, the infinite—restoration of religion and theology.

Feuerbach thus conceives the negation of the negation *only* as a contradiction of philosophy with itself—as the philosophy which affirms theology (the transcendent, etc.) after having denied it, and which it therefore affirms in opposition to itself.

The positive position or self-affirmation and self-confirmation contained in the negation of the negation is taken to be a position which is not yet sure of itself, which is therefore burdened with its opposite, which is doubtful of itself and therefore in need of proof, and which, therefore, is not a position demonstrating itself by its existence—not an acknowledged position; hence it is directly and immediately confronted by the position of sense-certainty based on itself. (Feuerbach also defines the negation of the negation, the definite concept, as thinking surpassing itself in thinking and as thinking wanting to be directly awareness, nature, reality.)

But because Hegel has conceived the negation of the negation, from the point of view of the positive relation inherent in it, as the true and only positive, and from the point of view of the negative relation inherent in it as the only true act and spontaneous activity of all being, he has only found the *abstract*, *logical*, *speculative* expression for the movement of history, which is not yet the *real* history of man as a given subject, but only the *act of creation*, the *history of the origin* of man.

We shall explain both the abstract form of this process and the difference between this process as it is in Hegel in contrast to modern criticism, in contrast to the same process in Feuerbach's *The Essence of Christianity*, or rather the *critical* form of this in Hegel still uncritical process.

Let us take a look at the Hegelian system. One must begin with Hegel's *Phenomenology*, the true point of origin and the secret of the Hegelian philosophy.

Phenomenology.

A. Self-consciousness.

I. *Consciousness*. a) Certainty at the level of sense-experience; or the "this" and *meaning*. b) *Perception*, or the thing with its properties, and *deception.* c) Force and understanding, appearance and the supersensible world.

II. *Self-consciousness.* The truth of certainty of self. a) Independence and dependence of self-consciousness; mastery and servitude. b) Freedom of self-consciousness. Stoicism, skepticism, the unhappy consciousness.

III. *Reason.* Reason's certainty and reason's truth. a) Observation as a process of reason. Observation of nature and of self-consciousness. b) Realization of rational self-consciousness through its own activity. Pleasure and necessity. The law of the heart and the insanity of self-conceit. Virtue and the course of the world. c) The individuality which is real in and for itself. The spiritual animal kingdom and the deception or the real fact. Reason as lawgiver. Reason which tests laws.

B. Mind.

I. *True* mind, ethics. **II.** Mind in self-estrangement, culture. **III.** Mind certain of itself, morality.

C. Religion. *Natural* religion; *religion of art; revealed* religion.

D. Absolute knowledge.

Hegel's *Encyclopedia*, beginning as it does with logic, with *pure speculative thought*, and ending with *absolute knowledge*—with the self-conscious, self-comprehending philosophic or absolute (i.e., superhuman) abstract mind—is in its entirety nothing but the *display*, the self-objectification, of the *essence* of the philosophic mind, and the philosophic mind is nothing but the estranged mind of the world thinking within its self-estrangement—i.e., comprehending itself abstractly.

Logic—mind's *coin of the realm*, the speculative or *mental value* of man and nature—its essence which has grown totally indifferent to all real determinateness, and hence unreal—is *alienated thinking*, and therefore thinking which abstracts from nature and from real man: *abstract thinking.*

Then: *The externality of this abstract thinking . . . nature*, as it is for this abstract thinking. Nature is external to it—its self-loss; and it apprehends nature also in an external fashion, as abstract thought, but as alienated abstract thinking. Finally, *mind*, this thinking returning home to its own point of origin—the thinking which as the anthropological, phenomenological, psychological, ethical, artistic and religious mind is not valid for itself, until ultimately it finds itself, and affirms itself, as *absolute* knowledge and hence absolute, i.e., abstract, mind, thus receiving its conscious embodiment in the mode of existence corresponding to it. For its real mode of existence is *abstraction*.

There is a double error in Hegel.

The first emerges most clearly in the *Phenomenology*, the birthplace of the Hegelian philosophy. When, for instance, wealth, state power, etc., are understood by Hegel as entities estranged from the *human* being, this only happens in their form as thoughts . . . They are thought-entities, and therefore merely an estrangement of *pure*, i.e., abstract, philosophical thinking. The whole process therefore ends with absolute knowledge. It is precisely abstract thought from which these objects are estranged and which they confront with their presumption of reality. The *philosopher*— who is himself an abstract form of estranged man—takes himself as the *criterion* of the estranged world. The whole *history of the alienation process* and the whole *process of the retraction* of the alienation is therefore nothing but the *history of the production* of abstract (i.e., absolute) thought—of logical, speculative thought. The *estrangement*, which therefore forms the real interest of the transcendence of this alienation, is the opposition of *in itself* and *for itself*, of *consciousness and self-consciousness*, of *object and subject*—that is to say, it is the opposition between abstract thinking and sensuous reality or real sensuousness within thought itself. All other oppositions and movements of these oppositions are but the *semblance*, the *cloak*, the *exoteric* shape of these oppositions which alone matter, and which constitute the *meaning* of these other, profane oppositions. It is not the fact that the human being objicifies himself *inhumanly*, in opposition to himself, but the fact that he objicifies himself in *distinction* from and in *opposition* to abstract thinking, that constitutes the posited essence of the estrangement and the thing to be superseded.

The appropriation of man's essential powers, which have become objects—indeed, alien objects—is thus, in the first place only an *appropriation* occurring in *consciousness*, in *pure thought*, i.e., in *abstraction*: it is the appropriation of these objects as *thoughts* and as *movements of thought*. Consequently, despite its thoroughly negative and critical appearance and despite the genuine criticism contained in it, which often anticipates far later development, there is already latent in the *Phenomenology* as a germ, a potentiality, a secret, the uncritical positivism and the equally uncritical idealism of Hegel's later works—that philosophic dissolution and restoration of the existing empirical world.

In the second place: the vindication of the objective world for man—for example, the realization that *sensuous* consciousness is not an *abstractly* sensuous consciousness but a *humanly* sensuous consciousness, that religion, wealth, etc., are but the estranged world of *human* objectification, of *man's* essential powers put to work and that they are therefore but the *path* to the true *human* world—this appropriation or the insight into this process appears in Hegel therefore in this form, that *sense, religion,* state power, etc., are *spiritual* entities; for only *mind* is the *true* essence of man, and the true form of mind is thinking mind, theological, speculative mind. The *human character* of nature and of the nature created by history— man's products—appears in the form that they are *products* of abstract mind and as such, therefore, phases of *mind—thought-entities.* The *Phenomenology* is, therefore, a hidden, mystifying and still uncertain criticism; but inasmuch as it depicts man's *estrangement,* even though man appears only as mind, there lie concealed in it *all* the elements of criticism, already *prepared* and *elaborated* in a manner often rising far above the Hegelian standpoint. The "unhappy consciousness," the "honest consciousness," the struggle of the "noble and base consciousness," etc., etc.—these separate sections contain, but still in an estranged form, the *critical* elements of whole spheres such as religion, the state, civil life, etc. Just as *entities, objects,* appear as thought-entities, so the *subject* is always *consciousness* or *self-consciousness*; or rather the object appears only as *abstract* consciousness, man only as *self-consciousness*: the distinct forms of estrangement which make their appearance are, therefore, only various forms of consciousness and self-consciousness. Just as *in itself* abstract consciousness—the form in which the object is conceived— is merely a moment of distinction of self-consciousness, what appears as the result of the movement is the identity of self-consciousness with consciousness (absolute knowledge) the movement of abstract thought no longer directed outwards but proceeding now only within its own self: that is to say, the dialectic of pure thought is the result.

The outstanding achievement of Hegel's *Phenomenology* and of its final outcome, the dialectic of negativity as the moving and generating principle, is thus first that Hegel conceives the self-creation of man as a process, conceives objectification as loss of the object, as alienation and as transcendence of this alienation; that he thus grasps the essence of *labor* and comprehends objective man—true, because real man—as the outcome of man's *own labor*. The *real, active* orientation of man to himself as a species-being, or his manifestation as a real species-being (i.e., as a human being), is only possible if he really brings out all his *species-powers*—something which in turn is only possible through the cooperative action of all of mankind, only as the result of history—and treats these powers as objects: and this, to begin with, is again only possible in the form of estrangement.

We shall now demonstrate in detail Hegel's one-sidedness and limitations as they are displayed in the final chapter of the *Phenomenology*, "Absolute Knowledge"—a chapter which contains the condensed spirit of the *Phenomenology*, the relationship of the *Phenomenology* to speculative dialectic, and also Hegel's *consciousness* concerning both and their relationship to one another.

Let us provisionally say just this much in advance: Hegel's standpoint is that of modern political economy. He grasps *labor* as the *essence* of man—as man's essence which stands the test: he sees only the positive, not the negative side of labor. Labor is *man's coming-to-be for himself* within *alienation*, or as *alienated* man. The only labor which Hegel knows and recognizes is *abstractly mental* labor. Therefore, that which constitutes the *essence* of philosophy—the *alienation of man who knows himself*, or *alienated* science *thinking itself*—Hegel grasps as its essence; and in contradistinction to previous philosophy he is therefore able to combine its separate aspects, and to present his philosophy as *the* philosophy. What the other philosophers did—that they grasped separate phases of nature and of abstract self-consciousness, namely, of human life as phases of self-consciousness—is *known* to Hegel as the *doings* of philosophy. Hence his science is absolute.

Let us now turn to our subject.

"Absolute Knowledge." The last chapter of the "Phenomenology."

The main point is that the *object of consciousness* is nothing else but *self-consciousness*, or that the object is only *objectified self-consciousness*—self-consciousness as object. (Positing of man = self-consciousness).

The issue, therefore, is to surmount the *object of consciousness*. *Objectivity* as such is regarded as an *estranged* human relationship which does not correspond to the *essence of man*, to self-consciousness. The *reappropriation* of the objective essence of man, produced within the orbit

of estrangement as something alien, therefore denotes not only the annulment of *estrangement*, but of *objectivity* as well. Man, that is to say, is
regarded as a *non-objective, spiritual* being.

The movement of *surmounting the object of consciousness* is now described by Hegel in the following way:

The *object* reveals itself not merely as *returning* into the *self*—this is
according to Hegel the *one-sided* way of apprehending this movement,
the grasping of only one side. Man is equated with self. The self, however, is only the *abstractly* conceived man—man created by abstraction.
Man *is* selfish. His eye, his ear, etc., are *selfish*. In him every one of his
essential powers has the quality of *selfhood*. But it is quite false to say
on that account "*self-consciousness* has eyes, ears, essential powers." *Self-
consciousness* is rather a quality of human nature, of the human eye, etc.;
it is not human nature that is a quality of *self-consciousness*.

The self-abstracted entity, fixed for itself, is man as *abstract egoist*—
egoism raised in its pure abstraction to the level of thought. (We shall
return to this point later.)

For Hegel the *human being—man*—equals *self-consciousness*. All estrangement of the human being is therefore *nothing* but *estrangement
of self-consciousness*. The estrangement of self-consciousness is not
regarded as an *expression*—reflected in the realm of knowledge and
thought—of the *real* estrangement of the human being. Instead, the *actual* estrangement—that which appears real—is according to its *inner-
most*, hidden nature (which is only brought to light by philosophy) nothing but the *manifestation* of the estrangement of the real human essence,
of *self-consciousness*. The science which comprehends this is therefore
called *phenomenology*. All reappropriation of the estranged objective essence appears therefore, as incorporation into self-consciousness: The
man who takes hold of his essential being is *merely* the self-consciousness which takes hold of objective essences. Return of the object into the
self is therefore the reappropriation of the object.

Expressed in *all its aspects*, the *surmounting of the object of consciousness* means:

1. That the object as such presents itself to consciousness as something vanishing.

2. That it is the alienation of self-consciousness which posits
   thinghood.

3. That this alienation has, not merely a *negative* but a *positive* significance.

4. That it has this meaning not merely *for us* or intrinsically, but *for self-consciousness itself.*

5. *For self-consciousness*, the negative of the object, or its annulling of itself, has *positive* significance—or it *knows* this futility of the object—because of the fact that it alienates itself, for in this alienation it posits *itself* as object, or, for the sake of the indivisible unity of *being-for-self*, posits the object as itself.

6. On the other hand, this contains likewise the other moment, that self-consciousness has also just as much superseded this alienation and objectivity and resumed them into itself, being thus *at home* in *its* other-being *as such.*

7. This is the movement of consciousness and this is therefore the totality of its moments.

8. Consciousness must similarly be related to the object in the totality of its determinations and have comprehended it in terms of each of them. This totality of its determinations makes the object *intrinsically a spiritual being*; and it becomes so in truth for consciousness through the apprehending of each one of the determinations as *self*, or through what was called above the *spiritual* attitude to them.

As to 1): That the object as such presents itself to consciousness as something vanishing—this is the above-mentioned *return of the object into the self.*

As to 2): The *alienation of self-consciousness* posits *thinghood.* Because man equals self-consciousness, his alienated, objective essence, or *thinghood*, equals *alienated self-consciousness*, and *thinghood* is thus posited through this alienation (thinghood being *that* which is an *object for man* and an object for him is really only that which is to him an essential object, therefore his *objective* essence. And since it is not *real man*, nor therefore *nature*—man being *human nature*—who as such is made the subject, but only the abstraction of man—self-consciousness—thinghood cannot be anything but alienated self-consciousness). It is only to be expected that a living, natural being equipped and endowed with objective (i.e., material) essential powers should have real natural objects of his essence; and that his self-alienation should lead to the positing of a *real*, objective world, but within the framework of *externality*, and, therefore, an overwhelming world not belonging to his own essential being. There is nothing incomprehensible or mysterious in this. It would be mysterious, rather, if it were otherwise. But it is equally clear that a *self-consciousness* by its alienation can posit only *thinghood*, i.e., only an abstract thing, a thing of abstraction and not a *real* thing. It is clear, further, that thinghood is therefore utterly without any *independence*, any *essentiality* vis-à-vis self-consciousness; that on the contrary it is a mere creature—something *posited* by self-consciousness. And what is posited, instead of confirming itself, is but confirmation of the act of positing which for a moment fixes its energy as the product, and gives it the *semblance*—but only for a moment—of an independent, real substance.

Whenever real, corporeal *man*, man with his feet firmly on the solid ground, man exhaling and inhaling all the forces of nature, *posits* his real, objective *essential powers* as alien objects by his externalization, it is not the *act of positing* which is the subject in this process: it is the subjectivity of *objective* essential powers, whose action, therefore, must also be something objective. An objective being acts objectively, and he would not act objectively if the objective did not reside in the very nature of his being. He only creates or posits objects, because he is posited by objects—because at bottom he is *nature*. In the act of positing, therefore, this objective being does not fall from his state of "pure activity" into *a creating of the object*; on the contrary, his *objective* product only confirms his *objective* activity, his activity as the activity of an objective, natural being.

Here we see how consistent naturalism or humanism is distinct from both idealism and materialism, and constitutes at the same time the unifying truth of both. We see also how only naturalism is capable of comprehending the action of world history.

Man is directly a *natural being*. As a natural being and as a living natural being he is on the one hand endowed with *natural powers, vital powers*—he is an *active* natural being. These forces exist in him as tendencies and abilities—as *instincts*. On the other hand, as a natural, corporeal, sensuous objective being he is a *suffering*, conditioned, and limited creature, like animals and plants. That is to say, the *objects* of his instincts exist outside him, as *objects* independent of him; yet these objects are *objects* that he *needs*—essential *objects*, indispensable to the manifestation and confirmation of his essential powers. To say that man is a *corporeal*, living, real, sensuous, objective being full of natural vigor is to say that he has *real, sensuous objects* as the object of his being or of his life, or that he can only *express* his life in real, sensuous objects. *To be* objective, natural and sensuous, and at the same time to have object, nature and sense outside oneself, or oneself to be object, nature, and sense for a third party, is one and the same thing.

Hunger is a natural *need*; it therefore needs a *nature* outside itself, an *object* outside itself, in order to satisfy itself, to be stilled. Hunger is an acknowledged need of my body for an *object* existing outside it, indispensable to its integration and to the expression of its essential being. The sun is the *object* of the plant—an indispensable object to it, confirming its life—just as the plant is an object of the sun, being an *expression* of the life-awakening power of the sun, of the sun's *objective* essential power.

A being which does not have its nature outside itself is not a *natural* being, and plays no part in the system of nature. A being which has no object outside itself is not an objective being. A being which is not itself an object for some third being has no being for its *object*; i.e., it is not objectively related. Its being is not objective.

A non-objective being is a *non-being*.

Suppose a being which is neither an object itself, nor has an object. Such a being, in the first place, would be the *unique* being: there would exist no being outside it —it would exist solitary and alone. For as soon as there are objects outside me, as soon as I am not *alone*, I am *another— another reality* than the object outside me. For this third object I am thus a *different reality* than itself; that is, I am *its* object. Thus, to suppose a being which is not the object of another being is to presuppose that *no* objective being exists. As soon as I have an object, this object has me for an object. But a *non-objective* being is an unreal, non-sensuous thing—a product of mere thought (i.e., of mere imagination)—an abstraction. To be *sensuous*, that is, to be really existing, means to be an object of sense, to be a *sensuous* object, to have sensuous objects outside oneself—objects of one's sensuousness. To be sensuous is to *suffer*.

Man as an objective, sensuous being is therefore a *suffering* being— and because he feels that he suffers, a *passionate* being. Passion is the essential power of man energetically bent on its object.

But man is not merely a natural being: he is a *human* natural being. That is to say, he is a being for himself. Therefore he is a *species-being*, and has to confirm and manifest himself as such both in his being and in his knowing. Therefore, *human* objects are not natural objects as they immediately present themselves, and neither is *human sense* as it immediately *is*—as it is objectively—*human* sensibility, human objectivity. Neither nature objectively nor nature subjectively is directly given in a form adequate to the *human* being. And as everything natural has to *come into being, man* too has his act of origin—*history*—which, however, is for him a known history, and hence as an act of origin it is a conscious self-transcending act of origin. History is the true natural history of man (on which more later).

Thirdly, because this positing of thinghood is itself only an illusion, an act contradicting the nature of pure activity, it has to be cancelled again and thinghood denied.

Re: 3, 4, 5 and 6. 3) This externalization of consciousness has not merely a *negative* but a *positive* significance, and 4) it has this meaning not merely *for us* or intrinsically, but for consciousness itself. *For consciousness* the negative of the object, its annulling of itself, has *positive* significance—i.e., consciousness *knows* this nullity of the object—because it alienates *itself*; for, in this alienation it *knows* itself as object, or, for the sake of the indivisible unity of *being-for-itself*, the object as itself. 6) On the other hand, there is also this other moment in the process, that consciousness has also just as much superseded this alienation and objectivity and resumed them into itself, being thus *at home* in its *other-being as such.*

As we have already seen, the appropriation of what is estranged and objective, or the annulling of objectivity in the form of *estrangement* (which has to advance from indifferent strangeness to real, antagonistic estrangement), means likewise or even primarily for Hegel that it is *objectivity* which is to be annulled, because it is not the *determinate* character of the object, but rather its *objective* character that is offensive and constitutes estrangement for self-consciousness. The object is therefore something negative, self-annulling—a *nullity*. This nullity of the object has not only a negative but a *positive* meaning for consciousness, since this nullity of the object is precisely the *self-confirmation* of the non-objectivity, of the *abstraction* of itself. For *consciousness itself* the nullity of the object has a positive meaning because it *knows* this nullity, the objective being, as *its self-alienation*; because it knows that it exists only as a result of its own self-alienation. . .

The way in which consciousness is, and in which something is for it, is *knowing*. Knowing is its sole act. Something therefore comes to be for consciousness insofar as the latter *knows* this *something*. Knowing is its sole objective relation.

It, consciousness, then, knows the nullity of the object (i.e., knows the non-existence of the distinction between the object and itself, the non-existence of the object for it) because it knows the object as its *self-alienation*; that is, it knows itself—knows knowing as object—because the object is only the *semblance* of an object, a piece of mystification, which in its essence, however, is nothing else but knowing itself, which has confronted itself with itself and hence has confronted itself with a *nullity*—a something which has *no* objectivity outside the knowing. Or: knowing knows that in relating itself to an object it is only *outside* itself—that it only externalizes itself; that *it itself* only *appears* to itself as an object—or that that which appears to it as an object is only itself.

On the other hand, says Hegel, there is here at the same time this other moment, that consciousness has just as much annulled and reabsorbed this externalization and objectivity, being thus *at home* in its *other-being as such*.

In this discussion all the illusions of speculation are brought together.

First of all: consciousness, self-consciousness, is *at home* in its *other-being as such*. It is therefore—or if we here abstract from the Hegelian abstraction and put the self-consciousness of man instead of self-consciousness—it is *at home* in its *other-being as such*. This implies, for one thing, that consciousness (knowing as knowing, thinking as thinking) pretends to be directly the *other* of itself—to be the world of sense, the real world, life—thought surpassing itself in thought (Feuerbach). This aspect is contained herein, inasmuch as consciousness as mere consciousness takes offense not at estranged objectivity, but at *objectivity as such*.

Secondly, this implies that self-conscious man, insofar as he has recognized and superseded the spiritual world (or his world's spiritual, general mode of being) as self-alienation, nevertheless again confirms it in this alienated shape and passes it off as his true mode of being—reestablishes it, and pretends to be *at home in his other-being as such*. Thus, for instance, after superseding religion, after recognizing religion to be a product of self-alienation he yet finds confirmation of himself in *religion as religion*. Here *is* the root of Hegel's *false* positivism, or of his merely *apparent* criticism: this is what Feuerbach designated as the positing, negating, and reestablishing of religion or theology—but it has to be expressed in more general terms. Thus reason is at home in unreason as unreason. The man who has recognized that he is leading an alienated life in law, politics, etc., is leading his true human life in this alienated life as such. Self-affirmation, self-confirmation *in contradiction* with itself—in contradiction both with the knowledge of and with the essential being of the object—is thus true *knowledge* and *life*.

There can therefore no longer be any question about an act of accommodation on Hegel's part vis-à-vis religion, the state, etc., since this lie is the lie of his principle.

If I *know* religion as *alienated* human self-consciousness, then what I know in it as religion is not my self-consciousness, but my alienated self-consciousness confirmed in it. I therefore know my self-consciousness that belongs to itself, to its very nature, confirmed not in *religion* but rather in *annihilated* and *superseded* religion.

In Hegel, therefore, the negation of the negation is not the confirmation of the true essence, effected precisely through negation of the pseudo-essence. With him the negation of the negation is the confirmation of the pseudo-essence, or of the self-estranged essence in its denial; or it is the denial of this pseudo-essence as an objective being dwelling outside man and independent of him, and its transformation into the subject.

A peculiar role, therefore, is played by the act of *superseding* in which denial and preservation, i.e., affirmation, are bound together.

Thus, for example, in Hegel's philosophy of law, *civil law* superseded equals *morality*, morality superseded equals the *family*, the family superseded equals *civil society*, civil society superseded equals the *state*, the state superseded equals *world history*. In the *actual world* civil law, morality, the family, civil society, the state, etc., remain in existence, only they have become *moments*—states of the existence and being of man—which have no validity in isolation, but dissolve and engender one another, etc. They have become *moments of motion*.

In their actual existence, this *mobile* nature of theirs is hidden. It appears and is made manifest only in thought, in philosophy. Hence my true religious existence is my existence in the *philosophy of religion*; my true political existence is my existence in the *philosophy of law*; my true natural existence, existence in the *philosophy of nature*; my true artistic existence, existence in the *philosophy of art*; my true human existence, my *existence in philosophy*. Likewise the true existence of religion, the state, nature, art, is the *philosophy* of religion, of nature, of the state, and of art. If, however, the philosophy of religion, etc., is for me the sole true existence of religion then, too, it is only as a *philosopher of religion* that I am truly religious, and so I deny *real* religious sentiment and the really *religious* man. But at the same time I *assert* them, in part within my own existence or within the alien existence which I oppose to them—for this *is* only their *philosophic* expression—and in part I assert them in their distinct original shape, since for me they represent merely the *apparent* other-being, allegories, forms of their own true existence (i.e., of my *philosophical* existence) hidden under sensuous disguises.

In just the same way, *quality* superseded equals *quantity*, quantity superseded equals *measure*, measure superseded equals *essence*, essence superseded equals *appearance*, appearance superseded equals *actuality*, actuality superseded equals the *concept*, the concept superseded equals *objectivity*, objectivity superseded equals the *absolute idea*, the absolute idea superseded equals *nature*, nature superseded equals *subjective* mind, subjective mind superseded equals *ethical* objective mind, ethical mind superseded equals *art*, art superseded equals *religion*, religion superseded equals *absolute knowledge*.

On the one hand, this act of superseding is a transcending of a conceptual entity; thus, private property as a concept is transcended in the *concept* of morality. And because thought imagines itself to be directly the other of itself, to be *sensuous reality*—and therefore takes its own action for *sensuous, real* action—this superseding in thought, which leaves its object in existence in the real world, believes that it has really overcome it. On the other hand, because the object has now become for it a moment of thought, thought takes it in its reality too to be self-confirmation of itself—of self-consciousness, of abstraction.

From the one point of view the entity which Hegel *supersedes* in philosophy is therefore not *real* religion, the *real* state, or *real* nature, but religion itself already as an object of knowledge, i.e., *dogmatics*; the same with *jurisprudence, political science,* and *natural science*. From the one point of view, therefore, he stands in opposition both to the *real* thing and to immediate, unphilosophic *science* or the unphilosophic *conceptions* of this thing. He therefore contradicts their conventional conceptions [The conventional conception of theology, jurisprudence, political science, natural science, etc.].

On the other hand, the religious, etc., man can find in Hegel his final confirmation.

It is now time to formulate the *positive* aspects of the Hegelian dialectic within the realm of estrangement.

A) *Supersession* as an objective movement of *retracting* the alienation *into self*. This is the insight, expressed within the estrangement, concerning the *appropriation* of the objective essence through the supersession of its estrangement; it is the estranged insight into the *real objectification* of man, into the real appropriation of his objective essence through the annihilation of the *estranged* character of the objective world, through the supersession of the objective world in its estranged mode of being. In the same way atheism, being the supersession of God, is the advent of theoretic humanism, and communism, as the supersession of private property, is the vindication of real human life as man's possession and thus the advent of practical humanism, or atheism is humanism mediated with itself through the supersession of religion, while communism is humanism mediated with itself through the supersession of private property. Only through the supersession of this mediation—which is itself, however, a necessary premise—does positively self-deriving humanism, *positive* humanism, come into being.

But atheism and communism are no flight, no abstraction, no loss of the objective world created by man—of man's essential powers born to the realm of objectivity; they are not a returning in poverty to unnatural, primitive simplicity. On the contrary, they are but the first real emergence, the actual realization for man of man's essence and of his essence as something real.

Thus, by grasping the *positive* meaning of self-referred negation (although again in estranged fashion) Hegel grasps man's self-estrangement, the alienation of man's essence, man's loss of objectivity and his loss of realness as self-discovery, manifestation of his nature, objectification and realization. In short, within the sphere of abstraction, Hegel conceives labor as man's act of *self-genesis*—conceives man's relation to himself as an alien being and the manifestation of himself as an alien being to be the emergence of *species-consciousness* and *species-life*.

B) However, apart from, or rather in consequence of, the referral already described, this act appears in Hegel:

First as a *merely formal*, because abstract, act, because the human being itself is taken to be only an *abstract, thinking being*, conceived merely as self-consciousness.

Secondly, because the exposition is *formal* and *abstract*, the supersession of the alienation becomes a confirmation of the alienation; or for Hegel this movement of *self-genesis* and *self-objectification* in the form of *self-alienation and self-estrangement* is the *absolute*, and hence final, *expression of human life*—of life with itself as its aim, of life at peace with itself, and in unity with its essence.

This movement, in its abstract form as dialectic, is therefore regarded as *truly human life*, and because it is nevertheless an abstraction—an estrangement of human life—it is regarded as a *divine process*, but as the divine process of man, a process traversed by man's abstract, pure, absolute essence that is distinct from himself.

Thirdly, this process must have a bearer, a subject. But the subject only comes into being as a result. This result—the subject knowing itself as absolute self-consciousness—is therefore *God, absolute Spirit, the self-knowing and self-manifesting idea*. Real man and real nature become mere predicates—symbols of this hidden, unreal man and of this unreal nature. Subject and predicate are therefore related to each other in absolute reversal—a *mystical subject-object* or a *subjectivity reaching beyond the object*—the *absolute subject* as a *process*, as *subject alienating* itself and returning from alienation into itself, but at the same time retracting this alienation into itself, and the subject as this process; a pure, *incessant* revolving within itself.

First. Formal and abstract conception of man's act of self-creation or self-objectification.

Hegel having posited man as equivalent to self-consciousness, the estranged object—the estranged essential reality of man—is nothing but *consciousness*, the thought of estrangement merely—estrangement's *abstract* and therefore empty and unreal expression, *negation*. The supersession of the alienation is therefore likewise nothing but an abstract, empty supersession of that empty abstraction—the *negation of the negation*. The rich, living, sensuous, concrete activity of self-objectification is therefore reduced to its mere abstraction, *absolute negativity*—an abstraction which is again fixed as such and considered as an independent activity—as sheer activity. Because this so-called negativity is nothing but the *abstract, empty* form of that real living act, its content can in consequence be merely a *formal* content produced by abstraction from all content. As a result therefore one gets general, abstract *forms of abstraction* pertaining to every content and on that account indifferent to, and, consequently, valid for, all content—the thought-forms or logical categories torn from *real* mind and from *real* nature. (We shall unfold the *logical* content of absolute negativity further on.)

Hegel's positive achievement here, in his speculative logic, is that the *definite concepts*, the universal *fixed thought-forms* in their independence vis-à-vis nature and mind are a necessary result of the general estrangement of the human being and therefore also of a human thought, and that Hegel has therefore brought these together and presented them as moments of the abstraction process. For example, superseded being is essence, superseded essence is concept, the concept superseded is . . . absolute idea. But what, then, is the absolute idea? It supersedes its own self again, if it does not want to traverse once more from the beginning the whole act of abstraction, and to satisfy itself with being a totality of abstractions or the self-comprehending abstraction. But abstraction comprehending itself as abstraction knows itself to be nothing: it must abandon itself—abandon abstraction—and so it arrives at an entity which is its exact opposite—at *nature*. Thus, the entire logic is the demonstration that abstract thought is nothing in itself; that the absolute idea is nothing for itself; that only *nature is* something.

The absolute idea, the abstract idea, which "*considered* with regard to its unity with itself is *intuiting* (*Logic*), and which in its own absolute truth resolves to let the moment of its particularity or of initial characterization and other-being, the *immediate idea*, as its reflection, *go forth* freely *from itself as nature*," this whole idea which behaves in such a strange and bizarre way, and which has given the Hegelians such terrible headaches, is from beginning to end nothing else but *abstraction* (i.e., the abstract thinker), which, made wise by experience and enlightened concerning its truth, resolves under various (false and themselves still abstract) conditions to *abandon itself* and to replace its self-absorption, nothingness, generality, and indeterminateness by its other-being, the particular, and the determinate; resolves to let *nature*, which it held hidden in itself only as an abstraction, as a thought-entity, *go forth freely from itself*; that is to say, this idea resolves to forsake abstraction and to have a look at nature *free* of abstraction. The abstract idea, which without mediation becomes *intuiting*, is indeed nothing else but abstract thinking that gives itself up and resolves on *intuition*. This entire transition from logic to natural philosophy is nothing else but the transition—so difficult to effect for the abstract thinker, who therefore describes it in such an adventurous way—from *abstracting* to *intuiting*. The *mystical* feeling which drives the philosopher forward from abstract thinking to intuiting is *boredom*—the longing for content.

The man estranged from himself is also the thinker estranged from his *essence*—that is, from the natural and human essence. His thoughts are therefore fixed mental forms dwelling outside nature and man. Hegel has locked up all these fixed mental forms together in his logic, interpreting each of them first as negation—that is, as an *alienation* of *human* thought—and then as negation of the negation—that is, as a superseding of this alienation, as a *real* expression of human thought. But as this still takes place within the confines of the estrangement, this negation of the negation is in part the restoring of these fixed forms in their estrangement; in part a stopping at the last act—the act of self-reference in alienation—as the true mode of being of these fixed mental forms;

[This means that what Hegel does is to put in place of these fixed abstractions the act of abstraction which revolves in its own circle. We must therefore give him the credit for having indicated the source of all these inappropriate concepts which originally appertained to particular philosophers; for having brought them together; and for having created the entire compass of abstraction as the object of criticism, instead of some specific abstraction. Why Hegel separates thought from the *subject* we shall see later; at this stage it is already clear, however, that when man is not, his characteristic expression cannot be human either, and so neither could thought be grasped as an expression of man as a human and natural subject endowed with eyes, ears, etc., and living in society, in the world, and in nature.—*Note by Marx*]

[. . .] and in part, to the extent that this abstraction apprehends itself and experiences an infinite weariness with itself, there makes its appearance in Hegel, in the form of the resolution to recognize *nature* as the essential being and to go over to intuition, the abandonment of abstract thought—the abandonment of thought revolving solely within the orbit of thought, of thought *sans* eyes, *sans* teeth, *sans* ears, *sans* everything.

But *nature* too, taken abstractly, for itself—nature fixed in isolation from man—is *nothing* for man. It goes without saying that the abstract thinker who has committed himself to intuiting, intuits nature abstractly. Just as nature lay enclosed in the thinker in the form of the absolute idea, in the form of a thought-entity—in a shape which was obscure and enigmatic even to him—so by letting it emerge from himself he has really let emerge only this *abstract nature*, only nature as a *thought-entity*—but now with the significance that it is the other-being of thought, that it is real, intuited nature—nature distinguished from abstract thought. Or, to talk in human language, the abstract thinker learns in his intuition of nature that the entities which he thought to create from nothing, from pure abstraction—the entities he believed he was producing in the divine dialectic as pure products of the labor of thought, for ever shuttling back and forth in itself and never looking outward into reality—are nothing else but *abstractions* from *characteristics of nature*. To him, therefore, the whole of nature merely repeats the logical abstractions in a sensuous, external form. He once more *resolves* nature into these abstractions. Thus, his intuition of nature is only the act of confirming his abstraction from the intuition of nature—is only the conscious repetition by him of the process of creating his abstraction. Thus, for example, time equals negativity referred to itself (Hegel, *Encyclopedia of the Philosophical Sciences*). To the superseded becoming as being there corresponds, in natural form, superseded movement as matter. Light is *reflection-in-itself*, the *natural* form. Body as *moon* and *comet* is the *natural* form of the *antithesis* which according to logic is on the one side the *positive resting on itself* and on the other side the *negative* resting on itself. The earth is the *natural* form of the logical *ground*, as the negative unity of the antithesis, etc.

Nature as nature—that is to say, insofar as it is still sensuously distinguished from that secret sense hidden within it—nature isolated, distinguished from these abstractions is *nothing*—a *nothing proving itself to be nothing*—is *devoid of sense*, or has only the sense of being an externality which has to be annulled.

> In the finite-*teleological* position is to be found the correct premise that nature does not contain within itself the absolute purpose.

Its purpose is the confirmation of abstraction.

> Nature has shown itself to be the idea in the *form of other-being*. Since the *idea* is in this form the negative of itself or *external to itself*, nature is not just relatively external vis-à-vis this idea, but *externality* constitutes the form in which it exists as nature.

Externality here is not to be understood as the *world of sense* which *manifests itself* and is accessible to the light, to the man endowed with senses.

It is to be taken here in the sense of alienation, of a mistake, a defect, which ought not to be. For what is true is still the idea. Nature is only the *form* of the idea's *other-being*. And since abstract thought is the essence, that which is external to it is by its essence something merely *external*. The abstract thinker recognizes at the same time that *sensuousness—externality* in contrast to thought shuttling back and forth *within itself*—is the essence of nature. But he expresses this contrast in such a way as to make this *externality of nature*, its *contrast* to thought, its *defect*, so that inasmuch as it is distinguished from abstraction, nature is something defective.

An entity which is defective not merely for me or in my eyes but in itself—intrinsically—has something outside itself which it lacks. That is, its essence is different from it itself. Nature has therefore to supersede itself for the abstract thinker, for it is already posited by him as a potentially *superseded* being.

> *For us*, mind has *nature* for its *premise*, being nature's *truth* and for that reason its *absolute prius* [first]. In this truth nature *has vanished*, and mind has resulted as the idea arrived at being-for-itself, the *object* of which, as well as the *subject*, is the *concept*. This identity is *absolute negativity*, for whereas in nature the concept has its perfect external objectivity, this its alienation has been superseded, and in this alienation the concept has become identical with itself. But it is this identity therefore, only in being a return out of nature.
>
> As the *abstract* idea, *revelation* is unmediated transition to, the *coming-to-be* of, nature; as the revelation of the mind, which is free, it is the *positing* of nature as the *mind's* world—a positing which, being reflection, is at the same time, a *presupposing* of the world as independently existing nature. Revelation in conception is the creation of nature as the mind's being, in which the mind procures the *affirmation* and the *truth* of its freedom.
>
> *The absolute is mind*. This is the highest definition of the absolute.

PHILOSOPHICAL NOTEBOOKS (EXCERPTS)

V.I. Lenin
1914–15

It is highly instructive that in 1914, at a time when World War I raged and the Second International had ignominiously collapsed, Lenin took the time to make a careful study of Hegel and his system of dialectics. To untangle the mess of contradictions facing the revolutionary internationalists and world working class, it was essential to go back to the fundamentals. This is always the case whenever earthshaking events confront Marxists, and it is no exaggeration to state that this study was part of Lenin's preparation for the October Revolution. We produce here three excerpts from Volume 38 of Lenin's Collected Works, *which are a brilliant summation of the essence of Hegelian dialectics.*

Summary of Dialectics (1914)

1) The determination of the concept out of itself—the thing itself must be considered in its relations and in its development;

2) the contradictory nature of the thing itself—the other of itself—the contradictory forces and tendencies in each phenomenon;

3) the union of analysis and synthesis.

Such apparently are the elements of dialectics.

One could perhaps present these elements in greater detail as follows:

1) the objectivity of consideration—not examples, not divergences, but the Thing-in-itself.

2) the entire totality of the manifold relations of this thing to others.

3) the development of this thing—phenomenon, respectively—its own movement, its own life.

4) the internally contradictory tendencies—and sides—in this thing.

5) the thing—phenomenon, etc.—as the sum and unity of opposites.

6) the struggle, respectively unfolding, of these opposites, contradictory strivings, etc.

7) the union of analysis and synthesis—the breakdown of the separate parts and the totality, the summation of these parts.

8) the relations of each thing—phenomenon, etc.—are not only manifold, but general, universal. Each thing—phenomenon, etc.—is connected with every other.

9) not only the unity of opposites, but the transitions of every determination, quality, feature, side, property into every other—into its opposite?

10) the endless process of the discovery of new sides, relations, etc.

11) the endless process of the deepening of man's knowledge of the thing, of phenomena, processes, etc., from appearance to essence and from less profound to more profound essence.

12) from coexistence to causality and from one form of connection and reciprocal dependence to another, deeper, more general form.

13) the repetition at a higher stage of certain features, properties, etc., of the lower and

14) the apparent return to the old—negation of the negation.

15) the struggle of content with form and conversely. The throwing off of the form, the transformation of the content.

16) the transition of quantity into quality and vice versa—15 and 16 are examples of 9

In brief, dialectics can be defined as the doctrine of the unity of opposites. This embodies the essence of dialectics, but it requires explanations and development.

On the Question of Dialectics (1915)

The splitting of a single whole and the cognition of its contradictory parts is the *essence*—one of the "essentials," one of the principal, if not the principal, characteristics or features—of dialectics. That is precisely how Hegel, too, put the matter.

The correctness of this aspect of the content of dialectics must be tested by the history of science. This aspect of dialectics—e.g., in Plekhanov—usually receives inadequate attention: the identity of opposites is taken as the sum total of *examples* ("for example, a seed," "for example, primitive communism." The same is true of Engels. But it is "in the interests of popularization . . .") and not as a *law of cognition—and* as a law of the objective world.

> In mathematics: + and −, differential and integral,
> In mechanics: action and reaction,
> In physics: positive and negative electricity,
> In chemistry: the combination and dissociation of atoms,
> In social science: the class struggle.

The identity of opposites (it would be more correct, perhaps, to say their "unity"—although the difference between the terms identity and unity is not particularly important here. In a certain sense both are correct) is the recognition (discovery) of the contradictory, *mutually exclusive*, opposite tendencies in *all* phenomena and processes of nature—*including* mind and society. The condition for the knowledge of all processes of the world in their "*self-movement*," in their spontaneous development, in their real life, is the knowledge of them as a unity of opposites. Development is the "struggle" of opposites. The two basic (or two possible? or two historically observable?) conceptions of development (evolution) are: development as decrease and increase, as repetition, and development as a unity of opposites—the division of a unity into mutually exclusive opposites and their reciprocal relation!

In the first conception of motion, self-movement, its driving force, its source, its motive, remains in the shade—or this source is made external—God, subject, etc. In the second conception the chief attention is directed precisely to knowledge of the source of "self-movement."

The first conception is lifeless, pale, and dry. The second is living. The second alone furnishes the key to the "self-movement" of everything existing; it alone furnishes the key to "leaps," to the "break in continuity," to the "transformation into the opposite," to the destruction of the old and the emergence of the new.

The unity—coincidence, identity, equal action—of opposites is conditional, temporary, transitory, relative. The struggle of mutually exclusive opposites is absolute, just as development and motion are absolute.

NB: The distinction between subjectivism—skepticism, sophistry, etc.,—and dialectics, incidentally, is that in objective dialectics the difference between the relative and the absolute is itself relative. For objective dialectics there is an absolute within the relative. For subjectivism and sophistry the relative is only relative and excludes the absolute.

In his *Capital*, Marx first analyzes the simplest, most ordinary and fundamental, most common and everyday *relation* of bourgeois (commodity) society, a relation encountered billions of times, viz., the exchange of commodities. In this very simple phenomenon, in this "cell" of bourgeois society, analysis reveals all the contradictions—or the germs of *all* contradictions—of modern society. The subsequent exposition shows us the development—*both* growth *and* movement—of these contradictions and of this society in the sum of its individual parts. From its beginning to its end.

Such must also be the method of exposition (or study) of dialectics in general—for with Marx the dialectics of bourgeois society is only a particular case of dialectics. To begin with what is the simplest, most ordinary, common, etc., with *any proposition*: the leaves of a tree are green; John is a man; Fido is a dog, etc. Here already we have *dialectics*—as Hegel's genius recognized; the individual is the universal.

The medieval scholastics cracked their brains over the question as to whether universals (abstractions) actually exist. Hegel solved this problem brilliantly by pointing out that the particular and the universal *are in fact the same*: every particular is, in one way or another, a universal. Every individual belongs to a genus or species that defines its true nature, however, genuses and species are made up of individual creatures. The limit of these categories in biology is determined by the ability to reproduce.

Consequently, the opposites—the particular as opposed to the universal—are identical: the individual exists only in the connection that leads to the universal. The universal exists only in the individual and through the individual. Every individual is—in one way or another—a universal. Every universal is a fragment, or an aspect, or the essence of an individual. Every universal only approximately embraces all the individual objects. Every individual enters incompletely into the universal, etc., etc. Every individual is connected by thousands of transitions with other kinds of individuals—things, phenomena, processes, etc. As Aristotle pointed out: "But of course, there cannot be a house in general, apart from individual houses" (*Metaphysics*).

Here already we have the elements, the germs, the concepts of *necessity*, of objective connection in nature, etc. Here already we have the contingent and the necessary, the phenomenon and the essence. This apparently contradictory assertion can be shown from even the simplest sentence. It is impossible to express the nature of any particular without immediately turning it into a universal. Such is the nature of any definition, for example when we say John is a man, Fido is a dog, *this* is a leaf of a tree", etc., we *disregard* a number of attributes as *contingent*; we separate the essence from the appearance, and counterpose the one to the other.

Thus, in any proposition we can—and must—disclose as in a "nucleus" ("cell") the germs of *all* the elements of dialectics, and thereby show that dialectics is a property of all human knowledge in general.

And natural science shows us—and here again it must be demonstrated in *any* simple instance—objective nature with the same qualities, the transformation of the individual into the universal, of the contingent into the necessary, transitions, modulations, and the reciprocal connection of opposites. Dialectics *is* the theory of knowledge of (Hegel and) Marxism. This is the "aspect" of the matter—it is not "an aspect" but the *essence* of the matter—to which Plekhanov, not to speak of other Marxists, paid no attention.

Knowledge is represented in the form of a series of circles both by Hegel (see *Logic*) and by the modern "epistemologist" of natural science, the eclectic and foe of Hegelianism—which he did not understand!!—Paul Volkmann.

"Circles" in philosophy: is a chronology of persons essential? No!
Ancient: from Democritus to Plato and the dialectics of Heraclitus.
Renaissance: Descartes versus Gassendi (Spinoza?)
Modern: Holbach-Hegel (via Berkeley, Hume, Kant).
Hegel—Feuerbach—Marx

Dialectics as living, many-sided knowledge—with the number of sides eternally increasing—with an infinite number of shades of every approach and approximation to reality—with a philosophical system growing into a whole out of each shade—here we have an immeasurably rich content as compared with metaphysical materialism, the fundamental misfortune of which is its inability to apply dialectics to the theory of reflection, to the process and development of knowledge.

Philosophical idealism is only nonsense from the standpoint of crude, simple, metaphysical materialism. From the standpoint of dialectical materialism, on the other hand, philosophical idealism is a one-sided, exaggerated, development—inflation, distension—of one of the features, aspects, facets of knowledge, into an absolute, divorced from matter, from nature, apotheosized. Idealism is clerical obscurantism. True. But philosophical idealism is—"more correctly" and "in addition"—a road to clerical obscurantism through one of the shades of the infinitely complex knowledge (dialectical) of man.

Human knowledge is not—or does not follow—a straight line, but a curve, which endlessly approximates a series of circles, a spiral. Any fragment, segment, section of this curve can be transformed—transformed one-sidedly—into an independent, complete, straight line, which then— if one does not see the wood for the trees—leads into the quagmire, into clerical obscurantism—where it is anchored by the class interests of the ruling classes. Rectilinearity and one-sidedness, woodenness and petrification, subjectivism and subjective blindness—voila the epistemological roots of idealism. And clerical obscurantism (= philosophical idealism), of course, has epistemological roots, it is not groundless; it is a sterile flower undoubtedly, but a sterile flower that grows on the living tree of living, fertile, genuine, powerful, omnipotent, objective, absolute human knowledge.

On Hegel's Dialectics in the "Shorter Logic" (1915)

The concept (cognition) reveals the essence—the law of causality, identity, difference, etc., in Being (in immediate phenomena). Such is actually the general course of all human cognition—of all science—in general. Such is the course also of natural science and political economy (and history). Insofar [as] Hegel's dialectic is a generalization of the history of thought.

To trace this more concretely and in greater detail in the history of the separate sciences seems an extraordinarily rewarding task. In logic, the history of thought must, by and large, coincide with the laws of thinking.

It is strikingly evident that Hegel sometimes passes from the abstract to the concrete:

Being (abstract)—Determinate Being (concrete)—Being-for-self

and sometimes the other way around:

The Subjective Notion—the Object—Truth (the Absolute Idea).

{Abstract Being only as a moment in πάντα ρεῖ [everything flows]}

Is this not inconsistency of an idealist—what Marx called the "mysticism of ideas"—in Hegel? Or are there deeper reasons? E.g., Being = Nothing—the idea of Becoming, of development.

First of all, impressions flash by, then Something emerges—afterwards the concepts of quality—the determination of the thing or the phenomenon—and quantity are developed. After that, study and reflection direct thought to cognition of identity—of difference—of Ground—of the Essence versus the Phenomenon—of causality, etc. All these moments—steps, stages, processes—of cognition move in the direction from the subject to the object, being tested in practice and arriving through this test at truth (= the Absolute Idea).

Quality and sensation are one and the same, says Feuerbach. The very first and most familiar to us is sensation, and in it is inevitably also quality...

If Marx did not leave behind him a "Logic" (with a capital letter), he did leave the logic of *Capital*, and this ought to be utilized to the full in this question. In *Capital*, Marx applied to a single science logic, dialectics, and the theory of knowledge of materialism [three words are not needed: it is one and the same thing] which has taken everything valuable in Hegel and developed it further.

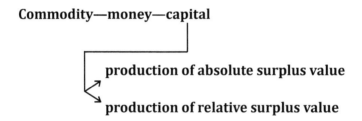

Commodity—money—capital

production of absolute surplus value

production of relative surplus value

The history of capitalism and the analysis of the *concepts* summing it up.

The beginning—the most simple, ordinary, mass, immediate "Being"— the single commodity ("Being" in political economy).
The analysis of it as a social relation.
A double analysis, deductive and inductive—logical and historical (forms of value).

Testing by facts or by practice respectively, is to be found here in each step of the analysis.

Cf. Concerning the question of Essence versus Appearance
- price and value
- demand and supply versus value
  (= crystallized labor)
- wages and the price of labor power.

TROTSKY'S NOTEBOOKS: EXCERPTS ON LENIN, DIALECTICS, AND EVOLUTIONISM

Leon Trotsky
1933–35

With fascism in power in Italy, Germany, and Spain, and Stalin consolidating his death grip on the USSR, Trotsky was living in exile, harried from country to country on a "planet without a visa." Fighting against such momentous odds to rebuild the forces of world Bolshevism, like Marx, Engels, and Lenin, Trotsky also went "back to basics" in the form of a critique of Hegelian dialectics.

In his Diary in Exile, *he wrote the following on May 16, 1935: "It's been about two weeks since I have written much of anything: it's too difficult. I read newspapers. French novels. Wittels's book about Freud (a bad book by an envious pupil), etc. Today I wrote a little about the interrelationship between the physiological determinism of brain processes and the 'autonomy' of thought, which is subject to the laws of logic. My philosophical interests have been growing during the last few years, but alas, my knowledge is too insufficient, and too little time remains for a big and serious work . . ."*

Discovered by chance in the Trotsky Archives at Harvard University, his notebooks on philosophy remained unknown until 1998, when they were translated from the Russian and annotated by Philip Pomper, who found them while researching a project on Lenin. They were subsequently published as Trotsky's Notebooks, 1933–1935 *by Columbia University Press. Not only does Trotsky anticipate his future debate with the anti-dialectics opposition of the Socialist Workers Party, he also takes up a wide range of topics including the history of philosophy, Darwin, the dialectics of consciousness, psychoanalysis, Lenin's dialectics versus Martov's, and much more. While the selections we have made focus on dialectics, this is a remarkable collection that deserves to be read in its entirety.*

Excerpt 1—Hegel

See the topic L. [Lenin]

Those who repudiate "dialectics" consider it to be simply superfluous, a useless playing with thought. Positive science is enough! Does positive science therefore exclude pure mathematics and *logic*?

In fact, dialectics is related to logic (formal) as higher mathematics is to lower.

Hegel himself viewed dialectics precisely as logic, as the science of the forms of human cognition, but in Hegel these forms are the ones in which the world develops, in that in logical forms it is only [realizing] its material content. Dialectics is summarized by Hegel in a work called *Science of Logic*.

For Hegel dialectics is a logic of broader dimensions—in space and in time—universal logic, the objective logic of the universe.

The negation of the concept in itself

If we visualize the fabric of life as a complex piece of knitting, then *the concept* can be equated with the separate stitches. Every concept seems to be independent and complete—formal logic operates with them this way—in reality every stitch has two ends, which connect it with adjacent stitches. If pulled at the end it unravels—the dialectical *negation* of a concept, in its *limitedness*, in its sham independence.

Some objects (phenomena) are confined easily within boundaries according to logical classification, others present difficulties: they can be put here or there, but within a stricter relationship—nowhere. While provoking the indignation of systematizers, such transitional forms are exceptionally interesting to dialecticians, for they smash the limited boundaries of classification, revealing the real connections and consecutiveness of a living process.

According to Hegel *being* and *thinking* are identical (absolute idealism). Materialism does not adopt this *identity*—it premises being to thought.

The identity of being and thinking according to H[egel] signifies the identity of objective and subjective logic, their ultimate congruence. Materialism accepts the correspondence of the subjective and objective, their unity, but not their identity, in other words, it does not liberate matter from its materiality, in order to keep only the logical framework of regularity, of which scientific thought (consciousness) is the expression.

The doctrine of the teacher is taken up only in ready-made results, which are transformed into a pillow for lazy thought. Hegel on Kant and his epigones.

From Kant to Hegel (from dualism to monism)

> Kant: Reason is self-legislating, it constructs its tools of cognition (the categories) by itself; only the thing-in-itself is located outside of consciousness.

> Hegel: But the thing-in-itself is only a logical abstraction, created by reason; consequently nothing exists aside from Reason.

Is it possible to say that Hegel's *absolute idealism* is a *self-legislating solipsism*?

The concept—is not a closed circle, but a loop, but you can also knot it. (this has been said once already!!)

Mikhailovsky and others deduce the [Hegelian] triad [of thesis, antithesis, and synthesis] from the *past, present,* and *future*. There is a shadow of truth here, but only a shadow. Our conceptualizing reflects *processes,* transforming them into "*objects.*" Not every present is suitable for the formation of a concept; a certain *stabilization* of the process is necessary in order for an enduring representation of it to form. This act of consciousness is thereby a rupture with the past, which prepared the stabilization. Our concept of the earth, the "most durable" of our conceptions, the "most durable" of the objects of our everyday conceptions, the "most durable" of the objects of our everyday milieu, is based upon a total rupture with the revolutionary formation of the solar system. The concept is conservative. Its conservatism issues: a) from its utilitarian purpose, b) from the fact that the memory of a person, like that of humankind, is short.

Thus, the triad does not at all correspond to an undifferentiated past, present, and future, but to the formative stages of the process.

Excerpt 2—The Second Notebook

$a = a$ is only a particular case of the law $a \neq a$.

Dialectics is the logic of motion, development, and evolution.

Formal logic involves stationary and unchanging quantities: $a = a$. Dialectics retorts: $a \neq a$. Both are correct: $a = a$ at every given moment; $a \neq a$ at two different moments. Everything flows, everything is changing. What does logic express? The law of the external world or the law of consciousness? The question is posed dualistically, [and] therefore not correctly [for] the laws of logic express the laws (rules, methods) of consciousness in its active relationship to the external world. The relationship of consciousness to the external world is a relationship of the part (the particular, specialized) to the whole.

Logic involves unchanging qualities ($a = a$) and the fixed quantities of these qualities. Dialectics is constructed on the transition of quantity into quality and the reverse.

The law of the transition of quantity into quality is (very likely) the fundamental law of dialectics.

In this sense dialectics is the logic of Darwinism (in opposition to Linnaeus), the logic of Marxism (in opposition to rationalistic, idealistic theories of the historical process), the logic of philosophical materialism (in opposition to Kantianism, etc.)

The dialectical relationship to quality signified an entirely new relationship to so-called moral values. Official, that is, bourgeois thought today still views justice, rights, honors, as absolute values, as higher criteria. Dialectical materialism razed to the ground the kingdom of idealistic mythology. It showed how imperceptible quantitative molecular changes in economics prepare the way for a radical change in moral criteria: the old values are transformed into their opposite, against them new values enter the scene, the carrier of which is a new class or stratum, not seldom a new generation of the [old] class itself. It is quite usual in philistine circles to accuse Lenin of *cynicism*, and this expresses precisely hostility to the dialectical worldview, a struggle for absolute values, [both] essential for covering up [their] pitiful, barren, self-interested practice.

Alexander III [in] the 1880s was much more confident and decisive in the defense of autocracy than his father. "The great reforms"—especially the *zemstvo*, the judiciary, the press—made it possible for the bureaucracy to distinguish the true strength of its enemies and allies. The balance proved to be a favorable one.

Dialectics

It must be recognized that the fundamental law of dialectics is the conversion of quantity into quality, for it gives [us] the general formula of all evolutionary processes—of nature as well as of society.

Cognition begins with the differentiation of things, with their opposition to each other, with a classification of their qualitative differences. The quantitative definitions operate with independent particulars, consequently they depend upon qualitative definitions (five fingers, ten years, 100 amperes).

Practical thought lives within these limits. For a cattle trader a cow is a cow; he is interested only in the individual qualities of its udder. From his practical point of view he is indifferent to the genetic links between the cow and an amoeba.

If we grasp the universe from the point of view of atomic theory, then it appears to us like a gigantic laboratory for the transformation of quantity into quality and the reverse.

It is possible to acknowledge this, but to fail to make it the fundamental principle of one's own thought. There are those who unite the Kant-Laplace worldview with biblical faiths or quasi-faiths and, while advertising themselves as Darwinists, believe in the higher principles, the moral innate in humanity.

The principle of the transition of quantity into quality has universal significance, insofar as we view the entire universe—without any exception—as the product of formation and transformation and not as the fruit of conscious creation.

Hegel himself undoubtedly did not give the law of the transition of quantity into quality the paramount importance which it fully deserves. Hegel relied upon the Kant-Laplace theory, but he did not yet know either Darwinism or Marxism. It is indeed sufficient to recall that the dialectician Hegel could consider the Prussian state the incarnation of the Absolute Idea.

Engels, following Hegel, called those who think in absolute and unchanging categories, that is, who visualize the world as an aggregate of unchanging qualities, metaphysicians.

In a more or less pure form, "metaphysical" thinking exists perhaps only in savages. Among civilized people eclecticism holds sway. The laws of "evolution," of "progress," on the whole are recognized, but independent of them several absolute categories are accepted—in the area of economics (private property), in the politics (democracy, patriotism), in morals (the categorical imperative).

Anglo-Saxon thinking is at the present moment the preserve of empiricism.

In the English scholar's head, just as on the shelves of his library, Darwin, the Bible, stand side by side, without disturbing each other. Anglo-Saxon thinking is constructed according to the system of the impermeable bulkhead. From this issues the most stubborn opposition in the conservative Anglo-Saxon world to dialectical thinking, which destroys all impermeable bulkheads.

The transition into its opposite

To view phenomena according to their resemblance or opposition means to see them according to their *quality*.

The transition of quality into quantity and the reverse presupposes the transition of one quality into another.

See Freud.

In primitive languages, big and small, high and low, etc., are expressed by *one word*, and the opposition between big and small is expressed by gestures, intonations, etc. In other words language, at a time when it was being developed, had only a general character, converting opposing qualities into quantitative differences.

The very same thing applies to the concepts of sweet and bitter, and at a later time—to good and evil, wealth and poverty, etc.

In these abstract formulas we have the most general laws (forms) of motion, change, the transformation of the stars of the heaven, of the earth, nature, and human society.

We have here the logical (dialectical) forms of the transformation of one regime into another. But in such general form it is a matter only of possibility.

The conversion of an abstract possibility into a concrete necessity—also an important law of dialectics—is defined each time by a combination of definite material conditions? Thus, from the possibility of a bourgeois victory over the feudal classes until the victory itself there were various time lapses, and the victory frequently looked like a semi-victory.

In order for a possibility to become a necessity there had to be a corresponding strengthening of some factors and the weakening of others, a definite interrelationship among these strengthenings and weakenings. In other words: it was necessary for several interconnected series of quantitative changes to prepare the way for a new constellation of forces.

The law of the conversion of possibility into necessity thus leads—in the last analysis—to the law of the conversion of quantity into quality.

Catastrophes

Everything flows, but not outside [its] banks. The world is not "fluid," there are changes in it, the crystallization of durable (congealed) elements, although indeed not "eternal" ones. Then life creates its own banks for itself in order later to wash them away. The quantitative changes of matter at a given stage push against those congealed forms, which sufficed for its previous state. Conflict. Catastrophe. Either the old form conquers (only partially conquers), necessitating the self-adaptation of the conquered (partially) process, or the process of movement explodes the old form and creates a new one, by way of its new crystallizations from its wombs and the assimilation of elements of the old form.

See in addition [John Stuart] Mill # The liberal (gradualist) conception of development, progress

The theory of revolutions

The logical antimony of *content* and *form* in this way loses its absolute character. Content and form change place. Content creates new forms from itself. In other words, the correlation of content and form leads, in the last analysis, to the conversion of quantity into quality.

Continue in relation to the other antinomies.

What is the aim of this? says the contemporary "positivist": I can give an excellent analysis of the world of phenomena without these contrivances and pedantic subtleties. With equal justification a butcher will say that he can sell veal without resorting to the Aristotelian syllogism. To the butcher we would try to make clear that in reality he is always relying on the syllogism without knowing it; if his trade is poor, then his personal ignorance cannot but affect it; but that, if he wants to set things up solidly, then he cannot avoid teaching his son the sciences, the composition of which includes the science of the syllogism (logic).

To the representative of positivism, with his limited point of view, we say that all the contemporary sciences use the laws of dialectical thinking at every step, just as the shopkeeper uses the syllogism or as Monsieur Jourdain uses prose: without ever knowing it. Precisely because of this the average scholar preserves many habitual [traits resembling those] of impermeable bulkheads, not posing those questions which issue from the *general* movement of scientific thought, and cravenly ceases to draw general conclusions, when they call for a dialectical leap.

The dialectic does not liberate the investigator from painstaking study of the facts—quite the contrary—it requires it. But in return it gives investigative thought elasticity, helps it cope with ossified prejudices, arms it with invaluable analogies, and educates it in a spirit of daring, grounded in circumspection.

The example of Mendeleev, whose lack of dialectical method prevented him from recognizing the mutual transformability of the elements, despite the fact that his discovery of the periodic table of elements connected the quantitative differences among them to the quantitative differences of atomic weights.

Excerpt 3—Lenin and Martov

If all contemporary thought is penetrated by elements of the dialectic, then this is even truer of the political thinking of the Mensheviks, who had passed through the school of Marxism and revolutionary events. But dialectics differ. [Julius] Martov very subtly, in many cases, with great virtuosity commanded the dialectic. But this was a dialectic close to his thinking about phenomena in the intelligentsia milieu connected with the intelligentsia of the top stratum of the workers.

Martov sometimes very intelligently analyzed regroupings in the sphere of parliamentary politics, changes in the tendencies of the press, the maneuvers of ruling circles—insofar as all this was limited to ongoing politics, the preparatory stage for distant events, or the peaceful conditions when only the leaders, deputies, journalists, and ministers of prewar Europe acted in the political arena, when the basic antagonists remained virtually unchanging.

Within these boundaries Martov swam about like a fish in water. His dialectic was a dialectic of derivative processes and limited scale, episodic changes. Beyond these boundaries he did not venture.

On the contrary, Lenin's dialectic had a massive character. His thought—his opponents often accused him of this—"simplified" reality, indeed swept aside the secondary and episodic in order to deal with the basic. Thus, Engels "simplified" reality when he defined the state as armed detachments of people with material appendages in the form of jails. But this was a *saving* simplification: true, insufficient in itself for an evaluation of the conjunctures of the day, it was decisive in the last historical analysis.

Lenin's thought operated with living classes as the basic factors of society and thus revealed *all* its power in those periods when the great masses entered the scene, that is, in periods of profound upheavals, wars, and revolutions. The Leninist dialectic was a dialectic for the large scale.

Although the fundamental laws of mechanics hold for all man's productive activity, in reality there is the mechanics of the watchmaker and the mechanics of [the] Dnieprostroi [hydroelectric dam]. Martov's thought was the thought of a watchmaker in politics. Lenin's thought worked on the scale of [the] Dnieprostroi. Is this a difference of a quantitative order? Quantity here passes over into quality.

The comparison with the watchmaker, however, has very conditional meaning. A watch's mechanism will live its self-contained life (so long as it is not ruined), and the watch's hands can correctly show the hour, even though the watchmaker is ignorant of the law of the earth's motion around its axis. But the politics of a minor scale (internal groupings within parties, parliamentary games, etc.) maintains its relative independence while the (relatively) large factors, that is, classes, are unchanging. Martov's dialectic therefore yielded the more tragic misfirings in matters of a minor scale as well, the closer the approach of stormy class conflicts, of perturbations in the life of society. And since our entire epoch since the first years of the century became one of ever more grandiose historical perturbations, Martov's thought increasingly showed its weakness, turned dialectics simply into a screen for inner uncertainty, and fell under the influence of vulgar empiricists, like [Fyodor] Dan.

To the contrary, Lenin's thought analyzed all the secondary phenomena, all the elements of the superstructure more penetratingly, the more immediately they depended upon the class movements that were occurring. From stage to stage, Lenin's thought became stronger, more courageous, and at the same time subtler and more flexible.

Martov's mistakes were always and invariably mistakes *to the right* of historical development, they grew in frequency and in scope, and soon outgrew the area of tactics and moved into that of strategy, and by virtue of that, rendered nil the tactical resourcefulness and wealth of his initiatives.

Lenin's political mistakes were always *to the left* of the line of development, thus the farther [along the line of development], the rarer they became, the smaller the angle of deviation, the sooner they were recognized and corrected; by virtue of which the relationship between strategy and tactics achieved a higher and more perfect correspondence.

Materialist dialectics (beginning)

Dialectics is the logic of development. It examines the world—completely without exception—not as a result of creation, of a sudden beginning, the realization of a plan, but as a result of motion, of transformation. Everything that is *became* the way it is as a result of lawlike development.

In this, its fundamental and most general sense, the dialectical view of nature and humanity coincides with the so-called "evolutionary" view of nature, the view of the contemporary natural and social sciences, insofar as they genuinely deserve this designation. One needs only to note that the philosophical conception of the development of all existence, representing a courageous generalization issuing from the preceding development of science, emerged before Darwinism and Marxism, and either indirectly or directly enriched them.

We further will see that "evolution" as a general formula for the origins of the world and society is more amorphous, less concrete, with less content, than the dialectical conception. Now it is quite enough for us that the dialectical (or evolutionary) point of view, consequently the suitable one, inevitably leads to materialism: the organic world emerged from the inorganic, consciousness is a capacity of living organisms depending upon organs that originated through evolution. In other words "the soul" of evolution (of dialectics) leads in the last analysis to matter. The evolutionary point of view carried to a logical conclusion leaves no room for either idealism or dualism, or for the other species of eclecticism.

Thus, "the materialist dialectic" (or "dialectical materialism") is not an arbitrary combination of two independent terms, but is a differentiated unity—a short formula for a whole and indivisible worldview, which rests exclusively on the entire development of scientific thought in all its branches, and which alone serves as a scientific support for human praxis.

. . .

Transpose here what was said about Clemenceau, his attitude toward evolutionism, etc. Note, how an egg "progresses" into a chicken.

The old sophism [paradox] about the bald man is the dialectical revelation of the unsoundness (= inadequacy) of formal categories.

Contrary to a photograph, which is the element of formal logic, the [motion-picture] film is "dialectical" (badly expressed).

Cognizing thought begins with differentiation, with the instantaneous photograph, with the establishment of terms—conceptions—in which the separate moments of a process are placed but from which the process as a whole escapes. These terms-conceptions, created by cognizing thought, are then transformed into its fetters. Dialectics removes these fetters, revealing the relativity of motionless concepts, their transition into each other (Hegel, *Logic*).

"We can investigate reality without the dialectic."

In the same way that we can walk without [knowing] anatomy and digest food without [knowing] physiology.

Hegel's absolute idealism is directed against dualism—against the thing-in-itself of dualism (Hegel, *Logic*). Isn't the recognition of the reality of the external world, outside a cognizing consciousness and independent of it, a return to dualism? Not at all, for cognition is in no respect an independent principle for us, but a specialized part of the objective world (make precise).

The evolutionary point of view is not at all hostile to our reason (Engels). Therefore we must study evolutionary logic (dialectics). [Max] Eastman scoffs at this.

Reason, which would be present at the most distant evolution of the earth, at the origin of the solar system, and at the development in it of organic life, etc., and would be able to embrace these processes, would be so to speak, dialectical reason immanent at birth. But our human reason is nature's youngest child. To human memory nature offered not so much a picture of change, as repeating cycles, "the wind returns to its circuits." Humanity itself is a consecutive succession of generations. Each generation starts the difficult work of cognition in a certain sense from the beginning. Within the boundaries of everyday praxis people are accustomed to dealing with unchanging objects. As a result of this innate, inherited, automatized [practice] there appears rational logic, which dismembers nature into autonomous and unchanging elements. The development of thought makes its way from vulgar logic to dialectics only on the basis of accumulated scientific experience, under the spur of historical (class) development.

Rationalism is an attempt to create a complete system on the basis of vulgar logic.

The chronology of evolutionism

> The *Kant-Laplace* theory of the origins of the solar system
> The dialectic of Hegel (after the French Revolution)
> The theory of [Charles] Lyell (the evolution of the earth)
> The theory of Darwin (the origin of species)
> The theory of Marx

In this fashion the transition from thinking in static categories to thinking in [terms of] development traces its lineage to the epoch after the Great French Revolution, which was the last great, brilliant burst of courageous rationalism.

Kant earlier believed that logic had been perfected because, since the time of *Aristotle*, that is, over a period of two thousand years, it hadn't changed.

Hegel, to the contrary, saw in this the enormous backwardness of logic.

The essence of the matter is that the rules and methods of a narrowly practical, common, or vulgar [mode] of thinking crystallized—entirely on the basis of praxis—and the theoretical work connected to it—very early, already in ancient times, and within the boundaries of this common thinking, change was neither demanded nor tolerated. But precisely the growth and development of cognition on the foundation of Aristotelian logic prepared the way for its explosion.

The triad is the "mechanism" of the transformation of quantity into quality.

Historically, humanity forms its "conceptions"—the basic elements of its thinking—on the foundation of experience, which is always incomplete, partial, one sided. It includes in "the concept" those features of a living, forever-changing process, which are important and significant for it at a given moment. Its future experience at first is enriched (quantitatively) and then outgrows the closed concept, that is, in practice negates it, by virtue of this necessitating a theoretical negation. But the negation does not signify a turning back to *tabula rasa* [blank slate]. Reason already possesses: a) the concept and b) the recognition of its unsoundness. This recognition is tantamount to the necessity to construct *a new concept*, and then it is inevitably revealed that the negation was not absolute, that it affected only certain features of the first concept. The new concept therefore has by necessity a *synthetic* character: into it enter those elements of the initial concept, which were able to withstand the trial by experience + those new elements of experience, which led to the negation of the initial concept.

Thus, in the domain of thinking (cognition) as well, the quantitative changes lead to qualitative ones, and then these transformations haven't a [steady] evolutionary character but are accompanied by breaks in gradualness, that is, by small or large intellectual catastrophes. In sum, this also means that the development of cognition has a *dialectical character*.

The new "synthetic" concept in turn becomes the point of departure for a new trial, enrichment, verification, and for a new negation. This is the place of the triad in the development of human thought. *But what is its place in the development of nature?*

Here we approach the most important problem of dialectical philosophy.

The interrelationship between consciousness (cognition) and nature is an independent realm with its own regularities.

Consciousness splits nature into fixed categories and in this way enters into contradiction with reality. Dialectics overcomes this contradiction—gradually and piecemeal— bringing consciousness nearer to the world's reality. The dialectic of consciousness (cognition) is not thereby a reflection of the dialectic of nature, but is a result of the lively interaction between consciousness and nature and—in addition—a method of cognition, issuing from this interaction.

Since cognition is not identical with the world (in spite of Hegel's idealistic postulation), dialectical cognition is not identical with the dialectic of nature. Consciousness is a quite original part of nature, possessing peculiarities and regularities that are completely absent in the remaining part of nature. Subjective dialectics must by virtue of this be a distinctive part of objective dialectics—with its own special forms and regularities. (The danger lies in the transference—under the guise of "objectivism"— of the birth pangs, the spasm of consciousness, to objective nature.)

The dialectic of cognition brings consciousness closer to the "secrets" of nature, that is, it helps it master the dialectic of nature too. But what does the *dialectic* of nature consist of? Where is the boundary separating it from the dialectic of cognition (a vacillating dialectical "boundary")?

Consciousness acts like a camera: it tears from nature "moments" and the ties and transitions among them are lost; but the object of photography, the living person, is not broken up into moments. Rather, motion-picture film gives us a crude "uninterruptedness" satisfactory for the retina of our eye and approaching the uninterruptedness of nature. True, cinematic uninterruptedness consists in fact of separate "moments" and short breaks between them. But both the former and latter are related to the technology of the cinema, which exploits the eye's imperfection.

Verify how this problem is treated by Lenin and Plekhanov.

Hegel himself spoke more than once about necessary concreteness, issuing from the immanent motion of "moments"—of motion which represents the direct opposite of an analytic procedure, that is, of an action external in relation to the object itself and innate in the subject.

The identity of *Being* and *Nothingness*, like the contradictoriness of the concept of the beginning, in which Being and Nothingness are united, seems at first glance a subtle but fruitless play of ideas. In fact, this "game" brilliantly exposes the failure of static thinking, which at first splits the world into motionless elements, and then seeks truth by way of a limitless expansion [of the process].

The role of the émigrés

All of the information about the West, including [what came] through the legal press (right up to the liberal [press]), came through them.

Legal and illegal Marxism 1905

Legal writers of tsarist Russia not only did not say everything, they didn't think things through. In essence, they didn't express fully and often did not think through the main point. Remaining within the boundaries of legality, they emasculated their thought. The illegal press seemed to them "simplistic," "fanatic," "rectilinear." But when the days of freedom began, it turned out that the undergrounders, the émigrés, swept the journalistic field. Only they knew how to write the language of the revolution. But this is the least of it: precisely from among the émigrés came the most talented journalists. This was no accident: politics calls for spirit, consequently, courage, and these qualities express themselves in style.

The identity of opposites

Little Paul says "*donne!*" ["give!"] both when he wants to take, and when he wants to give.

Excerpt 4

Why on a given stage of scientific thought in various areas is it necessary to put a theory "on its legs" (the presumption being that it has been standing on its head until that moment?)

Because humankind in its practical activity is inclined to view the entire world as a means, and itself as the end. Practical egocentrism (homocentrism)—is carried over into theory—turns the entire world structure on its head. From this issues the need for corrections (Kant-Laplace, Lyell, Darwin, Marx).

The brain is the material substrate of consciousness. Does this mean that consciousness is simply a form of "manifestation" of the physiological processes in the brain? If this were the state of affairs, then one would have to ask: What is the need for consciousness? If consciousness has no *independent* function, which rises *above* physiological processes in the brain and nerves, then it is unnecessary, useless; it is harmful because it is a superfluous complication—and what a complication!

The presence of consciousness and its crowning by logical thought can be biologically and socially "justified" only in the event that it yields positive vital results beyond those which are achieved by the system of unconscious reflexes. This presupposes not only the autonomy of consciousness (within certain limits) from automatic processes in the brain and nerves, but the ability of consciousness to influence the action and functions of the body as well. What kind of switches serving consciousness are there for achieving these goals? These switches clearly cannot possess a material character, or else they would be included in the chain of anatomic-physiological processes of the organism and could not play an independent role consisting of their prescribed functions. Thought operates by its own laws, which we can call the laws of logic; with their help achieving certain practical outcomes, it switches on the last (with more or less success) in the chain of our life activities.

It is well known that there is an entire school of psychiatry ("psychoanalysis." Freud) which in practice completely removes itself from physiology, basing itself upon the inner determinism of psychic phenomena, such as they are. Some critics therefore accuse the school of Freud of idealism. That psychoanalysts are frequently inclined toward dualism, idealism, and mystification . . . But by itself the method of psychoanalysis, taking as its point of departure "the autonomy" of psychological phenomena, in no way contradicts materialism. Quite the contrary, it is precisely dialectical materialism that prompts us to the idea that the psyche could not even be formed unless it played an autonomous, that is, within certain limits, an independent role in the life of the individual and the species.

All the same, we approach here some sort of critical point, a break in all the gradualness, a transition from quantity to quality: the psyche, arising from matter, is "freed" from the determinism of matter, so that it can independently—by its own laws—influence matter.

True, a dialectic of cause and effect, base and superstructure, is not news to us: politics grows out of economics in order for it in turn to influence the base by switches of a superstructural character. But here the interrelationships are real, for in both instances the actions of living people are involved; in one instance they are grouped together for production, in the other—under the pressure of the demands of the very same production—they are grouped politically and act with the switches of politics upon their own production grouping.

When we make the transition from the anatomy and physiology of the brain to intellectual activity, the interrelationship of "base" and "superstructure" is incomparably more puzzling.

The dualists divide the world into independent substances: matter and consciousness. If this is so, then what do we do with the unconscious?

Additional Notes

Dialectics

The syllogism is absolutely correct only when it is a tautology, that is, when it is fruitless.

The syllogism is "useful" when—it is incorrect, that is, when it admits into concepts "clearance [tolerance]."

The entire matter depends upon the permissible dimensions of "clearance [tolerance]." Here is where dialectics begins.

The fundamental "cell" of dialectical thinking is the syllogism. But it [too] undergoes transmutation, changes, like the basic cells in various tissues of an organism change.

"Philosophy" = a toolmaking guild in relation to all the remaining guilds of science.

A toolmaking guild is not a substitute for production as a whole. In order to use a tool one has to know a special area of production (metal work, lathe work). When an ignoramus, armed with the "materialistic dialectic" tries to solve complicated problems in special areas intuitively, he inevitably makes a fool of himself.

On the other hand, the "specialized" scholar can do without a toolmaking guild, that is, can use a tool of his own making, but his work will clearly suffer from it (Darwin, Mendeleev, and [others]).

[A.I.] Herzen called Hegel's philosophy the algebra of revolution.

Dialectics is the logic of development. Logic (formal) is the dialectic of motionlessness. Logic is a particular case of the dialectic, when motion and change enter into the formula as "0."

Cicero believed that between unquestionable truth and unquestionable falsehood there is a broad middle region of truth which depends upon the subject, on the person who is doing the reasoning:

Ista sunt ut disputantur [these are to be discussed] (a verbatim translation is impossible) depends upon the point of view

The "engineer" plays the very same universal role in the social constructions of M. Eastman and other Americans that Robinson Crusoe played in the constructions of bourgeois political economists.

People orient themselves toward ideas in two ways: treating them either as arbitrary, unreal shadows, standing outside the world of facts in their material conditionality, or as almighty "factors" which command reality. Both views are false. The idea is a fact in a chain of other facts.

> With Hegel the dialectic stands on its head. It has to be put on its feet in order to uncover the rational kernel under the mystical hull.

These words of Marx from the introduction to the second edition of *Capital* (1873) more than once inspired critical wits to refine them.

But in essence the very same operation—to turn something over from its head and stand it on its feet—has been repeated in every area of human thought.

God created man. Man created God.

The earth orbits around the sun. The sun orbits around the earth.

"To stand on its head. . ." Eastman scoffs at this. Nevertheless, science like art, is full of such reversals.

1. Cosmology until Galileo established the interdependence between movements of the sun and earth. Galileo did not repudiate this dependence, but turned it on its head.
2. Pre-Darwinian biology established the expediency of the structure of species, the correspondence (suitability) of organs to the conditions of life. From this it wound up with a preconceived system. Darwin did not reject the "expediency," the correspondence of organs, functions, environment, but turned the interdependence on its head. In this brilliant reversal lies the essence of Darwinism.
   a. To support this, citations about Darwinism.
3. Mendeleev and his periodic system of elements. For him the indecomposable individualities entered certain mathematical relationships to each other. Subsequent developments in chemistry turned these mutual relationships on their head.

All evolution is a transition from quantity into quality. The very concept of gradual, slow development signifies the achievement of qualitative values with the help of quantitative change. This works decisively in all areas.

Darwin's natural selection, which leads to the creation of various plant and animal species, is nothing other than the accumulation of quantitative changes, yielding as a result new qualities, a new species.

Whoever denies the dialectical law of the transition from quantity into quality must deny the genetic unity of plants and animal species, the chemical elements, etc. He must, in the last analysis, turn back to the biblical act of creation.

Teleological thinking

Tolstoy did not want to accept that he lived on this earth without a preset aim, like a bird that has fallen from its nest.

> It is important to recognize that god is the master and to know what he wants of me; but what he wants of me; but what he himself is, and how he lives, I will never know, because I am not his equal. I am the worker, he is the master (Tolstoy).

Teleology and Determinism

All schools of subjectivism in one or another fashion are based on the contradiction between objective cause and subjective purpose. Determinism is the philosophy of objective causality. Teleology is the philosophy of subjective purposes. The attempt to set up a hostile opposition between them or to combine them eclectically is itself a product of philosophical ignorance. The purpose is a partial aspect of the cause. Teleology is only a special department of determinism.

Darwinism

Everyone recognized the process of formation of *variations* by way of natural or artificial selection, but many categorically refused to recognize the very same process for the formation of *species*. As long as the transitional forms are there, the unity of a species seems stable. But should the transitional forms disappear, the varieties would become species.

Every process has its material or nonmaterial paleontology.

Darwin's doctrine started as a theory of the origin of species and became a theory of the evolution of the organic world.

The zoological geography of Darwin and Wallace—thanks to evolutionary theory separated by a gulf from the zoography of Linnaeus, etc. (The role of paleontology)

The intermediate links have died out.

The history of language—is the paleontology of thought.

Along what lines did the *objections against Darwinism* proceed? The Dutch botanist De Vries, the author of the so-called theory of mutations, tried to establish a *basic* distinction between the special features of variations and those of species, by virtue of which they could not cross from one to the other (But De Vries was an evolutionist all the same.)

Until Darwin, the question about the origins of species was considered to be "the secret of secrets."

Wallace on Darwin:

> I don't have . . . that inexhaustible patience for gathering a multitude of the most diverse facts, that surprising capacity to draw conclusions from those precise and rich physiological observations, that cleverness in designing a plan of experimentation and that gracefulness in execution, finally—that inimitable style—clear and at the same time cogent and precise—in a word, all those qualities that make Darwin a fully accomplished person.

(apply to a characterization of Lenin—show the consistency of [his] qualities in various areas)

Dialectics

Wallace—not only a Darwinist but a scientist who independently arrived at the theory of the evolutionary origin of species (among them, humanity), spent more than a little effort to adduce evidence that there was an impassable barrier between human beings and animals in the area of intellect and morality, in other words, evidence for the divine origin of the "soul."

Wallace makes the same leaps in relation to the transitions from inorganic to organic matter and the appearance of consciousness.

Evolution does not permit bargains: you either have to admit it or reject it.

Every reaction is bound to repudiate transformism. National Socialism cannot be reconciled with Darwinism.

III

MATERIALISM

vs

IDEALISM

ENGLAND AND MATERIALIST PHILOSOPHY

Karl Marx
1845

Marx wrote The Holy Family in 1844—his first collaboration with Friedrich Engels—as part of the process of working out their ideas on philosophy and communism. This amalgamated excerpt from the August 1923 issue of Labour Monthly *provides a compact overview of the development of materialism, comparing its British and French variants, and connecting this with the rise of utopian socialism.*

French materialism of the eighteenth century exhibits two currents, one having its origin in Descartes, the other in Locke. The latter exercised a dominating influence on the French mind and led directly to socialism. The former, the mechanical materialism, dominated French science. Both currents crossed in their courses . . .

Descartes, in his physics, endowed matter with creative power and conceived mechanical motion as its manifestation of life. He completely severed his physics from his metaphysics. Within his physics, matter is the only substance, the only reason of its existence and cognition. The French mechanical materialism adopted the physics of Descartes and rejected his metaphysics. His disciples were anti-metaphysicians by profession, namely, physicians. This school begins with the physician Leroy, reaches its culmination with the physician Cabanis, while the physician La Mettrie was its center . . .

But the man who destroyed the credit of the metaphysics of the seventeenth century was Pierre Bayle. The negative refutation of theology and metaphysics, however, sharpened the desire for a positive, anti-meta-physical system. And it was Locke who supplied it. His *Essay Concerning Human Understanding* came in the nick of time for the other side of the Channel. It was enthusiastically acclaimed as a long-expected guest.

Materialism is the born son of Britain. Even one of his great school-men, Duns Scotus, asked himself "whether matter cannot think." In per-forming this wonder, Duns had recourse to God's omnipotence, that is, he made theology itself preach materialism. He was, moreover, Nominalist. Nominalism is one of the main elements of the English materialists, as it is indeed the first expression of materialism in Christian Europe.

The real progenitor of English materialism is Francis Bacon. Natural science is to him the true science, and sensuous physics the foremost part of science. Anaxagoras with his *homoimeries* and Democritus with his atoms are often his authorities. According to Bacon, the senses are unerring and the source of all knowledge. Science is experimental and consists in the application of a rational method to sensuous data. Obser-vation, experiment, induction, analysis, are the main conditions of a ra-tional method. Of the qualities inherent in matter the foremost is motion, not only as mechanical and mathematical motion, but more as impulse, vital force, tension, or as Jacob Boehme said, pain of matter. The primi-tive forms of the latter are living, individualizing, inherent, and essential forces, which produce specific variations.

With Bacon as its pioneer, materialism contains in a naïve manner the germs of universal development. Matter is still smiling upon us in its poetic-sensuous charm. The aphoristic doctrine, on the other hand, teems with theological inconsistencies.

In its further development, materialism becomes one-sided. Hobbes is the systematizer of Baconian materialism. Sensuousness loses its bloom and is turned into the abstract sensuousness of geometry. The physical motion is sacrificed to the mechanical and mathematical one. Geometry is proclaimed the cardinal science . . . Materialism is rationalized, and it develops also the ruthless logicality of reason. Hobbes, starting from Bacon, argues that if all knowledge is supplied by the senses, then . . . only the corporeal is perceptible and knowable, therefore we can know noth-ing of the existence of God. Only my own existence is certain . . . Hobbes systematized Bacon, but did not establish the main principle, the origin of the ideas and knowledge of the sensuous world.

It was Locke who accomplished that work in his *Essay Concerning Hu-man Understanding.*

If Hobbes removed the theistic prejudices from Baconian materialism, Collins, Toland, Coward, Hartley, Priestley, etc. broke down the last theological barrier of Locke's sensualism. Theism is, for those materialists, merely a comfortable, lackadaisical way to get rid of religion . . .

The direct French disciple and interpreter of Locke was Condillac, who pitted Locke's sensualism against the metaphysics of the seventeenth century. He published a refutation of the system of Descartes, Spinoza, Leibniz, and Malebranche. In his *Essay on the Origin of Human Knowledge* he follows up the ideas of Locke and argues that not only the mind, but also the senses, not only the capacity for forming ideas, but also the capacity for sensuous perception, are a matter of experience and habit. On education and external circumstances depends the whole development of man.

The difference between French and English materialism is the difference between the two nationalities. The French endowed English materialism with esprit and eloquence, with flesh and blood, with temperament and grace.

In Helvetius, who likewise starts from Locke, materialism receives its proper French character. He envisages it in relation to social life. The sensuous qualities and self-love, enjoyment, and the well-understood personal interest are made into the foundations of morality. The natural equality of the human intelligence, the harmony between the progress of reason and the progress of manufactures, the natural goodness of man, the omnipotence of education, are the main points of his system . . .

It needs no special ingenuity to discover in the doctrines of materialism—concerning the natural goodness and the equal mental endowments of man, the omnipotence of experience, habit, and education, the influence of external circumstances on man, the great importance of manufactures, the legitimacy of enjoyment—the necessary connection with communism and socialism. If man receives from the external world and from his experience in the external world all his feelings, ideas, etc., then it is evidently our business to reorganize the empirical world in such a manner that man should only experience the really humane and acquire the habit of it. If the well-understood personal interest is the principle of all morality, then we must arrange society in such a manner as to make private interest fit in with social interest. If man is subject to the same laws as nature: if man is not free in a materialistic sense, that is, he is not free to do this or to avoid that, but that he is only free to assert his true individuality, then there is no sense in punishing the criminal, but we must rather destroy the antisocial breeding-places of vice and to allow to everybody social scope for his activities. If man is formed by circumstances, then we must humanize the circumstances. If man is social by nature, then man develops his true nature in society only, and we must not measure the power of his nature by the power of a single individual, but by the power of society.

These and similar views we find even literally in the works of the older French materialists. It is not the proper place here to sit in judgment upon them. Characteristic of the social-critical tendency of materialism is Mandeville's apology of vice. Mandeville, one of the earlier followers of Locke, demonstrates that in the present-day society vice is indispensable and useful. This was by no means an apology for present-day society.

Fourier starts directly from the doctrines of French materialism. The Babouvistes were raw, uncivilized materialists, but also the more advanced communism is based on French materialism. The latter, in the French garb, returned to its native country. Godwin and Bentham established their systems on the ethical philosophy of Helvetius, and Owen took it from Bentham and based upon it English communism. Etienne Corbet, banished to England, brought those ideas back to France and became here the most commonplace representative of communism. But also the more advanced of French communists, such as Dezamy, Gay, etc., developed, like Robert Owen, the materialist doctrine into real humanism and the logical basis of communism.

THE GERMAN IDEOLOGY (EXCERPTS)

Karl Marx and Friedrich Engels
1845

Unpublished in their lifetime, Engels commented that "We abandoned the manuscript to the gnawing criticism of the mice all the more willingly as we had achieved our main purpose—self-clarification!" Historical materialism first saw the light of day in this work as dialectics and materialism are applied to the development of human society, the historical process is illuminated, and idealism in historiography is pilloried. Foreshadowed by the Theses on Feuerbach *and anticipating the themes of the* Communist Manifesto, The German Ideology *turns Hegel's conception of history fully on its head.*

Preface

Hitherto men have constantly made up for themselves false conceptions about themselves, about what they are and what they ought to be. They have arranged their relationships according to their ideas of God, of normal man, etc. The phantoms of their brains have got out of their hands. They, the creators, have bowed down before their creations. Let us liberate them from the chimeras, the ideas, dogmas, imaginary beings under the yoke of which they are pining away. Let us revolt against the rule of thoughts. Let us teach men, says one, to exchange these imaginations for thoughts which correspond to the essence of man; says the second, to take up a critical attitude to them; says the third, to knock them out of their heads; and—existing reality will collapse.

These innocent and childlike fancies are the kernel of the modern

Young Hegelian philosophy, which not only is received by the German public with horror and awe, but is announced by our philosophic heroes with the solemn consciousness of its cataclysmic dangerousness and criminal ruthlessness. The first volume of the present publication has the aim of uncloaking these sheep, who take themselves and are taken for wolves; of showing how their bleating merely imitates in a philosophic form the conceptions of the German middle class; how the boasting of these philosophic commentators only mirrors the wretchedness of the real conditions in Germany. It is its aim to debunk and discredit the philosophic struggle with the shadows of reality, which appeals to the dreamy and muddled German nation.

Once upon a time, a valiant fellow had the idea that men were drowned in water only because they were possessed with the idea of gravity. If they were to knock this notion out of their heads, say, by stating it to be a superstition, a religious concept, they would be sublimely proof against any danger from water. His whole life long he fought against the illusion of gravity, of whose harmful results all statistics brought him new and manifold evidence. This valiant fellow was the type of the new revolutionary philosophers in Germany.

Part I: Feuerbach. Opposition of the Materialist and Idealist Outlook

A. Idealism and Materialism

. . .

First premises of the materialist method

The premises from which we begin are not arbitrary ones, not dogmas, but real premises from which abstraction can only be made in the imagination. They are the real individuals, their activity, and the material conditions under which they live, both those which they find already existing and those produced by their activity. These premises can thus be verified in a purely empirical way.

The first premise of all human history is, of course, the existence of living human individuals. Thus the first fact to be established is the physical organization of these individuals and their consequent relation to the rest of nature. Of course, we cannot here go either into the actual physical nature of man, or into the natural conditions in which man finds himself—geological, hydrographical, climatic, and so on. The writing of history must always set out from these natural bases and their modification in the course of history through the action of men.

Men can be distinguished from animals by consciousness, by religion, or anything else you like. They themselves begin to distinguish themselves from animals as soon as they begin to produce their means of subsistence, a step which is conditioned by their physical organization. By producing their means of subsistence, men are indirectly producing their actual material life.

The way in which men produce their means of subsistence depends, first of all, on the nature of the actual means of subsistence they find in existence and have to reproduce. This mode of production must not be considered simply as being the production of the physical existence of the individuals. Rather, it is a definite form of activity of these individuals, a definite form of expressing their life, a definite mode of life on their part. As individuals express their life, so they are. What they are, therefore, coincides with their production, both with what they produce and with how they produce. The nature of individuals thus depends on the material conditions determining their production.

This production only makes its appearance with the increase of population. In its turn, this presupposes the intercourse of individuals with one another. The form of this intercourse is again determined by production.

The essence of the materialist conception of history; social being and social consciousness

The fact is, therefore, that definite individuals who are productively active in a definite way enter into these definite social and political relations. Empirical observation must in each separate instance bring out empirically, and without any mystification and speculation, the connection of the social and political structure with production. The social structure and the state are continually evolving out of the life process of definite individuals, but of individuals, not as they may appear in their own or other people's imagination, but as they really are; i.e., as they operate, produce materially, and hence, as they work under definite material limits, presuppositions, and conditions independent of their will.

The ideas which these individuals form are ideas either about their relation to nature or about their mutual relations or about their own nature. It is evident that in all these cases their ideas are the conscious expression—real or illusory—of their real relations and activities, of their production, of their intercourse, of their social and political conduct. The opposite assumption is only possible if in addition to the spirit of the real, materially evolved individuals, a separate spirit is presupposed. If the conscious expression of the real relations of these individuals is illusory, if in their imagination they turn reality upside down, then this, in its turn, is the result of their limited material mode of activity and their limited social relations arising from it.

The production of ideas, of conceptions, of consciousness, is at first directly interwoven with the material activity and the material intercourse of men, the language of real life. Conceiving, thinking, the mental intercourse of men, appear at this stage as the direct efflux of their material behavior. The same applies to mental production as expressed in the language of politics, laws, morality, religion, metaphysics, etc., of a people. Men are the producers of their conceptions, ideas, etc.; real, active men, as they are conditioned by a definite development of their productive forces and of the intercourse corresponding to these, up to its furthest forms. Consciousness can never be anything else than conscious existence, and the existence of men is their actual life process. If in all ideology men and their circumstances appear upside down as in a camera obscura, this phenomenon arises just as much from their historical life process as the inversion of objects on the retina does from their physical life process.

In direct contrast to German philosophy, which descends from heaven to earth, here we ascend from earth to heaven. That is to say, we do not set out from what men say, imagine, conceive; nor from men as narrated, thought of, imagined, conceived, in order to arrive at men in the flesh. We set out from real, active men, and on the basis of their real life process we demonstrate the development of the ideological reflexes and echoes of this life process. The phantoms formed in the human brain are also, necessarily, sublimates of their material life process, which is empirically verifiable and bound to material premises. Morality, religion, metaphysics, all the rest of ideology and their corresponding forms of consciousness, thus no longer retain the semblance of independence. They have no history, no development; but men, developing their material production and their material intercourse, alter, along with this their real existence, their thinking, and the products of their thinking. Life is not determined by consciousness, but consciousness by life. In the first method of approach the starting point is consciousness taken as the living individual;

in the second method, which conforms to real life, it is the real living individuals themselves, and consciousness is considered solely as their consciousness.

This method of approach is not devoid of premises. It starts out from the real premises and does not abandon them for a moment. Its premises are men, not in any fantastic isolation and rigidity, but in their actual, empirically perceptible process of development under definite conditions. As soon as this active life process is described, history ceases to be a collection of dead facts, as it is with the empiricists—themselves still abstract—or an imagined activity of imagined subjects, as with the idealists.

Where speculation ends—in real life—there real, positive science begins: the representation of the practical activity, of the practical process of development of men. Empty talk about consciousness ceases, and real knowledge has to take its place. When reality is depicted, philosophy as an independent branch of knowledge loses its medium of existence. At the best its place can only be taken by a summing up of the most general results, abstractions which arise from the observation of the historical development of men. Viewed apart from real history, these abstractions have in themselves no value whatsoever. They can only serve to facilitate the arrangement of historical material, to indicate the sequence of its separate strata. But they by no means afford a recipe or schema, as does philosophy, for neatly trimming the epochs of history. On the contrary, our difficulties begin only when we set about the observation and the arrangement—the real depiction—of our historical material, whether of a past epoch or of the present. The removal of these difficulties is governed by premises which it is quite impossible to state here, but which only the study of the actual life process and the activity of the individuals of each epoch will make evident.

. . .

History as a continuous process

In history up to the present, it is certainly an empirical fact that separate individuals have, with the broadening of their activity into world-historical activity, become more and more enslaved under a power alien to them—a pressure which they have conceived of as a dirty trick on the part of the so-called universal spirit, etc.—a power which has become more and more enormous and, in the last instance, turns out to be the world market. But it is just as empirically established that, by the overthrow of the existing state of society by the communist revolution—of which more below—and the abolition of private property which is identical with it, this power, which so baffles the German theoreticians, will be dissolved; and that then the liberation of each single individual will be accomplished in the measure in which history becomes transformed into world history.

From the above it is clear that the real intellectual wealth of the individual depends entirely on the wealth of his real connections. Only then will the separate individuals be liberated from the various national and local barriers, be brought into practical connection with the material and intellectual production of the whole world, and be put in a position to acquire the capacity to enjoy this all-sided production of the whole earth—the creations of man. All-around dependence, this natural form of the world-historical cooperation of individuals, will be transformed by this communist revolution into the control and conscious mastery of these powers, which, born of the action of men on one another, have till now overawed and governed men as powers completely alien to them. Now this view can be expressed again in speculative-idealistic, i.e., fantastic, terms as "self-generation of the species"—"society as the subject"—and thereby, the consecutive series of interrelated individuals connected with each other can be conceived as a single individual, which accomplishes the mystery of generating itself. It is clear here that individuals certainly make one another, physically and mentally, but do not make themselves.

Development of the productive forces as a material premise of communism

This "alienation"—to use a term which will be comprehensible to the philosophers—can, of course, only be abolished given two practical premises. For it to become an "intolerable" power, i.e., a power against which men make a revolution, it must necessarily have rendered the great mass of humanity "propertyless," and produced, at the same time, the contradiction of an existing world of wealth and culture, both of which conditions presuppose a great increase in productive power, a high degree of its development. And, on the other hand, this development of productive forces—which itself implies the actual empirical existence of men in their world-historical, instead of local, being—is an absolutely necessary practical premise because without it want is merely made general, and with destitution the struggle for necessities and all the old filthy business would necessarily be reproduced; and furthermore, because only with this universal development of productive forces is a universal intercourse between men established, which produces in all nations simultaneously the phenomenon of the "propertyless" mass (universal competition), makes each nation dependent on the revolutions of the others, and finally has put world-historical, empirically universal individuals in place of local ones. Without this, 1) communism could only exist as a local event; 2) the forces of intercourse themselves could not have developed as universal, hence intolerable powers—they would have remained home-bred conditions surrounded by superstition; and 3) each extension of intercourse would abolish local communism. Empirically, communism is only possible as the act of the dominant peoples "all at once" and simultaneously, which presupposes the universal development of productive forces and the world intercourse bound up with communism.

Moreover, the mass of propertyless workers—the utterly precarious position of labor power on a mass scale cut off from capital or from even a limited satisfaction and, therefore, no longer merely temporarily deprived of work itself as a secure source of life—presupposes the world market through competition. The proletariat can thus only exist world-historically, just as communism, its activity, can only have a "world-historical" existence. World-historical existence of individuals means existence of individuals which is directly linked up with world history.

Communism is for us not a state of affairs which is to be established, an ideal to which reality [will] have to adjust itself. We call communism the real movement which abolishes the present state of things. The conditions of this movement result from the premises now in existence.

In the main we have so far considered only one aspect of human activity, the reshaping of nature by men. The other aspect, the reshaping of men by men . . . [Intercourse and productive power]

Origin of the state and the relation of the state to civil society . . .

B. The Illusion of the Epoch

Civil society and the conception of history

The form of intercourse determined by the existing productive forces at all previous historical stages, and in its turn determining these, is civil society. The latter, as is clear from what we have said above, has as its premises and basis the simple family and the multiple, the so-called tribe, the more precise determinants of this society are enumerated in our remarks above. Already here we see how this civil society is the true source and theater of all history, and how absurd is the conception of history held hitherto, which neglects the real relationships and confines itself to high-sounding dramas of princes and states.

Civil society embraces the whole material intercourse of individuals within a definite stage of the development of productive forces. It embraces the whole commercial and industrial life of a given stage and, insofar, transcends the state and the nation, though, on the other hand again, it must assert itself in its foreign relations as nationality, and inwardly must organize itself as state. The word "civil society" emerged in the eighteenth century, when property relationships had already extricated themselves from the ancient and medieval communal society. Civil society as such only develops with the bourgeoisie; the social organization evolving directly out of production and commerce, which in all ages forms the basis of the state and of the rest of the idealistic superstructure, has, however, always been designated by the same name.

Conclusions from the materialist conception of history

History is nothing but the succession of the separate generations, each of which exploits the materials, the capital funds, the productive forces handed down to it by all preceding generations, and thus, on the one hand, continues the traditional activity in completely changed circumstances and, on the other, modifies the old circumstances with a completely changed activity. This can be speculatively distorted so that later history is made the goal of earlier history, e.g., the goal ascribed to the discovery of America is to further the eruption of the French Revolution. Thereby, history receives its own special aims and becomes "a person rating with other persons" (to wit: "Self-Consciousness, Criticism, the Unique," etc.), while what is designated with the words "destiny," "goal," "germ," or "idea" of earlier history is nothing more than an abstraction formed from later history, from the active influence which earlier history exercises on later history.

The further the separate spheres, which interact on one another, extend in the course of this development, the more the original isolation of the separate nationalities is destroyed by the developed mode of production and intercourse, and the division of labor between various nations naturally brought forth by these, the more history becomes world history. Thus, for instance, if in England a machine is invented, which deprives countless workers of bread in India and China, and overturns the whole form of existence of these empires, this invention becomes a world-historical fact. Or again, take the case of sugar and coffee which have proved their world-historical importance in the nineteenth century by the fact that the lack of these products, occasioned by the Napoleonic Continental System, caused the Germans to rise against Napoleon, and thus became the real basis of the glorious wars of liberation of 1813. From this it follows that this transformation of history into world history is not indeed a mere abstract act on the part of the "self-consciousness," the world spirit, or of any other metaphysical specter, but a quite material, empirically verifiable act, an act the proof of which every individual furnishes as he comes and goes, eats, drinks, and clothes himself.

Summary of the materialist conception of history

This conception of history depends on our ability to expound the real process of production, starting out from the material production of life itself, and to comprehend the form of intercourse connected with this and created by this mode of production (i.e., civil society in its various stages), as the basis of all history; and to show it in its action as state, to explain all the different theoretical products and forms of consciousness, religion, philosophy, ethics, etc., etc., and trace their origins and growth from that basis; by which means, of course, the whole thing can be depicted in its totality—and therefore, too, the reciprocal action of these various sides on one another.

It has not, like the idealistic view of history, in every period to look for a category, but remains constantly on the real ground of history; it does not explain practice from the idea but explains the formation of ideas from material practice; and accordingly, it comes to the conclusion that all forms and products of consciousness cannot be dissolved by mental criticism, by resolution into "self-consciousness," or transformation into "apparitions," "specters," "fancies," etc., but only by the practical overthrow of the actual social relations which gave rise to this idealistic humbug; that not criticism but revolution is the driving force of history, also of religion, of philosophy, and all other types of theory. It shows that history does not end by being resolved into "self-consciousness as spirit of the spirit," but that in it, at each stage, there is found a material result: a sum of productive forces, a historically created relation of individuals to nature and to one another, which is handed down to each generation from its predecessor; a mass of productive forces, capital funds, and conditions, which, on the one hand, is indeed modified by the new generation, but also on the other prescribes for it its conditions of life and gives it a definite development, a special character. It shows that circumstances make men just as much as men make circumstances.

This sum of productive forces, capital funds, and social forms of intercourse, which every individual and generation finds in existence as something given, is the real basis of what the philosophers have conceived as "substance" and "essence of man," and what they have deified and attacked; a real basis which is not in the least disturbed, in its effect and influence on the development of men, by the fact that these philosophers revolt against it as "self-consciousness" and the "Unique." These conditions of life, which different generations find in existence, decide also whether or not the periodically recurring revolutionary convulsion will be strong enough to overthrow the basis of the entire existing system. And if these material elements of a complete revolution are not present—namely, on the one hand the existing productive forces, on the other the formation of a revolutionary mass, which revolts not only against separate conditions of society up till then, but against the very "production of life" till then, the "total activity" on which it was based— then, as far as practical development is concerned, it is absolutely immaterial whether the idea of this revolution has been expressed a hundred times already, as the history of communism proves.

The inconsistency of the idealist conception of history in general, and of German post-Hegelian philosophy in particular

In the whole conception of history up to the present this real basis of history has either been totally neglected or else considered as a minor matter quite irrelevant to the course of history. History must, therefore, always be written according to an extraneous standard; the real production of life seems to be primeval history, while the truly historical appears to be separated from ordinary life, something extra-superterrestrial. With this the relation of man to nature is excluded from history and hence the antithesis of nature and history is created. The exponents of this conception of history have consequently only been able to see in history the political actions of princes and states, religious and all sorts of theoretical struggles, and in particular, in each historical epoch have had to share the illusion of that epoch. For instance, if an epoch imagines itself to be actuated by purely "political" or "religious" motives, although "religion" and "politics" are only forms of its true motives, the historian accepts this opinion. The "idea," the "conception" of the people in question about their real practice is transformed into the sole determining, active force, which controls and determines their practice. When the crude form in which the division of labor appears with the Indians and Egyptians calls forth the caste system in their state and religion, the historian believes that the caste system is the power which has produced this crude social form.

While the French and the English at least hold by the political illusion, which is moderately close to reality, the Germans move in the realm of the "pure spirit," and make religious illusion the driving force of history. The Hegelian philosophy of history is the last consequence, reduced to its "finest expression," of all this German historiography, for which it is not a question of real, nor even of political, interests, but of pure thoughts, which consequently must appear to Saint Bruno as a series of "thoughts" that devour one another and are finally swallowed up in "self-consciousness."

> So-called *objective* historiography consisted precisely, in treating the historical relations separately from activity. Reactionary character. [Marginal note by Marx]

And even more consistently, the course of history must appear to Saint Max Stirner, who knows not a thing about real history, as a mere "tale of knights, robbers, and ghosts," from whose visions he can, of course, only save himself by "unholiness." This conception is truly religious: it postulates religious man as the primitive man, the starting point of history, and in its imagination puts the religious production of fancies in the place of the real production of the means of subsistence and of life itself.

This whole conception of history, together with its dissolution and the scruples and qualms resulting from it, is a purely national affair of the Germans and has merely local interest for Germany, as for instance the important question which has been under discussion in recent times: how exactly one "passes from the realm of God to the realm of Man" [Ludwig Feuerbach, *The Essense of Christianity*]—as if this "realm of God" had ever existed anywhere save in the imagination, and the learned gentlemen, without being aware of it, were not constantly living in the "realm of Man" to which they are now seeking the way; and as if the learned pastime—for it is nothing more—of explaining the mystery of this theoretical bubble-blowing did not, on the contrary, lie in demonstrating its origin in actual earthly relations. For these Germans, it is altogether simply a matter of resolving the ready-made nonsense they find into some other freak, i.e., of presupposing that all this nonsense has a special sense which can be discovered; while really it is only a question of explaining these theoretical phrases from the actual existing relations. The real, practical dissolution of these phrases, the removal of these notions from the consciousness of men, will, as we have already said, be effected by altered circumstances, not by theoretical deductions. For the mass of men, i.e., the proletariat, these theoretical notions do not exist and hence do not require to be dissolved, and if this mass ever had any theoretical notions, e.g., religion, these have now long been dissolved by circumstances.

The purely national character of these questions and solutions is moreover shown by the fact that these theorists believe in all seriousness that chimeras like "the God-Man," "Man," etc., have presided over individual epochs of history. Saint Bruno even goes so far as to assert that only "criticism and critics have made history." And when they themselves construct historical systems, they skip over all earlier periods in the greatest haste and pass immediately from "Mongolism" to history "with meaningful content," that is to say, to the history, of the *Hallische* and *Deutsche Jahrbücher* and the dissolution of the Hegelian school into a general squabble. They forget all other nations, all real events, and the *theatrum mundi* [world theater] is confined to the Leipzig book fair and the mutual quarrels of "criticism," [Bruno Bauer] "man," [Ludwig Feuerbach] and "the unique" [Max Stirner].

If for once these theorists treat really historical subjects, as for instance, the eighteenth century, they merely give a history of ideas, separated from the facts and the practical development underlying them; and even that merely in order to represent that period as an imperfect preliminary stage, the as yet limited predecessor of the truly historical age, i.e., the period of the German philosophic struggle from 1840 to 1844. As might be expected when the history of an earlier period is written with the aim of accentuating the brilliance of an unhistoric person and his fantasies, all the really historic events, even the really historic interventions of politics in history, receive no mention. Instead, we get a narrative based not on research but on arbitrary constructions and literary gossip, such as Saint Bruno provided in his now forgotten history of the eighteenth century.

These pompous and arrogant hucksters of ideas, who imagine themselves infinitely exalted above all national prejudices, are thus in practice far more national than the beer-swilling philistines who dream of a united Germany. They do not recognize the deeds of other nations as historical; they live in Germany, within Germany 1281 and for Germany; they turn the Rhine-song into a religious hymn, and conquer Alsace and Lorraine by robbing French philosophy instead of the French state, by Germanizing French ideas instead of French provinces. Herr Venedey is a cosmopolitan compared with the Saints Bruno and Max, who, in the universal dominance of theory, proclaim the universal dominance of Germany.

Feuerbach: philosophical, and real, liberation

It is also clear from these arguments how grossly Feuerbach is deceiving himself when, by virtue of the qualification "common man," he declares himself a communist, transforms the latter into a predicate of "man," and thereby thinks it possible to change the word "communist," which in the real world means the follower of a definite revolutionary party, into a mere category. Feuerbach's whole deduction with regard to the relation of men to one another goes only so far as to prove that men need and always have needed each other. He wants to establish consciousness of this fact, that is to say, like the other theorists, merely to produce a correct consciousness about an existing fact; whereas for the real communist it is a question of overthrowing the existing state of things. We thoroughly appreciate, moreover, that Feuerbach, in endeavoring to produce consciousness of just this fact, is going as far as a theorist possibly can, without ceasing to be a theorist and philosopher.

As an example of Feuerbach's acceptance and at the same time misunderstanding of existing reality, which he still shares with our opponents, we recall the passage in the *Philosophy of the Future* where he develops the view that the existence of a thing or a man is at the same time its or his essence, that the conditions of existence, the mode of life and activity of an animal or human individual are those in which its "essence" feels itself satisfied. Here every exception is expressly conceived as an unhappy chance, as an abnormality which cannot be altered. Thus, if millions of proletarians feel by no means contented with their living conditions, if their "existence" does not in the least correspond to their "essence," then, according to the passage quoted, this is an unavoidable misfortune, which must be borne quietly. The millions of proletarians and communists, however, think differently and will prove this in time, when they bring their "existence" into harmony with their "essence" in a practical way, by means of a revolution. Feuerbach, therefore, never speaks of the world of man in such cases, but always takes refuge in external nature, and moreover, in nature which has not yet been subdued by men. But every new invention, every advance made by industry, detaches another piece from this domain, so that the ground which produces examples illustrating such Feuerbachian propositions is steadily shrinking.

The "essence" of the fish is its "being"—water—to go no further than this one proposition. The "essence" of the freshwater fish is the water of a river. But the latter ceases to be the "essence" of the fish and is no longer a suitable medium of existence as soon as the river is made to serve industry, as soon as it is polluted by dyes and other waste products and navigated by steamboats, or as soon as its water is diverted into canals where simple drainage can deprive the fish of its medium of existence. The explanation that all such contradictions are inevitable abnormalities does not essentially differ from the consolation which Saint Max Stirner offers to the discontented, saving that this contradiction is their own contradiction, and this predicament their own predicament, whereupon, they should either set their minds at ease, keep their disgust to themselves, or revolt against it in some fantastic way. It differs just as little from Saint Bruno's allegation that these unfortunate circumstances are due to the fact that those concerned are stuck in the muck of "substance," have not advanced to "absolute self-consciousness and do not realize that these adverse conditions are spirit of their spirit.

Preconditions of the real liberation of man

We shall, of course, not take the trouble to enlighten our wise philosophers by explaining to them that the "liberation" of man is not advanced a single step by reducing philosophy, theology, substance, and all the trash to "self-consciousness," and by liberating man from the domination of these phrases, which have never held him in thrall. Nor will we explain to them that it is only possible to achieve real liberation in the real world and by employing real means, that slavery cannot be abolished without the steam engine, the mule, and spinning jenny; serfdom cannot be abolished without improved agriculture; and that, in general, people cannot be liberated as long as they are unable to obtain food and drink, housing and clothing in adequate quality and quantity. "Liberation" is an historical and not a mental act, and it is brought about by historical conditions, the development of industry, commerce, agriculture, the conditions of intercourse . . . [gap in the manuscript]

In Germany, a country where only a trivial historical development is taking place, these mental developments, these glorified and ineffective trivialities, naturally serve as a substitute for the lack of historical development, and they take root and have to be combated. But this fight is of local importance.

Feuerbach's contemplative and inconsistent materialism

In reality and for the practical materialist, i.e., the communist, it is a question of revolutionizing the existing world, of practically attacking and changing existing things. When occasionally we find such views with Feuerbach, they are never more than isolated surmises and have much too little influence on his general outlook to be considered here as anything else than embryos capable of development. Feuerbach's conception of the sensuous world is confined, on the one hand, to mere contemplation of it, and on the other, to mere feeling; he says "Man" instead of "real historical man." "Man" is really "the German." In the first case, the contemplation of the sensuous world, he necessarily lights on things which contradict his consciousness and feeling, which disturb the harmony he presupposes, the harmony of all parts of the sensuous world and especially of man and nature. To remove this disturbance, he must take refuge in a double perception, a profane one which only perceives the "flatly obvious," and a higher, philosophical, one which perceives the "true essence" of things. He does not see how the sensuous world around him is, not a thing given direct from all eternity, remaining ever the same, but the product of industry and of the state of society; and, indeed, in the sense that it is a historical product, the result of the activity of a whole succession of generations, each standing on the shoulders of the preceding one, developing its industry and its intercourse, modifying its social system according to the changed needs. Even the objects of the simplest "sensuous certainty" are only given him through social development, industry, and commercial intercourse. The cherry tree, like almost all fruit trees, was, as is well known, only a few centuries ago transplanted by commerce into our zone, and therefore, only by this action of a definite society in a definite age has it become "sensuous certainty" for Feuerbach.

Incidentally, when we conceive things thus—as they really are and happened—every profound philosophical problem is resolved, as will be seen even more clearly later, quite simply into an empirical fact. For instance, the important question of the relation of man to nature—Bruno [Bauer] goes so far as to speak of "the antitheses in nature and history," as though these were two separate "things," and man did not always have before him a historical nature and a natural history—out of which all the "unfathomably lofty works" on "substance" and "self-consciousness" were born, crumbles of itself when we understand that the celebrated "unity of man with nature" has always existed in industry and has existed in varying forms in every epoch according to the lesser or greater development of industry, just like the "struggle" of man with nature, right up to the development of his productive powers on a corresponding basis. Industry and commerce, production and the exchange of the necessities of life, themselves determine distribution, the structure of the different social classes, and are, in turn, determined by it as to the mode in which they are carried on. And so it happens that in Manchester, for instance, Feuerbach sees only factories and machines, where a hundred years ago only spinning wheels and weaving rooms were to be seen, or in the Campagna of Rome, he finds only pasture lands and swamps, where in the time of Augustus he would have found nothing but the vineyards and villas of Roman capitalists.

Feuerbach speaks in particular of the perception of natural science; he mentions secrets which are disclosed only to the eye of the physicist and chemist; but where would natural science be without industry and commerce? Even this pure natural science is provided with an aim, as with its material, only through trade and industry, through the sensuous activity of men. So much is this activity, this unceasing sensuous labor and creation, this production, the basis of the whole sensuous world as it now exists, that, were it interrupted only for a year, Feuerbach would not only find an enormous change in the natural world, but would very soon find that the whole world of men and his own perceptive faculty, nay his own existence, were missing. Of course, in all this the priority of external nature remains unassailed, and all this has no application to the original men produced by *generatio aequivoca* [spontaneous generation]; but this differentiation has meaning only insofar as man is considered to be distinct from nature. For that matter, nature, the nature that preceded human history, is not by any means the nature in which Feuerbach lives, it is nature which today no longer exists anywhere—except perhaps on a few Australian coral islands of recent origin—and which, therefore, does not exist for Feuerbach.

Certainly, Feuerbach has a great advantage over the "pure" materialists in that he realizes how man too is an "object of the senses." But apart from the fact that he only conceives him as an "object of the senses, not as sensuous activity," because he still remains in the realm of theory and conceives of men, not in their given social connection, not under their existing conditions of life, which have made them what they are, he never arrives at the really existing active men, but stops at the abstraction "Man," and gets no further than recognizing "the true, individual, corporeal man," emotionally, i.e., he knows no other "human relationships" "of man to man" than love and friendship, and even then idealized. He gives no criticism of the present conditions of life. Thus he never manages to conceive the sensuous world as the total living sensuous activity of the individuals composing it; and therefore, when, for example, he sees instead of healthy men a crowd of scrofulous, overworked, and consumptive starvelings, he is compelled to take refuge in the "higher perception" and in the ideal "compensation in the species," and thus to relapse into idealism at the very point where the communist materialist sees the necessity, and at the same time the condition, of a transformation both of industry and of the social structure.

As far as Feuerbach is a materialist he does not deal with history, and as far as he considers history he is not a materialist. With him materialism and history diverge completely, a fact which, incidentally, is already obvious from what has been said.

Ruling class and ruling ideas

The ideas of the ruling class are in every epoch the ruling ideas, i.e., the class which is the ruling material force of society, is at the same time its ruling intellectual force. The class which has the means of material production at its disposal, has control at the same time over the means of mental production, so that thereby, generally speaking, the ideas of those who lack the means of mental production are subject to it. The ruling ideas are nothing more than the ideal expression of the dominant material relationships, the dominant material relationships grasped as ideas; hence of the relationships which make the one class the ruling one, therefore, the ideas of its dominance. The individuals composing the ruling class possess among other things consciousness, and therefore, think. Insofar, therefore, as they rule as a class and determine the extent and compass of an epoch, it is self-evident that they do this in its whole range, hence among other things, rule also as thinkers, as producers of ideas, and regulate the production and distribution of the ideas of their age: thus their ideas are the ruling ideas of the epoch. For instance, in an age and in a country where royal power, aristocracy, and bourgeoisie are contending for mastery and where, therefore, mastery is shared, the doctrine of the separation of powers proves to be the dominant idea and is expressed as an "eternal law."

The division of labor, which we already saw above as one of the chief forces of history up till now, manifests itself also in the ruling class as the division of mental and material labor, so that inside this class one part appears as the thinkers of the class—its active, conceptive ideologists, who make the perfecting of the illusion of the class about itself their chief source of livelihood—while the others' attitude to these ideas and illusions is more passive and receptive, because they are in reality the active members of this class and have less time to make up illusions and ideas about themselves. Within this class this cleavage can even develop into a certain opposition and hostility between the two parts, which, however, in the case of a practical collision, in which the class itself is endangered, automatically comes to nothing, in which case there also vanishes the semblance that the ruling ideas were not the ideas of the ruling class and had a power distinct from the power of this class. The existence of revolutionary ideas in a particular period presupposes the existence of a revolutionary class; about the premises for the latter sufficient has already been said above.

If now, in considering the course of history, we detach the ideas of the ruling class from the ruling class itself and attribute to them an independent existence, if we confine ourselves to saying that these or those ideas were dominant at a given time, without bothering ourselves about the conditions of production and the producers of these ideas, if we thus ignore the individuals and world conditions which are the source of the ideas, we can say, for instance, that during the time that the aristocracy was dominant, the concepts honor, loyalty, etc., were dominant, during the dominance of the bourgeoisie the concepts freedom, equality, etc. The ruling class itself on the whole imagines this to be so. This conception of history, which is common to all historians, particularly since the eighteenth century, will necessarily come up against the phenomenon that increasingly abstract ideas hold sway, i.e., ideas which increasingly take on the form of universality. For each new class which puts itself in the place of one ruling before it, is compelled, merely in order to carry through its aim, to represent its interest as the common interest of all the members of society, that is, expressed in ideal form: it has to give its ideas the form of universality, and represent them as the only rational, universally valid ones. The class making a revolution appears from the very start, if only because it is opposed to a class, not as a class, but as the representative of the whole of society; it appears as the whole mass of society confronting the one ruling class.

> Universality corresponds to 1) the class versus the estate; 2) the competition, worldwide intercourse, etc.; 3) the great numerical strength of the ruling class; 4) the illusion of the common interests—in the beginning this illusion is true; 5) the delusion of the ideologists and the division of labor. [Marginal note by Marx]

It can do this because, to start with, its interest really is more connected with the common interest of all other non-ruling classes, because under the pressure of hitherto existing conditions its interest has not yet been able to develop as the particular interest of a particular class. Its victory, therefore, benefits also many individuals of the other classes which are not winning a dominant position, but only insofar as it now puts these individuals in a position to raise themselves into the ruling class. When the French bourgeoisie overthrew the power of the aristocracy, it thereby made it possible for many proletarians to raise themselves above the proletariat, but only insofar as they become bourgeois. Every new class, therefore, achieves its hegemony only on a broader basis than that of the class ruling previously, whereas the opposition of the non-ruling class against the new ruling class later develops all the more sharply and profoundly. Both these things determine the fact that the struggle to be waged against this new ruling class, in its turn, aims at a more decided and radical negation of the previous conditions of society than could all previous classes which sought to rule.

This whole semblance, that the rule of a certain class is only the rule of certain ideas, comes to a natural end, of course, as soon as class rule in general ceases to be the form in which society is organized, that is to say, as soon as it is no longer necessary to represent a particular interest as general or the "general interest" as ruling.

Once the ruling ideas have been separated from the ruling individuals and, above all, from the relationships which result from a given stage of the mode of production, and in this way, the conclusion has been reached that history is always under the sway of ideas, it is very easy to abstract from these various ideas "the idea," the notion, etc., as the dominant force in history, and thus, to understand all these separate ideas and concepts as "forms of self-determination" on the part of the concept developing in history. It follows then naturally, too, that all the relationships of men can be derived from the concept of man, man as conceived, the essence of man, Man. This has been done by the speculative philosophers. Hegel himself confesses at the end of the *History of Philosophy* that he "has considered the progress of the concept only" and has represented in history the "true theodicy." Now one can go back again to the producers of the "concept," to the theorists, ideologists, and philosophers, and one comes then to the conclusion that the philosophers, the thinkers as such, have at all times been dominant in history: a conclusion, as we see, already expressed by Hegel. The whole trick of proving the hegemony of the spirit in history—hierarchy, Stirner calls it—is thus confined to the following three efforts.

No. 1. One must separate the ideas of those ruling for empirical reasons, under empirical conditions and as empirical individuals, from these actual rulers, and thus recognize the rule of ideas or illusions in history.

No. 2. One must bring an order into this rule of ideas, prove a mystical connection among the successive ruling ideas, which is managed by understanding them as "acts of self-determination on the part of the concept." This is possible because by virtue of their empirical basis, these ideas are really connected with one another and because, conceived as mere ideas, they become self-distinctions, distinctions made by thought.

No. 3. To remove the mystical appearance of this "self-determining concept" it is changed into a person—"Self-Consciousness"—or, to appear thoroughly materialistic, into a series of persons, who represent the "concept" in history, into the "thinkers," the "philosophers," the ideologists, who again are understood as the manufacturers of history, as the "council of guardians," as the rulers. Thus, the whole body of materialistic elements has been removed from history and now full rein can be given to the speculative steed.

While in ordinary life every shopkeeper is very well able to distinguish between what somebody professes to be and what he really is, our historians have not yet won even this trivial insight. They take every epoch at its word and believe that everything it says and imagines about itself is true.

MATERIALISM AND EMPIRIOCRITICISM: CRITICAL COMMENTS ON A REACTIONARY PHILOSOPHY

V.I. Lenin
1908

During the period of reaction and ideological backsliding that followed the defeat of the 1905 revolution, Lenin, as always, went back to basics in this comprehensive defense of the fundamentals of Marxism against the encroachment of alien class ideas. Empiriocriticism was much in vogue at that time, having been popularized by the physicist Ernst Mach. Many Bolsheviks believed it represented something "new" that could and should be incorporated into Marxism—when in reality it was a rehash of Bishop Berkeley's and Immanuel Kant's variants of subjective idealism and agnosticism. In this work, Lenin meticulously dismantles these ideas and exposes their reactionary nature. Echoed yet again in more recent times by logical positivism and its variants, this classic of Marxist philosophy is a "must-read" for all those fighting against the dead end of agnosticism and its ultimate political offspring—reformism. We present here a hefty selection of material as an enticement to tackle this magnificent work in its entirety. Please note that the symbol § is used to indicate the section of a work being cited.

In Lieu of an Introduction

How certain "Marxists" in 1908 and certain idealists in 1710 refuted materialism

Anyone in the least acquainted with philosophical literature must know that scarcely a single contemporary professor of philosophy (or of theology) can be found who is not directly or indirectly engaged in refuting materialism. They have declared materialism refuted a thousand times, yet are continuing to refute it for the thousand and first time. All our revisionists are engaged in refuting materialism, pretending, however, that actually they are only refuting the materialist Plekhanov, and not the materialist Engels, nor the materialist Feuerbach, nor the materialist views of J. Dietzgen—and, moreover, that they are refuting materialism from the standpoint of "recent" and "modern" positivism, natural science, and so forth. Without citing quotations, which anyone desiring to do so could cull by the hundred from the books above mentioned, I shall refer to those arguments by which materialism is being combated by Bazarov, Bogdanov, Yushkevich, Valentinov, Chernov, and other Machians. I shall use this latter term throughout as a synonym for "empiriocriticist" because it is shorter and simpler and has already acquired rights of citizenship in Russian literature. That Ernst Mach is the most popular representative of empiriocriticism today is universally acknowledged in philosophical literature, while Bogdanov's and Yushkevich's departures from "pure" Machism are of absolutely secondary importance, as will be shown later.

The materialists, we are told, recognize something unthinkable and unknowable—"things-in-themselves"—matter "outside of experience" and outside of our knowledge. They lapse into genuine mysticism by admitting the existence of something beyond, something transcending the bounds of "experience" and knowledge. When they say that matter, by acting upon our sense organs, produces sensations, the materialists take as their basis the "unknown," nothingness; for do they not themselves declare our sensations to be the only source of knowledge? The materialists lapse into "Kantianism" (Plekhanov, by recognizing the existence of "things-in-themselves," i.e., things outside of our consciousness); they "duplicate" the world and preach "dualism," for the materialists hold that beyond the appearance there is the thing-in-itself; beyond the immediate sense data there is something else, some fetish, an "idol," an absolute, a source of "metaphysics," a double of religion ("holy matter," as Bazarov says).

Such are the arguments levelled by the Machians against materialism, as repeated and retold in varying keys by the aforementioned writers.

In order to test whether these arguments are new, and whether they are really directed against only one Russian materialist who "lapsed into Kantianism," we shall give some detailed quotations from the works of an old idealist, George Berkeley. This historical inquiry is all the more necessary in the introduction to our comments since we shall have frequent occasion to refer to Berkeley and his trend in philosophy, for the Machians misrepresent both the relation of Mach to Berkeley and the essence of Berkeley's philosophical line.

The work of Bishop George Berkeley, published in 1710 under the title *Treatise Concerning the Principles of Human Knowledge*, begins with the following argument:

> It is evident to anyone who takes a survey of the *objects* of human knowledge, that they are either ideas actually imprinted on the senses; or else such as are perceived by attending to the passions and operations of the mind; or lastly, ideas formed by help of memory and imagination . . . By sight I have the ideas of light and colors, with their several degrees and variations. By touch I perceive hard and soft, heat and cold, motion and resistance . . . Smelling furnishes me with odors; the palate with tastes; and hearing conveys sounds . . . And as several of these are observed to accompany each other, they come to be marked by one name, and so to be reputed as one thing. Thus, for example, a certain color, taste, smell, figure, and consistence having been observed to go together, are accounted one distinct thing, signified by the name apple; other collections of ideas constitute a stone, a tree, a book, and the like sensible things . . . (§ 1).

Such is the content of the first section of Berkeley's work. We must remember that Berkeley takes as the basis of his philosophy "hard, soft, heat, cold, colors, tastes, odors," etc. For Berkeley, things are "collections of ideas," this expression designating the aforesaid, let us say, qualities or sensations, and not abstract thoughts.

Berkeley goes on to say that besides these "ideas or objects of knowledge" there exists something that perceives them—"mind, spirit, soul, or *myself*" (§ 2). It is self-evident, the philosopher concludes, that "ideas" cannot exist outside of the mind that perceives them. In order to convince ourselves of this it is enough to consider the meaning of the word "exist."

"The table I write on I say exists, that is, I see and feel it; and if I were out of my study I should say it existed; meaning thereby that if I was in my study I might perceive it . . ." That is what Berkeley says in § 3 of his work and thereupon he begins a polemic against the people whom he calls materialists (§§ 18, 19, etc.). "For as to what is said of the absolute existence of unthinking things, without any relation to their being perceived," he says, "that is to me perfectly unintelligible." To exist means to be perceived ("Their *esse* is *percipi*," § 3—a dictum of Berkeley's frequently quoted in textbooks on the history of philosophy). "It is indeed an opinion strangely prevailing amongst men, that houses, mountains, rivers, and in a word, all sensible objects have an existence, natural or real, distinct from their being perceived by the understanding" (§ 4). This opinion is a "manifest contradiction," says Berkeley. "For, what are the aforementioned objects but the things we perceive by sense? and what do we perceive besides our own ideas or sensations? and is it not plainly repugnant that any one of these, or any combination of them, should exist unperceived?" (§ 4).

The expression "collection of ideas" Berkeley now replaces by what to him is an equivalent expression, *combination of sensations*, and accuses the materialists of a "repugnant" tendency to go still further, of seeking some source of this complex—that is, of this combination of sensations. In § 5 the materialists are accused of trifling with an abstraction, for to divorce the sensation from the object, according to Berkeley, is an empty abstraction. "In truth," he says at the end of § 5, omitted in the second edition, "the object and the sensation are the same thing, and cannot therefore be abstracted from each other." Berkeley goes on:

> But, say you, though the ideas themselves do not exist without the mind, yet there may be things like them, whereof they are copies or resemblances; which things exist without the mind, in an unthinking substance. I answer, an idea can be like nothing but an idea; a color or figure can be like nothing but another color or figure . . . I ask whether those supposed originals, or external things, of which our ideas are the pictures or representations, be themselves perceivable or not? If they are, then they are ideas and we have gained our point; but if you say they are not, I appeal to anyone whether it be sense to assert a color is like something which is invisible; hard or soft, like something which is intangible; and so of the rest. (§ 8).

As the reader sees, Bazarov's "arguments" against Plekhanov concerning the problem of whether things can exist outside of us apart from their action on us do not differ in the least from Berkeley's arguments against the materialists whom he does not mention by name. Berkeley considers the notion of the existence of "matter or corporeal substance" (§ 9) such a "contradiction," such a "repugnant" thing that it is really not worth wasting time exposing it. He says:

> But because the tenet of the existence of Matter seems to have taken so deep a root in the minds of philosophers, and draws after it so many ill consequences, I choose rather to be thought prolix and tedious than omit anything that might conduce to the full discovery and extirpation of that prejudice (§ 9).

We shall presently see to what ill consequences Berkeley is referring. Let us first finish with his theoretical arguments against the materialists. Denying the "absolute" existence of objects, that is, the existence of things outside human knowledge, Berkeley deliberately represents the viewpoint of his opponents as though they recognized the "thing-in-itself." In § 24 Berkeley writes in italics that the opinion which he is refuting recognizes *"the absolute existence of sensible objects in themselves, or without the mind."* The two fundamental lines of philosophical outlook are here depicted with the straightforwardness, clarity, and precision that distinguish the classical philosophers from the inventors of "new" systems in our day. Materialism is the recognition of "objects in themselves," or outside the mind; ideas and sensations are copies or images of those objects. The opposite doctrine (idealism) claims that objects do not exist "without the mind"; objects are "combinations of sensations."

This was written in 1710, fourteen years before the birth of Immanuel Kant, yet our Machians, supposedly on the basis of "recent" philosophy, have made the discovery that the recognition of "objects in themselves" is a result of the infection or distortion of materialism by Kantianism! The "new" discoveries of the Machians are the product of an astounding ignorance of the history of the basic philosophical trends.

Their next "new" thought consists in this: that the concepts "matter" or "substance" are remnants of old uncritical views. Mach and Avenarius, you see, advanced philosophical thought, deepened analysis, and eliminated these "absolutes," "unchangeable entities," etc. If you wish to check such assertions with the original sources, go to Berkeley and you will see that they are pretentious fictions. Berkeley says quite definitely that matter is "nonentity" (§ 68), that matter is *nothing* (§ 80). "You may," thus Berkeley ridicules the materialists, "if so it shall seem good, use the word *matter* in the same sense as other men use *nothing*." At the beginning, says Berkeley, it was believed that colors, odors, etc., "really exist," but subsequently such views were renounced, and it was seen that they only exist in dependence on our sensations. But this elimination of old errone- ous concepts was not completed; a remnant is the concept "substance" (§ 73), which is also a "prejudice," and which was finally exposed by Bishop Berkeley in 1710! In 1908 there are still wags who seriously believe Av- enarius, Petzoldt, Mach, and the rest, when they maintain that it is only "recent positivism" and "recent natural science" which have at last suc- ceeded in eliminating these "metaphysical" conceptions.

These same wags (Bogdanov among them) assure their readers that it was the new philosophy that explained the error of the "duplication of the world" in the doctrine of the eternally refuted materialists, who speak of some sort of a "reflection" by the human consciousness of things exist- ing outside the consciousness. A mass of sentimental verbiage has been written by the above-named authors about this "duplication." Owing to forgetfulness or ignorance, they failed to add that these new discoveries had already been discovered in 1710. Berkeley says:

"Our knowledge of these [i.e., ideas or things] has been very much obscured and confounded, and we have been led into very dangerous errors by supposing a twofold existence of the objects of sense—the one *intelligible* or in the mind, the other *real* and without the mind" (i.e., outside consciousness). And Berkeley ridicules this "repugnant" notion, which admits the possibility of thinking the unthinkable! The source of the "repugnancy," of course, follows from our supposing a difference be- tween *things* and *ideas* . . . "the supposition of external objects" (§ 87). This same source—as discovered by Berkeley in 1710 and rediscovered by Bogdanov in 1908—engenders a faith in fetishes and idols. "The exis- tence of Matter," says Berkeley, "or bodies unperceived, has not only been the main support of Atheists and Fatalists, but on the same principle doth Idolatry likewise in all its various forms depend" (§ 94).

Here we arrive at those "ill consequences" derived from the "absurd" doctrine of the existence of an external world which compelled Bishop Berkeley not only to refute this doctrine theoretically, but passionately to persecute its adherents as enemies.

> For as we have shown the doctrine of Matter or corporeal Substance to have been the main pillar and support of Skepticism, so likewise upon the same foundation have been raised all the impious schemes of Atheism and Irreligion . . . How great a friend material substance has

been to Atheists in all ages were needless to relate. All their monstrous systems have so visible and necessary a dependence on it, that when this cornerstone is once removed, the whole fabric cannot choose but fall to the ground, in so much that it is no longer worth while to bestow a particular consideration on the absurdities of every wretched sect of Atheists (§ 92).

Matter being once expelled out of nature drags with it so many skeptical and impious notions, such an incredible number of disputes and puzzling questions ["the principle of economy of thought," discovered by Mach in the seventies, "philosophy as a conception of the world according to the principle of minimum expenditure of effort"—Avenarius in 1876!] which have been thorns in the sides of divines as well as philosophers, and made so much fruitless work for mankind, that if the arguments we have produced against it are not found equal to demonstration (as to me they evidently seem), yet I am sure all friends to knowledge, peace, and religion have reason to wish they were (§ 96).

Frankly and bluntly did Bishop Berkeley argue! In our time these very same thoughts on the "economical" elimination of "matter" from philosophy are enveloped in a much more artful form, and confused by the use of a "new" terminology, so that these thoughts may be taken by naïve people for "recent" philosophy!

But Berkeley was not only candid as to the tendencies of his philosophy, he also endeavored to cover its idealistic nakedness, to represent it as being free from absurdities and acceptable to "common sense." Instinctively defending himself against the accusation of what would nowadays be called subjective idealism and solipsism, he says that by our philosophy "we are not deprived of any one thing in nature" (§ 34). Nature remains, and the distinction between realities and chimeras remains, only "they both equally exist in the mind."

I do not argue against the existence of any one thing that we can apprehend, either by sense or reflection. That the things I see with my eyes and touch with my hands do exist, really exist, I make not the least question. The only thing whose existence we deny is that which *philosophers* [Berkeley's italics] call Matter or corporeal substance. And in doing this there is no damage done to the rest of mankind, who, I dare say, will never miss it . . . The Atheist indeed will want the color of an empty name to support his impiety . . .

This thought is made still clearer in § 37, where Berkeley replies to the charge that his philosophy destroys corporeal substance:

> . . . if the word *substance* be taken in the vulgar sense, for a *combina-tion* of sensible qualities, such as extension, solidity, weight, and the like—this we cannot be accused of taking away; but if it be taken in a philosophic sense, for the support of accidents or qualities without the mind—then indeed I acknowledge that we take it away, if one may be said to take away that which never had any existence, not even in the imagination.

Not without good cause did the English philosopher, Fraser, an idealist and adherent of Berkeleianism, who published Berkeley's works and sup-plied them with his own annotations, designate Berkeley's doctrine by the term "natural realism." This amusing terminology must by all means be noted, for it in fact expresses Berkeley's intention to counterfeit real-ism. In our further exposition we shall frequently find "recent" "positiv-ists" repeating the same stratagem or counterfeit in a different form and in a different verbal wrapping. Berkeley does not deny the existence of real things! Berkeley does not go counter to the opinion of all humanity! Berkeley denies "only" the teaching of the philosophers, viz., the theory of knowledge, which seriously and resolutely takes as the foundation of all its reasoning the recognition of the external world and the reflection thereof in the minds of men. Berkeley does not deny natural science, which has always adhered (mostly unconsciously) to this, that is, the ma-terialist, theory of knowledge. We read in § 59:

> We may, from the experience [Berkeley—a philosophy of "pure experi-ence"] we have had of the train and succession of ideas in our minds . . . make . . . well-grounded predictions concerning the ideas we shall be affected with pursuant to a great train of actions, and be enabled to pass a right judgment of what would have appeared to us, in case we were placed in circumstances very different from those we are in at present. Herein consists the knowledge of nature, which [listen to this!] may preserve its use and certainty very consistently with what hath been said.

Let us regard the external world, nature, as "a combination of sensations" evoked in our mind by a deity. Acknowledge this and give up searching for the "ground" of these sensations outside the mind, outside man, and I will acknowledge within the framework of my idealist theory of knowl-edge *all* natural science and all the importance and certainty of its deduc-tions. It is precisely this framework, and only this framework, that I need for my deductions in favor of "peace and religion." Such is Berkeley's train of thought. It correctly expresses the essence of idealist philosophy and its social significance, and we shall encounter it later when we come to speak of the relation of Machism to natural science.

Let us now consider another recent discovery that was borrowed from Bishop Berkeley in the twentieth century by the recent positivist and critical realist, P. Yushkevich. This discovery is "empiriosymbolism." "Berkeley," says Fraser "thus reverts to his favorite theory of a Universal Natural Symbolism." Did these words not occur in an edition of 1871, one might have suspected the English fideist philosopher Fraser of plagiarizing both the modern mathematician and physicist Poincaré and the Russian "Marxist" Yushkevich!

This theory of Berkeley's, which threw Fraser into raptures, is set forth by the Bishop as follows:

> The connexion of ideas [do not forget that for Berkeley ideas and things are identical] does not imply the relation of *cause* and *effect*, but only of a mark or *sign* with the thing *signified* (§ 65).

> Hence, it is evident that those things, which under the notion of a cause cooperating or concurring to the production of effects, are altogether inexplicable, and run us into great absurdities, may be very naturally explained . . . when they are considered only as marks or signs for our information (§ 66).

Of course, in the opinion of Berkeley and Fraser, it is no other than the deity who informs us by means of these "empiriosymbols." The epistemological significance of *symbolism* in Berkeley's theory, however, consists in this, that it is to replace "the doctrine" which "pretends to explain things by corporeal causes" (§ 66).

We have before us two philosophical trends in the question of causality. One "pretends to explain things by corporeal causes." It is clear that it is connected with the "doctrine of matter" refuted as "repugnant" by Bishop Berkeley. The other reduces the "notion of cause" to the notion of a "mark or sign" which serves for "our information" (supplied by God). We shall meet these two trends in a twentieth-century garb when we analyze the attitudes of Machism and dialectical materialism to this question.

Further, as regards the question of reality, it ought also to be remarked that Berkeley, refusing as he does to recognize the existence of things outside the mind, tries to find a criterion for distinguishing between the real and the fictitious. In § 36 he says that those "ideas" which the minds of men evoke at pleasure "are faint, weak, and unsteady in respect to others they perceive by sense; which, being impressed upon them according to certain rules or laws of nature, speak themselves about the effects of a Mind more powerful and wise than human spirits. These latter are said to have *more reality* in them than the former; by which is meant that they are more affecting, orderly and distinct, and that they are not fictions of the mind perceiving them . . ." Elsewhere (§ 84) Berkeley tries to connect the notion of reality with the simultaneous perception of the same sensations by many people. For instance, how shall we resolve the question as to whether the transformation of water into wine, of which we are being told, is real? "If at table all who were present should see, and smell, and taste, and drink wine, and find the effects of it, with me there could be no doubt of its reality." And Fraser explains: "Simultaneous perception of the 'same' . . . *sense* ideas by different persons, as distinguished from purely individual consciousness of *imaginary* objects and emotions, is here referred to as a test of the *reality* of the former."

From this it is evident that Berkeley's subjective idealism is not to be interpreted as though it ignored the distinction between individual and collective perception. On the contrary, he attempts on the basis of this distinction to construct a criterion of reality. Deriving "ideas" from the action of a deity upon the human mind, Berkeley thus approaches objective idealism: the world proves to be not my idea but the product of a single supreme spiritual cause that creates both the "laws of nature" and the laws distinguishing "more real" ideas from less real, and so forth.

In another work, *The Three Dialogues Between Hylas and Philonous* (1713), where he endeavors to present his views in an especially popular form, Berkeley sets forth the opposition between his doctrine and the materialist doctrine in the following way:

> I assert as well as you [materialists] that, since we are affected from without, we must allow Powers to be without, in a Being distinct from ourselves . . . But then we differ as to the kind of this powerful being. I will have it to be Spirit, you Matter, or I know not what (I may add too, you know not what) third nature . . .

"This is the gist of the whole question," Fraser comments. "According to the Materialists, sensible phenomena are due to material substance, or to some unknown 'third nature'; according to Berkeley, to Rational Will; according to Hume and the Positivists, their origin is absolutely unknown, and we can only generalize them inductively, through custom, as facts."

Here the English Berkeleian, Fraser, approaches from his consistent idealist standpoint the same fundamental "lines" in philosophy which were so clearly characterized by the materialist Engels. In his work *Ludwig Feuerbach* Engels divides philosophers into "two great camps"—materialists and idealists. Engels—dealing with theories of the two trends much more developed, varied and rich in content than Fraser dealt with—sees the fundamental distinction between them in the fact that while for the materialists nature is primary and spirit secondary, for the idealists the reverse is the case. In between these two camps Engels places the adherents of Hume and Kant, who deny the possibility of knowing the world, or at least of knowing it fully, and calls them *agnostics*. In his *Ludwig Feuerbach*, Engels applies this term only to the adherents of Hume (those people whom Fraser calls, and who like to call themselves, "positivists"). But in his article "On Historical Materialism," Engels explicitly speaks of the standpoint of *"the Neo-Kantian agnostic"*—regarding Neo-Kantianism[1] as

---

1 Neo-Kantianism—a reactionary trend in bourgeois philosophy preaching subjective idealism under the slogan of a return to Kantian philosophy. It arose in the middle of the nineteenth century in Germany, where at this time there was an increased interest in Kantianism. In 1865, Otto Liebmann's book *Kant and the Epigones* was published, each chapter ending with the call: "Back to Kant." Liebmann put forward the task of correcting Kant's "main error"—the recognition of "things-in-themselves." The revival of Kantianism was helped by the works of Kuno Fischer and Eduard Zeller, and one of the early representatives of neo-Kantianism was Friedrich Albert Lange who tried to use physiology as a basis for agnosticism.

Later, two main schools of Neo-Kantianism were formed: that of Marburg and that of Freiburg or Baden. The former tried to substantiate idealism by speculating on the successes of natural science, especially on the penetration of mathematical methods into physics; the latter counterposed the social sciences to natural science, trying to prove that historical phenomena are strictly individual and not subject to the operation of any laws. Both schools put the question of the logical basis of science in place of the fundamental question of philosophy. Criticizing Kant "from the right," the neo-Kantians declared the "thing-in-itself" to be a "limiting concept" to which knowledge was tending. Denying the objective existence of the material world, they regarded as the object of knowledge not the laws of nature and society, but merely the phenomena of consciousness. In contrast to the agnosticism of the natural scientists, that of the neo Kantians was not "shamefaced materialism," for it asserted the impotence of science in regard to cognition and changes of reality. The neo-Kantians openly attacked Marxism, counterposing to it "ethical socialism." In accordance with their theory of knowledge they declared

a variety of agnosticism.

We cannot dwell here on this remarkably correct and profound judgment of Engels's—a judgment which is shamelessly ignored by the Machians. We shall discuss it in detail later on. For the present we shall confine ourselves to pointing to this Marxist terminology and to this meeting of extremes: the views of a consistent materialist and of a consistent idealist on the fundamental philosophical trends. In order to illustrate these trends—with which we shall constantly have to deal in our further exposition—let us briefly note the views of outstanding philosophers of the eighteenth century who pursued a different path from Berkeley.

Here are Hume's arguments. In his *An Enquiry Concerning Human Understanding*, in the chapter on skeptical philosophy, he says:

> It seems evident, that men are carried, by a natural instinct or prepossession, to repose faith in their senses; and that, without any reasoning, or even almost before the use of reason, we always suppose an external universe, which depends not on our perception, but would exist though we and every sensible creature were absent or annihilated. Even the animal creations are governed by a like opinion, and preserve this belief of external objects, in all their thoughts, designs, and actions
> ... But this universal and primary opinion of all men is soon destroyed by the slightest philosophy, which teaches us, that nothing can ever be present to the mind but an image or perception, and that the senses are only the inlets, through which these images are conveyed, without being able to produce any immediate intercourse between the mind and the object. The table, which we see, seems to diminish, as we remove farther from it: But the real table, which exists independent of us, suffers no alteration: It was, therefore, nothing but its image, which was present to the mind. These are the obvious dictates of reason; and no man, who reflects, ever doubted, that the existences, which we consider, when we say, "this house," and "that tree" are nothing but perceptions in the mind ...

---

socialism to be the "ethical ideal" of human social existence, an ideal to which mankind was striving but which it could not attain. This "theory" of the neo-Kantians was seized upon by the revisionists, headed by Eduard Bernstein, who put forward the slogan: "The movement is everything, the final goal is nothing." Neo-Kantianism was one of the philosophical pillars of the Second International. In Russia attempts to "combine" neo-Kantianism and Marxism were made by the "legal Marxists." G. V. Plekhanov, Paul Lafargue, and Franz Mehring opposed the neo-Kantian revision of Marxism. Lenin laid bare the reactionary nature of neo-Kantianism and showed its connection with other trends of bourgeois philosophy (immanentism, Machism, pragmatism, etc.).

By what argument can it be proved, that the perceptions of the mind must be caused by external objects, entirely different from them, though resembling them (if that be possible), and could not arise either from the energy of the mind itself, or from the suggestion of some invisible and unknown spirit, or from some other cause still more unknown to us?

How shall the question be determined? By experience surely; as all other questions of a like nature. But here experience is, and must be entirely silent. The mind has never anything present to it but the perceptions, and cannot possibly reach any experience of their connection with objects. This supposition of such a connection is, therefore, without any foundation in reasoning.

To have recourse to the veracity of the Supreme Being, in order to prove the veracity of our senses, is surely making a very unexpected circuit . . . if the external world be once called in question, we shall be at a loss to find arguments, by which we may prove the existence of that Being, or any of his attributes.

He says the same thing in his *Treatise of Human Nature*: "Our perceptions are our only objects." By skepticism Hume means refusal to explain sensations as the effects of objects, spirit, etc., refusal to reduce perceptions to the external world, on the one hand, and to a deity or to an unknown spirit, on the other. And the author of the introduction to the French translation of Hume, F. Pillon—a philosopher of a trend akin to Mach—as we shall see below—justly remarks that for Hume subject and object are reduced to "groups of various perceptions," to "elements of consciousness, to impressions, ideas, etc."; that the only concern should be with the "groupings and combinations of these elements." The English Humean, Huxley, who coined the apt and correct term "agnosticism," in his *Hume* also emphasizes the fact that Hume, regarding "sensations" as the "primary and irreducible states of consciousness," is not entirely consistent on the question how the origin of sensations is to be explained, whether by the effect of objects on man or by the creative power of the mind. "Realism and idealism are equally probable hypotheses" (i.e., for Hume). Hume does not go beyond sensations. "Thus the colors red and blue, and the odor of a rose, are simple impressions . . . A red rose gives us a complex impression, capable of resolution into the simple impressions of red color, rose scent, and numerous others." Hume admits both the "materialist position" and the "idealist position"; the "collection of perceptions" may be generated by the Fichtean "ego" or may be a "signification" and even a "symbol" of a "real something." This is how Huxley interprets Hume.

As for the materialists, here is an opinion of Berkeley given by Diderot, the leader of the Encyclopedists:

> Those philosophers are called *idealists* who, being conscious only of their existence and of the sensations which succeed each other within themselves, do not admit anything else. An extravagant system which, to my thinking, only the blind could have originated; a system which, to the shame of human intelligence and philosophy, is the most difficult to combat, although the most absurd of all.

And Diderot, who came very close to the standpoint of contemporary materialism—that arguments and syllogisms alone do not suffice to refute idealism, and that here it is not a question for theoretical argument—notes the similarity of the premises both of the idealist Berkeley, and the sensationalist Condillac. In his opinion, Condillac should have undertaken a refutation of Berkeley in order to avoid such absurd conclusions being drawn from the treatment of sensations as the only source of our knowledge.

In the "Conversation Between d'Alembert and Diderot," Diderot states his philosophical position thus:

> . . . Suppose a piano to be endowed with the faculty of sensation and memory, tell me, would it not of its own accord repeat those airs which you have played on its keys? We are instruments endowed with sensation and memory. Our senses are so many keys upon which surrounding nature strikes and which often strike upon themselves. And this is all, in my opinion, that occurs in a piano organized like you and me.

D'Alembert retorts that such an instrument would have to possess the faculty of finding food for itself and of reproducing little pianos. Undoubtedly, contends Diderot. But take an egg:

> This is what refutes all the schools of theology and all the temples on earth. What is this egg? A mass that is insensible until the embryo is introduced thither, and when this embryo is introduced, what is it then? An insensible mass, for in its turn, this embryo is only an inert and crude liquid. How does this mass arrive at a different organization, arrive at sensibility and life? By means of heat. And what produces heat? Motion . . .

The animal that is hatched from the egg is endowed with all your sensations; it performs all your actions.

Would you maintain with Descartes that this is a simple imitating machine? Little children will laugh at you, and the philosophers will reply that if this be a machine then you too are a machine. If you admit that the difference between these animals and you is only one of organization, you will prove your common sense and sagacity, you will be right. But from this will follow the conclusion that refutes you; namely, that from inert matter organized in a certain way, impregnated with another bit of inert matter, by heat and motion—sensibility, life, memory, consciousness, emotion, and thought are generated.

One of the two, continues Diderot, either admit some "hidden element" in the egg, that penetrates to it in an unknown way at a certain stage of development, an element about which it is unknown whether it occupies space, whether it is material or whether it is created for the purpose—which is contradictory to common sense, and leads to inconsistencies and absurdities; or we must make "a simple supposition which explains everything, namely, that the faculty of sensation is a general property of matter, or a product of its organization." To d'Alembert's objection that such a supposition implies a quality which in its essence is incompatible with matter, Diderot retorts:

> And how do you know that the faculty of sensation is essentially incompatible with matter, since you do not know the essence of anything at all, either of matter, or of sensation? Do you understand the nature of motion any better, its existence in a body, its communication from one body to another?

D'Alembert:

> Without knowing the nature of sensation, or that of matter, I see, however, that the faculty of sensation is a simple quality, single, indivisible, and incompatible with a divisible subject or substratum.

Diderot:

> Metaphysico-theological nonsense! What, do you not see that all qualities of matter, that all its forms accessible to our senses are in their essence indivisible? There cannot be a larger or a smaller degree of impenetrability. There may be half of a round body, but there is no half of roundness . . . Be a physicist and admit the derivative character of the given effect when you see how it is derived, though you may be unable to explain the relation between the cause and the effect. Be logical and do not replace a cause that exists and explains everything by some other cause which it is impossible to conceive, and the connection of which with the effect is even more difficult to conceive, and which

engenders an infinite number of difficulties without solving a single one of them.

D'Alembert:

And what if I abandon this cause?

Diderot:

There is only one substance in the universe, in men and in animals. A hand organ is of wood, man of flesh. A finch is of flesh, and a musician is of flesh, but differently organized; but both are of the same origin, of the same formation, have the same functions and the same purpose.

D'Alembert:

And what establishes the similarity of sounds between your two pianos?

Diderot:

. . . The instrument endowed with the faculty of sensation, or the animal, has learned by experience that after a certain sound certain consequences follow outside of it; that other sentient instruments, like itself, or similar animals, approach, recede, demand, offer, wound, caress;—and all these consequences are associated in its memory and in the memory of other animals with the formation of sounds. Mark, in intercourse between people there is nothing beside sounds and actions. And to appreciate all the power of my system, mark again that it is faced with that same insurmountable difficulty which Berkeley adduced against the existence of bodies. There was a moment of insanity when the sentient piano imagined that it was the only piano in the world, and that the whole harmony of the universe resided within it.

This was written in 1769. And with this we shall conclude our brief historical enquiry. We shall have more than one occasion to meet "the insane piano" and the harmony of the universe residing within man when we come to analyze "recent positivism."

For the present we shall confine ourselves to one conclusion: the "recent" Machians have not adduced a single argument against the materialists that had not been adduced by Bishop Berkeley.

Let us mention as a curiosity that one of these Machians, Valentinov, vaguely sensing the falsity of his position, has tried to "cover up the traces" of his kinship with Berkeley and has done so in a rather amusing manner. On page 150 of his book we read:

. . . When those who, speaking of Mach, point to Berkeley, we ask, which Berkeley do they mean? Do they mean the Berkeley who traditionally regards himself [Valentinov wishes to say who is regarded] as a solipsist; the Berkeley who defends the immediate presence and providence of the deity? Generally speaking [?], do they mean Berkeley, the philosophizing bishop, the destroyer of atheism, or Berkeley, the thoughtful analyzer? With Berkeley the solipsist and preacher of religious metaphysics Mach indeed has nothing in common.

Valentinov is muddled; he was unable to make clear to himself why he was obliged to defend Berkeley the "thoughtful analyzer" and idealist against the materialist Diderot. Diderot drew a clear distinction between the fundamental philosophical trends. Valentinov confuses them, and while doing so very amusingly tries to console us: "We would not consider the 'kinship' of Mach to the idealist views of Berkeley a philosophical crime," he says, "even if this actually were the case." To confound two irreconcilable fundamental trends in philosophy—really, what "crime" is that? But that is what the whole wisdom of Mach and Avenarius amounts to. We shall now proceed to an examination of this wisdom.

Chapter One: The Theory of Knowledge of Empiriocriticism and of Dialectical Materialism

1.1 Sensations and complexes of sensations

The fundamental premises of the theory of knowledge of Mach and Avenarius are frankly, simply, and clearly expounded by them in their early philosophical works. To these works we shall now turn, postponing for later treatment an examination of the corrections and emendations subsequently made by these writers.

Mach wrote in 1872:

The task of science can only be:

1. To determine the laws of connection of ideas (Psychology).

2. To discover the laws of connection of sensations (Physics).

3. To explain the laws of connection between sensations and ideas (Psycho-physics).

This is quite clear.

The subject matter of physics is the connection between sensations and not between things or bodies, of which our sensations are the image. And in 1883, in his *Mechanics*, Mach repeats the same thought:

> Sensations are not "symbols of things." The "thing" is rather a mental symbol for a complex of sensations of relative stability. Not the things (bodies) but colors, sounds, pressures, spaces, times (what we usually call sensations) are the real elements of the world.

About this word "elements," the fruit of twelve years of "reflection," we shall speak later. At present let us note that Mach explicitly states here that things or bodies are complexes of sensations, and that he quite clearly sets up his own philosophical point of view against the opposite theory which holds that sensations are "symbols" of things (it would be more correct to say images or reflections of things). The latter theory is *philosophical materialism*. For instance, the materialist Friedrich Engels—the not unknown collaborator of Marx and a founder of Marxism—constantly and without exception speaks in his works of things and their mental pictures or images, and it is obvious that these mental images arise exclusively from sensations. It would seem that this fundamental standpoint of the "philosophy of Marxism" ought to be known to everyone who speaks of it, and especially to anyone who comes out in print *in the name of* this philosophy. But because of the extraordinary confusion which our Machians have introduced, it becomes necessary to repeat what is generally known. We turn to the first section of *Anti-Dühring* and read: ". . . things and their mental images . . ."; or to the first section of the philosophical part, which reads:

> But whence does thought obtain these principles [*i.e.*, the fundamental principles of all knowledge]? From itself? No . . . these forms can never be created and derived by thought out of itself, but only from the external world . . . the principles are not the starting point of the investigation [as Dühring who would be a materialist, but cannot consistently adhere to materialism, holds], but its final result; they are not applied to nature and human history, but abstracted from them; it is not nature and the realm of humanity which conform to these principles, but the principles are only valid in so far as they are in conformity with nature and history. That is the only materialistic conception of the matter, and Herr Dühring's contrary conception is idealistic, makes things stand completely on their heads, and fashions the real world out of ideas.

Engels, we repeat, applies this "only materialistic conception" everywhere and without exception, relentlessly attacking Dühring for the least deviation from materialism to idealism. Anybody who reads *Anti-Dühring* and *Ludwig Feuerbach* with the slightest care will find scores of instances when Engels speaks of things and their reflections in the human brain, in our consciousness, thought, etc. Engels does not say that sensations or ideas are "symbols" of things, for consistent materialism must here use "image," picture, or reflection instead of "symbol," as we shall show in detail in the proper place. But the question here is not of this or that formulation of materialism, but of the opposition of materialism to idealism, of the difference between the two fundamental *lines* in philosophy. Are we to proceed from things to sensation and thought? Or are we to proceed from thought and sensation to things? The first line, i.e., the materialist line, is adopted by Engels. The second line, i.e., the idealist line, is adopted by Mach. No evasions, no sophisms—a multitude of which we shall yet encounter—can remove the clear and indisputable fact that Ernst Mach's doctrine that things are complexes of sensations is subjective idealism and a simple rehash of Berkeleianism. If bodies are "complexes of sensations," as Mach says, or "combinations of sensations," as Berkeley said, it inevitably follows that the whole world is but my idea. Starting from such a premise it is impossible to arrive at the existence of other people besides oneself: it is the purest solipsism. Much as Mach, Avenarius, Petzoldt, and the others may abjure solipsism, they cannot in fact escape solipsism without falling into howling logical absurdities. To make this fundamental element of the philosophy of Machism still clearer, we shall give a few additional quotations from Mach's works. Here is a sample from *The Analysis of Sensations*:

> We see a body with a point S. If we touch S, that is, bring it into contact with our body, we receive a prick. We can see S without feeling the prick. But as soon as we feel the prick we find S on the skin. Thus, the visible point is a permanent nucleus, to which, according to circumstances, the prick is attached as something accidental. By frequent repetitions of analogous occurrences we finally habituate ourselves to regard *all* properties of bodies as "effects" which proceed from permanent nuclei and are conveyed to the self through the medium of the body; which effects we call *sensations* . . .

In other words, people "habituate" themselves to adopt the standpoint of materialism, to regard sensations as the result of the action of bodies, things, nature on our sense organs. This "habit," so noxious to the philosophical idealists—a habit acquired by all mankind and all natural science!—is not at all to the liking of Mach, and he proceeds to destroy it:

> ... Thereby, however, these nuclei are deprived of their entire sensible content and are converted into naked abstract symbols ...

An old song, most worthy Professor! This is a literal repetition of Berkeley who said that matter is a naked abstract symbol. But it is Ernst Mach, in fact, who goes naked, for if he does not admit that the "sensible content" is an objective reality, existing independently of us, there remains only a "naked abstract" *I*, an I infallibly written with a capital letter and italicized, equal to "the insane piano, which imagined that it was the sole existing thing in this world." If the "sensible content" of our sensations is not the external world then nothing exists save this naked *I* engaged in empty "philosophical" acrobatics. A stupid and fruitless occupation!

> ... It is then correct that the world consists only of our sensations. In which case we have knowledge *only* of sensations, and the assumption of those nuclei, and of their interaction, from which alone sensations proceed, turns out to be quite idle and superfluous. Such a view can only appeal to *half-hearted* realism or *half-hearted* criticism.

We have quoted the sixth paragraph of Mach's "antimetaphysical observations" in full. It is a sheer plagiarism on Berkeley. Not a single idea, not a glimmer of thought, except that "we sense only our sensations." From which there is only one possible inference, namely, that the "world consists only of *my* sensations." The word "our" employed by Mach instead of "my" is employed illegitimately. By this word alone Mach betrays that "half-heartedness" of which he accuses others. For if the "assumption" of the existence of the external world is "idle," if the assumption that the needle exists independently of me and that an interaction takes place between my body and the point of the needle is really "idle and superfluous," then primarily the "assumption" of the existence of other people is idle and superfluous. Only *I* exist, and all other people, as well as the external world, come under the category of idle "nuclei." Holding this point of view one cannot speak of *"our"* sensations; and when Mach does speak of them, it is only a betrayal of his own amazing half-heartedness. It only proves that his philosophy is a jumble of idle and empty words in which their author himself does not believe.

Here is a particularly graphic example of Mach's half heartedness and confusion. In § 6 of Chapter XI of the *Analysis of Sensations* we read:

> If I imagine that while I am experiencing sensations, I or someone else

could observe my brain with all possible physical and chemical appliances, it would be possible to ascertain with what processes of the organism particular sensations are connected . . .

Very well! This means, then, that our sensations are connected with definite processes, which take place in the organism in general, and in our brain in particular? Yes, Mach very definitely makes this "assumption"—it would be quite a task not to make it from the standpoint of natural science! But is not this the very "assumption" of those very same "nuclei and their interaction" which our philosopher declared to be idle and superfluous? We are told that bodies are complexes of sensations; to go beyond that, Mach assures us, to regard sensations as a product of the action of bodies upon our sense organs, is metaphysics, an idle and superfluous assumption, etc., à la Berkeley. But the brain is a body. Consequently, the brain also is no more than a complex of sensations. It follows, then, that with the help of a complex of sensations I—and *I* also am nothing but a complex of sensations—sense complexes of sensations. A delightful philosophy! First sensations are declared to be "the real elements of the world"; on this an "original" Berkeleianism is erected—and then the very opposite view is smuggled in, viz., that sensations are connected with definite processes in the organism. Are not these "processes" connected with an exchange of matter between the "organism" and the external world? Could this exchange of matter take place if the sensations of the particular organism did not give it an objectively correct idea of this external world?

Mach does not ask himself such embarrassing questions when he mechanically jumbles fragments of Berkeleianism with the views of natural science, which instinctively adheres to the materialist theory of knowledge . . . In the same paragraph Mach writes: "It is sometimes also asked whether (inorganic) 'matter' experiences sensation . . ." Does this mean that there is no doubt that *organic* matter experiences sensation? Does this mean that sensation is not something primary but that it is one of the properties of matter? Mach skips over all the absurdities of Berkeleianism! . . . "The question," he avers, "is natural enough, if we proceed from the current widespread physical notions, according to which matter is the *immediate* and indisputably given *reality*, out of which everything, inorganic and organic, is constructed . . ." Let us bear in mind this truly valuable admission of Mach's that the current widespread *physical* notions regard matter as the immediate reality, and that only one variety of this reality (organic matter) possesses the well-defined property of sensation ... Mach continues:

> Then, indeed, sensation must suddenly arise somewhere in this structure [consisting of matter], or else have previously been present in the foundation. From *our* standpoint the question is a false one. For us matter is not what is primarily given. Rather, what is primarily given are the *elements* (which in a certain familiar relation are designated as sensations) ...

What is primarily given, then, are sensations, although they are "connected" only with definite processes in organic matter! And while uttering such absurdities Mach wants to blame materialism ("the current widespread physical notion") for leaving unanswered the question whence sensation "arises." This is a sample of the "refutation" of materialism by the fideists and their hangers-on. Does any other philosophical standpoint "solve" a problem before enough data for its solution has been collected? Does not Mach himself say in the very same paragraph: "So long as this problem (how far sensation extends in the organic world) has not been solved even in a single special case, no answer to the question is possible."

The difference between materialism and "Machism" in this particular question thus consists in the following. Materialism, in full agreement with natural science, takes matter as primary and regards consciousness, thought, sensation as secondary, because in its well-defined form sensation is associated only with the higher forms of matter (organic matter), while "in the foundation of the structure of matter" one can only surmise the existence of a faculty akin to sensation. Such, for example, is the supposition of the well-known German scientist Ernst Haeckel, the English biologist Lloyd Morgan, and others, not to speak of Diderot's conjecture mentioned above. Machism holds to the opposite, the idealist point of view, and at once lands into an absurdity: since, in the first place, sensation is taken as primary, in spite of the fact that it is associated only with definite processes in matter organized in a definite way; and since, in the second place, the basic premise that bodies are complexes of sensations is violated by the assumption of the existence of other living beings and, in general, of other "complexes" besides the given great *I*.

The word "element," which many naïve people (as we shall see) take to be some sort of a new discovery, in reality only obscures the question, for it is a meaningless term which creates the false impression that a solution or a step forward has been achieved. This impression is a false one, because there still remains to be investigated and reinvestigated how matter, apparently entirely devoid of sensation, is related to matter which, though composed of the same atoms (or electrons), is yet endowed with a well-defined faculty of sensation. Materialism clearly formulates the as yet unsolved problem and thereby stimulates the attempt to solve it, to undertake further experimental investigation. Machism, which is a species of muddled idealism, befogs the issue and sidetracks it by means of the futile verbal trick, "element."

Here is a passage from Mach's latest, comprehensive and conclusive philosophical work that clearly betrays the falsity of this idealist trick. In his *Knowledge and Error* we read:

> While there is no difficulty in constructing *every physical* experience out of sensations, *i.e., psychical elements*, it is impossible to imagine how any *psychical* experience can be composed of the elements employed in modern physics, i.e., mass and motion (in their rigidity—which is serviceable only for this special science).

Of the rigidity of the conceptions of many modern scientists and of their metaphysical (in the Marxist sense of the term, i.e., anti-dialectical) views, Engels speaks repeatedly and very precisely. We shall see later that it was just on this point that Mach went astray, because he did not understand or did not know the relation between relativism and dialectics. But this is not what concerns us here. It is important for us here to note how glaringly Mach's *idealism* emerges, in spite of the confused—ostensibly new—terminology. There is no difficulty, you see, in constructing any physical element out of sensations, i.e., psychical elements! Oh yes, such constructions, of course, are not difficult, for they are purely verbal constructions, shallow scholasticism, serving as a loophole for fideism. It is not surprising after this that Mach dedicates his works to the immanentists; it is not surprising that the immanentists, who profess the most reactionary kind of philosophical idealism, welcome Mach with open arms.

The "recent positivism" of Ernst Mach was only about two hundred years too late. Berkeley had already sufficiently shown that "out of sensations, i.e., psychical elements," nothing can be "built" except *solipsism*. As regards materialism, against which Mach here, too, sets up his own views, without frankly and explicitly naming the "enemy," we have already seen in the case of Diderot what the real views of the materialists are. These views do not consist in deriving sensation from the movement of matter or in reducing sensation to the movement of matter, but in recognizing sensation as one of the properties of matter in motion. On this question Engels shared the standpoint of Diderot. Engels dissociated himself from the "vulgar" materialists, Vogt, Büchner, and Moleschott, for the very reason, among others, that they erred in believing that the brain secretes thought *in the same way* as the liver secretes bile. But Mach, who constantly sets up his views in opposition to materialism, ignores, of course, all the great materialists—Diderot, Feuerbach, Marx, and Engels—just as all other official professors of official philosophy do.

In order to characterize Avenarius's earliest and basic view, let us take his first independent philosophical work, *Philosophy as a Conception of the World According to the Principle of the Minimum Expenditure of Effort: Prolegomena to a Critique of Pure Experience*, which appeared in 1876. Bogdanov in his *Empiriomonism* says that "in the development of Mach's views, the starting point was philosophical idealism, while a realistic tinge was characteristic of Avenarius from the very beginning." Bogdanov said so because he believed what Mach said (see *Analysis of Sensations.*) Bogdanov should not have believed Mach, and his assertion is diametrically opposed to the truth. On the contrary, Avenarius's idealism emerges so clearly in his work of 1876 that Avenarius himself in 1891 was obliged to admit it. In the introduction to *The Human Concept of the World* Avenarius says: "He who has read my first systematic work, *Philosophie, etc.*, will at once have presumed that I would have attempted to treat the problems of a criticism of pure experience from the 'idealist' standpoint" (*The Human Concept of the World*, 1891), but "the sterility of philosophical idealism compelled me to doubt the correctness of my previous path." This idealist starting point of Avenarius's is universally acknowledged in philosophical literature. Of the French writers I shall refer to Cauwelaert, who says that Avenarius' philosophical standpoint in the *Prolegomena* is "monistic idealism." Of the German writers, I shall name Rudolf Willy, Avenarius's disciple, who says that "Avenarius in his youth—and particularly in his work of 1876—was totally under the spell of so-called epistemological idealism."

And, indeed, it would be ridiculous to deny the idealism in Avenarius's *Prolegomena*, where he explicitly states that "*only sensation can be thought of as the existing*." This is how Avenarius himself presents the contents of § 116 of his work. Here is the paragraph in full:

> We have recognized that the existing is substance endowed with sensa-
> tion; the substance falls away [it is "more economical," don't you see,
> there is "a lesser expenditure of effort" in thinking that there is no
> "substance" and that no external world exists!], sensation remains; we
> must then regard the existing as sensation, at the basis of which there
> is nothing which does not possess sensation.

Sensation, then, exists without "substance," i.e., thought exists without
brain! Are there really philosophers capable of defending this brainless
philosophy? There are! Professor Richard Avenarius is one of them. And
we must pause for a while to consider this defense, difficult though it be
for a normal person to take it seriously. Here, in §§ 89 and 90 of this same
work, is Avenarius's argument:

> . . . The proposition that motion produces sensation is based on ap-
> parent experience only. This experience, which includes the act of per-
> ception, consists, presumably, in the fact that sensation is generated in
> a certain kind of substance (brain) as a result of transmitted motion
> (excitation) and with the help of other material conditions (e.g., blood).
> However—apart from the fact that such generation has never itself
> been observed—in order to construct the supposed experience, as an
> experience which is real in all its component parts, empirical proof, at
> least, is required to show that sensation, which assumedly is caused
> in a certain substance by transmitted motion, did not already exist in
> that substance in one way or another; so that the appearance of sensa-
> tion cannot be conceived of in any other way than as a creative act on
> the part of the transmitted motion. Thus only by proving that where a
> sensation now appears there was none previously, not even a minimal
> one, would it be possible to establish a fact which, denoting as it does
> some act of creation, contradicts all the rest of experience and radically
> changes all the rest of our conception of nature. But such proof is not
> furnished by any experience, and cannot be furnished by any experi-
> ence; on the contrary, the notion of a state of a substance totally devoid
> of sensation which subsequently begins to experience sensation is only
> a hypothesis. But this hypothesis merely complicates and obscures our
> understanding instead of simplifying and clarifying it.
>
> Should the so-called experience, viz., that the sensation is *caused*
> by a transmitted motion in a substance that begins to perceive from
> this moment, prove upon closer examination to be only apparent,
> there still remains sufficient material in the content of the experience
> to ascertain at least the relative origin of sensation from conditions
> of motion, namely, to ascertain that the sensation which is present,
> although latent or minimal, or for some other reason not manifest to
> the consciousness, becomes, owing to transmitted motion, released or

enhanced or made manifest to the consciousness. However, even this bit of the remaining content of experience is only an appearance. Were we even by an ideal observation to trace the motion proceeding from the moving substance A, transmitted through a series of intermediate centers and reaching the substance B, which is endowed with sensation, we should at best find that sensation in substance B is developed or becomes enhanced simultaneously with the reception of the incoming motion—but we should not find that this occurred as a *consequence* of the motion . . .

We have purposely quoted this refutation of materialism by Avenarius in full, in order that the reader may see to what truly pitiful sophistries "recent" empiriocritical philosophy resorts. We shall compare with the argument of the idealist Avenarius the *materialist* argument of—Bogdanov, if only to punish Bogdanov for his betrayal of materialism!

In long bygone days, fully nine years ago, when Bogdanov was half "a natural-historical materialist" (that is, an adherent of the materialist theory of knowledge, to which the overwhelming majority of contemporary scientists instinctively hold), when he was only half led astray by the muddled Ostwald, he wrote:

> From ancient times to the present day, descriptive psychology has adhered to the classification of the facts of consciousness into three categories: the domain of sensations and ideas, the domain of emotions, and the domain of impulses . . . To the first category belong the *images* of phenomena of the outer or inner world, as taken by themselves in consciousness . . . Such an image is called a "sensation" if it is directly produced through the sense organs by its corresponding external phenomenon.

And a little farther on he says: "Sensation . . . arises in consciousness as a result of a certain impulse from the external environment transmitted by the external sense organs." And further: "Sensation is the foundation of mental life; it is its immediate connection with the external world . . .At each step in the process of sensation a transformation of the energy of external excitation into a state of consciousness takes place." And even in 1905, when, with the gracious assistance of Ostwald and Mach, Bogdanov had abandoned the materialist standpoint in philosophy for the idealist standpoint, he wrote (from forgetfulness!) in his *Empiriomonism*:

> As is known, the energy of external excitation, transformed at the nerve-ends into a "telegraphic" form of nerve current (still insufficiently investigated but devoid of all mysticism), first reaches the neurons

that are located in the so-called "lower" centers—ganglial, cerebrospinal, subcortical, etc.

For every scientist who has not been led astray by professorial philosophy, as well as for every materialist, sensation is indeed the direct connection between consciousness and the external world; it is the transformation of the energy of external excitation into a state of consciousness. This transformation has been, and is, observed by each of us a million times on every hand. The sophism of idealist philosophy consists in the fact that it regards sensation as being not the connection between consciousness and the external world, but a fence, a wall, separating consciousness from the external world—not an image of the external phenomenon corresponding to the sensation, but as the "sole entity." Avenarius gave but a slightly changed form to this old sophism, which had been already worn threadbare by Bishop Berkeley. Since we do not yet know all the conditions of the connection we are constantly observing between sensation and matter organized in a definite way, let us therefore acknowledge the existence of sensation alone—that is what the sophism of Avenarius reduces itself to.

To conclude our description of the fundamental idealist premises of empiriocriticism, we shall briefly refer to the English and French representatives of this philosophical trend. Mach explicitly says of Karl Pearson, the Englishman, that he (Mach) is "in agreement with his epistemological views on all essential points" (*Mechanics*). Pearson in turn agrees with Mach. For Pearson "real things" are "sense impressions." He declares the recognition of things outside the boundaries of sense impressions to be metaphysics. Pearson fights materialism with great determination (although he does not know Feuerbach, or Marx, or Engels); his arguments do not differ from those analyzed above. However, the desire to masquerade as a materialist is so foreign to Pearson (that is a specialty of the Russian Machians), Pearson is so incautious—that he invents no "new" names for his philosophy and simply declares that his views and those of Mach are "*idealist*"! He traces his genealogy directly to Berkeley and Hume. The philosophy of Pearson, as we shall repeatedly find, excels that of Mach in integrity and consistency.

Mach explicitly declares his solidarity with the French physicists, Pierre Duhem and Henri Poincaré. We shall have occasion to deal with the particularly confused and inconsistent philosophical views of these

writers in the chapter on the new physics. Here we shall content ourselves with noting that for Poincaré things are "groups of sensations" and
that a similar view is casually expressed by Duhem.

We shall now proceed to examine how Mach and Avenarius, having
admitted the idealist character of their original views, *corrected* them in
their subsequent works.

1.2 "The discovery of the world-elements"

Such is the title under which Friedrich Adler, lecturer at the University
of Zürich, probably the only German author also anxious to supplement
Marx with Machism, writes of Mach. And this naïve university lecturer
must be given his due: in his simplicity of heart he does Machism more
harm than good. At least, he puts the question point-blank: did Mach really "discover the world-elements"? If so, then, only very backward and
ignorant people, of course, can still remain materialists. Or is this discovery a return on the part of Mach to the old philosophical errors?

We saw that Mach in 1872 and Avenarius in 1876 held a purely idealist view; for them the world is our sensation. In 1883 Mach's *Mechanics* appeared, and in the preface to the first edition Mach refers to Avenarius's *Prolegomena*, and greets his ideas as being "very close" to his
own philosophy. Here are the arguments in the *Mechanics* concerning the
elements:

> All natural science can only picture and represent complexes of those
> *elements* which we ordinarily call sensations. It is a matter of the con-
> nection of these elements ... The connection of A (heat) with B (flame)
> is a problem of physics, that of A and N (nerves) a problem of *physiol-
> ogy*. Neither exists separately; both exist in conjunction. Only tempo-
> rarily can we neglect either. Even processes that are apparently purely
> mechanical, are thus ... always physiological.

We find the same in *The Analysis of Sensations*:

> Wherever ... the terms "sensation," "complex of sensations," are used
> alongside of or in place of the terms "element," "complex of elements,"
> it must be borne in mind that it is *only* in this *connection* [namely, in
> the connection of A, B, C with K, L, M, that is, in the connection of "com-
> plexes which we ordinarily call bodies" with "the complex which we
> call our body"] and relation, only in this functional dependence that the
> elements are *sensations*. In another functional dependence they are at
> the same time physical objects."

A color is a physical object when we consider its dependence, for instance, upon the source of illumination (other colors, temperatures, spaces, and so forth). When we, however, consider its *dependence* upon the *retina* (the elements K, L, M), it is a *psychological* object, a *sensation*.

Thus the discovery of the world-elements amounts to this:

1.   all that exists is declared to be sensation,

2.   the sensations are called elements,

3.   elements are divided into the physical and the psychical; the latter is that which depends on the human nerves and the human organism generally; the former does not depend on them;

4.   the connection of physical elements and the connection of psychical elements, it is declared, do not exist separately from each other; they exist only in conjunction;

5.   it is possible only temporarily to leave one or the other connection out of account;

6.   the "new" theory is declared to be free from "one-sidedness."

Indeed, it is not one-sidedness we have here, but an in coherent jumble of antithetical philosophical points of view. Since you base yourself *only* on sensations you do not correct the "one-sidedness" of your idealism by the term "element," but only confuse the issue and cravenly hide from your own theory. In a word, you eliminate the antithesis between the physical and psychical, between materialism (which regards nature, matter, as primary) and idealism (which regards spirit, mind, sensation as primary); indeed, you promptly restore this antithesis; you restore it surreptitiously, retreating from your own fundamental premise! For, if elements are sensations, you have no right even for a moment to accept the existence of "elements" *independently* of my nerves and my mind. But if you do admit physical objects that are independent of my nerves and my sensations and that cause sensation only by acting upon my retina—you are disgracefully abandoning your "one-sided" idealism and adopting the standpoint of "one-sided" materialism! If color is a sensation only depending upon the retina (as natural science compels you to admit), then light rays, falling upon the retina, produce the sensation of color. This means that outside us, independently of us and of our minds, there exists a movement of matter, let us say of ether waves of a definite length and of a definite velocity, which, acting upon the retina, produce in man the sensation of a particular color. This is precisely how natural science regards it. It explains the sensations of various colors by the various lengths of light waves existing outside the human retina, outside man and independently of him. This is materialism: matter acting upon our sense organs produces sensation. Sensation depends on the brain, nerves, retina, etc., i.e., on matter organized in a definite way. The existence of matter does not depend on sensation. Matter is primary. Sensation, thought, consciousness are the supreme product of matter organized in a particular way. Such are the views of materialism in general, and of Marx and Engels in particular. Mach and Avenarius *secretly* smuggle in materialism by means of the word "element," which *supposedly* frees their theory of the "one-sidedness" of subjective idealism, *supposedly* permits the assumption that the mental is dependent on the retina, nerves and so forth, and the assumption that the physical is independent of the human organism.

In fact, of course, the trick with the word "element" is a wretched sophistry, for a materialist who reads Mach and Avenarius will immediately ask: what are the "elements"? It would, indeed, be childish to think that one can dispose of the fundamental philosophical trends by inventing a new word. Either the "element" is a *sensation*, as all empiriocriticists, Mach, Avenarius, Petzoldt, etc., maintain—in which case your philosophy, gentlemen, is *idealism* vainly seeking to hide the nakedness of its solipsism under the cloak of a more "objective" terminology; or the "element" is not a sensation—in which case *absolutely no thought whatever* is attached to the "new" term; it is merely an empty bauble.

Take Petzoldt, for instance, the last word in empiriocriticism, as V. Lesevich, the first and most outstanding Russian empiriocriticist describes him. Having defined elements as sensations, he says in the second volume of the work mentioned:

> In the statement that "sensations are the elements of the world" one must guard against taking the term "sensation" as denoting something only subjective and therefore ethereal, transforming the ordinary picture of the world into an illusion.

One speaks of what hurts one most! Petzoldt feels that the world "evaporates," or becomes transformed into an illusion, when world-elements are regarded as sensations. And the good Petzoldt imagines that he helps matters by the reservation that sensation must not be taken as something only subjective! Is this not a ridiculous sophistry? Does it make any difference whether we "take" sensation as sensation or whether we try to stretch the meaning of the term? Does this do away with the fact that sensations in man are connected with normally functioning nerves, retina, brain, etc., that the external world exists independently of our sensations? If you are not trying to evade the issue by a subterfuge, if you are really in earnest in wanting to "guard" against subjectivism and solipsism, you must above all guard against the fundamental idealist premises of your philosophy; you must replace the idealist line of your philosophy (from sensations to the external world) by the materialist line (from the external world to sensations); you must abandon that empty and muddled verbal embellishment, "element," and simply say that color is the result of the action of a physical object on the retina, which is the same as saying that sensation is a result of the action of matter on our sense organs.

Let us take Avenarius. The most valuable material on the question of the "elements" is to be found in his last work (and, it might be said, the most important for the comprehension of his philosophy), *Notes on the Concept of the Subject of Psychology*. The author, by the way, here gives a very "graphic" table, the main part of which we reproduce here:

I.	Things, or the substantial	Elements, complexes of elements Corporeal things
II.	Thoughts, or the mental	Incorporeal things, recollections and fantasies

Compare this with what Mach says after all his elucidation of the "elements" (*The Analysis of Sensations*): "It is not bodies that produce sensations, but complexes of elements (complexes of sensations) that make up bodies." Here you have the "discovery of the world-elements" that overcomes the one-sidedness of idealism and materialism! At first we are assured that the "elements" are something new, both physical and psychical at the same time; then a little correction is surreptitiously inserted: instead of the crude, materialist differentiation of matter (bodies, things) and the psychical (sensations, recollections, fantasies) we are presented with the doctrine of "recent positivism" regarding elements substantial and elements mental. Adler (Fritz) did not gain very much from "the discovery of the world-elements"!

Bogdanov, arguing against Plekhanov in 1906, wrote:

> . . . I cannot own myself a Machian in philosophy. In the general philosophical conception there is only one thing I borrowed from Mach—the idea of the neutrality of the elements of experience in relation to the "physical" and "psychical" and the dependence of these characteristics solely on the *connection* of experience (*Empiriomonism*, Book III).

This is as though a religious man were to say—I cannot own myself a believer in religion, for there is "only one thing" I have borrowed from the believers—the belief in God. This "only one thing" which Bogdanov borrowed from Mach is the *basic error* of Machism, the basic falsity of its entire philosophy. Those deviations of Bogdanov's from empiriocriticism to which he himself attaches great significance are in fact of entirely secondary importance and amount to nothing more than inconsiderable private and individual differences between the various empiriocriticists who are approved by Mach and who approve Mach (we shall speak of this in greater detail later). Hence when Bogdanov was annoyed at being confused with the Machians he only revealed his failure to understand what *radically* distinguishes materialism from what is common to Bogdanov and to all other Machians. How Bogdanov developed, improved, or worsened Machism is not important. What is important is that he has abandoned the materialist standpoint and has thereby inevitably condemned himself to confusion and idealist aberrations.

In 1899, as we saw, Bogdanov had the correct standpoint when he wrote: "The image of the man before me, directly given to me by vision, is a sensation." Bogdanov did not trouble to give a criticism of this earlier position of his. He blindly believed Mach and began to repeat after him that the "elements" of experience are neutral in relation to the physical and psychical. "As has been established by recent positivist philosophy," wrote Bogdanov in Book I of *Empiriomonism*, "the elements of psychical experience are identical with the elements of experience in general, as they are identical with the elements of physical experience." Or in 1906: "as to 'idealism,' can it be called idealism merely on the grounds that the elements of 'physical experience' are regarded as identical with the elements of 'psychical experience,' or with elementary sensations—when this is simply an indubitable fact?"

Here we have the true source of all Bogdanov's philosophical misadventures, a source which he shares with the rest of the Machians. We can and must call it idealism when "the elements of physical experience" (i.e., the physical, the external world, matter) are regarded as identical with sensations, for this is sheer Berkeleianism. There is not a trace here of recent philosophy, or positivist philosophy, or of indubitable fact. It is merely an old, old idealist sophism. And were one to ask Bogdanov how he would prove the "indubitable fact" that the physical is identical with sensations, one would get no other argument save the eternal refrain of the idealists: I am aware only of my sensations; the "testimony of self-consciousness" of Avenarius in his *Prolegomena*; or: "in our experience [which testifies that "we are sentient substance"] sensation is given us with more certainty than is substantiality," and so on and so forth. Bogdanov (trusting Mach) accepted a reactionary philosophical trick as an "indubitable fact." For, indeed, not a single fact was or could be cited which would refute the view that sensation is an image of the external world—a view which was shared by Bogdanov in 1899 and which is shared by natural science to this day. In his philosophical wanderings the physicist Mach has completely strayed from the path of "modern science." Regarding this important circumstance, which Bogdanov overlooked, we shall have much to say later.

One of the circumstances which helped Bogdanov to jump so quickly from the materialism of the natural scientists to the muddled idealism of Mach was (apart from the influence of Ostwald) Avenarius's doctrine of the dependent and independent series of experience. Bogdanov himself expounds the matter in Book I of his *Empiriomonism* thus:

> Insofar as the data of experience appear in *dependence upon the state of the particular nervous system*, they form the *psychical world* of the particular person; insofar as the data of experience are taken *outside of such a dependence*, we have before us the *physical world*. Avenarius therefore characterizes these two realms of experience respectively as the *dependent series* and the *independent series* of experience.

That is just the whole trouble, the doctrine of the *independent* (i.e., independent of human sensation) "series" is a surreptitious importation of materialism, which, from the standpoint of a philosophy that maintains that bodies are complexes of sensations, that sensations are "identical" with physical "elements," is illegitimate, arbitrary, and eclectic. For once you have recognized that the source of light and light waves exists *independently* of man and the human consciousness, that color is dependent on the action of these waves upon the retina, you have in fact adopted the materialist standpoint and have *completely destroyed* all the "indubitable facts" of idealism, together with all "the complexes of sensations," the elements discovered by recent positivism, and similar nonsense.

That is just the whole trouble. Bogdanov (like the rest of the Russian Machians) has never looked into the idealist views originally held by Mach and Avenarius, has never understood their fundamental idealist premises, and has therefore failed to discover the illegitimacy and eclecticism of their subsequent attempts to smuggle in materialism surreptitiously. Yet, just as the initial idealism of Mach and Avenarius is generally acknowledged in philosophical literature, so is it generally acknowledged that subsequently empiriocriticism endeavored to swing towards materialism. Cauwelaert, the French writer quoted above, asserts that Avenarius' *Prolegomena* is "monistic idealism," *The Critique of Pure Experience* (1888–90) is "absolute realism," while *The Human Concept of the World* (1891) is an attempt "to explain" the change. Let us note that the term realism is here employed as the antithesis of idealism. Following Engels, I use *only* the term materialism in this sense, and consider it the sole correct terminology, especially since the term "realism" has been bedraggled by the positivists and the other muddleheads who oscillate between materialism and idealism. For the present it will suffice to note that Cauwelaert had the indisputable fact in mind that in the *Prolegomena* (1876) sensation, according to Avenarius, is the only entity, while "substance"—in accordance with the principle of "the economy of thought"!—is eliminated, and that in the *Critique of Pure Experience* the physical is taken as the *independent series*, while the psychical and, consequently, sensations, are taken as the dependent series.

Avenarius's disciple Rudolf Willy likewise admits that Avenarius was a "complete" idealist in 1876, but subsequently "reconciled" "naïve realism" (i.e., the instinctive, unconscious materialist standpoint adopted by humanity, which regards the external world as existing independently of our minds) with this teaching.

Oskar Ewald, the author of the book *Avenarius as the Founder of Empiriocriticism*, says that this philosophy combines contradictory idealist and "realist" (he should have said materialist) elements (not in Mach's sense, but in the human sense of the term element). For example, "the absolute [method of consideration] would perpetuate naïve realism, the relative would declare exclusive idealism as permanent." Avenarius calls the absolute method of consideration that which corresponds to Mach's connection of "elements" outside our body, and the relative that which corresponds to Mach's connection of "elements" dependent on our body.

But of particular interest to us in this respect is the opinion of Wundt, who himself, like the majority of the above mentioned writers, adheres to the confused idealist standpoint, but who has analyzed empiriocriticism perhaps more attentively than all the others. P. Yushkevich has the following to say in this connection: "It is interesting to note that Wundt regards empiriocriticism as the most scientific form of the latest type of materialism," i.e., the type of those materialists who regard the spiritual as a function of corporeal processes (and whom—we would add— Wundt defines as standing midway between Spinozism and absolute materialism).

True, this opinion of Wundt's is extremely interesting. But what is even more "interesting" is Mr. Yushkevich's attitude towards the books and articles on philosophy of which he treats. This is a typical example of the attitude of our Machians to such matters. Gogol's Petrushka used to read and find it interesting that letters always combined to make words. Mr. Yushkevich read Wundt and found it "interesting" that Wundt accused Avenarius of materialism. If Wundt is wrong, why not refute him? If he is right, why not explain the antithesis between materialism and empiriocriticism? Mr. Yushkevich finds what the idealist Wundt says "interesting," but this Machian regards it as a waste of effort to endeavor to go to the root of the matter (probably on the principle of "the economy of thought") . . .

The point is that by informing the reader that Wundt accuses Avenarius of materialism, and by not informing him that Wundt regards some aspects of empiriocriticism as materialism and others as idealism and holds that the connection between the two is artificial, Yushkevich entirely *distorted the matter*. Either this gentleman absolutely does not understand what he reads, or he was prompted by a desire to indulge in false self-praise with the help of Wundt, as if to say: you see, the official professors regard us, too, as materialists, and not as muddleheads.

The above-mentioned article by Wundt constitutes a large book (more than 300 pages), devoted to a detailed analysis first of the immanentist school, and then of the empiriocriticists. Why did Wundt connect these two schools? Because he considers them *closely akin*; and this opinion, which is shared by Mach, Avenarius, Petzoldt, and the immanentists is, as we shall see later, entirely correct. Wundt shows in the first part of this article that the immanentists are idealists, subjectivists, and adherents of fideism. This, too, as we shall see later, is a perfectly correct opinion, although Wundt expounds it with a superfluous ballast of professorial erudition, with superfluous niceties and reservations, which is to be explained by the fact that Wundt himself is an idealist and fideist. He reproaches the immanentists not because they are idealists and adherents of fideism, but because, in his opinion, they arrive at these great principles by incorrect methods. Further, the second and third parts of Wundt's article are devoted to empiriocriticism. There he quite definitely points out that very important theoretical propositions of empiriocriticism—e.g., the interpretation of "experience" and the "principal coordination," of which we shall speak later—are identical with those held by the immanentists. Other of Avenarius's theoretical propositions are borrowed from materialism, and in general empiriocriticism is a "*motley*," in which the "various component elements *are entirely heterogeneous*."

Wundt regards Avenarius's doctrine of the "*independent vital series*," in particular, as one of the materialist morsels of the Avenarius-Mach hodgepodge. If you start from the "system C" (that is how Avenarius—who was very fond of making erudite play of new terms—designates the human brain or the nervous system in general), and if the mental is for you a function of the brain, then this "system C" is a "metaphysical substance"—says Wundt, and your doctrine is materialism. It should be said that many idealists and all agnostics (Kantians and Humeans included) call the materialists metaphysicians, because it seems to them that to recognize the existence of an external world independent of the human mind is to transcend the bounds of experience. As to this terminology and its utter incorrectness from the point of view of Marxism, we shall speak in its proper place. Here it is important to note that the recognition of the "independent" series by Avenarius (and also by Mach, who expresses the same idea in different words) is, according to the general opinion of philosophers of various parties, i.e., of various trends in philosophy, an *appropriation from materialism*. If you assume that everything that exists is sensation, or that bodies are complexes of sensations, you cannot, without violating all your fundamental premises, all "your" philosophy, arrive at the conclusion that the *physical* exists *independently* of our minds, and that sensation is a *function* of matter organized in a definite way. Mach and Avenarius, in their philosophy, combine fundamental idealist premises with individual materialist deductions for the very reason that their theory is an example of that "pauper's broth of eclecticism" of which Engels speaks with just contempt.

This eclecticism is particularly marked in Mach's latest philosophical work, *Knowledge and Error*. We have already seen that Mach there declared that "there is no difficulty in constructing every physical element out of sensation, i.e., out of psychical elements," and in the same book we read: "Dependencies outside the boundary U [= *Umgrenzung*, i.e., "the spatial boundary of our body,"] are *physics in the broadest sense. . .* To obtain those dependencies in a pure state it is necessary as much as possible to eliminate the influence of the observer, that is, of those elements that lie within U."

Well, well, the titmouse first promised to set the sea on fire . . . i.e., to construct physical elements from psychical elements, and then it turns out that physical elements lie beyond the boundary of psychical elements, "which lie within our body"! A remarkable philosophy!

Another example:

> A perfect gas, a perfect liquid, a perfect elastic body, does not exist; the physicist knows that his fictions only approximate to the facts and arbitrarily simplify them; he is aware of the divergence, which cannot be eliminated.

What divergence is meant here? The divergence of what from what? Of thought (physical theory) from the facts. And what are thoughts, ideas? Ideas are the "tracks of sensations." And what are facts? Facts are "complexes of sensations." And so, the divergence of the tracks of sensations from complexes of sensations cannot be eliminated.

What does this mean? It means that Mach *forgets* his own theory and, when treating of various problems of physics, speaks plainly, without idealist twists, i.e., materialistically. All the "complexes of sensations" and the entire stock of Berkeleian wisdom vanish. The physicists' theory proves to be a reflection of bodies, liquids, gases existing outside us and independently of us, a reflection which is, of course, approximate; but to call this approximation or simplification "arbitrary" is wrong. *In fact*, sensation is here regarded by Mach just as it is regarded by all science which has not been "purified" by the disciples of Berkeley and Hume, viz., as an *image of the external world*. Mach's own theory is subjective idealism; but when the factor of objectivity is required, Mach unceremoniously inserts into his arguments the premises of the contrary, i.e., the materialist, theory of knowledge. Eduard von Hartmann, a consistent idealist and consistent reactionary in philosophy, *who sympathizes with the Machians' fight against materialism*, comes very close to the truth when he says that Mach's philosophical position is a "mixture of naïve realism and absolute illusionism." That is true. The doctrine that bodies are complexes of sensations, etc., is absolute illusionism, i.e., solipsism; for from this standpoint the world is nothing but my illusion. On the other hand, Mach's aforementioned argument, as well as many other of his fragmentary arguments, is what is known as "naïve realism," i.e., the materialist theory of knowledge unconsciously and instinctively taken over from the scientists.

Avenarius and the professors who follow in his footsteps attempt to disguise this mixture by the theory of the "principal coordination." We shall proceed to examine this theory presently, but let us first finish with the charge that Avenarius is a materialist. Mr. Yushkevich, to whom Wundt's opinion which he failed to understand seemed so interesting, was either himself not enough interested to learn, or else did not condescend to inform the reader, how Avenarius's nearest disciples and successors reacted to this charge. Yet this is necessary to clarify the matter if we are interested in the relation of Marx's philosophy, i.e., materialism, to the philosophy of empiriocriticism. Moreover, if Machism is a muddle, a mixture of materialism and idealism, it is important to know whither this current turned—if we may so express it—after the official idealists began to disown it because of its concessions to materialism.

Wundt was answered, among others, by two of Avenarius's purest and most orthodox disciples, J. Petzoldt and Fr. Carstanjen. Petzoldt, with haughty resentment, repudiated the charge of materialism, which is so degrading to a German professor, and in support referred to—what do you think?—Avenarius's *Prolegomena*, where, supposedly, the concept of substance has been annihilated! A convenient theory, indeed, that can be made to embrace both purely idealist works and arbitrarily assumed materialist premises! Avenarius's *Critique of Pure Experience*, of course, does not contradict this teaching, i.e., materialism, writes Petzoldt, but neither does it contradict the directly opposite spiritualist doctrine. An excellent defense! This is exactly what Engels called "a pauper's broth of eclecticism." Bogdanov, who refuses to own himself a Machian and who wants to be considered a Marxist (*in philosophy*), follows Petzoldt. He asserts that "empiriocriticism is not . . . concerned with materialism, or with spiritualism, or with metaphysics in general," that "truth . . . does not lie in the 'golden mean' between the conflicting trends [materialism and spiritualism], but lies outside of both." What appeared to Bogdanov to be truth is, as a matter of fact, confusion, a wavering between materialism and idealism.

Carstanjen, rebutting Wundt, said that he absolutely repudiated this "importation of a materialist element" which is utterly foreign to the critique of pure experience." "Empiriocriticism is skepticism [preeminently] in relation to the content of the concepts." There is a grain of truth in this insistent emphasis on the neutrality of Machism; the amendment made by Mach and Avenarius to their original idealism amounts to partial concessions to materialism. Instead of the consistent standpoint of Berkeley—the external world is my sensation—we sometimes get the Humean standpoint—I exclude the question whether or not there is anything beyond my sensations. And this agnostic standpoint inevitably condemns one to vacillate between materialism and idealism.

1.3　The principal coordination and "naïve realism"

Avenarius's doctrine of the principal coordination is expounded in *The Human Concept of the World* and in the *Notes*. The second was written later, and in it Avenarius emphasizes that he is expounding, it is true in a somewhat altered form, something that is not different from the *Critique of Pure Experience* and *The Human Concept of the World*, but *exactly the same* (*Notes*, 1894). The essence of this doctrine is the thesis of "the *indissoluble* coordination [i.e., the correlative connection] of the self and the environment." "Expressed philosophically," Avenarius says here, one can say the "*self* and *not-self*." We "*always* find together" the one and the other, the *self* and the environment. "No full description of what we find can contain an 'environment' without some self whose environment it is, even though it be only the *self* that is describing what is found." The *self* is called the *central term* of the coordination, the environment the counterterm (*The Human Concept of the World*).

Avenarius claims that by this doctrine he recognizes the full value of what is known as *naïve realism*, that is, the ordinary, nonphilosophical, naïve view which is entertained by all people who do not trouble themselves as to whether they themselves exist and whether the environment, the external world, exists. Expressing his solidarity with Avenarius, Mach also tries to represent himself as a defender of "naïve realism"

(*The Analysis of Sensations*). The Russian Machians, without exception, believed Mach's and Avenarius's claim that this was indeed a defense of "naïve realism": the *self* is acknowledged, the environment is acknowledged—what more do you want?

In order to decide who actually possesses the greatest degree of *naïveté*, let us proceed from a somewhat remote starting point. Here is a popular dialogue between a certain philosopher and his reader:

> *Reader*: The existence of a system of things [according to ordinary philosophy] is required and from them only is consciousness to be derived.

> *Author*: Now you are speaking in the spirit of a professional philosopher . . . and not according to human common sense and actual consciousness . . .

> Tell me, and reflect well before you answer: Does a thing appear in you and become present in you and for you otherwise than simultaneously with and through your consciousness of the thing? . . .

> *Reader*: Upon sufficient reflection, I must grant you this.

> *Author*: Now you are speaking from yourself, from your heart. Take care, therefore, not to jump out of yourself and to apprehend anything otherwise than you are able to apprehend it, as consciousness *and* [the italics are the philosopher's] the thing, the thing *and* consciousness; or, more precisely, neither the one nor the other, but that which only subsequently becomes resolved into the two, that which is the absolute subjective-objective and objective-subjective.

Here you have the whole essence of the empiriocritical principal coordination, the latest defense of "naïve realism" by the latest positivism! The idea of "indissoluble" coordination is here stated very clearly and as though it were a genuine defense of the point of view of the common man, undistorted by the subtleties of "the professional philosophers." But, as a matter of fact, this dialogue is taken from the work of a classical representative of *subjective idealism*, Johann Gottlieb Fichte, published in 1801.

There is nothing but a paraphrase of subjective idealism in the teachings of Mach and Avenarius we are examining. The claim that they have risen above materialism and idealism, that they have eliminated the opposition between the point of view that proceeds from the thing *to* consciousness and the contrary point of view—is but the empty claim of a renovated Fichteanism. Fichte too imagined that he had "indissolubly" connected the "self" and the "environment," the consciousness and the thing; that he had "solved" the problem by the assertion that a man cannot jump out of himself. In other words, the Berkeleian argument is repeated: I perceive only my sensations, I have no right to assume "objects in themselves" outside of my sensation. The different methods of expression used by Berkeley in 1710, by Fichte in 1801, and by Avenarius in 1891–94 do not in the least change the essence of the matter, viz., the fundamental philosophical line of subjective idealism. The world is my sensation; the non-*self* is "postulated" (is created, produced) by the self; the thing is indissolubly connected with the consciousness; the indissoluble coordination of the *self* and the environment is the empiriocritical principal coordination;—this is all one and the same proposition, the same old trash with a slightly refurbished, or repainted, signboard.

The reference to "naïve realism," supposedly defended by this philosophy, is *sophistry* of the cheapest kind. The "naïve realism" of any healthy person who has not been an inmate of a lunatic asylum or a pupil of the idealist philosophers consists in the view that things, the environment, the world, exist *independently* of our sensation, of our consciousness, of our *self* and of man in general. The same *experience* (not in the Machian sense, but in the human sense of the term) that has produced in us the firm conviction that *independently* of us there exist other people, and not mere complexes of my sensations of high, short, yellow, hard, etc.—this same *experience* produces in us the conviction that things, the world, the environment exist independently of us. Our sensation, our consciousness is only *an image* of the external world, and it is obvious that an image cannot exist without the thing imaged, and that the latter exists independently of that which images it. Materialism *deliberately* makes the "naïve" belief of mankind the foundation of its theory of knowledge.

Is not the foregoing evaluation of the "principal coordination" a product of the materialist prejudice against Machism? Not at all. Specialists in philosophy who cannot be accused of partiality towards materialism, who even detest it and who accept one or other of the idealist systems, agree that the principal coordination of Avenarius and Co. is subjective idealism. Wundt, for instance, whose interesting opinion was not understood by Mr. Yushkevich, explicitly states that Avenarius's theory, according to which a full description of the given or the found is impossible without some self, an observer or describer, is "a false confusion of the content of real experience with reflections about it." Natural science, says Wundt, completely abstracts from every observer.

> Such abstraction is possible only because the attribution of an experiencing individual to every content of experience, which the empiriocritical philosophy, in agreement with the immanentist philosophy, assumes, is in general an empirically unfounded assumption arising from a false confusion of the content of real experience with reflections about it.

For the immanentists (Schuppe, Rehmke, Leclair, Schubert-Soldern), who themselves voice—as we shall see later—their hearty sympathy with Avenarius, proceed from *this very* idea of the "indissoluble" connection between subject and object. And W. Wundt, before analyzing Avenarius, demonstrated in detail that the immanentist philosophy is only a "modification" of Berkeleianism, that however much the immanentists may deny their kinship with Berkeley we should not allow verbal differences to conceal from us the "deeper content of these philosophical doctrines," viz., Berkeleianism or Fichteanism.

The English writer Norman Smith, analyzing Avenarius's *Philosophy of Pure Experience*, puts this criticism in an even more straightforward and emphatic form:

> Most readers of Avenarius's *The Human Concept of the World* will probably agree that, however convincing as criticism [of idealism], it is tantalizingly illusive in its positive teaching. So long as we seek to interpret his theory of experience in the form in which it is avowedly presented, namely, as genuinely realistic, it eludes all clear comprehension: its whole meaning seems to be exhausted in negation of the subjectivism which it overthrows. It is only when we translate Avenarius's technical terms into more familiar language that we discover where the real source of the mystification lies. Avenarius has diverted attention from the defects of his position by directing his main attack against the very weakness [i.e., of the idealist position] which is fatal to his own theory.
>
> Throughout the whole discussion the vagueness of the term experience stands him in good stead. Sometimes it means experiencing and at other times the experienced, the latter meaning being emphasized when the nature of the self is in question. These two meanings of the term experience practically coincide with his important distinction between the absolute and the relative standpoints [I have examined above what significance this distinction has for Avenarius]; and these two points of view are not in his philosophy really reconciled. For when he allows as legitimate the demand that experience be ideally completed

in thought [the full description of the environment is ideally completed by thinking of an observing self], he makes an admission which he cannot successfully combine with his assertion that nothing exists save in relation to the self. The ideal completion of given reality which results from the analysis of material bodies into elements which no human senses can apprehend [here are meant the material elements discovered by natural science, the atoms, electrons, etc., and not the fictitious elements invented by Mach and Avenarius], or from following the earth back to a time when no human being existed upon it, is, strictly, not a completion of experience but only of what is experienced.

It completes only one of the two aspects which Avenarius has asserted to be inseparable. It leads us not only to what has not been experienced but to what can never by any possibility be experienced by beings like ourselves. But here again the ambiguities of the term experience come to Avenarius's rescue. He argues that thought is as genuine a form of experience as sense perception, and so in the end falls back on the timeworn argument of subjective idealism, that thought and reality are inseparable, because reality can only be conceived in thought, and thought involves the presence of the thinker. Not, therefore, any original and profound reestablishment of realism, but only the restatement in its crudest form of the familiar position of subjective idealism is the final outcome of Avenarius's positive speculations."

The mystification wrought by Avenarius, who completely duplicates Fichte's error, is here excellently exposed. The much-vaunted elimination of the antithesis between materialism (Norman Smith should not have used the term realism) and idealism by means of the term "experience" instantly proves to be a myth as soon as we proceed to definite and concrete problems. Such, for instance, is the problem of the existence of the earth *prior* to man, *prior* to any sentient being. We shall presently speak of this point in detail. Here we will note that not only Norman Smith, an opponent of his theory, but also W. Schuppe, the immanentist, who warmly greeted the appearance of *The Human Concept of the World* as *a confirmation of naïve realism* unmasks Avenarius and his fictitious "realism." The fact of the matter is that Schuppe *fully* agrees with *such* "realism," i.e., the mystification of materialism dished out by Avenarius. Such "realism," he wrote to Avenarius, I, the immanentist philosopher, who have been slandered as a subjective idealist, have always claimed with as much right as yourself, *hochverehrter Herr Kollege*. "My conception of thought . . . excellently harmonizes with your 'theory of pure experience' . . . The connection and inseparability of the two terms of the coordination" are in fact provided only by the *self* (*das Ich*, the abstract, Fichtean self-consciousness, thought divorced from the brain). "That which you desired to eliminate you have tacitly assumed"—so Schuppe wrote to Avenarius. And it is difficult to say who more rudely unmasks Avenarius the mystifier—Smith by his straightforward and clear refutation, or Schuppe by his enthusiastic opinion of Avenarius's crowning work. The kiss of Wilhelm Schuppe in philosophy is no better than the kiss of Peter Struve or Menshikov in politics.

O. Ewald, who praises Mach for not succumbing to materialism, speaks of the principal coordination in a similar manner:

> If one declares the correlation of central term and counter-term to be an epistemological necessity which cannot be avoided, then, even though the word "empiriocriticism" be inscribed on the signboard in shrieking letters, one is adopting a standpoint that differs in no way from absolute idealism. [The term is incorrect; he should have said subjective idealism, for Hegel's absolute idealism is reconcilable with the existence of the earth, nature, and the physical universe without man, since nature is regarded as the "otherness" of the absolute idea.] On the other hand, if we do not hold fast to this coordination and grant the counter-terms their independence, then the way is at once opened for every metaphysical possibility, especially in the direction of transcendental realism.

By metaphysics and transcendental realism, Herr Friedländer, who is disguised under the pseudonym Ewald, means *materialism*. Himself professing one of the varieties of idealism, he fully agrees with the Machians and the Kantians that materialism is metaphysics—"from beginning to end the wildest metaphysics." On the question of the "transcendence" and the metaphysical character of materialism he is in agreement with Bazarov and all our Machians, and of this we shall have occasion to say more later. Here again it is important to note how *in fact* the shallow and pedantic claim to have transcended idealism and materialism vanishes, and how the question arises inexorably and irreconcilably. "To grant the counter-terms their independence" means (if one translates the pretentious language of the affected Avenarius into common parlance) to regard nature and the external world as independent of human consciousness and sensation. And that is materialism. To build a theory of knowledge on the hypothesis of the indissoluble connection between the object and human sensation ("complexes of sensations" as identical with bodies; "world-elements" that are identical both psychically and physically;

Avenarius's coordination, and so forth) is to land inevitably into idealism. Such is the simple and unavoidable truth that with a little attention may be easily detected beneath the piles of affected quasi-erudite terminology of Avenarius, Schuppe, Ewald, and the others, which deliberately obscures matters and frightens the general public away from philosophy.

The "reconciliation" of Avenarius's theory with "naïve realism" in the end aroused misgivings even among his own disciples. For instance, R. Willy says that the common assertion that Avenarius came to adopt "naïve realism" should be taken *cum grano salis* [with a grain of salt]. "As a dogma, naïve realism would be nothing but the belief in things-in-themselves existing outside man in their perceptible form." In other words, the only theory of knowledge that is really created by an actual and not fictitious agreement with "naïve realism" is, according to Willy, materialism! And Willy, of course, rejects materialism. But he is compelled to admit that Avenarius in *The Human Concept of the World* restores the unity of "experience," the unity of the "self" and the environment "by means of a series of complicated and extremely artificial subsidiary and intermediary conceptions." *The Human Concept of the World*, being a reaction against the original idealism of Avenarius, "entirely bears the character of a *reconciliation* between the naïve realism of common sense and the epistemological idealism of school philosophy. But that such a reconciliation could restore the unity and integrity of experience [Willy calls it *Grunderfahrung*, that is, basic experience—another new world!], I would not assert."

A valuable admission! Avenarius's "experience" failed to reconcile idealism and materialism. Willy, it seems, repudiates the *school philosophy* of experience in order to replace it by a philosophy of "basic" experience, which is confusion thrice confounded . . .

1.4 Did nature exist prior to man?

We have already seen that this question is particularly repugnant to the philosophy of Mach and Avenarius. Natural science positively asserts that the earth once existed in such a state that no man or any other creature existed or could have existed on it. Organic matter is a later phenomenon, the fruit of a long evolution. It follows that there was no sentient matter, no "complexes of sensations," no *self* that was supposedly "indissolubly" connected with the environment in accordance with Avenarius's doctrine. Matter is primary, and thought, consciousness, sensation are products of a very high development. Such is the materialist theory of knowledge, to which natural science instinctively subscribes.

The question arises, have the eminent representatives of empiriocriticism observed this contradiction between their theory and natural science? They have observed it, and they have definitely asked themselves by what arguments this contradiction can be removed. Three attitudes to this question are of particular interest from the point of view of materialism, that of Avenarius himself and those of his disciples J. Petzoldt and R. Willy.

Avenarius tries to eliminate the contradiction to natural science by means of the theory of the "potential" central term in the coordination. As we know, coordination is the "indissoluble" connection between *self* and environment. In order to eliminate the obvious absurdity of this theory the concept of the "potential" central term is introduced. For instance, what about man's development from the embryo? Does the environment (the "counter-term") exist if the "central term" is represented by an embryo? The embryonic system C—Avenarius replies—is the "potential central term in relation to the future individual environment." The potential central term is never equal to zero, even when there are as yet no parents, but only the "integral parts of the environment" capable of becoming parents.

The coordination then is indissoluble. It is essential for the empiriocriticist to assert this in order to save the fundamentals of his philosophy—sensations and their complexes. Man is the central term of this coordination. But when there is no man, when he has not yet been born, the central term is nevertheless not equal to zero; it has only become a *potential* central term! It is astonishing that there are people who can take seriously a philosopher who advances such arguments! Even Wundt, who stipulates that he is not an enemy of every form of metaphysics (i.e., of fideism), was compelled to admit "the mystical obscuration of the concept experience" by the word "potential," which destroys coordination entirely.

And, indeed, how can one seriously speak of a coordination the indissolubility of which consists in one of its terms being potential?

Is this not mysticism, the very antechamber of fideism? If it is possible to think of the potential central term in relation to a future environment, why not think of it in relation to a *past* environment, that is, *after man's death*? You will say that Avenarius did not draw this conclusion from his theory? Granted, but that absurd and reactionary theory became the more cowardly and not any the better for that. Avenarius, in 1894, did not carry this theory to its logical conclusion, or perhaps feared to do so. But R. Schubert Soldern, as we shall see, resorted in 1896 *to this very theory* to arrive at theological conclusions, which in 1906 earned the *approval* of Mach, who said that Schubert-Soldern was following "*very close paths*" (to Machism) (*Analysis of Sensations*) Engels was quite right in attacking Dühring, an avowed atheist, for inconsistently *leaving loopholes* for fideism in his philosophy. Engels several times, and justly, brought this accusation against the materialist Dühring, although the latter had not drawn any theological conclusions, in the seventies at least. But we have among us people who would have us regard them as Marxists, yet who bring to the masses a philosophy which comes very close to fideism.

Avenarius wrote in the *Notes*:

> ... It would seem that from the empiriocritical standpoint natural science is not entitled to enquire about periods of our present environment which in time preceded the existence of man.

Avenarius answers:

> The enquirer cannot avoid mentally projecting himself (i.e., imagining oneself to be present) ... for what the scientist wants (although he may not be clearly aware of it) is essentially only this: how is the earth ... to be defined prior to the appearance of living beings or man if I were mentally to project myself in the role of a spectator—in much the same way as though it were thinkable that we could from our earth follow the history of another star or of another solar system with the help of perfected instruments.

An object cannot exist independently of our consciousness. "We always mentally project ourselves as the intelligence endeavoring to apprehend the object."

This theory of the necessity of "mentally projecting" the human mind to every object and to nature prior to man is given by me in the first paragraph in the words of the "recent positivist," R. Avenarius, and in the second, in the words of the subjective idealist, J. G. Fichte. The sophistry of this theory is so manifest that it is embarrassing to analyze it. If we "mentally project" ourselves, our presence will be *imaginary*—but the existence of the earth prior to man is *real*. Man *could not* in practice be an observer, for instance, of the earth in an incandescent state, and to "imagine" his being present at the time is *obscurantism*, exactly as though I were to endeavor to prove the existence of hell by the argument that if I "mentally projected" myself thither as an observer I could observe hell. The "reconciliation" of empiriocriticism and natural science amounts to this, that Avenarius graciously consents to "mentally project" something the possibility of admitting which is *excluded* by natural science. No man at all educated or sound-minded doubts that the earth existed at a time when there *could not* have been any life on it, any sensation or any "central term," and consequently the whole theory of Mach and Avenarius, from which it follows that the earth is a complex of sensations ("bodies are complexes of sensations") or "complexes of elements in which the psychical and physical are identical," or "a counter-term of which the central term can never be equal to zero," is *philosophical obscurantism*, the carrying of subjective idealism to absurdity.

J. Petzoldt perceived the absurdity of the position into which Avenarius had fallen and felt ashamed. In his *Introduction to the Philosophy of Pure Experience* he devotes a whole paragraph "to the question of the reality of earlier periods of the earth." Petzoldt says:

> In the teaching of Avenarius the self (*das Ich*) plays a role different from that which it plays with Schuppe [let us note that Petzoldt openly and repeatedly declares: our philosophy was founded by *three* men—Avenarius, Mach, and Schuppe], yet it is a role which, perhaps, possesses too much importance for his theory [Petzoldt was evidently influenced by the fact that Schuppe had unmasked Avenarius by showing that with him too everything rests entirely on the self; and Petzoldt wishes to make a correction] . . . Avenarius said on one occasion that we can think of a "region" where no human foot has yet trodden, but to be able *to think* (italicized by Avenarius) of such an environment there is required what we designate by the term self (*Ich-Bezeichnetes*), *whose* (italicized by Avenarius) thought the thinking is.

Petzoldt replies:

> The epistemologically important question, however, is not whether we can think of such a region at all, but whether we are entitled to think of it as existing, or as having existed, independently of any individual mind.

What is true, is true! People can think and "mentally project" for themselves any kind of hell and any kind of devil. Lunacharsky even "mentally projected" for himself—well, to use a mild expression—religious conceptions. But it is precisely the purpose of the theory of knowledge to show the unreal, fantastic, and reactionary character of such projections.

> . . . For, that the system C [i.e., the brain] is necessary for thought is obvious both for Avenarius and for the philosophy which is here presented. . .

That is not true. Avenarius's theory of 1876 is a theory of thought without brain. And in his theory of 1891–94, as we shall presently see, there is a similar element of idealist nonsense.

> . . . But is this system C a condition of *existence* [italicized by Petzoldt] of, say, the Mesozoic period of the earth?

And Petzoldt, presenting the argument of Avenarius I have already cited on the subject of what science actually wants and how we can "mentally project" the spectator, objects:

> No, we wish to know whether I have the right to think that the earth at that remote epoch existed in the same way as I think of it as having existed yesterday or a minute ago. Or must the existence of the earth be really made conditional, as Willy claimed, on our right at least to assume that at the given period there coexisted some system C, even though at the lowest stage of its development?

Of this idea of Willy's we shall speak presently.

Avenarius evades Willy's strange conclusion by the argument that the person who puts the question cannot mentally remove himself (*sich wegdenken*, i.e., think himself as absent), nor can he avoid mentally projecting himself (*sich hinzuzudenken*, see Avenarius, *The Human Concept of the World*). But then Avenarius makes the individual self of the person who puts the question, or the thought of such a self, the condition not only of the act of thought regarding the uninhabitable earth, but also of the justification for believing in the existence of the earth at that time.

> These false paths are easily avoided if we do not ascribe so much theoretical importance to the self. The only thing the theory of knowledge should demand of the various conceptions of that which is remote in space or time is that it be conceivable and uniquely determined; the rest is the affair of the special sciences.

Petzoldt rechristened the law of causality the law of unique determination and imported into his theory, as we shall see later, the *apriority* of this law. This means that Petzoldt saves himself from Avenarius's subjective idealism and solipsism ("he attributes an exaggerated importance to the self," as the professorial jargon has it) with the help of *Kantian* ideas. The absence of the objective factor in Avenarius's doctrine, the impossibility of reconciling it with the demands of natural science, which declares the earth (object) to have existed long before the appearance of living beings (subject), compelled Petzoldt to resort to causality (unique determination). The earth existed, for its existence prior to man is causally connected with the present existence of the earth. Firstly, where does causality come from? *A priori*, says Petzoldt. Secondly, are not the ideas of hell, devils, and Lunacharsky's "mental projections" also connected by causality? Thirdly, the theory of the "complexes of sensations" in any case turns out to be destroyed by Petzoldt. Petzoldt failed to resolve the contradiction he observed in Avenarius, and only entangled himself still more, for only one solution is possible, viz., the recognition that the external world reflected by our mind exists independently of our mind. This materialist solution alone is really compatible with natural science, and it alone eliminates both Petzoldt's and Mach's idealist solution of the question of causality, which we shall speak of separately.

The third empiriocriticist, R. Willy, first raised the question of this difficulty in Avenarius's philosophy in 1896, in an article entitled "Empiriocriticism as the Only Scientific Standpoint." What about the world prior to man?—Willy asks here, and at first answers according to Avenarius: "we project ourselves *mentally* into the past." But then he goes on to say that we are not necessarily obliged to regard *experience* as human experience. "For we must simply regard the animal kingdom—be it the most insignificant worm—as primitive fellow men if we regard animal life in connection with general experience." Thus, prior to man the earth was the "experience" of a worm, which discharged the functions of the "central term" in order to save Avenarius's "coordination" and Avenarius's philosophy! No wonder Petzoldt tried to dissociate himself from an argument which is not only the height of absurdity (ideas of the earth corresponding to the theories of the geologists attributed to a worm), but which does not in any way help our philosopher, for the earth existed not only before man but before any living being generally.

Willy returned to the question in 1905. The worm was now removed. But Petzoldt's "law of unique determination" could not, of course, satisfy Willy, who regarded it merely as "logical formalism." The author says— will not the question of the world prior to man, as Petzoldt puts it, lead us "back again to the things-in-themselves of common sense"? (i.e., to materialism! How terrible indeed!). What does millions of years without life mean?

> Is time perhaps a thing-in-itself? Of course not! And that means that things outside men are only impressions, bits of fantasy fabricated by men with the help of a few fragments we find about us. And why not? Need the philosopher fear the stream of life? . . . And so I say to myself: abandon all this love of systems and grasp the moment, the moment you are living in, the moment which alone brings happiness.

Well, well! Either materialism or solipsism—this, in spite of his vociferous phrases, is what Willy arrives at when he analyzes the question of the existence of nature before man.

To summarize. Three augurs of empiriocriticism have appeared before us and have labored in the sweat of their brow to reconcile their philosophy with natural science, to patch up the holes of solipsism. Avenarius repeated Fichte's argument and substituted an imaginary world for the real world. Petzoldt withdrew from Fichtean idealism and moved towards Kantian idealism. Willy, having suffered a fiasco with the "worm," threw up the sponge and inadvertently blurted out the truth: either materialism or solipsism, or even the recognition of nothing but the present moment.

It only remains for us to show the reader how this problem was understood and treated by our own native Machians. Here is Bazarov in the *Studies "in" the Philosophy of Marxism*:

> It remains for us now, under the guidance of our faithful *vademecum* [i.e., Plekhanov], to descend into the last and most horrible circle of the solipsist inferno, into that circle where, as Plekhanov assures us, every subjective idealism is menaced with the necessity of conceiving the world as it was contemplated by the ichthyosauruses and archaeopteryxes. "Let us mentally transport ourselves," writes Plekhanov, "to that epoch when only very remote ancestors of man existed on the earth, for instance, to the Mesozoic period. The question arises, what was the status of space, time, and causality *then*? *Whose* subjective forms were they then? Were they the subjective forms of the ichthyosauruses? And *whose intelligence* at that time dictated its laws to nature? The intelligence of the archaeopteryx? To these queries the Kantian philosophy *can give no answer*. And it must be rejected as absolutely incompatible with modern science" (*L. Feuerbach*).

Here Bazarov breaks the quotation from Plekhanov just before a very important passage—as we shall soon see—namely:

> Idealism says that without subject there is no object. The history of the earth shows that the object existed long before the subject appeared, i.e., long before the appearance of organisms possessing a perceptible degree of consciousness . . . The history of development reveals the truth of materialism.

We continue the quotation from Bazarov:

> . . . But does Plekhanov's thing-in-itself provide the desired solution? Let us remember that even according to Plekhanov we can have no idea of things as they are in themselves; we know only their manifestations, only the results of their action on our sense organs. "Apart from this action they possess no aspect" (*L. Feuerbach*). What sense organs existed in the period of the ichthyosauruses? Evidently, only the sense organs of the ichthyosauruses and their like. Only the ideas of the ichthyosauruses were then the actual, the real manifestations of things-in-themselves. Hence, according to Plekhanov also, if the paleontologist desires to remain on "real" ground he must write the story of the Mesozoic period in the light of the contemplations of the ichthyosaurus. And, consequently, not a single step forward is made in comparison with solipsism.

Such is the complete argument (the reader must pardon the lengthy quotation—we could not avoid it) of a Machian, an argument worthy of perpetuation as a first-class example of muddleheadedness.

Bazarov imagines that Plekhanov gave himself away. If things-in-themselves, apart from their action on our sense organs, have no aspect of their own, then in the Mesozoic period they did not exist except as the "aspect" of the sense organs of the ichthyosaurus. And this is the argument of a materialist! If an "aspect" is the result of the action of "things-in-themselves" on sense organs—it follow that things *do not exist independently* of sense organs of one kind or another!

Let us assume for a moment that Bazarov indeed "misunderstood" Plekhanov's words (improbable as such an assumption may seem), that they did appear obscure to him. Be it so. We ask: is Bazarov engaged in a fencing bout with Plekhanov (whom the Machians exalt to the position of the only representative of materialism!), or is he endeavoring to clear up the problem *of materialism*? If Plekhanov seemed obscure to you, or contradictory, and so forth, why did you not turn to other materialists? Is it because you do not know them? But ignorance is no argument.

If Bazarov indeed does not know that the fundamental premise of materialism is the recognition of the external world, of the existence of *things* outside and independent of our mind, this is truly a striking case of crass ignorance. We would remind the reader of Berkeley, who in 1710 rebuked the materialists for their recognition of "objects in themselves" existing independently of our mind and reflected by our mind. Of course, everybody is free to side with Berkeley or anyone else *against* the materialists; that is unquestionable. But it is equally unquestionable that to speak of the materialists and distort or ignore the fundamental premise of *all* materialism is to import preposterous confusion into the problem.

Was Plekhanov right when he said that for idealism there is no object without a subject, while for materialism the object exists independently of the subject and is reflected more or less adequately in the subject's mind? If this is *wrong*, then any man who has the slightest respect for Marxism should have pointed out *this* error of Plekhanov's, and should have dealt *not* with him, but with someone else, with Marx, Engels, or Feuerbach, on the question of materialism and the existence of nature prior to man. But if this is right, or, at least, if you are unable to find an error here, then your attempt to shuffle the cards and to confuse in the reader's mind the most elementary conception of materialism, as distinguished from idealism, is a literary indecency.

As for the Marxists who are interested in the question *apart* from every little word uttered by Plekhanov, we shall quote the opinion of L. Feuerbach, who, as is known (perhaps not to Bazarov?), was a materialist, and through whom Marx and Engels, as is well known, came from the idealism of Hegel to their materialist philosophy. In his rejoinder to R. Haym, Feuerbach wrote:

> Nature, which is not an object of man or mind, is for speculative philosophy, or at least for idealism, a Kantian thing-in-itself [we shall speak later in detail of the fact that our Machians confuse the Kantian thing-in-itself with the materialist thing-in-itself], an abstraction without reality, but it is nature that causes the downfall of idealism. Natural science, at least in its present state, necessarily leads us back to a point when the conditions for human existence were still absent, when nature, i.e., the earth, was not yet an object of the human eye and mind, when, consequently, nature was an absolutely nonhuman entity. Idealism may retort: but nature also is something thought of by you. Certainly, but from this it does not follow that this nature did not at one time actually exist, just as from the fact that Socrates and Plato do not exist for me if I do not think of them, it does not follow that Socrates

and Plato did not actually at one time exist without me.

This is how Feuerbach regarded materialism and idealism from the standpoint of the existence of nature prior to the appearance of man. Avenarius's sophistry (the "mental projection of the observer") was refuted by Feuerbach, who did not know the "recent positivism" but who thoroughly knew the old idealist sophistries. And Bazarov offers us absolutely nothing new, but merely repeats this sophistry of the idealists: "Had I been there [on earth, prior to man], I would have seen the world so-and-so" (*Studies "in" the Philosophy of Marxism*). In other words: if I make an assumption that is obviously absurd and contrary to natural science (that man can be an observer in an epoch before man existed), I shall be able to patch up the breach in my philosophy!

This gives us an idea of the extent of Bazarov's knowledge of the subject and of his literary methods. Bazarov did not even hint at the "difficulty" with which Avenarius, Petzoldt, and Willy wrestled; and, moreover, he made such a hash of the whole subject, placed before the reader such an incredible hodgepodge, that there ultimately appears to be no difference between materialism and solipsism! Idealism is represented as "realism," and to materialism is ascribed the denial of the existence of things outside of their action on the sense organs! Truly, either Feuerbach did not know the elementary difference between materialism and idealism, or else Bazarov and Co. have completely altered the elementary truths of philosophy.

Or let us take Valentinov, a philosopher who, naturally, is delighted with Bazarov:

1. "Berkeley is the founder of the correlativist theory of the relativity of subject and object." This is not Berkeleian idealism, oh, no! This is a "profound analysis."

2. "In the most realistic aspect, irrespective of the forms [!] of their usual idealist interpretation [only interpretation!], the fundamental premises of the theory are formulated by Avenarius." Infants, as we see, are taken in by the mystification!

3. "Avenarius's conception of the starting point of knowledge is that each individual finds himself in a definite environment, in other words, the individual and the environment are represented as connected and inseparable [!] terms of one and the same coordination." Delightful! This is not idealism—Bazarov and Valentinov

have risen above materialism and idealism—this "inseparability" of the subject and object is "realism" itself.

4.   "Is the reverse assertion correct, namely, that there is no counter-term to which there is no corresponding central term—an individual? Naturally [!] not . . . In the Archean period the woods were verdant . . . yet there was no man." That means that the inseparable can be separated! Is that not "natural"?

5.   "Yet from the standpoint of the theory of knowledge, the question of the object in itself is absurd." Of course! When there were no sentient organisms objects were nevertheless "complexes of elements" identical with sensations!

6.   "The immanentist school, in the person of Schubert-Soldern and Schuppe, clad these [!] thoughts in an unsatisfactory form and found itself in the cul-de-sac of solipsism." But "these thoughts" themselves, of course, contain no solipsism, and empiriocriticism, of course, is not a paraphrase of the reactionary theories of the immanentists, who lie when they declare themselves to be in sympathy with Avenarius!

This, Messrs. Machians, is not philosophy, but an incoherent jumble of words.

1.5 Does man think with the help of the brain?

Bazarov emphatically answers this question in the affirmative. He writes:

If Plekhanov's thesis that "consciousness is an internal [? Bazarov] state of matter" be given a more satisfactory form, e.g., that "every mental process is a function of the cerebral process," then neither Mach nor Avenarius would dispute it (*Studies "in" the Philosophy of Marxism*).

To the mouse no beast is stronger than the cat. To the Russian Machians there is no materialist stronger than Plekhanov. Was Plekhanov really the *only* one, or the first, to advance the materialist thesis that consciousness is an internal state of matter? And if Bazarov did not like Plekhanov's formulation of materialism, why did he take Plekhanov and not Engels or Feuerbach?

Because the Machians are afraid to admit the truth. They are fighting materialism, but pretend that it is only Plekhanov they are fighting. A cowardly and unprincipled method.

But let us turn to empiriocriticism. Avenarius "would not dispute" the statement that thought is a function of the brain. These words of Bazarov's contain a direct untruth. Not only does Avenarius dispute the materialist thesis, but invents a whole "theory" in order to refute it. "The brain," says Avenarius in *The Human Concept of the World*, "is not the habitation, the seat, the creator, it is not the instrument or organ, the supporter or substratum, etc., of thought" (approvingly quoted by Mach in the *Analysis of Sensations*). "Thought is not an inhabitant, or commander, or the other half, or side, etc., nor is it a product or even a physiological function, or a state in general of the brain" (ibid.). And Avenarius expresses himself no less emphatically in his *Notes*: "presentations" are "not functions (physiological, psychical, or psycho-physical) of the brain" (op. cit., § 115). Sensations are not "psychical functions of the brain" (§ 116).

Thus, according to Avenarius, the brain is not the organ of thought, and thought is not a function of the brain. Take Engels, and we immediately find directly contrary, frankly materialist formulations. "Thought and consciousness," says Engels in *Anti-Dühring*, "are products of the human brain." This idea is often repeated in that work. In *Ludwig Feuerbach* we have the following exposition of the views of Feuerbach and Engels: ". . . the material, sensuously perceptible world to which we ourselves belong is the only reality . . . our consciousness and thinking, however suprasensuous they may seem, are the product of a material, bodily organ, the brain. Matter is not a product of mind, but mind itself is merely the highest product of matter. This is, of course, pure materialism." Or on p. 4, where he speaks of the reflection of the processes of nature in "the thinking brain," etc., etc.

Avenarius rejects this materialist standpoint and says that "the thinking brain" is a *"fetish of natural science"* (*The Human Concept of the World*). Hence, Avenarius cherishes no illusions concerning his absolute disagreement with natural science on this point. He admits, as do Mach and all the immanentists, that natural science holds an instinctive and unconscious materialist point of view. He admits and explicitly declares that *he absolutely differs from the "prevailing psychology"* (*Notes*). This prevailing psychology is guilty of an inadmissible "introjection"—such is the new term contrived by our philosopher—i.e., the insertion of thought into the brain, or of sensations into us. These "two words" (into us), Avenarius goes on to say, contain the assumption that empiriocriticism disputes. "This insertion of the visible, etc., into man is what we call *introjection*" (§ 45).

Introjection deviates "in principle" from the "natural conception of the world" by substituting "in me" for "before me" "by turning a component part of the (real) environment into a component part of (ideal) thought" (ibid.). "Out of the *amechanical* [a new word in place of "mental"] which manifests itself freely and clearly in the experienced [or, in what is found], introjection makes something which hides itself [*Latitierendes*, says Avenarius—another new word] mysteriously in the central nervous system."

Here we have the same *mystification* that we encountered in the famous defense of "naïve realism" by the empiriocriticists and immanentists. Avenarius here acts on the advice of the charlatan in Turgenev: denounce most of all those vices which you yourself possess. Avenarius tries to pretend that he is combating idealism: philosophical idealism, you see, is usually deduced from introjection, the external world is converted into sensation, into ideas, and so forth, while I defend "naïve realism," the equal reality of everything presented, both "*self*" and environment, without inserting the external world into the human brain.

The sophistry here is the same as that which we observed in the case of the famous coordination. While distracting the attention of the reader by attacking idealism, Avenarius is in fact defending idealism, albeit in slightly different words: thought is not a function of the brain; the brain is not the organ of thought; sensations are not a function of the nervous system, oh, no! sensations are—"elements," psychical only in one connection, while in another connection (although the elements are "*identical*") they are physical. With his new and muddled terminology, with his new and pompous epithets, supposedly expressing a new "theory," Avenarius merely beat about the bush and returned to his fundamental idealist premise.

And if our Russian Machians (e. g., Bogdanov) failed to notice the "mystification" and discerned a refutation of idealism in the "new" defense of idealism, in the analysis of empiriocriticism given by the professional philosophers we find a sober estimate of the true nature of Avenarius's ideas, which is laid bare when stripped of its pretentious terminology.

In 1903 Bogdanov wrote ("Authoritative Thinking," an article in the symposium *From the Psychology of Society*):

> Richard Avenarius presented a most harmonious and complete philosophical picture of the development of the dualism of spirit and body.

The gist of his "doctrine of introjection" is the following: [we observe only physical bodies directly, and we infer the experiences of others, i.e., the mind of another person, only by hypothesis] . . . The hypothesis is complicated by the fact that the experiences of the other person are assumed to be located in his body, are inserted (introjected) into his organism. This is already a superfluous hypothesis and even gives rise to numerous contradictions. Avenarius systematically draws attention to these contradictions by unfolding a series of successive historical facts in the development of dualism and of philosophical idealism. But here we need not follow Avenarius . . . Introjection serves as an explanation of the dualism of mind and body.

Bogdanov swallowed the bait of professorial philosophy in believing that "introjection" was aimed against idealism. He accepted the evaluation of introjection given by Avenarius himself *at its face value* and failed to notice the *barb* directed against materialism. Introjection denies that thought is a function of the brain, that sensations are a function of man's central nervous system: that is, it denies the most elementary truth of physiology in order to destroy materialism. "Dualism," it appears, is refuted *idealistically* (notwithstanding all Avenarius's diplomatic rage against idealism), for sensation and thought prove to be not secondary, not a product of matter, but *primary*. Dualism is here refuted by Avenarius only insofar as he "refutes" the existence of the object without the subject, matter without thought, the external world independent of our sensations; that is, it is refuted idealistically. The absurd denial of the fact that the visual image of a tree is a function of the retina, the nerves, and the brain, was required by Avenarius in order to bolster up his theory of the "indissoluble" connection of the "complete" experience, which includes not only the self but also the tree, i.e., the environment.

The doctrine of introjection is a muddle; it smuggles in idealistic rubbish and is contradictory to natural science, which inflexibly holds that thought is a function of the brain, that sensations, i.e., the images of the *external world*, exist *within us*, produced by the action of things on our sense organs. The materialist elimination of the "dualism of mind and body" (i.e., materialist monism) consists in the assertion that the mind does not exist independently of the body, that mind is secondary, a function of the brain, a reflection of the external world. The idealist elimination of the "dualism of mind and body" (i.e., idealist monism) consists in the assertion that mind *is not* a function of the body, that, consequently, mind is primary, that the "environment" and the "self" exist only in an inseparable connection of one and the same "complexes of elements." Apart from these two diametrically opposed methods of eliminating "the dualism of mind and body," there can be no third method, unless it be eclecticism, which is a senseless jumble of materialism and idealism. And it was this jumble of Avenarius's that seemed to Bogdanov and Co. "the truth transcending materialism and idealism."

But the professional philosophers are not as naïve and credulous as are the Russian Machians. True, each of these professors-in-ordinary advocates his "*own*" system of refuting materialism, or, at any rate, of "reconciling" materialism and idealism. But when it comes to a competitor they unceremoniously expose the unconnected fragments of materialism and idealism that are contained in all the "recent" and "original" systems. And if a few young intellectuals swallowed Avenarius's bait, that old bird Wundt was not to be enticed so easily. The idealist Wundt tore the mask from the poseur Avenarius very unceremoniously *when he praised him for the anti-materialist tendency of the theory of introjection*. Wundt wrote:

> If empiriocriticism reproaches vulgar materialism because by such expressions as the brain "has" thought, or the brain "produces" thought, it expresses a relation which generally cannot be established by factual observation and description [evidently, for Wundt it is a "fact" that a person thinks without the help of a brain!] . . . this reproach, of course, is well founded.

Well, of course! The idealists will always join the half-hearted Avenarius and Mach in attacking materialism! It is only a pity, Wundt goes on to say, that this theory of introjection "does not stand in any relation to the doctrine of the independent vital series, and was, to all appearances, only tacked on to it as an afterthought and in a rather artificial fashion."

Introjection, says O. Ewald, "is to be regarded as nothing but a fiction of empiriocriticism, which the latter requires in order to shield its own fallacies."

> We observe a strange contradiction: on the one hand, the elimination of introjection and the restoration of the natural world conception is intended to restore to the world the character of living reality; on the other hand, in the principal coordination empiriocriticism is leading to a purely idealist theory of an absolute correlation of the counter-term and the central term. Avenarius is thus moving in a circle. He set out to do battle against idealism but laid down his arms before it came to an open skirmish. He wanted to liberate the world of objects from the yoke of the subject, but again bound that world to the subject. What he

has actually destroyed by his criticism is a caricature of idealism rather than its genuine epistemological expression.

"In his [Avenarius's] frequently quoted statement," Norman Smith says, "that the brain is not the seat, organ, or supporter of thought, he rejects the only terms which we possess for defining their connection."

Nor is it surprising that the theory of introjection approved by Wundt excites the sympathy of the outspoken spiritualist, James Ward, who wages systematic war on "naturalism and agnosticism," and especially on Thomas Huxley (not because he was an insufficiently outspoken and determined materialist, for which Engels reproached him, but) because his agnosticism served in fact to conceal materialism.

Let us note that Karl Pearson, the English Machian, who avoids all philosophical artifices, and who recognizes neither introjection, nor co-ordination, nor yet "the discovery of the world-elements," arrives at the inevitable outcome of Machism when it is stripped of such "disguises," namely, pure subjective idealism. Pearson knows no "elements"; "sense impressions" are his alpha and omega. He never doubts that man thinks with the help of the brain. And the contradiction between this thesis (which alone conforms with science) and the basis of his philosophy remains naked and obvious. Pearson spares no effort in combating the concept that matter exists independently of our sense impressions (*The Grammar of Science*). Repeating all Berkeley's arguments, Pearson declare that matter is a nonentity. But when he comes to speak of the relation of the brain to thought, Pearson emphatically declares: "From will and consciousness associated with material machinery we can infer nothing whatever as to will and consciousness without that machinery." He even advances the following thesis as a summary of his investigations in this field:

> Consciousness has no meaning beyond nervous systems akin to our own; it is illogical to assert that all matter is conscious [but it is logical to assert that all matter possesses a property which is essentially akin to sensation, the property of reflection], still more that consciousness or will can exist outside matter.

Pearson's muddle is glaring! Matter is nothing but groups of sense impressions. That is his premise, that is his philosophy. Hence, sensation and thought should be primary; matter, secondary. But no, consciousness without matter does not exist, and apparently not even without a nervous system! That is, consciousness and sensation are secondary. The waters rest on the earth, the earth rests on a whale, and the whale rests on the waters. Mach's "elements" and Avenarius's coordination and introjection do not clear up this muddle, all they do is to obscure the matter, to cover up traces with the help of an erudite philosophical gibberish.

Just such gibberish, and of this a word or two will suffice, is the special terminology of Avenarius, who coined a plenitude of diverse "notals," "securals," "fidentials," etc., etc. Our Russian Machians for the most part shamefacedly avoid this professorial rigmarole, and only now and again bombard the reader (in order to stun him) with an "existential" and such like. But if naïve people take these words for a species of biomechanics, the German philosophers, who are themselves lovers of "erudite" words, laugh at Avenarius. To say "notal" (*notus* = known), or to say that this or the other thing is known to me, is absolutely one and the same, says Wundt in the section entitled "Scholastic Character of the Empiriocritical System." And, indeed, it is the purest and most dreary scholasticism. One of Avenarius's most faithful disciples, R. Willy, had the courage to admit it frankly. He says:

> Avenarius dreamed of a bio-mechanics but an understanding of the life of the brain can be arrived at only by actual discoveries, and not by the way in which Avenarius attempted to arrive at it. Avenarius's biomechanics is not grounded on any new observations whatever; its characteristic feature is purely schematic constructions of concepts, and, indeed, constructions that do not even bear the nature of hypotheses that open up new vistas, but rather of stereotyped speculations, which, like a wall, conceal our view.

The Russian Machians will soon be like fashion lovers who are moved to ecstasy over a hat which has already been discarded by the bourgeois philosophers of Europe.

1.6 The solipsism of Mach and Avenarius

We have seen that the starting point and the fundamental premise of the philosophy of empiriocriticism is subjective idealism. The world is our sensation—this is the fundamental premise, which is obscured but in no wise altered by the word "element" and by the theories of the "independent series," "coordination," and "introjection." The absurdity of this philosophy lies in the fact that it leads to solipsism, to the recognition of the existence of the philosophizing individual only. But our Russian

Machians assure their readers that to "charge" Mach "with idealism and even solipsism" is "extreme subjectivism." So says Bogdanov in the introduction to the Russian translation of *Analysis of Sensations*, and the whole Machian troop repeat it in a great variety of keys.

Having examined the methods whereby Mach and Avenarius disguise their solipsism, we have now to add only one thing: the "extreme subjectivism" of assertion lies entirely with Bogdanov and Co.; for in philosophical literature writers of the most varied trends have long since disclosed the fundamental sin of Machism beneath all its disguises. We shall confine ourselves to a mere *summary* of opinions which sufficiently indicate the "subjective" *ignorance* of our Machians. Let us note in passing that nearly every professional philosopher sympathizes with one or another brand of idealism: in their eyes idealism is not a reproach, as it is with us Marxists; but they point out Mach's *actual* philosophical trend and oppose one system of idealism by another system, also idealist, but to them more consistent.

O. Ewald, in the book devoted to an analysis of Avenarius's teachings, writes:

> The creator of empiriocriticism commits himself *volens nolens* to solipsism.

Hans Kleinpeter, a disciple of Mach with whom Mach in his preface to *Knowledge and Error* explicitly declares his solidarity, says:

> It is precisely Mach who is an example of the compatibility of epistemological idealism with the demands of natural science [for the eclectic everything is "compatible"!], and of the fact that the latter can very well start from solipsism without stopping there (*Archive for Systematic Philosophy*, 1900).

E. Lucka, analyzing Mach's *Analysis of Sensations*, says:

> Apart from this . . . misunderstandings Mach adopts the ground of pure idealism . . . It is incomprehensible that Mach denies that he is a Berkeleian.

W. Jerusalem, a most reactionary Kantian with whom Mach in the above-mentioned preface expresses his solidarity ("a closer kinship" of thought than Mach had previously suspected—*Foreword to Knowledge and Error*, 1906) says: "Consistent phenomenalism leads to solipsism." And therefore one must borrow a little from Kant! (See *Critical Idealism and Pure Logic*)

R. Hönigswald says:

> ... the immanentists and the empiriocriticists face the alternative of solipsism or metaphysics in the spirit of Fichte, Schelling, or Hegel *Hume's Doctrine of the Reality of the External World*, 1904).

The English physicist Oliver Lodge, in his book denouncing the materialist Haeckel, speaks in passing, as though of something generally known, of "solipsists such as Mach and Karl Pearson" (*Life and Matter*, 1907).

Nature, the organ of the English scientists, through the mouth of the geometrician E. T. Dixon, pronounced a very definite opinion of the Machian Pearson, one worth quoting, not because it is new, but because the Russian Machians have naïvely accepted Mach's philosophical muddle as the "philosophy of natural science" (A. Bogdanov, introduction to *Analysis of Sensations*). Dixon writes:

> The foundation of the whole book is the proposition that since we cannot directly apprehend anything but sense impressions, therefore the things we commonly speak of as objective, or external to ourselves, and their variations, are nothing but groups of sense impressions and sequences of such groups. But Professor Pearson admits the existence of other consciousness than his own, not only by implication in addressing his book to them, but explicitly in many passages.

Pearson infers the existence of the consciousness of others by analogy, by observing the bodily motions of other people; but since the consciousness of others is real, the existence of people outside myself must be granted!

> Of course it would be impossible thus to refute a consistent idealist, who maintained that not only external things but all other consciousness were unreal and existed only in his imagination, but to recognize the reality of other consciousness is to recognize the reality of the means by which we become aware of them, which . . . is the external aspect of men's bodies.

The way out of the difficulty is to recognize the "hypothesis" that to our sense impressions there corresponds an objective reality outside of us. This hypothesis satisfactorily explains our sense impressions. "I cannot seriously doubt that Professor Pearson himself believes in them as much as anyone else. Only, if he were to acknowledge it explicitly, he would have to rewrite almost every page of *The Grammar of Science*."

Ridicule—that is the response of the thinking scientists to the idealist philosophy over which Mach waxes so enthusiastic.

And here, finally, is the opinion of a German physicist, L. Boltzmann. The Machians will perhaps say, as Friedrich Adler said, that he is a physicist of the old school. But we are concerned now not with theories of physics but with a fundamental philosophical problem. Writing against people who "have been carried away by the new epistemological dogmas," Boltzmann says:

> Mistrust of conceptions which we can derive only from immediate sense impressions has led to an extreme which is the direct opposite of former naïve belief. Only sense impressions are given us, and, therefore, it is said, we have no right to go a step beyond. But to be consistent, one must further ask: are our sense impressions of yesterday also given? What is immediately given is only the one sense impression, or only the one thought, namely, the one we are thinking at the present moment. Hence, to be consistent, one would have to deny not only the existence of other people outside one's self, but also all conceptions we ever had in the past.

This physicist rightly ridicules the supposedly "new" "phenomenalist" view of Mach and Co. as the old absurdity of philosophical subjective idealism.

No, it is those who "failed to note" that solipsism is Mach's fundamental error who are stricken with "subjective" blindness.

Chapter Two: The Theory of Knowledge of Empiriocriticism and of Dialectical Materialism II

* * *

2.5 Absolute and relative truth, or the eclecticism of Engels as discovered by A. Bogdanov

Bogdanov made his discovery in 1906, in the preface to Book III of his *Empiriomonism*. "Engels in *Anti-Dühring*," writes Bogdanov, "expresses himself *almost* in the same sense in which I have just described the relativity of truth"—that is, in the sense of denying all eternal truth, "denying the unconditional objectivity of all truth whatsoever." "Engels is wrong in his indecision, in the fact that in spite of his irony he recognizes certain 'eternal truths,' wretched though they may be . . . Only inconsistency can here permit such eclectic reservations as those of Engels . . ." Let us cite one instance of Bogdanov's refutation of Engels's eclecticism. "Napoleon died on May 5, 1821," says Engels in *Anti-Dühring*, in the chapter "Eternal Truths," where he reminds Dühring of the "platitudes" (*Plattheiten*) to which he who claims to discover eternal truths in the historical sciences has to confine himself. Bogdanov thus answers Engels: "What sort of 'truth' is that? And what is there 'eternal' about it? The recording of a single correlation, which perhaps even has no longer any real significance for our generation, cannot serve as a basis for any activity, and leads nowhere." And "Can *Plattheiten* be called *Wahrheiten*? Are 'platitudes' truths? Truth is a vital organizing form of experience; it *leads* us somewhere in our activity and provides a point of support in the struggle of life."

It is quite clear from these two quotations that Bogdanov, instead of refuting Engels, makes a mere *declamation*. If you cannot assert that the proposition "Napoleon died on May 5, 1821," is false or inexact, you acknowledge that it is true. If you do not assert that it may be refuted in the future, you acknowledge this truth to be eternal. But to call phrases such as truth is a "vital organizing form of experience" an answer, is to palm off a mere *jumble of words* as philosophy. Did the earth have the history which is expounded in geology, or was the earth created in seven days? Is one to be allowed to dodge this question by talking about "vital" ('what does that mean?) truth which "leads" somewhere, and the like? Can it be that knowledge of the history of the earth and of the history of humanity "has no real significance"? This is just turgid nonsense, used by Bogdanov to cover his *retreat*. For it is a retreat, when, having taken it upon himself to prove that the admission of eternal truths by Engels is eclecticism, he dodges the issue by a mere noise and clash of words and leaves unrefuted the fact that Napoleon did die on May 5, 1821, and that to regard this *truth* as refutable in the future is absurd.

The example given by Engels is elementary, and anybody without the slightest difficulty can think of scores of similar *truths* that are eternal and absolute and that only insane people can doubt (as Engels says, citing another example: "Paris is in France"). Why does Engels speak here of "platitudes"? Because he refutes and ridicules the dogmatic, metaphysical materialist Dühring, who was incapable of applying dialectics to the relation between absolute and relative truth. To be a materialist is to acknowledge objective truth, which is revealed to us by our sense organs. To acknowledge objective truth, i.e., truth not dependent upon man and mankind, is, in one way or another, to recognize absolute truth. And it is this "one way or another" which distinguishes the metaphysical materialist Dühring from the dialectical materialist Engels. On the most complex questions of science in general, and of historical science in particular, Dühring scattered words right and left: ultimate, final, and eternal truth. Engels jeered at him. Of course there are eternal truths, Engels said, but it is unwise to use high-sounding words in connection with simple things. If we want to advance materialism, we must drop this trite play with the words "eternal truth"; we must learn to put, and answer, the question of the relation between absolute and relative truth dialectically. It was on this issue that the fight between Dühring and Engels was waged thirty years ago. And Bogdanov, who managed *"not to notice"* Engels's explanation of the problem of absolute and relative truth given *in this very same chapter*, and who managed to accuse Engels of "eclecticism" for his admission of a proposition which is a truism for all forms of materialism, only once again betrays his utter ignorance of both materialism and dialectics.

". . . Now we come to the question," Engels writes in *Anti-Dühring*, in the beginning of the chapter mentioned, "whether any, and if so which, products of human knowledge ever can have sovereign validity and an unconditional claim to truth." And Engels answers the question thus:

"The sovereignty of thought is realized in a number of extremely unsovereignly thinking human beings; the knowledge which has an unconditional claim to truth is realized in a number of relative errors; neither the one nor the other [i.e., neither absolutely true knowledge, nor sovereign thought] can be fully realized except through an endless eternity of human existence.

"Here once again we find the same contradiction as we found above, between the character of human thought, necessarily conceived as absolute, and its reality in individual human beings with their extremely limited thought. This is a contradiction which can only be solved in the infinite progression, or what is for us, at least from a practical standpoint, the endless succession, of generations of mankind. In this sense human thought is just as much sovereign as not sovereign, and its capacity for knowledge just as much unlimited as limited. It is sovereign and unlimited in its disposition, its vocation, its possibilities, and its historical ultimate goal; it is not sovereign and it is limited in its individual expression and in its realization at each particular moment." Chernov, the Machian, fully shares the position of Bogdanov who does not wish to own himself a Machian. The difference is that Bogdanov *tries to cover up* his disagreement with Engels, to present it as a casual matter, etc., while Chernov feels that it is a question of a struggle against both materialism and dialectics.]

"It is just the same," Engels continues, "with eternal truths."

This argument is extremely important for the question of *relativism*, i.e., the principle of the relativity of our knowledge, which is stressed by all Machians. The Machians one and all insist that they are relativists, but the Russian Machians, while repeating the words of the Germans, are afraid, or unable to propound the question of the relation of relativism to dialectics clearly and straightforwardly. For Bogdanov (as for all the Machians) recognition of the relativity of our knowledge *excludes* even the least admission of absolute truth. For Engels absolute truth is compounded from relative truths. Bogdanov is a relativist; Engels is a dialectician. Here is another, no less important, argument of Engels from the chapter of *Anti-Dühring* already quoted:

". . . Truth and error, like all thought concepts which move in polar opposites, have absolute validity only in an extremely limited field, as we have just seen, and as even Herr Dühring would realize if he had any acquaintance with the first elements of dialectics, which deal precisely with the inadequacy of all polar opposites. As soon as we apply the antithesis between truth and error outside of that narrow field which has been referred to above it becomes relative and therefore unserviceable for exact scientific modes of expression; and if we attempt to apply it as absolutely valid outside that field we really find ourselves altogether beaten: both poles of the antithesis become transformed into their opposites, truth becomes error and error truth." Here follows the example of Boyle's law (the volume of a gas is inversely proportional to its pressure). The "grain of truth" contained in this law is only absolute truth within certain limits. The law, it appears, is a truth "only approximately."

Human thought then by its nature is capable of giving, and does give, absolute truth, which is compounded of a sum total of relative truths. Each step in the development of science adds new grains to the sum of absolute truth, but the limits of the truth of each scientific proposition are relative, now expanding, now shrinking with the growth of knowledge. "Absolute truth," says J. Dietzgen in his *Excursions*,— "can be seen, heard, smelt, touched and, of course, also be *known*, but it is not entirely absorbed into knowledge." "It goes without saying that a picture does not exhaust its object and the artist remains behind his model . . . How can a picture 'coincide' with its model? Approximately it can." "Hence, we can know nature and her parts only relatively; since even a part, though only a relation of nature, possesses nevertheless the nature of the absolute, the nature of nature as a whole which cannot be exhausted by knowledge . . . How, then, do we know that behind the phenomena of nature, behind the relative truths, there is a universal, unlimited, absolute nature which does not reveal itself to man completely? . . . Whence this knowledge? It is innate; it is given us with consciousness." This last statement is one of the inexactitudes of Dietzgen's which led Marx, in one of his letters to Kugelmann, to speak of the confusion in Dietzgen's views. Only by seizing upon such incorrect passages can one speak of a specific philosophy of Dietzgen differing from dialectical materialism. But Dietzgen corrects himself *on the same page*: "When I say that the consciousness of eternal, absolute truth is innate in us, that it is the one and only *a priori* knowledge, experience also confirms this innate consciousness."

From all these statements by Engels and Dietzgen it is obvious that for dialectical materialism there is no impassable boundary between relative and absolute truth. Bogdanov entirely failed to grasp this if he could write: "It [the world outlook of the old materialism] sets itself up as the absolute *objective knowledge of the essence of things* [Bogdanov's italics] and is incompatible with the historically conditional nature of all ideologies" (*Empiriomonism*). From the standpoint of modern materialism i.e., Marxism, the *limits* of approximation of our knowledge to objective, absolute truth are historically conditional, but the existence of such truth is *unconditional*, and the fact that we are approaching nearer to it is also unconditional. The contours of the picture are historically conditional, but the fact that this picture depicts an objectively existing model is unconditional. When and under what circumstances we reached, in our knowledge of the essential nature of things, the discovery of alizarin in coal tar or the discovery of electrons in the atom is historically conditional; but that every such discovery is an advance of "absolutely objective knowledge" is unconditional. In a word, every ideology is historically conditional, but it is unconditionally true that to every scientific ideology (as distinct, for instance, from religious ideology), there corresponds an objective truth, absolute nature. You will say that this distinction between relative and absolute truth is indefinite. And I shall reply: yes, it is sufficiently "indefinite" to prevent science from becoming a dogma in the bad sense of the term, from becoming something dead, frozen, ossified; but it is at the same time sufficiently "definite" to enable us to dissociate ourselves in the most emphatic and irrevocable manner from fideism and agnosticism, from philosophical idealism and the sophistry of the followers of Hume and Kant. Here is a boundary which you have not noticed, and not having noticed it, you have fallen into the swamp of reactionary philosophy. It is the boundary between dialectical materialism and relativism.

We are relativists, proclaim Mach, Avenarius, Petzoldt. We are relativists, echo Mr. Chernov and certain Russian Machians, would-be Marxists. Yes, Mr. Chernov and Comrades Machians—and therein lies your error. For to make relativism the basis of the theory of knowledge is inevitably to condemn oneself either to absolute skepticism, agnosticism, and sophistry, or to subjectivism. Relativism as a basis of the theory of knowledge is not only the recognition of the relativity of our knowledge, but also a denial of any objective measure or model existing independently of humanity to which our relative knowledge approximates. From the standpoint of naked relativism one can justify any sophistry; one may regard it as "conditional" whether Napoleon died on May 5, 1821, or not; one may declare the admission, alongside of scientific ideology ("convenient" in one respect), of religious ideology (very "convenient" in another respect) a mere "convenience" for man or humanity, and so forth.

Dialectics—as Hegel in his time explained—*contains* the element of relativism, of negation, of skepticism, but *is not reducible* to relativism. The materialist dialectics of Marx and Engels certainly does contain relativism, but is not reducible to relativism, that is, it recognizes the relativity of all our knowledge, not in the sense of denying objective truth, but in the sense that the limits of approximation of our knowledge to this truth are historically conditional.

Bogdanov writes in italics: "*Consistent Marxism does not admit such dogmatism and such static concepts*" as eternal truths (*Empiriomonism*). This is a muddle. If the world is eternally moving and developing matter (as the Marxists think), reflected by the developing human consciousness, what is there "static" here? The point at issue is not the immutable essence of things, or an immutable consciousness, but the *correspondence* between the consciousness which reflects nature and the nature which is reflected by consciousness. In connection with this question, and this question alone, the term "dogmatism" has a specific, characteristic philosophical flavor: it is a favorite word used by the idealists and the agnostics *against* the materialists, as we have already seen in the case of the fairly "old" materialist, Feuerbach. The objections brought against materialism from the standpoint of the celebrated "recent positivism" are just ancient trash.

Chapter Three: The Theory of Knowledge of Dialectical Materialism and of Empiriocriticism.

3.1 What is matter? What is experience?

The first of these questions is constantly being hurled by the idealists and agnostics, including the Machians, at the materialists; the second question by the materialists at the Machians. Let us try to make the point at issue clear.

Avenarius says on the subject of matter:

> Within the purified, "complete experience" there is nothing "physical"— "matter" in the metaphysical absolute conception—for "matter" according to this conception is only an abstraction; it would be the total of the counter-terms abstracted from every central term. Just as in the principal coordination, that is, "complete experience," a counter-term is inconceivable without a central term, so "matter" in the metaphysical absolute conception is a complete chimera (*Notes*).

In all this gibberish one thing is evident, namely, that Avenarius designates the physical or matter by the terms absolute and metaphysics, for, according to his theory of the principal coordination (or, in the new way, "complete experience"), the counter-term is inseparable from the central term, the environment from the *self*; the *non-self* is inseparable from the *self* (as J. G. Fichte said). That this theory is disguised subjective idealism we have already shown, and the nature of Avenarius's attacks on "matter" is quite obvious: the idealist denies physical being that is independent of the psychical and therefore rejects the concept elaborated by philosophy for such being. That matter is "physical" (i.e., that which is most familiar and immediately given to man, and the existence of which no one save an inmate of a lunatic asylum can doubt) is not denied by Avenarius; he only insists on the acceptance of "*his*" theory of the indissoluble connection between the environment and the self.

Mach expresses the same thought more simply, without philosophical flourishes: "What we call matter is a certain systematic combination of the *elements* (sensations)" (*Analysis of Sensations*). Mach thinks that by this assertion he is effecting a "radical change" in the usual world outlook. In reality this is the old, old subjective idealism, the nakedness of which is concealed by the word "element."

And lastly, the English Machian, Pearson, a rabid antagonist of materialism, says: "Now there can be no scientific objection to our classifying certain more or less permanent groups of sense impressions together and terming them matter,—to do so indeed leads us very near to John Stuart Mill's definition of matter as a 'permanent possibility of sensation,'—but this definition of matter then leads us entirely away from matter as the thing which moves" (*The Grammar of Science*, 1900). Here there is not even the figleaf of the "elements," and the idealist openly stretches out a hand to the agnostic.

As the reader sees, all these arguments of the founders of empiriocriticism entirely and exclusively revolve around the old epistemological question of the relation of thinking to being, of sensation to the physical. It required the extreme naïveté of the Russian Machians to discern anything here that is even remotely related to "recent science," or "recent positivism." All the philosophers mentioned by us, some frankly, others guardedly, replace the fundamental philosophical line of materialism (from being to thinking, from matter to sensation) by the reverse line of idealism. Their denial of matter is the old answer to epistemological problems, which consists in denying the existence of an external, objective source of our sensations, of an objective reality corresponding to our sensations. On the other hand, the recognition of the philosophical line denied by the idealists and agnostics is expressed in the definitions: matter is that which, acting upon our sense organs, produces sensation; matter is the objective reality given to us in sensation, and so forth.

Bogdanov, pretending to argue only against Beltov and cravenly ignoring Engels, is indignant at such definitions, which, don't you see, "prove to be simple repetitions" (*Empiriomonism*) of the "formula" (of Engels, our "Marxist" forgets to add) that for one trend in philosophy matter is primary and spirit secondary, while for the other trend the reverse is the case. All the Russian Machians exultantly echo Bogdanov's "refutation"!

But the slightest reflection could have shown these people that it is impossible, in the very nature of the case, to give any definition of these two ultimate concepts of epistemology save one that indicates which of them is taken as primary. What is meant by giving a "definition"? It means essentially to bring a given concept within a more comprehensive concept. For example, when I give the definition "an ass is an animal," I am bringing the concept "ass" within a more comprehensive concept. The question then is, are there more comprehensive concepts, with which the theory of knowledge could operate, than those of being and thinking, matter and sensation, physical and mental? No. These are the ultimate concepts, the most comprehensive concepts which epistemology has in point of fact so far not surpassed (apart from changes in *nomenclature*, which are *always* possible). One must be a charlatan or an utter blockhead to demand a "definition" of these two "series" of concepts of ultimate comprehensiveness which would not be a "mere repetition": one or the other must be taken as the primary. Take the three aforementioned arguments on matter. What do they all amount to? To this, that these philosophers proceed from the mental or the self, to the physical, or environment, as from the central term to the counter-term—or from sensation to matter, or from sense perception to matter. Could Avenarius, Mach, and Pearson in fact have given any other "definition" of these fundamental concepts, save by pointing to the *trend* of their philosophical line? Could they have defined in any other way, in any specific way, what the *self* is, what sensation is, what sense perception is? One has only to formulate the question clearly to realize what utter nonsense the Machians are talking when they demand that the materialists give a definition of matter which would not amount to a repetition of the proposition that matter, nature, being, the physical—is primary, and spirit, consciousness, sensation, the psychical—is secondary.

One expression of the genius of Marx and Engels was that they despised pedantic playing with new words, erudite terms, and subtle "isms," and said simply and plainly: there is a materialist line and an idealist line in philosophy, and between them there are various shades of agnosticism. The painful quest for a "new" point of view in philosophy betrays the same poverty of mind that is revealed in the painful effort to create a "new" theory of value, or a "new" theory of rent, and so forth.

Of Avenarius, his disciple Carstanjen says that he once expressed himself in private conversation as follows: "I know neither the physical nor the mental, but only some third." To the remark of one writer that the concept of this third was not given by Avenarius, Petzoldt replied: "We know why he could not advance such a concept. The third lacks a counter concept . . . The question, what is the third? is illogically put" (*Introduction to the Philosophy of Pure Experience*). Petzoldt understands that an ultimate concept cannot be defined. But he does not understand that the resort to a "third" is a mere subterfuge, for every one of us knows what is physical and what is mental, but none of us knows at present what that "third" is. Avenarius was merely covering up his tracks by this subterfuge and *actually* was declaring that the self is the primary (central term) and nature (environment) the secondary (counter-term).

Of course, even the antithesis of matter and mind has absolute significance only within the bounds of a very limited field—in this case exclusively within the bounds of the fundamental epistemological problem of what is to be regarded as primary and what as secondary. Beyond these bounds the relative character of this antithesis is indubitable.

Let us now examine how the word "experience" is used in empiriocritical philosophy. The first paragraph of *The Critique of Pure Experience* expounds the following "assumption": "Any part of our environment stands in relation to human individuals in such a way that, the former having been given, the latter speak of their experience as follows: 'this is experienced,' 'this is an experience'; or 'it followed from experience,' or 'it depends upon experience.'" Thus experience is defined in terms of these same concepts: *self* and environment; while the "doctrine" of their "indissoluble" connection is for the time being tucked out of the way. Further: "The synthetic concept of pure experience"—namely, experience "as a predication for which, in all its components, only parts of the environment serve as a premise." If we assume that the environment exists independently of "declarations" and "predications" of man, then it becomes possible to interpret experience in a materialist way! "The analytical concept of pure experience"—"namely, as a predication to which nothing is admixed that would not be in its turn experience and which, therefore, in itself is nothing but experience." Experience is experience. And there are people who take this quasi-erudite rigmarole for true wisdom!

It is essential to add that in the second volume of *The Critique of Pure Experience* Avenarius regards "experience" as a "special case" of the mental; that he divides experience into *thing values* and *thought values*; that "experience in the broad sense" includes the latter; that "complete experience" is identified with the principal coordination (*Notes*). In short, you pay your money and take your choice. "Experience" embraces both the materialist and the idealist line in philosophy and sanctifies the muddling of them. But while our Machians confidingly accept "pure experience" as pure coin of the realm, in philosophical literature the representatives of the various trends are alike in pointing to Avenarius' abuse of this concept. "What pure experience is," A. Riehl writes, "remains vague with Avenarius, and his explanation that 'pure experience is experience to which nothing is admixed that is not in its turn experience' obviously revolves in a circle" (*Systematic Philosophy*, 1907). Pure experience for Avenarius, writes Wundt, is at times any kind of fantasy, and at others, a predication with the character of "corporeality" (*Philosophical Studies*). Avenarius stretches the concept experience. "On the precise definition of the terms experience and pure experience," writes Cauwelaert, "depends the meaning of the whole of this philosophy. Avenarius does not give a precise definition" (*Neoscholastic Review*, February 1907). "The vagueness of the term 'experience' stands him in good stead, and so in the end Avenarius falls back on the timeworn argument of subjective idealism" (under the pretence of combating it), says Norman Smith (*Mind*).

"I openly declare that the inner sense, the soul of my philosophy consists in this that a human being possesses nothing save experience; a human being comes to everything to which he comes only through experience ..." A zealous philosopher of pure experience, is he not? The author of these words is the subjective idealist Fichte (*Sonnenklarer Bericht*). We know from the history of philosophy that the interpretation of the concept experience divided the classical materialists from the idealists. Today professorial philosophy of all shades disguises its reactionary nature by declaiming on the subject of "experience." All the immanentists fall back on experience. In the preface to the second edition of his *Knowledge and Error*, Mach praises a book by Professor Wilhelm Jerusalem in which we read: "The acceptance of a divine original being is not contradictory to experience" (*Critical Idealism and Pure Logic*).

One can only commiserate with people who believed Avenarius and Co. that the "obsolete" distinction between materialism and idealism can be surmounted by the word "experience." When Valentinov and Yushkevich accuse Bogdanov, who departed somewhat from pure Machism, of abusing the word experience, these gentlemen are only betraying their ignorance. Bogdanov is "not guilty" in this case; he *only* slavishly borrowed the muddle of Mach and Avenarius. When Bogdanov says that "consciousness and immediate mental experience are identical concepts" (*Empiriomonism*) while matter is "not experience" but "the unknown which evokes everything known" (*Empiriomonism*), he is interpreting experience *idealistically*. And, of course, he is not the first [In England Comrade Belfort Bax has been exercising himself in this way for a long time. A French reviewer of his book, *The Roots of Reality*, rather bitingly remarked: "experience is only another word for consciousness"; then come forth as an open idealist! (*Review of Philosophy*, 1907)—Note by Lenin] nor the last to build petty idealist systems on the word experience. When he replies to the reactionary philosophers by declaring that attempts to transcend the boundaries of experience lead in fact "only to empty abstractions and contradictory images, all the elements of which have nevertheless been taken from experience," he is drawing a contrast between the empty abstractions of the human mind and that which exists outside of man and independently of his mind, in other words, he is interpreting experience as a materialist.

Similarly, even Mach, although he makes idealism his starting point (bodies are complexes of sensations or "elements") frequently strays into a materialist interpretation of the word experience. "We must not *philosophize out of ourselves*, but must take from experience," he says in the *Mechanics*. Here a contrast is drawn between experience and philosophizing out of ourselves, in other words, experience is regarded as something objective, something given to man from the outside; it is interpreted materialistically. Here is another example: "What we observe in nature is imprinted, although uncomprehended and unanalyzed, upon our ideas, which, then, in their most general and strongest features imitate the processes of nature. In these experiences we possess a treasure store which is ever to hand . . ." Here nature is taken as primary and sensation and experience as products. Had Mach consistently adhered to this point of view in the fundamental questions of epistemology, he would have spared humanity many foolish idealist "complexes." A third example: "The close connection of thought and experience creates modern natural science. Experience gives rise to a thought. The latter is further elaborated and is again compared with experience" (*Knowledge and Error*). Mach's special "philosophy" is here thrown overboard, and the author instinctively accepts the customary standpoint of the scientists, who regard experience materialistically.

To summarize: The word "experience," on which the Machians build their systems, has long been serving as a shield for idealist systems, and is now serving Avenarius and Co. in eclectically passing to and fro between the idealist position and the materialist position. The various "definitions" of this concept are only expressions of those two fundamental lines in philosophy which were so strikingly revealed by Engels.

3.3 Causality and necessity in nature

The question of causality is particularly important in determining the philosophical line of any new "*ism*," and we must therefore dwell on it in some detail.

Let us begin with an exposition of the materialist theory of knowledge on this point. L. Feuerbach's views are expounded with particular clarity in his reply to R. Haym already referred to.

> "Nature and human reason," says Haym, "are for him (Feuerbach) completely divorced, and between them a gulf is formed which cannot be spanned from one side or the other." Haym grounds this reproach on § 48 of my *Essence of Religion* where it is said that "nature may be conceived only through nature itself, that its necessity is neither human nor logical, neither metaphysical nor mathematical, that nature alone is the being to which it is impossible to apply any human measure, although we compare and give names to its phenomena, in order to make them comprehensible to us, and in general apply human expressions and conceptions to them, as for example: order, purpose, law; and are obliged to do so because of the character of our language." What does this mean? Does it mean that there is no order in nature, so that, for example, autumn may be succeeded by summer, spring by winter, winter by autumn? That there is no purpose, so that, for example, there is no coordination between the lungs and the air, between light and the eye, between sound and the ear? That there is no law, so that, for example, the earth may move now in an ellipse, now in a circle, that it may revolve around the sun now in a year, now in a quarter of an hour? What nonsense! What then is meant by this passage? Nothing more than to distinguish between that which belongs to nature and that which belongs to man; it does not assert that there is actually nothing in nature corresponding to the words or ideas of order, purpose, law. All that it does is to deny the identity between thought and being; it denies that they exist in nature exactly as they do in the head or mind of man. Order, purpose, law are words used by man to translate the acts of nature into *his own* language in order that he may understand them. These

words are not devoid of meaning or of objective content; nevertheless, a distinction must be made between the original and the translation. Order, purpose, law in the human sense express something arbitrary.

From the contingency of order, purpose, and law in nature, theism expressly infers their arbitrary origin; it infers the existence of a being distinct from nature which brings order, purpose, law into a nature that is in itself chaotic (*dissolute*) and indifferent to all determination. The reason of the theists . . . is reason contradictory to nature, reason absolutely devoid of understanding of the essence of nature. The reason of the theists splits nature into two beings—one material, and the other formal or spiritual (*Works*).

Thus Feuerbach recognizes objective law in nature and objective causality, which are reflected only with approximate fidelity by human ideas of order, law, and so forth. With Feuerbach the recognition of objective law in nature is inseparably connected with the recognition of the objective reality of the external world, of objects, bodies, things, reflected by our mind. Feuerbach's views are consistently materialistic. All other views, or rather, any other philosophical line on the question of causality, the denial of objective law, causality, and necessity in nature, are justly regarded by Feuerbach as belonging to the fideist trend. For it is, indeed, clear that the subjectivist line on the question of causality, the deduction of the order and necessity of nature not from the external objective world, but from consciousness, reason, logic, and so forth, not only cuts human reason off from nature, not only opposes the former to the latter, but makes nature a *part* of reason, instead of regarding reason as a part of nature. The subjectivist line on the question of causality is philosophical idealism (varieties of which are the theories of causality of Hume and Kant), i.e., fideism, more or less weakened and diluted. The recognition of objective law in nature and the recognition that this law is reflected with approximate fidelity in the mind of man is materialism.

As regards Engels, he had, if I am not mistaken, no occasion to contrast his materialist view with other trends on the particular question of causality. He had no need to do so, since he had definitely dissociated himself from all the agnostics on the more fundamental question of the objective reality of the external world in general. But to anyone who has read his philosophical works at all attentively it must be clear that Engels does not admit even the shadow of a doubt as to the existence of objective law, causality, and necessity in nature. We shall confine ourselves to a few examples. In the first section of *Anti-Dühring* Engels says: "In order to understand these details [of the general picture of the world phenomena], we must detach them from their natural or historical connection and examine each one separately, its nature, special causes, effects, etc." That this natural connection, the connection between natural phenomena, exists objectively, is obvious. Engels particularly emphasizes the dialectical view of cause and effect: "And we find, in like manner, that cause and effect are conceptions which only hold good in their application to individual cases, but as soon as we consider the individual cases in their general connection with the universe as a whole, they run into each other, and they become confounded when we contemplate that universal action and reaction in which causes and effects are eternally changing places, so that what is effect here and now will be cause there and then, and vice versa." Hence, the human conception of cause and effect always somewhat simplifies the objective connection of the phenomena of nature, reflecting it only approximately, artificially isolating one or another aspect of a single world process. If we find that the laws of thought correspond with the laws of nature, says Engels, this becomes quite conceivable when we take into account that reason and consciousness are "products of the human brain and that man himself is a product of nature." Of course, "the products of the human brain, being in the last analysis also products of nature, do not contradict the rest of nature's interconnections but are in correspondence with them." There is no doubt that there exists a natural, objective interconnection between the phenomena of the world. Engels constantly speaks of the "laws of nature," of the "necessities of nature," without considering it necessary to explain the generally known propositions of materialism.

In *Ludwig Feuerbach* also we read that "the general laws of motion—both of the external world and of human thought—[are] two sets of laws which are identical in substance but differ in their expression in so far as the human mind can apply them consciously, while in nature and also up to now for the most part in human history, these laws assert themselves unconsciously in the form of external necessity in the midst of an endless series of seeming accidents." And Engels reproaches the old natural philosophy for having replaced "the real but as yet unknown interconnections" (of the phenomena of nature) by "ideal and imaginary ones." Engels's recognition of objective law, causality, and necessity in nature is absolutely clear, as is his emphasis on the relative character of our, i.e., man's approximate reflections of this law in various concepts.

Passing to Joseph Dietzgen, we must first note one of the innumerable distortions committed by our Machians. One of the authors of the *Studies "in" the Philosophy of Marxism*, Mr. Helfond, tells us: "The basic points of Dietzgen's world outlook may be summarized in the following propositions: . . . The causal dependence which we ascribe to things is in reality not contained in the things themselves." *This is sheer nonsense.* Mr. Helfond, whose own views represent a veritable hash of materialism and agnosticism, *has outrageously falsified* J. Dietzgen. Of course, we can find plenty of confusion, inexactnesses, and errors in Dietzgen, such as gladden the hearts of the Machians and oblige materialists to regard Dietzgen as a philosopher who is not entirely consistent. But to attribute to the materialist J. Dietzgen a direct denial of the materialist view of causality—only a Helfond, only the Russian Machians are capable of that.

"Objective scientific knowledge," says Dietzgen in his *The Nature of the Workings of the Human Mind*, "seeks for causes not by faith or speculation, but by experience and induction, not *a priori*, but *a posteriori*. Natural science looks for causes not outside or back of phenomena, but within or by means of them . . . Causes are the products of the faculty of thought. They are, however, not its pure products, but are produced by it in conjunction with sense material. This sense material gives the causes thus derived their objective existence. Just as we demand that a truth should be the truth of an objective phenomenon, so we demand that a cause should be real, that it should be the cause of some objective effect . . . The cause of the thing is its connection."

It is clear from this that Mr. Helfond has made a statement which is *directly contrary to fact*. The world outlook of materialism expounded by J. Dietzgen recognizes that "the causal dependence" *is contained* "in the things themselves." It was necessary for the Machian hash that Mr. Helfond should confuse the materialist line with the idealist line on the question of causality.

Let us now proceed to the latter line.

A clear statement of the starting point of Avenarius's philosophy on this question is to be found in his first work, *Philosophy as a Way of Thinking About the World According to the Principle of the Smallest Measure of Force*: "Just as we do not experience force as causing motion, so we do not experience the *necessity* for any motion . . . All we experience is that the one follows the other." This is the Humean standpoint in its purest form: sensation, experience tell us nothing of any necessity. A philosopher who asserts (on the principle of "the economy of thought") that only sensation exists could not have come to any other conclusion. "Since the idea of *causality*," we read further, "demands force and necessity or constraint as integral parts of the effect, so it falls together with the latter" (§ 82). "Necessity therefore expresses a particular degree of probability with which the effect is, or may be, expected" (§ 83).

This is outspoken subjectivism on the question of causality. And if one is at all consistent one cannot come to any other conclusion unless one recognizes objective reality as the source of our sensations.

Let us turn to Mach. In a special chapter, "Causality and Explanation," we read: "The Humean criticism (of the conception of causality) nevertheless retains its validity." Kant and Hume (Mach does not trouble to deal with other philosophers) solve the problem of causality differently. "We prefer" Hume's solution. "Apart from *logical* necessity [Mach's italics] no other necessity, for instance physical necessity, exists." This is exactly the view which was so vigorously combated by Feuerbach. It never even occurs to Mach to deny his kinship with Hume. Only the Russian Machians could go so far as to assert that Hume's agnosticism could be "combined" with Marx's and Engels's materialism. In Mach's *Mechanics*, we read: "In nature there is neither cause nor effect . . . I have repeatedly demonstrated that all forms of the law of causality spring from subjective motives and that there is no necessity for nature to correspond with them."

We must here note that our Russian Machians with amazing naïveté replace the question of the materialist or idealist trend of all arguments on the law of causality by the question of one or another formulation of this law. They believed the German empiriocritical professors that merely to say "functional correlation" was to make a discovery in "recent positivism" and to release one from the "fetishism" of expressions like "necessity," "law," and so forth. This of course is utterly absurd, and Wundt was fully justified in ridiculing such a *change of words* (in the article, quoted above, in *Philosophical Studies*), which in fact changes nothing. Mach himself speaks of "all forms" of the law of causality and in his *Knowledge and Error* makes the self-evident reservation that the concept function can express the "dependence of elements" more precisely only when the possibility is achieved of expressing the results of investigation in *measurable* quantities, which even in sciences like chemistry has only partly been achieved. Apparently, in the opinion of our Machians, who are so credulous as to professorial discoveries, Feuerbach (not to mention Engels) did not know that the concepts order, law, and so forth, can under certain conditions be expressed as a mathematically defined functional relation!

The really important epistemological question that divides the philosophical trends is not the degree of precision attained by our descriptions of causal connections, or whether these descriptions can be expressed in exact mathematical formulas, but whether the source of our knowledge of these connections is objective natural law or properties of our mind, its innate faculty of apprehending certain *a priori* truths, and so forth. This is what so irrevocably divides the materialists Feuerbach, Marx, and Engels from the agnostics (Humeans) Avenarius and Mach.

In certain parts of his works, Mach, whom it would be a sin to accuse of consistency, frequently "forgets" his agreement with Hume and his own subjectivist theory of causality and argues "simply" as a natural scientist, i.e., from the instinctive materialist standpoint. For instance, in his *Mechanics*, we read of "the uniformity which nature teaches us to find in its phenomena." But if we *do find* uniformity in the phenomena of nature, does this mean that uniformity exists objectively outside our mind? No. On the question of the uniformity of nature Mach also delivers himself thus: "The power that prompts us to complete in thought facts only partially observed is the power of association. It is greatly strengthened by repetition. It then appears to us to be a power which is independent of our will and of individual facts, a power which directs thoughts *and* [Mach's italics] facts, which keeps both in mutual correspondence as a *law* governing both. That we consider ourselves capable of making predictions with the help of such a law only [!] proves that there is sufficient uniformity in our environment, but it does not prove the *necessity* of the success of our predictions" (*Thermodynamics*).

It follows that we may and ought to look for a necessity *apart from* the uniformity of our environment, i.e.., of nature! Where to look for it is the secret of idealist philosophy which is afraid to recognize man's perceptive faculty as a simple reflection of nature. In his last work, *Knowledge and Error*, Mach even defines a law of nature as a "limitation of expectation"! Solipsism claims its own.

Let us examine the position of other writers of the same philosophical trend. The Englishman, Karl Pearson, expresses himself with characteristic precision (*The Grammar of Science*): "The laws of science are products of the human mind rather than factors of the external world . . . Those, whether poets or materialists, who do homage to nature, as the sovereign of man, too often forget that the order and complexity they admire are at least as much a product of man's perceptive and reasoning faculties as are their own memories and thoughts . . . The comprehensive character of natural law is due to the ingenuity of the human mind." "*Man is the maker of natural law*," it is stated in Chapter III, § 4. "There is more meaning in the statement that man gives laws to nature than in its converse that nature gives laws to man," although the worthy professor is regretfully obliged to admit, the latter (materialist) view is "unfortunately far too common today." In the fourth chapter, which is devoted to the question of causality, Pearson formulates the following thesis(§ 11): "*The necessity lies in the world of conceptions*" *and not in the world of perceptions*. It should be noted that for Pearson perceptions or sense impressions are *the* reality existing outside us. "In the uniformity with which sequences of perception are repeated (the routine of perceptions) there is also no inherent necessity, but it is a necessary condition for the existence of thinking beings that there should be a routine in the perceptions. The necessity thus lies in the nature of the thinking being and not in the perceptions themselves; thus it is conceivably a product of the perceptive faculty.

Our Machian, with whom Mach himself frequently expresses complete solidarity, thus arrives safely and soundly at pure Kantian idealism: it is man who dictates laws to nature and not nature that dictates laws to man! The important thing is not the repetition of Kant's doctrine of apriorism—which does not define the idealist line in philosophy as such, but only a particular formulation of this line—but the fact that reason, mind, consciousness are here primary, and nature secondary. It is not reason that is a part of nature, one of its highest products, the reflection of its processes, but nature that is a part of reason, which thereby is stretched from the ordinary, simple human reason known to us all to a "stupendous," as Dietzgen puts it, mysterious, divine reason. The Kantian-Machian formula, that "man gives laws to nature," is a fideist formula. If our Machians stare wide-eyed on reading Engels's statement that the fundamental characteristic of materialism is the acceptance of nature and not spirit as primary, it only shows how incapable they are of distinguishing the really important philosophical trends from the mock erudition and sage jargon of the professors.

J. Petzoldt, who in his two-volume work analyzed and developed Avenarius, may serve as an excellent example of reactionary Machian scholasticism. "Even to this day," says he, "one hundred and fifty years after Hume, substantiality and causality paralyze the daring of the thinker" (*Introduction to the Philosophy of Pure Experience*). It goes without saying that those who are most "daring" are the solipsists who discovered sensation without organic matter, thought without brain, nature without objective law! "And the last formulation of causality, which we have not yet mentioned, necessity, or *necessity in nature*, contains something vague and mystical"—(the idea of "fetishism," "anthropomorphism," etc.). Oh, the poor mystics, Feuerbach, Marx, and Engels! They have been talking all the time of necessity in nature, and have even been calling those who hold the Humean position theoretical reactionaries! Petzoldt rises above all "anthropomorphism." He has discovered the great "*law of unique determination*," which eliminates every obscurity, every trace of "fetishism," etc., etc., etc. For example, the parallelogram of forces. This cannot be "proven"; it must be accepted as a "fact of experience." It cannot be conceded that a body under like impulses will move in different ways. "We cannot concede nature such indefiniteness and arbitrariness; we must demand from it definiteness and law." Well, well! We demand of nature obedience to law. The bourgeoisie demands reaction of its professors. "Our thought demands definiteness from nature, and nature always conforms to this demand; we shall even see that in a certain sense it is compelled to conform to it." Why, having received an impulse in the direction of the line AB, does a body move towards C and not towards D or F, etc.?

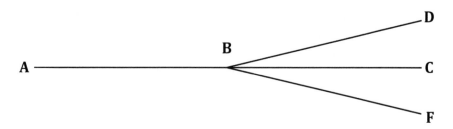

"Why does nature not choose any of the countless other directions?" Because that would be "multiple determination," and the great empiriocritical discovery of Joseph Petzoldt demands *unique determination*.

The "empiriocriticists" fill scores of pages with such unutterable trash!

"... We have remarked more than once that our thesis does not derive its force from a sum of separate experiences, but that, on the contrary, we demand that nature should recognize its validity. Indeed, even before it becomes a law it has already become for us a principle with which we approach reality, a postulate. It is valid, so to speak, *a priori*, independently of all separate experiences. It would, indeed, be unbefitting for a philosophy of pure experience to preach *a priori* truths and thus relapse into the most sterile metaphysics. Its apriorism can only be a logical one, never a psychological, or metaphysical one." Of course, if we call apriorism logical, then the reactionary nature of the idea disappears and it becomes elevated to the level of "recent positivism"!

There can be no unique determination of psychical phenomena, Petzoldt further teaches us; the role of imagination, the significance of great inventions, etc., here create exceptions, while the law of nature, or the law of spirit, tolerates "no exceptions." We have before us a pure metaphysician, who has not the slightest inkling of the relativity of the difference between the contingent and the necessary.

I may, perhaps, be reminded—continues Petzoldt—of the motivation of historical events or of the development of character in poetry. "If we examine the matter carefully we shall find that there is no such unique determination. There is not a single historical event or a single drama in which we could not imagine the participants acting differently under similar psychical conditions ... Unique determination is not only absent in the realm of the psychical, but we are also entitled to *demand* its absence from reality [Petzoldt's italics]. Our doctrine is thus elevated to the rank of a *postulate*, i.e., to the rank of a fact, which we regard as a necessary condition of a much earlier experience, as its *logical a priori*" (Petzoldt's italics).

And Petzoldt continues to operate with this "logical *a priori*" in both volumes of his *Introduction*, and in the booklet issued in 1906, *The World Problem from the Positivist Standpoint*. Here is a second instance of a noted empiriocriticist who has imperceptibly slipped into Kantianism and who serves up the most reactionary doctrines with a somewhat different sauce. And this is not fortuitous, for at the very foundations of Mach's and Avenarius's teachings on causality there lies an idealist falsehood, which no high-flown talk of "positivism" can cover up. The distinction between the Humean and the Kantian theories of causality is only a secondary difference of opinion between agnostics who are basically at one, viz., in their denial of objective law in nature, and who thus inevitably condemn themselves to idealist conclusions of one kind or another. A rather more "scrupulous" empiriocriticist than J. Petzoldt, Rudolf Willy, who is ashamed of his kinship with the immanentists, rejects, for example, Petzoldt's whole theory of "unique determination" as leading to nothing but "logical formalism." But does Willy improve his position by disavowing Petzoldt? Not in the least, for he disavows Kantian agnosticism solely for the sake of Humean agnosticism. "We have known from the time of Hume," he writes, "that 'necessity' is a purely logical (not a 'transcendental') characteristic, or, as I would rather say and have already said, a purely verbal characteristic" (R. Willy, *Against School Knowledge*).

The agnostic calls our materialist view of necessity "transcendental," for from the standpoint of Kantian and Humean "school wisdom," which Willy does not reject but only furbishes up, any recognition of objective reality given us in experience is an illicit "transcendence."

Among the French writers of the philosophical trend we are analyzing, we find Henri Poincaré constantly straying into this same path of agnosticism. Henri Poincaré is an eminent physicist but a poor philosopher, whose errors Yushkevich, of course, declared to be the last word of recent positivism, so "recent," indeed, that it even required a new "*ism*," viz., empiriosymbolism. For Poincaré (with whose views as a whole we shall deal in the chapter on the new physics), the laws of nature are symbols, conventions, which man creates for the sake of "*convenience*." "The only true objective reality is the internal harmony of the world." By "objective," Poincaré means that which is generally   regarded as valid, that which is accepted by the majority of men, or by all; that is to say, in a purely subjectivist manner he destroys objective truth, as do all the Machians. And as regards "harmony," he categorically declares in answer to the question whether it exists *outside of us*—"undoubtedly, no." It is perfectly obvious that the new terms do not in the least change the ancient philosophical position of agnosticism, for the essence of Poincaré's "original" theory amounts to a denial (although he is far from consistent) of objective reality and of objective law in nature. It is, therefore, perfectly natural that in contradistinction to the Russian Machians, who accept new formulations of old errors as the latest discoveries, the German Kantians greeted such views as a conversion to their own views, i.e., to agnosticism, on a fundamental question of philosophy. "The French mathematician Henri

Poincaré," we read in the work of the Kantian, Philipp Frank, "holds the point of view that many of the most general laws of theoretical natural science (e.g., the law of inertia, the law of the conservation of energy, etc.), of which it is so often difficult to say whether they are of empirical or of *a priori* origin, are, in fact, neither one nor the other, but are purely conventional propositions depending upon human discretion . . ." "Thus [exults the Kantian] the latest *Naturphilosophie* unexpectedly renews the fundamental idea of critical idealism, namely, that experience merely fills in a framework which man brings with him from nature . . ."

We quote this example in order to give the reader a clear idea of the degree of naïveté of our Yushkeviches, who take a "theory of symbolism" for something genuinely new, whereas philosophers in the least versed in their subject say plainly and explicitly: he has become converted to the standpoint of critical idealism! For the essence of this point of view does not necessarily lie in the repetition of Kant's formulations, but in the recognition of the fundamental idea *common* to both Hume and Kant, viz., the denial of objective law in nature and the deduction of particular "conditions of experience," particular principles, postulates, and propositions *from the subject*, from human consciousness, and not from nature. Engels was right when he said that it is not important to which of the numerous schools of materialism or idealism a particular philosopher belongs, but rather whether he takes nature, the external world, matter in motion, or spirit, reason, consciousness, etc., as primary.

Another characterization of Machism on this question, in contrast to the other philosophical lines, is given by the expert Kantian, E. Lucka. On the question of causality "Mach entirely agrees with Hume." "P. Volkmann derives the necessity of thought from the necessity of the processes of nature—a standpoint that, in contradistinction to Mach and in agreement with Kant, recognizes the fact of necessity; but contrary to Kant, it seeks the source of necessity not in thought, but in the processes of nature."

Volkmann is a physicist who writes fairly extensively on epistemological questions, and who tends, as do the vast majority of scientists, to materialism, albeit an inconsistent, timid, and incoherent materialism. The recognition of necessity in nature and the derivation from it of necessity in thought is materialism. The derivation of necessity, causality, law, etc., from thought is idealism. The only inaccuracy in the passage quoted is that a total denial of all necessity is attributed to Mach. We have already seen that this is not true either of Mach or of the empiriocritical trend generally, which, having definitely departed from materialism, is inevitably sliding into idealism.

It remains for us to say a few words about the Russian Machians in particular. They would like to be Marxists; they have all "read" Engels's decisive demarcation of materialism from the Humean trend; they could not have failed to learn both from Mach himself and from everybody in the least acquainted with his philosophy that Mach and Avenarius follow the line of Hume. Yet they are all careful *not to say a single word* about Humism and materialism on the question of causality! Their confusion is utter. Let us give a few examples. Mr. P. Yushkevich preaches the "new" empiriosymbolism. The "sensations of blue, hard, etc.—these supposed data of pure experience" and "the creations supposedly of pure reason, such as a chimera or a chess game"—all these are "empiriosymbols" (*Studies, etc.*). "Knowledge is empiriosymbolic, and as it develops leads to empirio-symbols of a greatest degree of symbolization . . . The so-called laws of nature . . . are these empiriosymbols . . ." (ibid.). "The so-called true reality, being in itself, is that infinite [a terribly learned fellow, this Mr. Yushkevich!] ultimate system of symbols to which all our knowledge is striving." "The stream of experience . . . which lies at the foundation of our knowledge is . . . irrational . . . illogical." Energy "is just as little a thing, a substance, as time, space, mass and the other fundamental concepts of science: energy is a constancy, an empiriosymbol, like other empiriosymbols that for a time satisfy the fundamental human need of introducing reason, Logos, into the irrational stream of experience."

Clad like a harlequin in a garish motley of shreds of the "latest" terminology, there stands before us a subjective idealist, for whom the external world, nature, and its laws are all symbols of our knowledge. The stream of experience is devoid of reason, order, and law: our knowledge brings reason into it. The celestial bodies are symbols of human knowledge, and so is the earth. If science teaches us that the earth existed long before it was possible for man and organic matter to have appeared, we, you see, have changed all that! The order of the motion of the planets is brought about *by us*, it is a product of our knowledge. And sensing that human reason is being inflated by such a philosophy into the author and founder of nature, Mr. Yushkevich puts alongside of reason the word *Logos*, that is, reason in the abstract, not reason, but Reason, not a function of the human brain, but something existing prior to any brain, something divine.

The last word of "recent positivism" is that old formula of fideism which Feuerbach had already exposed.

Let us take A. Bogdanov. In 1899, when he was still a semi-materialist and had only just begun to go astray under the influence of a very great chemist and very muddled philosopher, Wilhelm Ostwald, he wrote: "The general causal connection of phenomena is the last and best child of human knowledge; it is the universal law, the highest of those laws which, to express it in the words of a philosopher, human reason dictates to nature" (*Fundamental Elements, etc.*).

Allah alone knows from what source Bogdanov took this reference. But the fact is that "the words of a philosopher" trustingly repeated by the "Marxist"—are the words of Kant. An unpleasant event! And all the more unpleasant in that it cannot even be explained by the "mere" influence of Ostwald.

In 1904, having already managed to discard both natural-historical materialism and Ostwald, Bogdanov wrote: ". . . Modern positivism regards the law of causality only as a means of cognitively connecting phenomena into a continuous series, only as a form of coordinating experience" (*From the Psychology of Society*). Bogdanov either did not know, or would not admit, that this modern positivism is agnosticism and that it denies the objective necessity of nature, which existed prior to, and outside of, "knowledge" and man. He accepted on faith what the German professors called "modern positivism." Finally, in 1905, having passed through all the previous stages and the stage of empiriocriticism, and being already in the stage of "empiriomonism," Bogdanov wrote: "Laws do not belong to the sphere of experience . . . they are not given in it, but are created by thought as a means of organizing experience, of harmoniously coordinating it into a symmetrical whole" (*Empiriomonism*). "Laws are abstractions of knowledge; and physical laws possess physical properties just as little as psychological laws possess psychical properties."

And so, the law that winter succeeds autumn and the spring winter is not given us in experience but is created by thought as a means of organizing, harmonizing, coordinating . . . what with what, Comrade Bogdanov?

"Empiriomonism is possible only because knowledge actively harmonizes experience, eliminating its infinite contradictions, creating for it universal organizing forms, replacing the primeval chaotic world of elements by a derivative, ordered world of relations." That is not true. The idea that knowledge can "create" universal forms, replace the primeval chaos by order, etc., is the idea of idealist philosophy. The world is matter moving in conformity to law, and our knowledge, being the highest product of nature, is in a position only to *reflect* this conformity to law.

In brief, our Machians, blindly believing the "recent" reactionary professors, repeat the mistakes of Kantian and Humean agnosticism on the question of causality and fail to notice either that these doctrines are in absolute contradiction to Marxism, i.e., materialism, or that they themselves are rolling down an inclined plane towards idealism.

. . .

Conclusion

There are four standpoints from which a Marxist must proceed to form a judgment of empiriocriticism.

First and foremost, the theoretical foundations of this philosophy must be compared with those of dialectical materialism. Such a comparison, to which the first three chapters were devoted, reveals, *along the whole line* of epistemological problems, the *thoroughly reactionary* character of empiriocriticism, which uses new artifices, terms, and subtleties to disguise the old errors of *idealism and agnosticism*. Only utter ignorance of the nature of philosophical materialism generally and of the nature of Marx's and Engels's dialectical method can lead one to speak of "combining" empiriocriticism and Marxism.

Secondly, the place of empiriocriticism, as one very small school of specialists in philosophy, in relation to the other modern schools of philosophy must be determined. Both Mach and Avenarius started with Kant and, leaving him, proceeded not towards materialism, but in the opposite direction, towards Hume and Berkeley. Imagining that he was "purifying experience" generally, Avenarius was in fact only purifying agnosticism of Kantianism. The whole school of Mach and Avenarius is moving more and more definitely towards idealism, hand in hand with one of the most reactionary of the idealist schools, viz., the so-called immanentists.

Thirdly, the indubitable connection between Machism and one school in one branch of modern science must be borne in mind. The vast majority of scientists, both generally and in this special branch of science in question, viz., physics, are invariably on the side of materialism. A minority of new physicists, however, influenced by the breakdown of old theories brought about by the great discoveries of recent years, influenced by the crisis in the new physics, which has very clearly revealed the relativity of our knowledge, have, owing to their ignorance of dialectics, slipped into idealism by way of relativism. The physical idealism in vogue today is as reactionary and transitory an infatuation as was the fashionable physiological idealism of the recent past.

Fourthly, behind the epistemological scholasticism of empiriocriticism one must not fail to see the struggle of parties in philosophy, a struggle which in the last analysis reflects the tendencies and ideology of the antagonistic classes in modern society. Recent philosophy is as partisan as was philosophy two thousand years ago. The contending parties are essentially, although it is concealed by a pseudo-erudite quackery of new terms or by a feeble-minded non-partisanship, materialism and idealism. The latter is merely a subtle, refined form of fideism, which stands fully armed, commands vast organizations, and steadily continues to exercise influence on the masses, turning the slightest vacillation in philosophical thought to its own advantage. The objective, class role of empiriocriticism consists entirely in rendering faithful service to the fideists in their struggle against materialism in general and historical materialism in particular.

IV

THE CLASS STRUGGLE, PARTY BUILDING, AND THE SOCIALIST TRANSITION

REFORM OR REVOLUTION

Rosa Luxemburg
1900

In this short but sharp excerpt from Rosa Luxemburg's classic work on reformism, she excoriates the revisionism of Eduard Bernstein—in the sense that he attempts to "revise" Marxism to make it compatible with the continuation of capitalism—and connects his theoretical and practical errors with his rejection of the dialectic.

Chapter IX | Collapse

... Bernstein's conception of socialism collapses entirely. The proud and admirable symmetric construction of socialist thought becomes for him a pile of rubbish in which the debris of all systems, the pieces of thought of various great and small minds, find a common resting place. Marx and Proudhon, Leon von Buch and Franz Oppenheimer, Friedrich Albert Lange and Kant, Herr Prokopovich and R. Ritter von Neupauer, Herkner, and Schulze-Gävernitz, Lassalle and Professor Julius Wolff: all contribute something to Bernstein's system. From each he takes a little. There is nothing astonishing about that. For when he abandoned scientific socialism he lost the axis of intellectual crystallization around which isolated facts group themselves in the organic whole of a coherent conception of the world.

His doctrine, composed of bits of all possible systems, seems upon first consideration to be completely free from prejudices. For Bernstein does not like talk of "party science," or to be more exact, of class science, any more than he likes to talk of class liberalism or class morality. He thinks he succeeds in expressing human, general, abstract science, abstract liberalism, abstract morality. But since the society of reality is made up of classes which have diametrically opposed interests, aspirations, and conceptions, a general human science in social questions, an abstract liberalism, an abstract morality, are at present illusions, pure utopia. The science, the democracy, the morality, considered by Bernstein as general, human, are merely the dominant science, dominant democracy, and dominant morality, that is, bourgeois science, bourgeois democracy, bourgeois morality.

When Bernstein rejects the economic doctrine of Marx in order to swear by the teachings of Bretano, Böhm-Bawerk, Jevons, Say, and Julius Wolff, he exchanges the scientific base of the emancipation of the working class for the apologetics of the bourgeoisie. When he speaks of the generally human character of liberalism and transforms socialism into a variety of liberalism, he deprives the socialist movement (generally) of its class character and consequently of its historic content, consequently of all content; and conversely, recognizes the class representing liberalism in history, the bourgeoisie, as the champion of the general interests of humanity.

And when he wars against "raising of the material factors to the rank of an all-powerful force of development," when he protests against the so-called "contempt for the ideal" that is supposed to rule the Social Democracy, when he presumes to talk for idealism, for morals, pronouncing himself at the same time against the only source of the moral rebirth of the proletariat—a revolutionary class struggle—he does no more than the following: preach to the working class the quintessence of the morality of the bourgeoisie, that is, reconciliation with the existing social order and the transfer of the hopes of the proletariat to the limbo of ethical simulacra.

When he directs his keenest arrows against our dialectic system, he is really attacking the specific mode of thought employed by the conscious proletariat in its struggle for liberation. It is an attempt to break the sword that has helped the proletariat to pierce the darkness of its future. It is an attempt to shatter the intellectual arm with the aid of which the proletariat, though materially under the yoke of the bourgeoisie, is yet enabled to triumph over the bourgeoisie. For it is our dialectical system that shows to the working class the transitory nature of this yoke, proving to workers the inevitability of their victory, and is already real-izing a revolution in the domain of thought. Saying goodbye to our system of dialectics and resorting instead to the intellectual see-saw of the well known "on the one hand, on the other hand," "yes, but," "although, how-ever," "more, less," etc., he quite logically lapses into a mode of thought that belongs historically to the bourgeoisie in decline, being the faithful intellectual reflection of the social existence and political activity of the bourgeoisie at that stage. The political "on the one hand, on the other hand," "yes, but" of the bourgeoisie today resembles, in a marked degree, Bernstein's manner of thinking, which is the sharpest and surest proof of the bourgeois nature of his conception of the world.

But, as it is used by Bernstein, the word "bourgeois" itself is not a class expression but a general social notion. Logical to the end, he has exchanged, together with his science, politics, morals, and mode of think-ing, the historic language of the proletariat for that of the bourgeoisie. When he uses, without distinction, the term "citizen" in reference to the bourgeois as well as to the proletarian, intending, thereby, to refer to man in general, he identifies man in general with the bourgeois and human society with bourgeois society.

HISTORY OF THE RUSSIAN REVOLUTION TO BREST-LITOVSK

Leon Trotsky
1918

Trotsky's "shorter history" of the Russian Revolution is an excellent introduction to his masterpiece, The History of the Russian Revolution, *both of which are "must reads" for anyone wishing to understand the dialectical process of revolutions. In this brief excerpt, part of a speech to the Central Executive Committee which Trotsky delivered in February 1918 in his capacity as People's Commissar for Foreign Affairs, he touches on the contradictions and tensions of the class struggle, as the Russian Bolsheviks faced down German imperialism in a high-stakes game of "chicken," as each side waited for the coming of their salvation or ruin—the German Revolution.*

Speech of the People's Commissar for Foreign Affairs

. . . One may complain that the proletariat of other countries, especially of the Central Empires, is passing to an open revolutionary struggle too slowly. Yes, the *tempo* of its advance is much too slow. But in Austria-Hungary we saw a movement which assumed the proportions of a national event and which was a direct and immediate result of the Brest-Litovsk negotiations.

Before we departed from here we discussed the matter together, and we said that we had no reason to believe that that wave would sweep away the Austro-Hungarian militarism. Had we been convinced to the contrary, we should have certainly given the pledge so eagerly demanded from us by certain persons, namely, that we should never sign a separate treaty with Germany. I said at the time that it was impossible for us to make such a pledge, as it would have been tantamount to pledging ourselves to defeat German imperialism. We held the secret of no such victory in our hands, and insofar as we could not pledge ourselves to change the balance and correlation of the world's powers in a very short period of time, we openly and honestly declared that the revolutionary government might, under certain circumstances, be compelled to accept an annexationist peace. For, not the acceptance of a peace forced upon us by the course of events, but an attempt to hide its predatory character from our own people would have been the beginning of the end of the revolutionary government.

At the same time, we pointed out that we were departing for Brest in order to continue the negotiations in circumstances which were apparently becoming more favorable to us and less advantageous to our adversaries. We were watching the events in Austria-Hungary, and various circumstances made us think that, as hinted at by Socialist spokesmen in the Reichstag, Germany was on the eve of similar events. Such were our hopes, and then in the course of the first days of our new stay at Brest the wireless brought us via Vilna the first news that a tremendous strike movement had broken out in Berlin, which, like the movement in Austria-Hungary, was the direct result of the Brest-Litovsk negotiations. But, as it often happens, in consequence of the "dialectical," double-edged, character of the class struggle, it was just this powerful swing of the proletarian movement, such as Germany had never seen before, that aroused the propertied classes and caused them to close their ranks and to take up a more irreconcilable attitude.

The German ruling classes are only too well-imbued with the instinct of self-preservation, and they understood that any, even partial concession, under such circumstances, when they were being pressed by the masses of their own people, would have been tantamount to a capitulation before the idea of revolution. That is why, after the first period of conferences, when Kühlmann had been deliberately delaying the negotiations by either postponing the sittings or wasting them on minor questions of form, he, as soon as the strike had been suppressed, and his masters, he felt, were for the time being out of danger, reverted to his old accents of complete self-confidence, and redoubled his aggressiveness.

IN DEFENSE OF MARXISM (EXCERPTS)

Leon Trotsky
1939–40

In Defense of Marxism, *a collection of articles and letters written by Trotsky during a bitter factional struggle in the US Socialist Workers Party, is a true treasure for revolutionary socialists. Covering a wide range of topics—from the class nature of the USSR to the healthy functioning of internal party democracy—it is an object lesson in the application of the Marxist method to the problems of building a revolutionary leadership. A petty-bourgeois opposition had developed in the US section of the Fourth International, and Trotsky participated energetically in the debate. Trotsky traced the consistent errors of the anti-Marxist intellectuals to the fact that some of them rejected dialectical materialism outright, whereas others took an agnostic, "take it or leave it" approach. In the excerpts compiled below, one can see the great efforts Trotsky made to politicize the debate and to try to win his opponents on a principled basis. For example, in his classic "the ABC of Materialist Dialectics," Trotsky summarizes the key ideas of Marxist philosophy with easy to understand examples from everyday life. In the end, as is so often the case with petty-bourgeois individualists who recoil at voluntary collective discipline, the opposition split away. It should be noted that, to minimize the chance of having his correspondence intercepted, Trotsky often signed with a pseudonym.*

The USSR in War (September 1939)

Proletariat and its leadership

We shall very soon devote a separate article to the question of the relation between the class and its leadership. We shall confine ourselves here to the most indispensable. Only vulgar "Marxists" who take it that politics is a mere and direct "reflection" of economics, are capable of thinking that leadership reflects the class directly and simply. In reality, leadership, having risen above the oppressed class, inevitably succumbs to the pressure of the ruling class. The leadership of the American trade unions, for instance, "reflects" not so much the proletariat, as the bourgeoisie.

The selection and education of a truly revolutionary leadership, capable of withstanding the pressure of the bourgeoisie, is an extraordinarily difficult task. The dialectics of the historic process expressed itself most brilliantly in the fact that the proletariat of the most backward country, Russia, under certain historic conditions, has put forward the most far-sighted and courageous leadership. On the contrary, the proletariat in the country of the oldest capitalist culture, Great Britain, has even today the most dull-witted and servile leadership.

The crisis of capitalist society which assumed an open character in July 1914, from the very first day of the war produced a sharp crisis in the proletarian leadership. During the 25 years that have elapsed since that time, the proletariat of the advanced capitalist countries has not yet created a leadership that could rise to the level of the tasks of our epoch. The experience of Russia testifies, however, that such a leadership can be created. (This does not mean, of course, that it will be immune to degeneration.) The question consequently stands as follows: Will objective historical necessity in the long run cut a path for itself in the consciousness of the vanguard of the working class; that is, in the process of this war and those profound shocks which it must engender will a genuine revolutionary leadership be formed capable of leading the proletariat to the conquest of power?

The Fourth International has replied in the affirmative to this question, not only through the text of its program, but also through the very fact of its existence. All the various types of disillusioned and frightened representatives of pseudo-Marxism proceed *on the contrary* from the assumption that the bankruptcy of the leadership only "reflects" the incapacity of the proletariat to fulfill its revolutionary mission. Not all our opponents express this thought clearly, but all of them—ultralefts, centrists, anarchists, not to mention Stalinists and social democrats—shift the responsibility for the defeats from themselves to the shoulders of the proletariat. None of them indicate under precisely what conditions the proletariat will be capable of accomplishing the socialist overturn.

If we grant as true that the cause of the defeats is rooted in the social qualities of the proletariat itself then the position of modern society will have to be acknowledged as hopeless. Under conditions of decaying capitalism the proletariat grows neither numerically nor culturally. There are no grounds, therefore, for expecting that it will sometime rise to the level of the revolutionary tasks. Altogether differently does the case present itself to him who has clarified in his mind the profound antagonism between the organic, deep going, insurmountable urge of the toiling masses to tear themselves free from the bloody capitalist chaos, and the conservative, patriotic, utterly bourgeois character of the outlived labor leadership. We must choose one of these two irreconcilable conceptions.

* * *

Again and Once More Again on the Nature of the USSR (October 1939)

Psychoanalysis and Marxism

Certain comrades, or former comrades, such as Bruno R., having forgotten the past discussions and decisions of the Fourth International, attempt to explain my personal estimate of the Soviet state psychoanalytically. "Since Trotsky participated in the Russian Revolution, it is difficult for him to lay aside the idea of the workers' state inasmuch as he would have to renounce his whole life's cause," etc. I think that old Freud, who was very perspicacious, would have cuffed the ears of psychoanalysts of this ilk a little. Naturally I would never risk taking such action myself. Nevertheless I dare assure my critics that subjectivity and sentimentality are not on my side but on theirs.

Moscow's conduct, which has passed all bounds of abjectness and cynicism, calls forth an easy revolt within every proletarian revolutionary. Revolt engenders need for rejection. When the forces for immediate action are absent, impatient revolutionaries are inclined to resort to artificial methods. Thus arises, for example, the tactic of individual terror. More frequently resort is taken to strong expressions, to insults, and to imprecation. In the case which concerns us, certain comrades are manifestly inclined to seek compensation through "terminological" terror. However, even from this point of view the mere fact of qualifying the bureaucracy as a class is worthless. If the Bonapartist riff-raff is a class this means that it is not an abortion but a viable child of history. If its marauding parasitism is "exploitation" in the scientific sense of the term, this means that the bureaucracy possesses a historical future as the ruling class indispensable to the given system of economy. Here we have the end to which impatient revolt leads when it cuts itself loose from Marxist discipline!

When an emotional mechanic considers an automobile in which, let us say, gangsters have escaped from police pursuit over a bad road, and finds the frame bent, the wheels out of line, and the motor partially damaged, he might quite justifiably say: "It is not an automobile—devil knows what it is!" Such an estimate would lack any technical and scientific value, but it would express the legitimate reaction of the mechanic at the work of the gangsters. Let us suppose, however, that this same mechanic must recondition the object which he named "devil-knows-what-it-is." In this case he will start with the recognition that it is a damaged automobile before him. He will determine which parts are still good and which are beyond repair in order to decide how to begin work. The class-conscious worker will have a similar attitude toward the USSR. He has full right to say that the gangsters of the bureaucracy have transformed the workers' state into "devil-knows-what-it-is." But when he passes from this explosive reaction to the solution of the political problem, he is forced to recognize that it is a damaged workers' state before him, in which the motor of economy is damaged, but which still continues to run and which can be completely reconditioned with the replacement of some parts. Of course this is only an analogy. Nevertheless it is worth reflecting over.

* * *

A Petty-Bourgeois Opposition in the Socialist Workers Party (December 1939)

It is necessary to call things by their right names. Now that the positions of both factions in the struggle have become determined with complete clearness, it must be said that the minority of the National Committee is leading a typical petty-bourgeois tendency. Like any petty-bourgeois group inside the socialist movement, the present opposition is character-ized by the following features: a disdainful attitude toward theory and an inclination toward eclecticism; disrespect for the tradition of their own organization; anxiety for personal "independence" at the expense of anxiety for objective truth; nervousness instead of consistency; readiness to jump from one position to another; lack of understanding of revolu-tionary centralism and hostility toward it; and finally, inclination to sub-stitute clique ties and personal relationships for party discipline. Not all the members of the opposition, of course, manifest these features with identical strength. Nevertheless, as always in a variegated bloc the tinge is given by those who are most distant from Marxism and proletarian policy. A prolonged and serious struggle is obviously before us. I make no at-tempt to exhaust the problem in this article, but I will endeavor to outline its general features.

Theoretical skepticism and eclecticism

In the January 1939 issue of the *New International* a long article was pub-lished by comrades Burnham and Shachtman, "Intellectuals in Retreat." The article, while containing many correct ideas and apt political charac-terizations, was marred by a fundamental defect if not flaw. While polem-icizing against opponents who consider themselves—without sufficient reason—above all as proponents of "theory," the article deliberately did not elevate the problem to a theoretical height. It was absolutely neces-sary to explain why the American "radical" intellectuals accept Marxism without the dialectic (a clock without a spring). The secret is simple. In no other country has there been such rejection of the class struggle as in the land of "unlimited opportunity." The denial of social contradictions as the moving force of development led to the denial of the dialectic as the logic of contradictions in the domain of theoretical thought. Just as in the sphere of politics it was thought possible everybody could be convinced of the correctness of a "just" program by means of clever syllogisms and society could be reconstructed through "rational" measures, so in the sphere of theory it was accepted as proved that Aristotelian logic, low-ered to the level of "common sense," was sufficient for the solution of all questions.

Pragmatism, a mixture of rationalism and empiricism, became the national philosophy of the United States. The theoretical methodology of Max Eastman is not fundamentally different from the methodology of Henry Ford—both regard living society from the point of view of an "engineer" (Eastman—platonically). Historically, the present disdainful attitude toward the dialectic is explained simply by the fact that the grandfathers and great-grandmothers of Max Eastman and others did not need the dialectic in order to conquer territory and enrich themselves. But times have changed and the philosophy of pragmatism has entered a period of bankruptcy just as has American capitalism.

The authors of the article did not show, could not and did not care to show, this internal connection between philosophy and the material development of society, and they frankly explained why.

"The two authors of the present article," they wrote of themselves, "differ thoroughly on their estimate of the general theory of dialectical materialism, one of them accepting it and the other rejecting it . . . There is nothing anomalous in such a situation. Though theory is doubtless always in one way or another related to practice, the relation is not invariably direct or immediate; and as we have before had occasion to remark, human beings often act inconsistently. From the point of view of each of the authors there is in the other a certain such inconsistency between 'philosophical theory' and political practice, which might on some occasion lead to decisive concrete political disagreement. But it does not now, nor has anyone yet demonstrated that agreement or disagreement on the more abstract doctrines of dialectical materialism necessarily affects today's and tomorrow's concrete political issues—and political parties, programs, and struggles are based on such concrete issues. We all may hope that as we go along or when there is more leisure, agreement may also be reached on the more abstract questions. Meanwhile there is fascism and war and unemployment."

What is the meaning of this thoroughly astonishing reasoning? Inasmuch as *some* people through a bad method *sometimes* reach correct conclusions, and inasmuch as some people through a correct method *not infrequently* reach incorrect conclusions, therefore . . . the method is not of great importance. We shall meditate upon methods sometime when we have more leisure, but now we have other things to do. Imagine how a worker would react upon complaining to his foreman that his tools were bad and receiving the reply: With bad tools it is possible to turn out a good job, and with good tools many people only waste material. I am afraid that such a worker, particularly if he is on piecework, would re-spond to the foreman with an unacademic phrase. A worker is faced with refractory materials which show resistance and which because of that compel him to appreciate fine tools, whereas a petty-bourgeois intellec-tual—alas!—utilizes as his "tools" fugitive observations and superficial generalizations—until major events club him on the head.

To demand that every party member occupy himself with the phi-losophy of dialectics naturally would be lifeless pedantry. But a worker who has gone through the school of the class struggle gains from his own experience an inclination toward dialectical thinking. Even if unaware of this term, he readily accepts the method itself and its conclusions. With a petty bourgeois it is worse. There are of course petty-bourgeois elements organically linked with the workers, who go over to the proletarian point of view without an internal revolution. But these constitute an insignifi-cant minority. The matter is quite different with the academically trained petty bourgeoisie. Their theoretical prejudices have already been given finished form at the school bench. Inasmuch as they succeeded in gain-ing a great deal of knowledge both useful and useless without the aid of the dialectic, they believe that they can continue excellently through life without it. In reality they dispense with the dialectic only to the ex-tent they fail to check, to polish, and to sharpen theoretically their tools of thought, and to the extent that they fail to break practically from the narrow circle of their daily relationships. When thrown against great events they are easily lost and relapse again into petty-bourgeois ways of thinking.

Appealing to "inconsistency" as justification for an unprincipled theoretical bloc, signifies giving oneself bad credentials as a Marxist. In-consistency is not accidental, and in politics it does not appear solely as an individual symptom. Inconsistency usually serves a social function. There are social groupings which cannot be consistent. Petty-bourgeois elements who have not rid themselves of hoary petty-bourgeois tenden-cies are systematically compelled within a workers' party to make theo-retical compromises with their own conscience.

Comrade Shachtman's attitude toward the dialectic method, as mani-fested in the above-quoted argumentation, cannot be called anything but eclectical skepticism. It is clear that Shachtman became infected with this attitude not in the school of Marx but among the petty-bourgeois intellectuals to whom all forms of skepticism are proper.

Warning and verification

The article astonished me to such an extent that I immediately wrote to Comrade Shachtman:

> I have just read the article you and Burnham wrote on the intellectuals. Many parts are excellent. However, the section on the dialectic is the greatest blow that you, personally, as the editor of the *New International*, could have delivered to Marxist theory. Comrade Burnham says: "I don't recognize the dialectic." It is clear and everybody has to acknowledge it. But you say: "I recognize the dialectic, but no matter; it does not have the slightest importance." Reread what you wrote. This section is terribly misleading for the readers of the *New International* and the best of gifts to the Eastmans of all kinds. Good! We will speak about it publicly.

My letter was written January 20, some months before the present discussion. Shachtman did not reply until March 5, when he answered in effect that he couldn't understand why I was making such a stir about the matter. On March 9, I answered Shachtman in the following words:

> I did not reject in the slightest degree the possibility of collaboration with the anti-dialecticians, but only the advisability of writing an article together where the question of the dialectic plays, or should play, a very important role. The polemic develops on two planes: political and theoretical. Your political criticism is OK. Your theoretical criticism is insufficient; it stops at the point at which it should just become aggressive. Namely, the task consists of showing that their mistakes (insofar as they are *theoretical* mistakes) are products of their incapacity and unwillingness to think things through dialectically. This task could be accomplished with a very serious pedagogical success. Instead of this you declare that dialectics is a private matter and that one can be a very good fellow without dialectic thinking.

By allying himself in *this* question with the anti-dialectician Burnham, Shachtman deprived himself of the possibility of showing why Eastman, Hook, and many others began with a philosophical struggle against the dialectic but finished with a political struggle against the socialist revolution. That is, however, the essence of the question.

The present political discussion in the party has confirmed my apprehensions and warning in an incomparably sharper form than I could have expected, or, more correctly, feared. Shachtman's methodological skepticism bore its deplorable fruits in the question of the nature of the Soviet state. Burnham began some time ago by constructing purely empirically, on the basis of his immediate impressions, a non-proletarian and non-bourgeois state, liquidating in passing the Marxist theory of the state as the organ of class rule. Shachtman unexpectedly took an evasive position: "The question, you see, is subject to further consideration"; moreover, the sociological definition of the USSR does not possess any direct and immediate significance for our "political tasks" in which Shachtman agrees completely with Burnham. Let the reader again refer to what these comrades wrote concerning the dialectic. Burnham rejects the dialectic. Shachtman seems to accept, but . . . the divine gift of "inconsistency" permits them to meet on common political conclusions. *The attitude of each of them toward the nature of the Soviet state reproduces point for point their attitude toward the dialectic.*

In both cases Burnham takes the leading role. This is not surprising; he *possesses* a method—pragmatism. Shachtman has no method. He adapts himself to Burnham. Without assuming complete responsibility for the anti-Marxian conceptions of Burnham, he defends his bloc of aggression against the Marxian conceptions with Burnham in the sphere of philosophy as well as in the sphere of sociology. In both cases Burnham appears as a pragmatist and Shachtman as an eclectic. This example has the invaluable advantage that the complete parallelism between Burnham's and Shachtman's positions upon two different planes of thought and upon two questions of primary importance, will strike the eyes even of comrades who have had no experience in purely theoretical thinking. The method of thought can be dialectic or vulgar, conscious or unconscious, but it exists and makes itself known.

Last January we heard from our authors: "But it does not now, nor has anyone yet demonstrated that agreement or disagreement on the more abstract doctrines of dialectical materialism necessarily affects today's and tomorrow's concrete political issues." Nor has anyone yet demonstrated! Not more than a few months passed before Burnham and Shachtman themselves demonstrated that their attitude toward such an "abstraction" as dialectical materialism found its precise manifestation in their attitude toward the Soviet state.

To be sure, it is necessary to mention that the difference between the two instances is rather important, but it is of a political and not a theoretical character. In both cases Burnham and Shachtman formed a bloc on the basis of rejection and semi-rejection of the dialectic. But in the first instance that bloc was directed against the opponents of the proletarian party. In the second instance the bloc was concluded against the Marxist wing of their own party. The front of military operations, so to speak, has changed but the weapon remains the same.

True enough, people are often inconsistent. Human consciousness nevertheless tends toward a certain homogeneity. Philosophy and logic are compelled to rely upon this homogeneity of human consciousness and not upon what this homogeneity lacks, that is, inconsistency. Burnham does not recognize the dialectic, but the dialectic recognizes Burnham, that is, extends its sway over him. Shachtman thinks that the dialectic has no importance in political conclusions, but in the political conclusions of Shachtman himself we see the deplorable fruits of his disdainful attitude toward the dialectic. We should include this example in the textbooks on dialectical materialism.

Last year I was visited by a young British professor of political economy, a sympathizer of the Fourth International. During our conversation on the ways and means of realizing socialism, he suddenly expressed the tendencies of British utilitarianism in the spirit of Keynes and others: "It is necessary to determine a clear economic end, to choose the most reasonable means for its realization," etc. I remarked: "I see that you are an adversary of dialectics." He replied, somewhat astonished: "Yes, I don't see any use in it." "However," I replied to him, "the dialectic enabled me on the basis of a few of your observations upon economic problems to determine what category of philosophical thought you belong to—this alone shows that there is an appreciable value in the dialectic." Although I have received no word about my visitor since then, I have no doubt that this anti-dialectic professor maintains the opinion that the USSR is not a workers' state, that unconditional defense of the USSR is an "outmoded" opinion, that our organizational methods are bad, etc. If it is possible to place a given person's general type of thought on the basis of his relation to concrete practical problems, it is also possible to predict approximately, knowing his general type of thought, how a given individual will approach one or another practical question. That is the incomparable educational value of the dialectical method of thought.

The ABC of materialist dialectics

Gangrenous skeptics like Souvarine believe that "nobody knows" what the dialectic is. And there are "Marxists" who kowtow reverently before Souvarine and hope to learn something from him. And these Marxists hide not only in the *Modern Monthly*. Unfortunately, a current of Souvarin-ism exists in the present opposition of the SWP. And here it is necessary to warn young comrades: Beware of this malignant infection!

The dialectic is neither fiction nor mysticism, but a science of the forms of our thinking insofar as it is not limited to the daily problems of life but attempts to arrive at an understanding of more complicated and drawn-out processes. The dialectic and formal logic bear a relationship similar to that between higher and lower mathematics.

I will here attempt to sketch the substance of the problem in a very concise form. The Aristotelian logic of the simple syllogism starts from the proposition that "A" is equal to "A." This postulate is accepted as an axiom for a multitude of practical human actions and elementary gen-eralizations. But in reality "A" is not equal to "A." This is easy to prove if we observe these two letters under a lens—they are quite different from each other. But, one can object, the question is not of the size or the form of the letters, since they are only symbols for equal quantities, for instance, a pound of sugar. The objection is beside the point; in reality a pound of sugar is never equal to a pound of sugar—a more delicate scale always discloses a difference. Again one can object: but a pound of sugar is equal to itself. Neither is this true—all bodies change uninterruptedly in size, weight, color, etc. They are never equal to themselves. A sophist will respond that a pound of sugar is equal to itself "at any given moment." Aside from the extremely dubious practical value of this "axiom," it does not withstand theoretical criticism either. How should we really conceive the word "moment"? If it is an infinitesimal interval of time, then a pound of sugar is subjected during the course of that "moment" to inevitable changes. Or is the "moment" a purely mathematical abstraction, that is, a zero of time? But everything exists in time; and existence itself is an unin-terrupted process of transformation; time is consequently a fundamental element of existence. Thus the axiom "A" is equal to "A" signifies that a thing is equal to itself if it does not change, that is, if it does not exist.

At first glance it could seem that these "subtleties" are useless. In real-ity they are of decisive significance. The axiom "A" is equal to "A" appears on one hand to be the point of departure for all our knowledge, on the other hand the point of departure for all the errors in our knowledge. To make use of the axiom "A" is equal to "A" with impunity is possible only within certain *limits*. When quantitative changes in "A" are negligible for the task at hand then we can presume that "A" is equal to "A." This is, for example, the manner in which a buyer and a seller consider a pound of sugar. We consider the temperature of the sun likewise. Until recently we considered the buying power of the dollar in the same way. But quantitative changes beyond certain limits become converted into qualitative. A pound of sugar subjected to the action of water or kerosene ceases to be a pound of sugar. A dollar in the embrace of a president ceases to be a dollar. To determine at the right moment the critical point where quantity changes into quality is one of the most important and difficult tasks in all the spheres of knowledge including sociology.

Every worker knows that it is impossible to make two completely equal objects. In the elaboration of bearing-brass into cone bearings, a certain deviation is allowed for the cones which should not, however, go beyond certain limits (this is called tolerance). By observing the norms of tolerance, the cones are considered as being equal. ("A" is equal to "A.") When the tolerance is exceeded the quantity goes over into quality; in other words, the cone bearings become inferior or completely worthless.

Our scientific thinking is only a part of our general practice including techniques. For concepts there also exists "tolerance" which is established not by formal logic issuing from the axiom "A" is equal to "A," but by dialectical logic issuing from the axiom that everything is always changing. "Common sense" is characterized by the fact that it systematically exceeds dialectical "tolerance."

Vulgar thought operates with such concepts as capitalism, morals, freedom, workers' state, etc., as fixed abstractions, presuming that capitalism is equal to capitalism, morals are equal to morals, etc. Dialectical thinking analyzes all things and phenomena in their continuous change, while determining in the material conditions of those changes that critical limit beyond which "A" ceases to be "A," a workers' state ceases to be a workers' state.

The fundamental flaw of vulgar thought lies in the fact that it wishes to content itself with motionless imprints of a reality which consists of eternal motion. Dialectical thinking gives to concepts, by means of closer approximations, corrections, concretizations, a richness of content and flexibility; I would even say a succulence which to a certain extent brings them close to living phenomena. Not capitalism in general, but a given capitalism at a given stage of development. Not a workers' state in general, but a given workers' state in a backward country in an imperialist encirclement, etc.

Dialectical thinking is related to vulgar thinking in the same way that a motion picture is related to a still photograph. The motion picture does not outlaw the still photograph but combines a series of them according to the laws of motion. Dialectics does not deny the syllogism, but teaches us to combine syllogisms in such a way as to bring our understanding closer to the eternally changing reality. Hegel in his *Logic* established a series of laws: change of quantity into quality, development through contradictions, conflict of content and form, interruption of continuity, change of possibility into inevitability, etc., which are just as important for theoretical thought as is the simple syllogism for more elementary tasks.

Hegel wrote before Darwin and before Marx. Thanks to the powerful impulse given to thought by the French Revolution, Hegel anticipated the general movement of science. But because it was only an *anticipation*, although by a genius, it received from Hegel an idealistic character. Hegel operated with ideological shadows as the ultimate reality. Marx demonstrated that the movement of these ideological shadows reflected nothing but the movement of material bodies.

We call our dialectic, materialist, since its roots are neither in heaven nor in the depths of our "free will," but in objective reality, in nature. Consciousness grew out of the unconscious, psychology out of physiology, the organic world out of the inorganic, the solar system out of nebulae. On all the rungs of this ladder of development, the quantitative changes were transformed into qualitative. Our thought, including dialectical thought, is only one of the forms of the expression of changing matter. There is place within this system for neither God, nor Devil, nor immortal soul, nor eternal norms of laws and morals. The dialectic of thinking, having grown out of the dialectic of nature, possesses consequently a thoroughly materialist character.

Darwinism, which explained the evolution of species through quantitative transformations passing into qualitative, was the highest triumph of the dialectic in the whole field of organic matter. Another great triumph was the discovery of the table of atomic weights of chemical elements, and further, the transformation of one element into another.

With these transformations (species, elements, etc.) is closely linked the question of classification, equally important in the natural as in the social sciences. Linnaeus' system (18th century), utilizing as its starting point the immutability of species, was limited to the description and classification of plants according to their external characteristics. The infantile period of botany is analogous to the infantile period of logic, since the forms of our thought develop like everything that lives. Only decisive repudiation of the idea of fixed species, only the study of the history of the evolution of plants and their anatomy prepared the basis for a really scientific classification.

Marx, who in distinction from Darwin was a conscious dialectician, discovered a basis for the scientific classification of human societies in the development of their productive forces and the structure of the relations of ownership which constitute the anatomy of society. Marxism substituted for the vulgar descriptive classification of societies and states, which even up to now still flourishes in the universities, a materialistic dialectical classification. Only through using the method of Marx is it possible correctly to determine both the concept of a workers' state and the moment of its downfall.

All this, as we see, contains nothing "metaphysical" or "scholastic," as conceited ignorance affirms. Dialectic logic expresses the laws of motion in contemporary scientific thought. The struggle against materialist dialectics, on the contrary, expresses a distant past, conservatism of the petty bourgeoisie, the self-conceit of university routinists and—a spark of hope for an afterlife.

The nature of the USSR

The definition of the USSR given by comrade Burnham—"not a workers' and not a bourgeois state"—is purely negative, wrenched from the chain of historical development, left dangling in midair, void of a single particle of sociology, and represents simply a theoretical capitulation of pragmatism before a *contradictory* historical phenomenon.

If Burnham were a dialectical materialist, he would have probed the following three questions: 1) What is the historical origin of the USSR? 2) What changes has this state suffered during its existence? 3) Did these changes pass from the quantitative stage to the qualitative? That is, did they create a historically necessary domination by a new exploiting class? Answering these questions would have forced Burnham to draw the only possible conclusion—the USSR is still a degenerated workers' state.

The dialectic is not a magic master key for all questions. It does not replace concrete scientific analysis. But it directs this analysis along the correct road, securing it against sterile wanderings in the desert of subjectivism and scholasticism.

Bruno R. places both the Soviet and fascist regimes under the category of "bureaucratic collectivism," because the USSR, Italy, and Germany are all ruled by bureaucracies; here and there are the principles of planning; in one case private property is liquidated, in another limited, etc. Thus, on the basis of the *relative* similarity of *certain* external characteristics of *different* origin, of *different* specific weight, of *different* class significance, a fundamental *identity* of social regimes is constructed, completely in the spirit of bourgeois professors who construct categories of "controlled economy," "centralized state," without taking into consideration whatsoever the class nature of one or the other. Bruno R. and his followers, or semi-followers like Burnham, at best remain in the sphere of social classification on the level of Linnaeus in whose justification it should be remarked, however, that he lived before Hegel, Darwin, and Marx.

Even worse and more dangerous, perhaps, are those eclectics who express the idea that the class character of the Soviet state "does not matter," and that the direction of our policy is determined by "the character of the war." As if the war were an independent super-social substance; as if the character of the war were not determined by the character of the ruling class, that is, by the same social factor that also determines the character of the state. Astonishing how easily some comrades forget the ABCs of Marxism under the blows of events.

It is not surprising that the theoreticians of the opposition who reject dialectic thought capitulate lamentably before the contradictory nature of the USSR. However, the contradiction between the social basis laid down by the revolution, and the character of the caste which arose out of the degeneration of the revolution, is not only an irrefutable historical fact but also a motor force. In our struggle for the overthrow of the bureaucracy we base ourselves on this contradiction. Meanwhile, some ultralefts have already reached the ultimate absurdity by affirming that it is necessary to sacrifice the social structure of the USSR in order to overthrow the Bonapartist oligarchy! They have no suspicion that the USSR minus the social structure founded by the October Revolution would be a fascist regime.

Evolution and dialectics

Comrade Burnham will probably protest that as an evolutionist he is interested in the development of society and state forms not less than we dialecticians. We will not dispute this. Every educated person since Darwin has labeled himself an "evolutionist." But a real evolutionist must apply the idea of evolution to his own forms of thinking. Elementary logic, founded in the period when the idea of evolution itself did not yet exist, is evidently insufficient for the analysis of evolutionary processes. Hegel's logic is the logic of evolution. Only one must not forget that the concept of "evolution" itself has been completely corrupted and emasculated by university professors and liberal writers to mean peaceful "progress." Whoever has come to understand that evolution proceeds through the struggle of antagonistic forces; that a slow accumulation of changes at a certain moment explodes the old shell and brings about a catastrophe, revolution; whoever has learned finally to apply the general laws of evolution to thinking itself, he is a dialectician, as distinguished from vulgar evolutionists. Dialectic training of the mind, as necessary to a revolutionary fighter as finger exercises to a pianist, demands approaching all problems as *processes* and not as *motionless categories*. Whereas vulgar evolutionists, who limit themselves generally to recognizing evolution in only certain spheres, content themselves in all other questions with the banalities of "common sense."

The American liberal, who has reconciled himself to the existence of the USSR, more precisely to the Moscow bureaucracy, believes, or at least believed until the Soviet-German pact, that the Soviet regime on the whole is a "progressive thing," that the repugnant features of the bureaucracy ("well, naturally they exist!") will progressively slough away and that peaceful and painless "progress" is thus assured.

A vulgar petty-bourgeois radical is similar to a liberal "progressive" in that he takes the USSR as a whole, failing to understand its internal contradictions and dynamics. When Stalin concluded an alliance with Hitler, invaded Poland, and now Finland, the vulgar radicals triumphed; the identity of the methods of Stalinism and fascism was proved. They found themselves in difficulties, however, when the new authorities invited the population to expropriate the landowners and capitalists—they had not foreseen this possibility at all! Meanwhile, the social revolutionary measures, carried out via bureaucratic military means, not only did not disturb *our*, dialectic, definition of the USSR as a degenerated workers' state, but gave it the most incontrovertible corroboration. Instead of utilizing this triumph of Marxian analysis for persevering agitation, the petty-bourgeois oppositionists began to shout with criminal light-mindedness that events have refuted our prognosis, that our old formulas are no longer applicable, that new words are necessary. What words? They haven't decided yet themselves.

* * *

Letter to the National Committee Majority
(January 3, 1940)

Dear Friends,

I received the two documents of the opposition, studied that on bureaucratic conservatism and am now studying the second on the Russian question. What lamentable writings! It is difficult to find a sentence expressing a correct idea or placing a correct idea in the correct place. Intelligent and even talented people occupied an evidently false position and push themselves more and more into a blind alley.

The phrase of Abern about the "split" can have two senses: either he wishes to frighten you with a split as he did during the entry discussion or he wishes really to commit political suicide. In the first case, he will of course not prevent our giving a Marxist appreciation of the opposition politics. In the second case, nothing can be done; if an adult person wishes to commit suicide it is difficult to hinder him.

The reaction of Burnham is a brutal challenge to all Marxists. If dialectics is a religion, and if it is true that religion is the opium of the people, how can he refuse to fight for liberating his own party from this venom? I am now writing an open letter to Burnham on this question. I don't believe that the public opinion of the Fourth International would permit the editor of the theoretical Marxist magazine to limit himself to rather cynical aphorisms about the foundation of scientific socialism. In any case, I will not rest until the anti-Marxist conceptions of Burnham are unmasked to the end before the Party and the International. I hope to send the open letter, at least the Russian text, the day after tomorrow.

Simultaneously, I am writing an analysis of the two documents. Excellent is the explanation why they agree to disagree about the Russian question.

I grit my teeth upon losing my time in the reading of these absolutely stale documents. The errors are so elementary that it is necessary to make an effort to remember the necessary argument from the ABC of Marxism.

W. RORK [Leon Trotsky]

Coyoacán, D.F.

* * *

An Open Letter to Comrade Burnham
(January 1940)

Dear Comrade:

You have expressed as your reaction to my article on the petty-bourgeois opposition, I have been informed, that you do not intend to argue over the dialectic with me and that you will discuss only the "concrete questions." "I stopped arguing about religion long ago," you added ironically. I once heard Max Eastman voice this same sentiment.

Is there logic in identifying logic with religion?

As I understand this, your words imply that the dialectic of Marx, Engels, and Lenin belongs to the sphere of religion. What does this assertion signify? The dialectic, permit me to recall once again, is the *logic of evolution*. Just as a machine shop in a plant supplies instruments for all departments, so logic is indispensable for all spheres of human knowledge. If you do not consider logic in general to be a religious prejudice (sad to say, the self-contradictory writings of the opposition incline one more and more toward this lamentable idea), then just which logic do you accept? I know of two systems of logic worthy of attention: the logic of Aristotle (formal logic) and the logic of Hegel (the dialectic). Aristotelian logic takes as its starting point immutable objects and phenomena. The scientific thought of our epoch studies all phenomena in their origin, change, and disintegration. Do you hold that the progress of the sciences, including Darwinism, Marxism, modern physics, chemistry, etc., has not influenced in any way the forms of our thought? In other words, do you hold that in a world where everything changes, the syllogism alone re-mains unchanging and eternal? The Gospel according to St. John begins with the words: "In the beginning was the Word," i.e., in the beginning was Reason or the Word (reason expressed in the word, namely, the syl-logism). To St. John the syllogism is one of the literary pseudonyms for God. If you consider that the syllogism as immutable, i.e., has neither origin nor development, then it signifies that to you it is the product of divine revelation. But if you acknowledge that the logical forms of our thought develop in the process of our adaptation to nature, then please take the trouble to inform us just who following Aristotle analyzed and systematized the subsequent progress of logic. So long as you do not clarify this point, I shall take the liberty of asserting that to identify logic (the dialectic) with religion reveals utter ignorance and superficiality in the basic questions of human thought.

Is the revolutionist not obliged to fight against religion?

Let us grant, however, that your more than presumptuous innuendo is correct. But this does not improve affairs to your advantage. Religion, as I hope you will agree, diverts attention away from real to fictitious knowl-edge, away from the struggle for a better life to false hopes for reward in the Hereafter. Religion is the opium of the people. Whoever fails to struggle against religion is unworthy of bearing the name of revolution-ist. On what grounds, then, do you justify your refusal to fight against the dialectic if you deem it one of the varieties of religion?

You stopped bothering yourself long ago, as you say, about the ques-tion of religion. But you stopped only *for yourself*. In addition to you, there exist all the others. Quite a few of them. We revolutionists never "stop" bothering ourselves about religious questions, inasmuch as our task consists in emancipating from the influence of religion, not only our-selves but also the masses. If the dialectic is a religion, how is it possible to renounce the struggle against this opium within one's own party?

Or perhaps you intended to imply that religion is of no political im-portance? That it is possible to be religious and at the same time a con-sistent communist and revolutionary fighter? You will hardly venture so rash an assertion. Naturally, we maintain the most considerate attitude toward the religious prejudices of a backward worker. Should he desire to fight for our program, we would accept him as a party member; but at the same time, our party would persistently educate him in the spirit of materialism and atheism. If you agree with this, how can you refuse to struggle against a "religion," held, to my knowledge, by the overwhelming majority of those members of your own party who are interested in theoretical questions? You have obviously overlooked this most important aspect of the question.

Among the educated bourgeoisie there are not a few who have broken personally with religion, but whose atheism is solely for their own private consumption; they keep thoughts like these to themselves but in public often maintain that it is well the people have a religion. Is it possible that you hold such a point of view toward your own party? Is it possible that this explains your refusal to discuss with us the philosophic foundations of Marxism? If that is the case, under your scorn for the dialectic rings a note of contempt for the party.

Please do not make the objection that I have based myself on a phrase expressed by you in private conversation, and that you are not concerned with publicly refuting dialectic materialism. This is not true. Your winged phrase serves only as an illustration. Whenever there has been an occasion, for various reasons you have proclaimed your negative attitude toward the doctrine which constitutes the theoretical foundation of our program. This is well known to everyone in the party. In the article "Intellectuals in Retreat," written by you in collaboration with Shachtman and published in the party's theoretical organ, it is categorically affirmed that you reject dialectic materialism. Doesn't the party have the right, after all, to know just why? Do you really assume that in the Fourth International an editor of a theoretical organ can confine himself to the bare declaration: "I decisively reject dialectical materialism"—as if it were a question of a proffered cigarette: "Thank you, I don't smoke." The question of a correct philosophical doctrine, that is, a correct method of thought, is of decisive significance to a revolutionary party, just as a good machine shop is of decisive significance to production. It is still possible to defend the old society with the material and intellectual methods inherited from the past. It is absolutely unthinkable that this old society can be overthrown and a new one constructed without first critically analyzing the current methods. If the party errs in the very foundations of its thinking it is your elementary duty to point out the correct road. Otherwise your conduct will be interpreted inevitably as the cavalier attitude of an academician toward a proletarian organization which, after all, is incapable of grasping a real "scientific" doctrine. What could be worse than that?

Instructive examples

Anyone acquainted with the history of the struggles of tendencies within workers' parties knows that desertions to the camp of opportunism and even to the camp of bourgeois reaction began not infrequently with rejection of the dialectic. Petty-bourgeois intellectuals consider the dialectic the most vulnerable point in Marxism and at the same time they take advantage of the fact that it is much more difficult for workers to verify differences on the philosophical than on the political plane. This long-known fact is backed by all the evidence of experience. Again, it is impermissible to discount an even more important fact, namely, that all the great and outstanding revolutionists—first and foremost, Marx, Engels, Lenin, Luxemburg, Franz Mehring—stood on the ground of dialectic materialism. Can it be assumed that all of them were incapable of distinguishing between science and religion? Isn't there too much presumptuousness on your part, Comrade Burnham? The examples of Bernstein, Kautsky, and Franz Mehring are extremely instructive. Bernstein categorically rejected the dialectic as "scholasticism" and "mysticism." Kautsky maintained indifference toward the question of the dialectic, somewhat like Comrade Shachtman. Mehring was a tireless propagandist and defender of dialectic materialism. For decades he followed all the innovations of philosophy and literature, indefatigably exposing the reactionary essence of idealism, neo-Kantianism, utilitarianism, all forms of mysticism, etc. The political fate of these three individuals is very well known. Bernstein ended his life as a smug petty-bourgeois democrat. Kautsky, from a centrist, became a vulgar opportunist. As for Mehring, he died a revolutionary communist.

In Russia, three very prominent academic Marxists, Struve, Bulgakov, and Berdyaev began by rejecting the philosophic doctrine of Marxism and ended in the camp of reaction and the Orthodox Church. In the United States, Eastman, Sidney Hook, and their friends utilized opposition to the dialectic as cover for their transformation from fellow travellers of the proletariat to fellow travellers of the bourgeoisie. Similar examples by the score could be cited from other countries.

The example of Plekhanov, which appears to be an exception, in reality only proves the rule. Plekhanov was a remarkable propagandist of dialectic materialism, but during his whole life he never had the opportunity of participating in the actual class struggle. His thinking was divorced from practice. The revolution of 1905 and subsequently the World War flung him into the camp of petty-bourgeois democracy and forced him in actuality to renounce dialectic materialism. During the World War, Plekhanov came forward openly as the protagonist of the Kantian categorical imperative in the sphere of international relations: "Do not do unto others as you would not have them do unto you." The example of Plekhanov only proves that dialectic materialism *in and of itself* still does not make a man a revolutionist.

Shachtman, on the other hand, argues that Liebknecht left a posthumous work against dialectic materialism which he had written in prison. Many ideas enter a person's mind while in prison which cannot be checked by association with other people. Liebknecht, whom nobody, least of all himself, considered a theoretician, became a symbol of heroism in the world labor movement. Should any of the American opponents of the dialectic display similar self-sacrifice and independence from patriotism during war, we shall render what is due him as a revolutionist. But that will not thereby resolve the question of the dialectic method.

It is impossible to say what Liebknecht's own final conclusions would have been had he remained at liberty. In any case before publishing his work, undoubtedly he would have shown it to his more competent friends, namely, Franz Mehring and Rosa Luxemburg. It is quite probable that on their advice he would have simply tossed the manuscript into the fire. Let us grant, however, that against the advice of people far excelling him in the sphere of theory he nevertheless had decided to publish his work. Mehring, Luxemburg, Lenin, and others would not, of course, have proposed that he be expelled for this from the party; on the contrary, they would have intervened decisively on his behalf had anyone made such a foolish proposal. But at the same time they would not have formed a philosophical bloc with him, but rather, would have differentiated themselves decisively from his theoretical mistakes.

Comrade Shachtman's behavior, we note, is quite otherwise. "You will observe," he says—and this to teach the youth(!)—"that Plekhanov was an outstanding theoretician of dialectic materialism but ended up an opportunist; Liebknecht was a remarkable revolutionist but he had his doubts about dialectic materialism." This argument, if it means anything at all, signifies that dialectic materialism is of no use whatsoever to a revolutionist. With these examples of Liebknecht and Plekhanov, artificially torn out of history, Shachtman reinforces and "deepens" the idea of his last year's article, namely, that politics does not depend on method, inasmuch as method is divorced from politics through the divine gift of inconsistency. By falsely interpreting two "exceptions," Shachtman seeks to overthrow the rule. If this is the argument of a "supporter" of Marxism, what can we expect from an opponent? The revision of Marxism passes here into its downright liquidation; more than that, into the liquidation of every doctrine and every method.

What do you propose instead?

Dialectic materialism is not, of course, an eternal and immutable philosophy. To think otherwise is to contradict the spirit of the dialectic. Further development of scientific thought will undoubtedly create a more profound doctrine into which dialectic materialism will enter merely as structural material. However, there is no basis for expecting that this philosophic revolution will be accomplished under the decaying bourgeois regime, without mentioning the fact that a Marx is not born every year or every decade. The life-and-death task of the proletariat now consists not in *interpreting* the world anew but in *remaking* it from top to bottom. In the next epoch we can expect great revolutionists of action but hardly a new Marx. Only on the basis of socialist culture will mankind feel the need to review the ideological heritage of the past and undoubtedly will far surpass us not only in the sphere of economy but also in the sphere of intellectual creation. The regime of the Bonapartist bureaucracy in the USSR is criminal not only because it creates an ever-growing inequality in all spheres of life but also because it degrades the intellectual activity of the country to the depths of the unbridled blockheads of the GPU.

Let us grant, however, that contrary to our supposition, the proletariat is so fortunate during the present epoch of wars and revolutions as to produce a new theoretician or a new constellation of theoreticians who will surpass Marxism and, in particular, advance logic beyond materialist dialectics. It goes without saying that all advanced workers will learn from the new teachers and the old men will have to reeducate themselves again. But in the meantime, this remains the music of the future. Or am I mistaken? Perhaps you will call my attention to those works which should supplant the system of dialectic materialism for the proletariat? Were these at hand surely you would not have refused to conduct a struggle against the opium of the dialectic. But none exist. While attempting to discredit the philosophy of Marxism you do not propose anything with which to replace it.

Picture to yourself a young amateur physician who proceeds to argue with a surgeon using a scalpel that modern anatomy, neurology, etc., are worthless, that much in them remains unclear and incomplete and that only "conservative bureaucrats" could set to work with a scalpel on the basis of these pseudosciences, etc. I believe that the surgeon would ask his irresponsible colleague to leave the operating room. We too, Comrade Burnham, cannot yield to cheap innuendos about the philosophy of scientific socialism. On the contrary, since in the course of the factional struggle the question has been posed point-blank, we shall say, turning to all members of the party, especially the youth: Beware of the infiltration of bourgeois skepticism into your ranks. Remember that socialism to this day has not found higher scientific expression than Marxism. Bear in mind that the method of scientific socialism is dialectic materialism. Occupy yourselves with serious study! Study Marx, Engels, Plekhanov, Lenin, and Franz Mehring. This is a hundred times more important for you than the study of tendentious, sterile, and slightly ludicrous treatises on the conservatism of Cannon. Let the present discussion produce at least this positive result, that the youth attempt to embed in their minds a serious theoretical foundation for revolutionary struggle!

False political "realism"

In your case, however, the question is not confined to the dialectic. The remarks in your resolution to the effect that you do not now pose for the decision of the party the question of the nature of the Soviet state signify, in reality, that you *do pose* this question, if not juridically then theoretically and politically. Only infants can fail to understand this. This very statement, likewise, has another meaning, far more outrageous and pernicious. It means that you divorce politics from Marxist sociology. Yet for us the crux of the matter lies precisely in this. If it is possible to give a correct definition of the state without utilizing the method of dialectic materialism; if it is possible correctly to determine politics without giving a class analysis of the state, then the question arises: Is there any need whatsoever for Marxism?

Disagreeing among themselves on the class nature of the Soviet state, the leaders of the opposition agree on this, that the foreign policy of the

Kremlin must be labelled "imperialist" and that the USSR cannot be supported "unconditionally." (Vastly substantial platform!) When the opposing "clique" raises the question of the nature of the Soviet state point-blank at the convention (what a crime!) you have in advance agreed . . . to disagree, i.e., to vote differently. In the British "national" government this precedent occurs of ministers who "agree to disagree," i.e., to vote differently. But His Majesty's ministers enjoy this advantage, that they are well aware of the nature of *their* state and can afford the luxury of disagreement on *secondary* questions. The leaders of the opposition are far less favorably situated. They permit themselves the luxury of differing on the fundamental question in order to solidarize on secondary questions. If this is Marxism and principled politics then I don't know what unprincipled combinationism means.

You seem to consider apparently that by refusing to discuss dialectic materialism and the class nature of the Soviet state and by sticking to "concrete" questions you are acting the part of a realistic politician. This self-deception is a result of your inadequate acquaintance with the history of the past 50 years of factional struggles in the labor movement. In every principled conflict, without a single exception, the Marxists invariably sought to face the party squarely with the fundamental problems of doctrine and program, considering that only under this condition could the "concrete" questions find their proper place and proportion. On the other hand, the opportunists of every shade, especially those who had already suffered a few defeats in the sphere of principled discussion, invariably counterposed to the Marxist class analysis "concrete" conjunctural appraisals which they, as is the custom, formulated under the pressure of bourgeois democracy. Through decades of factional struggle this division of roles has persisted. The opposition, permit me to assure you, has invented nothing new. It is continuing the tradition of revisionism in theory and opportunism in politics.

Toward the close of the last century the revisionist attempts of Bernstein, who in England came under the influence of Anglo-Saxon empiricism and utilitarianism—the most wretched of philosophies—were mercilessly repulsed. Whereupon the German opportunists suddenly recoiled from philosophy and sociology. At conventions and in the press they did not cease to berate the Marxist "pedants," who replaced the "concrete political questions" with general principled considerations. Read over the records of the German Social Democracy toward the close of the last and the beginning of the present century—and you will be astonished yourself at the degree to which, as the French say, *le mort saisit le vif* (the dead grip the living)!

You are not unacquainted with the great role played by *Iskra* in the development of Russian Marxism. *Iskra* began with the struggle against so-called "Economism" in the labor movement and against the Narodniks (party of the Social Revolutionaries). The chief argument of the "Economists" was that *Iskra* floats in the sphere of theory while they, the "Economists," propose leading the concrete labor movement. The main argument of the Social Revolutionaries was as follows: *Iskra* wants to found a school of dialectic materialism while we want to overthrow tsarist autocracy. It must be said that the Narodnik terrorists took their own words very seriously: bomb in hand they sacrificed their lives. We argued with them: "Under certain circumstances a bomb is an excellent thing but we should first clarify our own minds." It is historical experience that the greatest revolution in all history was not led by the party which started out with bombs but by the party which started out with dialectic materialism.

When the Bolsheviks and the Mensheviks were still members of the same party, the pre convention periods and the convention itself invariably witnessed an embittered struggle over the agenda. Lenin used to propose as first on the agenda such questions as clarification of the nature of the tsarist monarchy, the analysis of the class character of the revolution, the appraisal of the stages of the revolution we were passing through, etc. Martov and Dan, the leaders of the Mensheviks, invariably objected: We are not a sociological club but a political party; we must come to an agreement not on the class nature of tsarist economy but on the "concrete political tasks." I cite this from memory but I do not run any risk of error since these disputes were repeated from year to year and became stereotyped in character. I might add that I personally committed not a few sins on this score myself. But I have learned something since then.

To those enamored with "concrete political questions," Lenin invariably explained that our politics is not of conjunctural but of principled character; that tactics are subordinate to strategy; that for us the primary concern of every political campaign is that it guide the workers from the particular questions to the general, that it teach them the nature of modern society and the character of its fundamental forces. The Mensheviks always felt the need urgently to slur over principled differences in their unstable conglomeration by means of evasions, whereas Lenin, on the contrary, posed principled questions point blank. The current arguments of the opposition against philosophy and sociology in favor of "concrete political questions" is a belated repetition of Dan's arguments. Not a single new word! How sad it is that Shachtman respects the principled politics of Marxism only when it has aged long enough for the archives.

Especially awkward and inappropriate does the appeal to shift from Marxist theory to "concrete political questions" sound on your lips, Comrade Burnham, for it was not I but you who raised the question of the character of the USSR, thereby forcing me to pose the question of the method through which the class character of the state is determined. True enough, you withdrew your resolution. But this factional maneuver has no objective meaning whatsoever. You draw your *political* conclusions from your *sociological* premise, even if you have temporarily slipped it into your briefcase. Shachtman draws exactly the same political conclusions without a sociological premise: he adapts himself to you. Abern seeks to profit equally both from the hidden premise and the absence of a premise for his "organizational" combinations. This is the real and not the diplomatic situation in the camp of the opposition. You proceed as an anti-Marxist; Shachtman and Abern—as *platonic* Marxists. Who is worse, it is not easy to determine.

The dialectic of the present discussion

When confronted with the diplomatic front covering the hidden premises and lack of premises of our opponents, we, the "conservatives," naturally reply: A fruitful dispute over "concrete questions" is possible only if you clearly specify what class premises you take as your starting point. We are not compelled to confine ourselves to those topics in this dispute which you have selected artificially. Should someone propose that we discuss as "concrete" questions the invasion of Switzerland by the Soviet fleet or the length of a tail of a Bronx witch, then I am justified in posing in advance such questions as, does Switzerland have a sea coast? Are there witches at all?

Every serious discussion develops from the particular and even the accidental to the general and fundamental. The immediate causes and motives of a discussion are of interest, in most cases, only symptomatically. Of actual political significance are only those problems which the discussion raises in its development. To certain intellectuals, anxious to indict "bureaucratic conservatism" and to display their "dynamic spirit," it might seem that questions concerning the dialectic, Marxism, the nature of the state, and centralism are raised "artificially" and that the discussion has taken a "false" direction. The nub of the matter, however, consists in this, that discussion has its own objective logic which does not coincide at all with the subjective logic of individuals and groupings. The *dialectic* character of the discussion proceeds from the fact that its objective course is determined by the living conflict of opposing tendencies and not by a preconceived logical plan. The *materialist* basis of the discussion consists in its reflecting the pressure of different classes. Thus, the present discussion in the SWP, like the historic process as a whole, develops—with or without your permission, Comrade Burnham—according to the laws of dialectic materialism. There is no escape from these laws.

"Science" against Marxism and "experiments" against program

Accusing your opponents of "bureaucratic conservatism" (a bare psychological abstraction insofar as no specific social interests are shown underlying this "conservatism"), you demand in your document that conservative politics be replaced by "critical and experimental politics—in a word, scientific politics." This statement, at first glance so innocent and meaningless with all its pompousness, is in itself a complete exposure. You don't speak of Marxist politics. You don't speak of proletarian politics. You speak of "experimental," "critical," "scientific" politics. Why this pretentious and deliberately abstruse terminology so unusual in our ranks? I shall tell you. It is the product of your adaptation, Comrade Burnham, to bourgeois public opinion, and the adaptation of Shachtman and Abern to your adaptation. Marxism is no longer fashionable among the broad circles of bourgeois intellectuals. Moreover if one should mention Marxism, God forbid, he might be taken for a dialectic materialist. It is better to avoid this discredited word. What to replace it with? Why, of course, with "science," even with Science capitalized. And science, as everybody knows, is based on "criticism" and "experiments." It has its own ring; so solid, so tolerant, so unsectarian, so professorial! With this formula one can enter any democratic salon.

Reread, please, your own statement once again: "In place of

conservative politics, we must put bold, flexible, critical, and experimental politics—in a word, scientific politics." You couldn't have improved it! But this is precisely the formula which all petty-bourgeois empiricists, all revisionists and, last but not least, all political adventurers have counterpoised to "narrow," "limited," "dogmatic," and "conservative" Marxism.

Buffon once said: The style is the man. Political terminology is not only the man but the party. Terminology is one of the elements of the class struggle. Only lifeless pedants can fail to understand this. In your document you painstakingly expunge—yes, no one else but you, Comrade Burnham—not only such terms as the dialectic and materialism but also Marxism. You are above all this. You are a man of "critical," "experimental" science. For exactly the same reason you culled the label "imperialism" to describe the foreign policy of the Kremlin. This innovation differentiates you from the too-embarrassing terminology of the Fourth International by creating less "sectarian," less "religious," less rigorous formulas, common to you and—oh happy coincidence—bourgeois democracy.

You want to experiment? But permit me to remind you that the workers' movement possesses a long history with no lack of experience and, if you prefer, experiments. This experience so dearly bought has been crystallized in the shape of a definite doctrine, the very Marxism whose name you so carefully avoid. Before giving you the right to experiment, the party has the right to ask: What method will you use? Henry Ford would scarcely permit a man to experiment in his plant who had not assimilated the requisite conclusions of the past development of industry and the innumerable experiments already carried out. Furthermore, experimental laboratories in factories are carefully segregated from mass production. Far more impermissible even are witch doctor experiments in the sphere of the labor movement—even though conducted under the banner of anonymous "science." For us the science of the workers' movement is Marxism. Nameless social science, Science with a capital letter, we leave these completely at the disposal of Eastman and his ilk.

I know that you have engaged in disputes with Eastman and in some questions you have argued very well. But you debate with him as a representative of your own circle and not as an agent of the class enemy. You revealed this conspicuously in your joint article with Shachtman when you ended up with the unexpected invitation to Eastman, Hook, Lyons, and the rest that they take advantage of the pages of the *New International* to promulgate their views. It did not even concern you that they might pose the question of the dialectic and thus drive you out of your diplomatic silence.

On January 20 of last year, hence, long prior to this discussion, in a letter to Comrade Shachtman, I insisted on the urgent necessity of attentively following the internal developments of the Stalinist party. I wrote:

"It would be a thousand times more important than inviting Eastman, Lyons, and the others to present their personal sweatings. I was wondering a bit why you gave space to Eastman's last insignificant and arrogant article; he has at his disposal *Harper's Magazine*, *Modern Monthly*, *Common Sense*, etc. But I am absolutely perplexed that you personally *invited* these people to besmirch the not-so-numerous pages of the *New International*. The perpetuation of this polemic can interest some *petty-bourgeois intellectuals* but not the revolutionary elements. It is my firm conviction that a certain reorganization of the *New International* and the *Socialist Appeal* is necessary: more distance from Eastman, Lyons, etc.; and nearer to the workers and, in this sense, to the Stalinist party."

As always in such cases, Shachtman replied inattentively and carelessly. In actuality, the question was resolved by the fact that the enemies of Marxism whom you invited refused to accept your invitation. This episode, however, deserves closer attention. On the one hand, you, Comrade Burnham, bolstered by Shachtman, invite bourgeois democrats to send in friendly explanations to be printed in the pages of our party organ. On the other hand, you, bolstered by this same Shachtman, refuse to engage in a debate with me over the dialectic and the class nature of the Soviet state. Doesn't this signify that you, together with your ally Shachtman, have turned your faces somewhat toward the bourgeois semi-opponents and your backs toward your own party? Abern long ago came to the conclusion that Marxism is a doctrine to be honored but a good oppositional combination is something far more substantial. Meanwhile, Shachtman slips and slides downward, consoling himself with wisecracks. I feel, however, that his heart is a trifle heavy. Upon reaching a certain point, Shachtman will, I hope, pull himself together and begin the upward climb again. Here is the hope that his "experimental" factional politics will at least turn out to the profit of "Science."

"An unconscious dialectician"

Using as his text my remark concerning Darwin, Shachtman has stated, I have been informed, that you are an "unconscious dialectician." This ambiguous compliment contains an iota of truth. Every individual is a dialectician *to some extent or other*, in most cases, unconsciously. A housewife knows that a certain amount of salt flavors soup agreeably but that added salt makes the soup unpalatable. Consequently, an illiterate peasant woman guides herself in cooking soup by the Hegelian law of the transformation of quantity into quality. Similar examples from daily life could be cited without end. Even animals arrive at their practical conclusions not only on the basis of the Aristotelian syllogism but also on the basis of the Hegelian dialectic. Thus, a fox is aware that quadrupeds and birds are nutritious and tasty. On sighting a hare, a rabbit, or a hen, a fox concludes: this particular creature belongs to the tasty and nutritive type, and—chases after the prey. We have here a complete syllogism, although the fox, we may suppose, never read Aristotle. When the same fox, however, encounters the first animal which exceeds it in size, for example, a wolf, it quickly concludes that quantity passes into quality, and turns to flee. Clearly, the legs of a fox are equipped with Hegelian tendencies, even if not fully conscious ones. All this demonstrates, in passing, that our methods of thought, both formal logic and the dialectic, are not arbitrary constructions of our reason, but rather, expressions of the actual interrelationships in nature itself. In this sense, the universe throughout is permeated with "unconscious" dialectics. But nature did not stop there. No little development occurred before nature's inner relationships were converted into the language of the consciousness of foxes and men, and man was then enabled to generalize these forms of consciousness and transform them into logical (dialectical) categories, thus creating the possibility for probing more deeply into the world about us.

The most finished expression to date of the laws of the dialectic which prevail in nature and in society has been given by Hegel and Marx. Despite the fact that Darwin was not interested in verifying his logical methods, his empiricism—that of a genius—in the sphere of natural science reached the highest dialectic generalizations. In this sense, Darwin was, as I stated in my previous article, an "unconscious dialectician." We do not, however, value Darwin for his inability to rise to the dialectic, but for having, despite his philosophical backwardness, explained to us the origin of species. Engels was, it might be pointed out, exasperated by the narrow empiricism of the Darwinian method, although he, like Marx, immediately appreciated the greatness of the theory of natural selection. Darwin, on the contrary, remained, alas, ignorant of the meaning of Marx's sociology to the end of his life. Had Darwin come out in the press against the dialectic or materialism, Marx and Engels would have attacked him with redoubled force so as not to allow his authority to cloak ideological reaction.

In the attorney's plea of Shachtman to the effect that you are an "unconscious dialectician," the stress must be laid on the word *unconscious*. Shachtman's aim (also partly unconscious) is to defend his bloc with you by degrading dialectic materialism. For in reality, Shachtman is saying: The difference between a "conscious" and an "unconscious" dialectician is not so great that one must quarrel about it. Shachtman thus attempts to discredit the Marxist method.

But the evil goes beyond even this. Very many unconscious or semi-unconscious dialecticians exist in this world. Some of them apply the materialist dialectic excellently to politics, even though they have never concerned themselves with questions of method. It would obviously be pedantic blockheadedness to attack such comrades. But it is otherwise with you, Comrade Burnham. You are an editor of the theoretical organ whose task it is to educate the party in the spirit of the Marxist method. Yet you are a *conscious opponent of the dialectic and not at all an unconscious dialectician*. Even if you had, as Shachtman insists, successfully followed the dialectic in political questions, i.e., even if you were endowed with a dialectic "instinct," we would still be compelled to begin a struggle against you, because your dialectic instinct, like other individual qualities, cannot be transmitted to others, whereas the conscious dialectic method can, to one degree or another, be made accessible to the entire party.

The dialectic and Mr. Dies[1]

Even if you have a dialectic instinct—and I do not undertake to judge this—it is well-nigh stifled by academic routine and intellectual hauteur.

---

1 The Dies Committee, the precursor to the House Committee on Un-American Activities, set up by Congressman Martin Dies. In October 1939, it invited Trotsky to give public testimony on Stalinism. Trotsky accepted the invitation, which he viewed as an opportunity to educate a broad audience on the history of the Russian Revolution and the rise of Stalinism, much as he had previously used his trials as political platforms, despite having no illusions in tsarist "justice." In the end, his visa to the US fell through and he never gave his testimony.

What we term the class instinct of the worker, accepts with relative ease the dialectic approach to questions. There can be no talk of such a class instinct in a bourgeois intellectual. Only by *consciously* surmounting his petty-bourgeois spirit can an intellectual divorced from the proletariat rise to Marxist politics. Unfortunately, Shachtman and Abern are doing everything in their power to bar this road to you. By their support they render you a very bad service, Comrade Burnham.

Bolstered by your bloc, which might be designated as the "League of Factional Abandon," you commit one blunder after another: in philosophy, in sociology, in politics, in the organizational sphere. Your errors are not accidental. You approach each question by isolating it, by splitting it away from its connection with other questions, away from its connection with social factors, and, independently of international experience. You lack the dialectic method. Despite all your education, in politics you proceed like a witch doctor.

In the question of the Dies Committee your mumbo jumbo manifested itself no less glaringly than in the question of Finland. To my arguments in favor of utilizing this parliamentary body, you replied that the question should be decided not by principled considerations but by some special circumstances known to you alone but which you refrained from specifying. Permit me to tell you what these circumstances were: your ideological dependence on bourgeois public opinion. Although bourgeois democracy, in all its sections, bears full responsibility for the capitalist regime, including the Dies Committee, it is compelled, in the interests of this very same capitalism, shamefacedly to distract attention away from the too-naked organs of the regime. A simple division of labor! An old fraud which still continues, however, to operate effectively! As for the workers, to whom you refer vaguely, a section of them, and a very considerable section, is like yourself under the influence of bourgeois democracy. But the average worker, not infected with the prejudices of the labor aristocracy, would joyfully welcome every bold revolutionary word thrown in the very face of the class enemy. And the more reactionary the institution which serves as the arena for the combat, all the more complete is the satisfaction of the worker. This has been proved by historical experience. Dies himself, becoming frightened and jumping back in time, demonstrated how false your position was. It is always better to compel the enemy to retreat than to hide oneself without a battle.

But at this point I see the irate figure of Shachtman rising to stop me with a gesture of protest: "The opposition bears no responsibility for Burnham's views on the Dies Committee. This question did not assume a factional character," and so forth and so on. I know all this. As if the only thing that lacked was for the entire opposition to express itself in favor of the tactic of boycott, so utterly senseless in this instance! It is sufficient that the leader of the opposition, who has views and openly expressed them, came out in favor of boycott. If you happened to have outgrown the age when one argues about "religion," then, let me confess, I had considered that the entire Fourth International had outgrown the age when abstentionism is accounted the most revolutionary of policies. Aside from your lack of method, you revealed in this instance an obvious lack of political sagacity. In the given situation, a revolutionist would not have needed to discuss long before springing through a door flung open by the enemy and making the most of the opportunity. For those members of the opposition who together with you spoke against participation in the Dies Committee—and their number is not so small—it is necessary in my opinion to arrange special elementary courses in order to explain to them the elementary truths of revolutionary tactics which have nothing in common with the pseudo-radical abstentionism of the intellectual circles.

"Concrete political questions"

The opposition is weakest precisely in the sphere where it imagines itself especially strong—the sphere of day-to-day revolutionary politics. This applies above all to you, Comrade Burnham. Impotence in the face of great events manifested itself in you as well as in the entire opposition most glaringly in the questions of Poland, the Baltic states, and Finland. Shachtman began by discovering a philosopher's stone: the achievement of a simultaneous insurrection against Hitler and Stalin in occupied Poland. The idea was splendid; it is only too bad that Shachtman was deprived of the opportunity of putting it into practice. The advanced workers in eastern Poland could justifiably say: "A simultaneous insurrection against Hitler and Stalin in a country occupied by troops might perhaps be arranged very conveniently from the Bronx; but here, locally, it is more difficult. We should like to hear Burnham's and Shachtman's answer to a 'concrete political question': What shall we do between now and the coming insurrection?" In the meantime, the commanding staff of the Soviet army called upon the peasants and workers to seize the land and the factories. This call, supported by armed force, played an enormous role in the life of the occupied country. Moscow papers were filled to overflowing with reports of the boundless "enthusiasm" of workers and poor peasants. We should and must approach these reports with justifiable distrust—there is no lack of lies. But it is nevertheless impermissible to close one's eyes to facts. The call to settle accounts with the landlords and to drive out the capitalists could not have failed to rouse the spirit of the hounded and crushed Ukrainian and Belarusian peasants and workers who saw in the Polish landlord a double enemy.

In the Parisian organ of the Mensheviks, who are in solidarity with the bourgeois democracy of France and not the Fourth International, it was stated categorically that the advance of the Red Army was accompanied by a wave of revolutionary upsurge, echoes of which penetrated even the peasant masses of Romania. What adds special weight to the dispatches of this organ is the close connection with the Mensheviks and the leaders of the Jewish Bund, the Polish Socialist Party, and other organizations who are hostile to the Kremlin and who fled from Poland. We were therefore completely correct when we said to the Bolsheviks in eastern Poland:

> Together with the workers and peasants, and in the forefront, you must conduct a struggle against the landlords and the capitalists; do not tear yourself away from the masses, despite all their illusions, just as the Russian revolutionists did not tear themselves away from the masses who had not yet freed themselves from their hopes in the tsar (Bloody Sunday, January 22, 1905); educate the masses in the course of the struggle, warn them against naïve hopes in Moscow, but do not tear yourself away from them, fight in their camp, try to extend and deepen their struggle, and to give it the greatest possible independence. Only in this way will you prepare the coming insurrection against Stalin.

The course of events in Poland has completely confirmed this directive, which was a continuation and a development of all our previous policies, particularly in Spain.

Since there is no principled difference between the Polish and Finnish situations, we can have no grounds for changing our directive. But the opposition, who failed to understand the meaning of the Polish events, now tries to clutch at Finland as a new anchor of salvation. "Where is the civil war in Finland? Trotsky talks of a civil war. We have seen nothing about it in the press," and so on. The question of Finland appears to the opposition as in principle different from the question of western Ukraine and Belarus. Each question is isolated and viewed aside and apart from the general course of development. Confounded by the course of events, the opposition seeks each time to support itself on some accidental, secondary, temporary, and conjunctural circumstances.

Do these cries about the absence of civil war in Finland signify that the opposition would adopt our policy if civil war were actually to unfold in Finland? Yes or no? If yes, then the opposition thereby condemns its own policy in relation to Poland, since there, despite the civil war, they limited themselves to refusal to participate in the events, while they waited for a simultaneous uprising against Stalin and Hitler. It is obvious, Comrade Burnham, that you and your allies have not thought this question through to the end.

What about my assertion concerning a civil war in Finland? At the very inception of military hostilities, one might have conjectured that Moscow was seeking through a "small" punitive expedition to bring about a change of government in Helsingfors and to establish the same relations with Finland as with the other Baltic states. But the appointment of the Kuusinen government in Terijoki demonstrated that Moscow had other plans and aims. Dispatches then reported the creation of a Finnish "Red Army." Naturally, it was only a question of small formations set up from above. The program of Kuusinen was issued. Next the dispatches appeared of the division of large estates among poor peasants. In their totality, these dispatches signified an attempt on the part of Moscow to organize a civil war. Naturally, this is a civil war of a special type. It does not arise spontaneously from the depths of the popular masses. It is not conducted under the leadership of the Finnish revolutionary party based on mass support. It is introduced on bayonets from without. It is controlled by the Moscow bureaucracy. All this we know, and we dealt with all this in discussing Poland. Nevertheless, it is precisely a question of civil war, of an appeal to the lowly, to the poor, a call to them to expropriate the rich, drive them out, arrest them, etc. I know of no other name for these actions except civil war.

"But, after all, the civil war in Finland did not unfold," object the leaders of the opposition. "This means that your predictions did not materialize." With the defeat and the retreat of the Red Army, I reply, the civil war in Finland cannot, of course, unfold under the bayonets of Mannerheim. This fact is an argument not against me but against Shachtman; since it demonstrates that in the first stages of war, at a time when discipline in armies is still strong, it is much easier to organize insurrection, and on two fronts to boot, from the Bronx than from Terijoki.

We did not foresee the defeats of the first detachments of the Red Army. We could not have foreseen the extent to which stupidity and demoralization reign in the Kremlin and in the tops of the army beheaded by the Kremlin. Nevertheless, what is involved is only a military episode, which cannot determine our political line. Should Moscow, after its first unsuccessful attempt, refrain entirely from any further offensive against Finland, then the very question which today obscures the entire world situation to the eyes of the opposition would be removed from the order of the day. But there is little chance for this. On the other hand, if England, France, and the United States, basing themselves on Scandinavia, were to aid Finland with military force, then the Finnish question would be submerged in a war between the USSR and the imperialist countries. In this case, we must assume that even a majority of the oppositionists would remind themselves of the program of the Fourth International.

At the present time, however, the opposition is not interested in these two variants: either the suspension of the offensive on the part of the USSR, or the outbreak of hostilities between the USSR and the imperialist democracies. The opposition is interested only in the isolated question of the USSR's invasion of Finland. Very well, let us take this as our starting point. If the second offensive, as may be assumed, is better prepared and conducted, then the advance of the Red Army into the country will again place the question of civil war on the order of the day, and moreover, on a much broader scale than during the first and ignominiously unsuccessful attempt. Our directive, consequently, remains completely valid so long as the question itself remains on the agenda. But what does the opposition propose in the event the Red Army successfully advances into Finland and civil war unfolds there? The opposition apparently doesn't think about this at all, for they live from one day to the next, from one incident to another, clutching at episodes, clinging to isolated phrases in an editorial, feeding on sympathies and antipathies, and thus creating for themselves the semblance of a platform. The weakness of empiricists and impressionists is always revealed most glaringly in their approach to "concrete political questions."

Theoretical bewilderment and political abstentionism

Throughout all the vacillations and convulsions of the opposition, contradictory though they may be, two general features run like a guiding thread from the pinnacles of theory down to the most trifling political episodes. The first general feature is the absence of a unified conception. The opposition leaders split sociology from dialectic materialism. They split politics from sociology. In the sphere of politics they split our tasks in Poland from our experience in Spain—our tasks in Finland from our position on Poland. History becomes transformed into a series of exceptional incidents; politics becomes transformed into a series of improvisations. We have here, in the full sense of the term, the disintegration of Marxism, the disintegration of theoretical thought, the disintegration of politics into its constituent elements. Empiricism and its foster brother, impressionism, dominate from top to bottom. That is why the ideological leadership, Comrade Burnham, rests with you as an opponent of the dialectic, as an empiricist, unabashed by his empiricism.

Throughout the vacillations and convulsions of the opposition, there is a second general feature intimately bound to the first, namely, a tendency to refrain from active participation, a tendency to self-elimination, to abstentionism, naturally under cover of ultraradical phrases. You are in favor of overthrowing Hitler and Stalin in Poland; Stalin and Mannerheim in Finland. And until then, you reject both sides *equally*, in other words, you withdraw from the struggle, including the civil war. Your citing the absence of civil war in Finland is only an accidental conjunctural argument. Should the civil war unfold, the opposition will attempt not to notice it, as they tried not to notice it in Poland, or they will declare that inasmuch as the policy of the Moscow bureaucracy is "imperialist" in character "we" do not take part in this filthy business. Hot on the trail of "concrete" political tasks in words, the opposition actually places itself outside the historical process. Your position, Comrade Burnham, in relation to the Dies Committee merits attention precisely because it is a graphic expression of this same tendency of abstentionism and bewilderment. Your guiding principle still remains the same: "Thank you, I don't smoke."

Naturally, any man, any party, and even any class can become bewildered. But with the petty bourgeoisie, bewilderment, especially in the face of great events, is an inescapable and, so to speak, congenital condition. The intellectuals attempt to express their state of bewilderment in the language of "science." The contradictory platform of the opposition reflects petty-bourgeois bewilderment expressed in the bombastic language of the intellectuals. There is nothing proletarian about it.

The petty bourgeoisie and centralism

In the organizational sphere, your views are just as schematic, empiric, and nonrevolutionary as in the sphere of theory and politics. A Stolberg[2], lantern in hand, chases after an ideal revolution, unaccompanied by any excesses, and guaranteed against Thermidor and counterrevolution; you, likewise, seek an ideal party democracy which would secure forever and for everybody the possibility of saying and doing whatever popped into his head, and which would insure the party against bureaucratic degeneration. You overlook a trifle, namely, that the party is not an arena for the assertion of free individuality, but an instrument of the proletarian revolution; that only a victorious revolution is capable of preventing the degeneration not only of the party but of the proletariat itself and of modern civilization as a whole. You do not see that our American section is not sick from too much centralism—it is laughable even to talk about it—but from a monstrous abuse and distortion of democracy on the part of petty-bourgeois elements. This is at the root of the present crisis.

A worker spends his day at the factory. He has comparatively few hours left for the party. At the meetings he is interested in learning the most important things: the correct evaluation of the situation and the political conclusions. He values those leaders who do this in the clearest and the most precise form and who keep in step with events. Petty-bourgeois, and especially declassed elements, divorced from the proletariat, vegetate in an artificial and shut-in environment. They have ample time to dabble in politics or its substitute. They pick out faults, exchange all sorts of tidbits and gossip concerning happenings among the party "tops." They always locate a leader who initiates them into all the "secrets." Discussion is their native element. No amount of democracy is ever enough for them. For their war of words they seek the fourth dimension. They become jittery, they revolve in a vicious circle, and they quench their thirst with salt water. Do you want to know the organizational program of the opposition? It consists of a mad hunt for the fourth dimension of party democracy.

---

2 Benjamin Stolberg, a liberal American author and journalist, who served as a member of the Commission of Inquiry on Leon Trotsky investigating the Moscow trials.

In practice this means burying politics beneath discussion; and burying centralism beneath the anarchy of the intellectual circles. When a few thousand workers join the party, they will call the petty-bourgeois anarchists severely to order. The sooner, the better.

Conclusions

Why do I address you and not the other leaders of the opposition? Because you are the ideological leader of the bloc. Comrade Abern's faction, destitute of a program and a banner, is ever in need of cover. At one time Shachtman served as cover, then came Muste with Spector, and now you, with Shachtman adapting himself to you. Your ideology I consider the expression of bourgeois influence in the proletariat.

To some comrades, the tone of this letter may perhaps seem too sharp. Yet, let me confess, I did everything in my power to restrain myself. For, after all, it is a question of nothing more or less than an attempt to reject, disqualify and overthrow the theoretical foundations, the political principles, and organizational methods of our movement.

In reaction to my previous article, Comrade Abern, it has been reported, remarked: "This means split." Such a response merely demonstrates that Abern lacks devotion to the party and the Fourth International; he is a circle man. In any case, threats of split will not deter us from presenting a Marxist analysis of the differences. For us Marxists, it is a question not of split but of educating the party. It is my firm hope that the coming convention will ruthlessly repulse the revisionists.

The convention, in my opinion, must declare categorically that in their attempts to divorce sociology from dialectic materialism and politics from sociology, the leaders of the opposition have broken from Marxism and become the transmitting mechanism for petty-bourgeois empiricism. While reaffirming, decisively and completely, its loyalty to the Marxist doctrine and the political and organizational methods of Bolshevism, while binding the editorial boards of its official publications to promulgate and defend this doctrine and these methods, the party will, of course, extend the pages of its publications in the future to those of its members who consider themselves capable of adding something new to the doctrine of Marxism. But it will not permit a game of hide-and-seek with Marxism and light-minded gibes concerning it.

The politics of a party has a class character. Without a class analysis of the state, the parties and ideological tendencies, it is impossible to arrive at a correct political orientation. The party must condemn as vulgar opportunism the attempt to determine policies in relation to the USSR from incident to incident and independently of the class nature of the Soviet state.

The disintegration of capitalism, which engenders sharp dissatisfaction among the petty bourgeoisie and drives its bottom layers to the left, opens up broad possibilities but it also contains grave dangers. The Fourth International needs only those emigrants from the petty bourgeoisie who have broken completely with their social past and who have come over decisively to the standpoint of the proletariat.

This theoretical and political transit must be accompanied by an actual break with the old environment and the establishment of intimate ties with workers, in particular, by participation in the recruitment and education of proletarians for their party. Emigrants from the petty-bourgeois milieu who prove incapable of settling in the proletarian milieu must after the lapse of a certain period of time be transferred from membership in the party to the status of sympathizers.

Members of the party untested in the class struggle must not be placed in responsible positions. No matter how talented and devoted to socialism an emigrant from the bourgeois milieu may be, before becoming a teacher, he must first go to school in the working class. Young intellectuals must not be placed at the head of the intellectual youth but sent out into the provinces for a few years, into the purely proletarian centers, for hard practical work.

The class composition of the party must correspond to its class program. The American section of the Fourth International will either become proletarian or it will cease to exist.

Comrade Burnham! If we can arrive at an agreement with you on the basis of these principles, then without difficulty we shall find a correct policy in relation to Poland, Finland, and even India. At the same time, I pledge myself to help you conduct a struggle against any manifestations whatsoever of bureaucratism and conservatism. These in my opinion are the conditions necessary to end the present crisis.

With Bolshevik greetings,
L. TROTSKY

Coyoacán, D.F.

* * *

A Letter to James P. Cannon
(January 9, 1940)

Dear Friend,

Yesterday I sent the Russian text of my new article written in the form of a letter to Burnham. Not all comrades possibly are content with the fact that I give the predominant place in the discussion to the matter of dialectics. But I am sure it is now the only way to begin the theoretical education of the Party, especially of the youth and to inject a reversion to empiricism and eclectics.

W. RORK [Leon Trotsky]

* * *

A Letter to Joseph Hansen
(January 18, 1940)

Dear Joe,

My article against Shachtman is already written. I need now to polish it for two days, and I will try to use some of your quotations. But I wish to speak here about another more important question. Some of the leaders of the opposition are preparing a split; whereby they represent the opposition in the future as a persecuted minority. It is very characteristic of their state of mind. I believe we must answer them approximately as follows:

"You are already afraid of our future repressions? We propose to you mutual guarantees for the future minority, independently of who might be this minority, you or we. These guarantees could be formulated in four points: 1) No prohibition of factions; 2) No other restrictions on factional activity than those dictated by the necessity for common action; 3) The official publications must represent, of course, the line established by the new convention; 4) The future minority can have, if it wishes, an internal bulletin destined for party members, or a common discussion bulletin with the majority."

The continuation of discussion bulletins immediately after a long discussion and a convention is, of course, not a rule but an exception, a rather deplorable one. But we are not bureaucrats at all. We don't have immutable rules. We are dialecticians also in the organizational field. If we have in the party an important minority which is dissatisfied with the decisions of the convention, it is incomparably more preferable to legalize the discussion after the convention than to have a split.

We can go, if necessary, even further and propose to them to publish, under the supervision of the new National Committee, special discussion symposiums, not only for party members, but for the public in general. We should go as far as possible in this respect in order to disarm their at least premature complaints and handicap them in provoking a split.

For my part I believe that the prolongation of the discussion, if it is channelized by the good will of both sides, can only serve in the present conditions the education of the party. I believe that the majority should make these propositions officially in the National Committee in a written form. Whatever might be their answer, the party could only win.

With best greetings,
CORNELL [Leon Trotsky]

Coyoacán, D.F.

* * *

From a Scratch—To the Danger of Gangrene
(January 1940)

The discussion is developing in accordance with its own internal logic. Each camp, corresponding to its social character and political physiognomy, seeks to strike at those points where its opponent is weakest and most vulnerable. It is precisely this that determines the course of the discussion and not *a priori* plans of the leaders of the opposition. It is belated and sterile to lament now over the flaring up of the discussion. It is necessary only to keep a sharp eye on the role played by Stalinist provocateurs who are unquestionably in the party and who are under orders to poison the atmosphere of the discussion and to head the ideological struggle toward split. It is not so very difficult to recognize these gentlemen; their zeal is excessive and, of course, artificial; they replace ideas and arguments with gossip and slander. They must be exposed and thrown out through the joint efforts of both factions. But the principled struggle must be carried through to the end, that is, to serious clarification of the more important questions that have been posed. It is necessary to so utilize the discussion that it raises the theoretical level of the party.

A considerable proportion of the membership of the American section as well as our entire young International, came to us either from the Comintern in its period of decline or from the Second International. These are bad schools. The discussion has revealed that wide circles of the party lack a sound theoretical education. It is sufficient, for instance, to refer to the circumstance that the New York local of the party did not respond with a vigorous defensive reflex to the attempts at light-minded revision of Marxist doctrine and program but on the contrary, gave support in the majority to the revisionists. This is unfortunate but remediable to the degree that our American section and the entire International consist of honest individuals sincerely seeking their way to the revolutionary road. They have the desire and the will to learn. But there is no time to lose. It is precisely the party's penetration into the trade unions, and into the workers' milieu in general that demands heightening the theoretical qualification of our cadres. I do not mean by cadres the "apparatus" but the party as a whole. Every party member should and must consider himself an officer in the proletarian army.

"Since when have you become specialists in the question of philosophy?" the oppositionists now ironically ask the majority representatives. Irony here is completely out of place. Scientific socialism is the conscious expression of the unconscious historical process; namely, the instinctive and elemental drive of the proletariat to reconstruct society on communist beginnings. These organic tendencies in the psychology of workers spring to life with utmost rapidity today in the epoch of crises and wars. The discussion has revealed beyond all question a clash in the party between a petty-bourgeois tendency and a proletarian tendency. The petty-bourgeois tendency reveals its confusion in its attempt to reduce the program of the party to the small coin of "concrete" questions. The proletarian tendency, on the contrary, strives to correlate all the partial questions into theoretical unity. At stake at the present time is not the extent to which individual members of the majority consciously apply the dialectic method. What is important is the fact that the majority as a whole pushes toward the proletarian posing of the questions and by very reason of this tends to assimilate the dialectic, which is the "algebra of the revolution." The oppositionists, I am informed, greet with bursts of laughter the very mention of "dialectics." In vain. This unworthy method will not help. The dialectic of the historic process has more than once cruelly punished those who tried to jeer at it.

Comrade Shachtman's latest article, "An Open Letter to Leon Trotsky," is an alarming symptom. It reveals that Shachtman refuses to learn from the discussion and persists instead in deepening his mistakes, exploiting thereby not only the inadequate theoretical level of the party but also the specific prejudices of its petty-bourgeois wing. Everybody is aware of the facility with which Shachtman is able to weave various historical episodes around one or another axis. This ability makes Shachtman a talented journalist. Unfortunately, this by itself is not enough. The main question is what axis to select. Shachtman is absorbed always by the reflection of politics in literature and in the press. He lacks interest in the actual processes of the class struggle, the life of the masses, the interrelationships between the different layers within the working class itself, etc. I have read not a few excellent and even brilliant articles by Shachtman but I have never seen a single commentary of his which actually probed into the life of the American working class or its vanguard.

A qualification must be made to this extent—that not only Shachtman's personal failing is embodied therein, but the fate of a whole revolutionary generation which, because of a special conjuncture of historical conditions, grew up outside the labor movement. More than once in the past I have had occasion to speak and write about the danger of these valuable elements degenerating *despite* their devotion to the revolution. What was an inescapable characteristic of adolescence in its day has become a weakness. Weakness invites disease. If neglected, the disease can become fatal. To escape this danger it is necessary to open a new chapter consciously in the development of the party. The propagandists and journalists of the Fourth International must begin a new chapter in their own consciousness. It is necessary to rearm. It is necessary to make an about-face on one's own axis: to turn one's back to the petty-bourgeois intellectuals, and to face toward the workers.

To view as the cause of the present party crisis—the conservatism of its worker section; to seek a solution to the crisis through the victory of the petty-bourgeois bloc—it would be difficult to conceive a mistake more dangerous to the party. As a matter of fact, the gist of the present crisis consists in the conservatism of the petty-bourgeois elements who have passed through a purely propagandistic school and who have not yet found a pathway to the road of class struggle. The present crisis is the final battle of these elements for self-preservation. Every oppositionist as an individual can, if he firmly desires, find a worthy place for himself in the revolutionary movement. As a faction they are doomed. In the struggle that is developing, Shachtman is not in the camp where he ought to be. As always in such cases, his strong sides have receded into the background, while his weak traits, on the other hand, have assumed an especially finished expression. His "Open Letter" represents, so to speak, a crystallization of his weak traits.

Shachtman has left out a trifle: his class position. Hence his extraordinary zigzags, his improvisations, and leaps. He replaces class analysis with disconnected historical anecdotes for the sole purpose of covering up his own shift, for camouflaging the contradiction between his yesterday and today. This is Shachtman's procedure with the history of Marxism, the history of his own party, and the history of the Russian Opposition. In carrying this out, he heaps mistakes upon mistakes. All the historical analogies to which he resorts, speak, as we shall see, against him.

It is much more difficult to correct mistakes than to commit them. I must ask patience from the reader in following with me step by step all the zigzags of Shachtman's mental operations. For my part I promise not to confine myself merely to exposing mistakes and contradictions, but to counterpose from beginning to end the proletarian position against the petty-bourgeois, the Marxist position against the eclectic. In this way, all of us, perhaps, may learn something from the discussion.

. . .

The philosophic bloc against Marxism

The opposition circles consider it possible to assert that the question of dialectic materialism was introduced by me only because I lacked an answer to the "concrete" questions of Finland, Latvia, India, Afghanistan, Baluchistan, and so on. This argument, void of all merit in itself, is of interest, however, in that it characterizes the level of certain individuals in the opposition, their attitude toward theory and toward elementary ideological loyalty. It would not be amiss, therefore, to refer to the fact that my first serious conversation with Comrades Shachtman and Warde [George Novack], in the train immediately after my arrival in Mexico in January 1937, was devoted to the necessity of persistently propagating dialectic materialism. After our American section split from the Socialist Party I insisted most strongly on the earliest possible publication of a theoretical organ, having again in mind the need to educate the party, first and foremost its new members, in the spirit of dialectic materialism. In the United States, I wrote at that time, where the bourgeoisie systematically instills vulgar empiricism in the workers, more than anywhere else, is it necessary to speed the elevation of the movement to a proper theoretical level. On January 20, 1939, I wrote to Comrade Shachtman concerning his joint article with Comrade Burnham, "Intellectuals in Retreat":

> The section on the dialectic is the greatest blow that you, personally, as the editor of the *New International* could have delivered to Marxist theory . . . Good! We will speak about it publicly.

Thus, a year ago I gave open notice in advance to Shachtman that I intended to wage a public struggle against his eclectic tendencies. At that time there was no talk whatever of the coming opposition; in any case, furthest from my mind was the supposition that the philosophic bloc against Marxism prepared the ground for a political bloc against the program of the Fourth International.

The character of the differences which have risen to the surface has only confirmed my former fears both in regard to the social composition of the party and in regard to the theoretical education of the cadres. There was nothing that required a change of mind or "artificial" introduction. This is how matters stand in actuality. Let me also add that I feel somewhat abashed over the fact that it is almost necessary to justify coming out in defense of Marxism within one of the sections of the Fourth International

In his "Open Letter," Shachtman refers particularly to the fact that comrade Vincent Dunne expressed satisfaction over the article on the intellectuals. But I too praised it: "Many parts are excellent." However, as the Russian proverb puts it, a spoonful of tar can spoil a barrel of honey. It is precisely this spoonful of tar that is involved. The section devoted to dialectic materialism expresses a number of conceptions monstrous from the Marxist standpoint, whose aim, it is now clear, was to prepare the ground for a political bloc. In view of the stubbornness with which Shachtman persists that I seized upon the article as a pretext, let me once again quote the central passage in the section of interest to us:

> . . . nor has anyone yet demonstrated that agreement or disagreement on the more abstract doctrines of dialectic materialism necessarily affects (!) today's and tomorrow's concrete political issues—and political parties, programs, and struggles are based on such concrete issues.

Isn't this alone sufficient? What is above all astonishing is this formula, unworthy of revolutionists: ". . . political parties, programs, and struggles are based on such concrete issues." What parties? What programs? What struggles? All parties and all programs are here lumped together. The party of the proletariat is a party unlike all the rest. It is not at all based upon "such concrete issues." In its very foundation it is diametrically opposed to the parties of bourgeois horse traders and petty-bourgeois rag patchers. Its task is the preparation of a social revolution and the regeneration of mankind on new material and moral foundations. In order not to give way under the pressure of bourgeois public opinion and police repression, the proletarian revolutionist, a leader all the more, requires a clear, farsighted, completely thought-out world outlook. Only upon the basis of a unified Marxist conception is it possible to correctly approach "concrete" questions.

Precisely here begins Shachtman's betrayal—not a mere mistake as I wished to believe last year—but, it is now clear, an outright theoretical betrayal. Following in the footsteps of Burnham, Shachtman teaches the young revolutionary party that "no one has yet demonstrated" presumably that dialectic materialism affects the political activity of the party. "No one has yet demonstrated," in other words, that Marxism is of any use in the struggle of the proletariat. The party consequently does not have the least motive for acquiring and defending dialectic materialism. This is nothing else than the renunciation of Marxism, of the scientific method in general, a wretched capitulation to empiricism. Precisely this constitutes the philosophic bloc of Shachtman with Burnham and through Burnham with the priests of bourgeois "Science." It is precisely this and only this to which I referred in my January 20 letter of last year. On March 5, Shachtman replied:

> I have reread the January article of Burnham and Shachtman to which you referred, and while in the light of which you have written I might

have proposed a different formulation here (!) and there (!) if the article were to be done over again, I cannot agree with the substance of your criticism.

This reply, as is always the case with Shachtman in a serious situation, in reality expresses nothing whatsoever; but it still gives the impression that Shachtman has left a bridge open for retreat. Today, seized with factional frenzy, he promises to "do it again and again tomorrow." Do what? Capitulate to bourgeois "Science"? Renounce Marxism?

Shachtman explains at length to me (we shall see presently with what foundation) the utility of this or that *political bloc*. I am speaking about the deadliness of *theoretical betrayal*. A bloc can be justified or not depending upon its content and the circumstances. Theoretical betrayal cannot be justified by any bloc. Shachtman refers to the fact that his article is of a purely political character. I do not speak of the article but of that section which renounces Marxism. If a textbook on physics contained only two lines on God as the first cause it would be my right to conclude the author is an obscurantist.

Shachtman does not reply to the accusation but tries to distract attention by turning to irrelevant matters. "Wherein does what you call my 'bloc with Burnham in the sphere of philosophy' differ," he asks, "from Lenin's bloc with Bogdanov? Why was the latter principled and ours unprincipled? I should be very much interested to know the answer to this question." I shall deal presently with the political difference, or rather the political polar opposite between the two blocs. We are here interested in the question of Marxist method. Wherein is the difference you ask? In this, that Lenin never declaimed for Bogdanov's profit that dialectic materialism is superfluous in solving "concrete political questions." In this, that Lenin never theoretically confounded the Bolshevik Party with parties in general. He was organically incapable of uttering such abominations. And not he alone but not a single one of the serious Bolsheviks. That is the difference. Do you understand? Shachtman sarcastically promised me that he would be "interested" in a clear answer. The answer, I trust, has been given. I don't demand the "interest."

The abstract and the concrete; economics and politics

The most lamentable section of Shachtman's lamentable opus is the chapter, "The State and the Character of the War."

> What, then, is our position? Simply this: It is impossible to deduce *directly* our policy towards a *specific* war from an *abstract* characterization of the class character of the state involved in the war, more particularly, from the property forms prevailing in that state. Our policy must flow from a *concrete* examination of the character of the war in relation to the interests of the international socialist revolution (Trotsky's emphasis).

What a muddle! What a tangle of sophistry! If it is impossible to deduce our policy *directly* from the class character of a state, then why can't this be done *nondirectly*? Why must the analysis of the character of the state be abstract whereas the analysis of the character of the war is *concrete*? Formally speaking, one can say with equal, in fact with much more right, that our policy in relation to the USSR can be deduced not from an *abstract* characterization of war as "imperialist," but only from a *concrete* analysis of the character of the state in the given historical situation. The fundamental sophistry upon which Shachtman constructs everything else is simple enough: Inasmuch as the economic basis determines events in the superstructure not *immediately*; inasmuch as the mere class characterization of the state is *not enough* to solve the practical tasks, therefore ... therefore we can get along without examining economics and the class nature of the state; by replacing them, as Shachtman phrases it in his journalistic jargon, with the "realities of living events."

The very same artifice circulated by Shachtman to justify his philosophic bloc with Burnham—dialectical materialism determines our politics not immediately, consequently ... it does not *in general* affect the "concrete political tasks"—is repeated here word for word in relation to Marxist sociology: Inasmuch as property forms determine the policy of a state not immediately it is possible therefore to throw Marxist sociology overboard in general in determining "concrete political tasks."

But why stop there? Since the law of labor value determines prices not "directly" and not "immediately"; since the laws of natural selection determine not "directly" and not "immediately" the birth of a suckling pig; since the laws of gravity determine not "directly" and not "immediately" the tumble of a drunken policeman down a flight of stairs, therefore ... therefore let us leave Marx, Darwin, Newton, and all the other lovers of "abstractions" to collect dust on a shelf. This is nothing less than the solemn burial of science for, after all, the entire course of the development of science proceeds from "direct" and "immediate" causes to the more remote and profound ones, from multiple varieties and kaleidoscopic events—to the unity of the driving forces.

The law of labor value determines prices not "immediately," but it nevertheless does determine them. Such "concrete" phenomena as the bankruptcy of the New Deal find their explanation in the final analysis in the "abstract" law of value. Roosevelt does not know this, but a Marxist dare not proceed without knowing it. Not immediately but through a whole series of intermediate factors and their reciprocal interaction, property forms determine not only politics but also morality. A proletarian politician seeking to ignore the class nature of the state would invariably end up like the policeman who ignores the laws of gravitation; that is, by smashing his nose.

Shachtman obviously does not take into account the distinction between the abstract and the concrete. Striving toward concreteness, our mind operates with abstractions. Even "this," "given," "concrete" dog is an abstraction because it proceeds to change, for example, by dropping its tail the "moment" we point a finger at it. Concreteness is a relative concept and not an absolute one: what is concrete in one case turns out to be abstract in another: that is, insufficiently defined for a given purpose. In order to obtain a concept "concrete" enough *for a given need* it is necessary to correlate several abstractions into one—just as in reproducing a segment of life upon the screen, which is a picture in movement, it is necessary to combine a number of still photographs.

The concrete is a combination of abstractions—not an arbitrary or subjective combination but one that corresponds to the laws of the movement of a given phenomenon.

"The interests of the international socialist revolution," to which Shachtman appeals against the class nature of the state, represent in this given instance the vaguest of all abstractions. After all, the question which occupies us is precisely this, in what concrete way can we further the interests of the revolution? Nor would it be amiss to remember, too, that the task of the socialist revolution is to create a workers' state. Before talking about the socialist revolution it is necessary consequently to learn how to distinguish between such "abstractions" as the bourgeoisie and the proletariat, the capitalist state and the workers' state.

Shachtman indeed squanders his own time and that of others in proving that nationalized property does not determine "in and of itself," "automatically," "directly," "immediately" the policies of the Kremlin. On the question as to how the economic "base" determines the political, juridical, philosophical, artistic, and so on "superstructure" there exists a rich Marxist literature. The opinion that economics presumably determines directly and immediately the creativeness of a composer or even the verdict of a judge, represents a hoary caricature of Marxism which the bourgeois professordom of all countries has circulated time out of end to mask their intellectual impotence.

As for the question which immediately concerns us, the interrelationship between the social foundations of the Soviet state and the policy of the Kremlin, let me remind the absentminded Shachtman that for seventeen years we have already been establishing, publicly, the growing *contradiction* between the foundation laid down by the October Revolution and the tendencies of the state "superstructure." We have followed step by step the increasing independence of the bureaucracy from the Soviet proletariat and the growth of its dependence upon other classes and groups both inside and outside the country. Just what does Shachtman wish to add in this sphere to the analysis already made?

However, although economics determines politics not directly or immediately, but only in the last analysis, *nevertheless economics does determine politics*. The Marxists affirm precisely this in contrast to the bourgeois professors and their disciples. While analyzing and exposing the growing political independence of the bureaucracy from the proletariat, we have never lost sight of the objective social boundaries of this "independence"; namely, nationalized property supplemented by the monopoly of foreign trade.

It is astonishing! Shachtman continues to support the slogan for a political revolution against the Soviet bureaucracy. Has he ever seriously thought out the meaning of this slogan? If we hold that the social foundations laid down by the October Revolution were "automatically" reflected in the policy of the state, then why would a *revolution* against the bureaucracy be necessary? If the USSR, on the other hand, has completely ceased being a workers' state, not a *political* revolution would be required but a *social* revolution. Shachtman consequently continues to defend the slogan which follows 1) from the character of the USSR as a workers' state and 2) from the irreconcilable antagonism between the social foundations of the state and the bureaucracy. But as he repeats this slogan, he tries to undermine its theoretical foundation. Is it perhaps in order to demonstrate once again the independence of his politics from scientific "abstractions"?

Under the guise of waging a struggle against the bourgeois caricature of dialectic materialism, Shachtman throws the doors wide open to historical idealism. Property forms and the class character of the state are a matter of *indifference* to him in analyzing the policy of a government. The state itself appears to him an animal of indiscriminate sex. Both feet planted firmly on this bed of chicken feathers, Shachtman pompously explains to us—today in the year 1940—that in addition to the nationalized property there is also the Bonapartist filth and their reactionary politics. How new! Did Shachtman perchance think that he was speaking in a nursery?

* * *

"Science and Style" (February 23, 1940)

Dear Comrades,

I received Burnham's "Science and Style." The abscess is open and this is an important political advantage. The theoretical backwardness of the American "radical" opinion is expressed by the fact that Burnham repeats only—with some "modernized" illustrations—what Struve wrote in Russia more than forty years ago and to a great degree what Dühring tried to teach German Social Democracy three-quarters of a century ago. So much from the point of view of "science." As far as "style" is concerned, I frankly prefer Eastman.

The interest of the document is not at all of a theoretical character: the thousand and first professorial refutation of dialectics has no more worth than all its precedents. But, from the political point of view the importance of the document is indisputable. It shows that the theoretical inspirer of the opposition is not at all nearer to scientific socialism than was Muste, the former associate of Abern. Shachtman mentioned Bogdanov's philosophy. But it is absolutely impossible to imagine Bogdanov's signature under such a document, even after his definite rupture with Bolshevism. I believe the Party should ask Comrades Abern and Shachtman, as I do at this moment: What do you think of Burnham's "science" and of Burnham's "style"? The question of Finland is important but it is finally only an episode and the change of the international situation, revealing the genuine factors of events, can at once dissipate the divergences on this concrete issue. But can Comrades Abern and Shacht-man now, after the appearance of "Science and Style," continue to carry the slightest responsibility, not for the poor document as such, but for Burnham's entire conception on science, Marxism, politics, and "morals"? Those minorityites who prepared themselves for a split should consider that they would be connected not for a week and not for the duration of the Soviet-Finnish War, but for years with a "leader" who has in his entire conception nothing in common with the proletarian revolution.

The abscess is open. Abern and Shachtman can no longer repeat that they wish only to discuss Finland and Cannon a bit. They can no longer play blind man's buff with Marxism and with the Fourth International. Should the Socialist Workers Party remain in the tradition of Marx, Engels, Franz Mehring, Lenin, and Rosa Luxemburg—a tradition which Burnham proclaims "reactionary"—or should it accept Burnham's conceptions which are only a belated reproduction of pre-Marxian petty-bourgeois socialism?

We know too well what such revisionism signified *politically* in the past. Now in the epoch of the death agony of bourgeois society, the political consequences of Burnhamism would be incomparably more immediate and antirevolutionary. Comrades Abern and Shachtman, you have the floor!

LEON TROTSKY

Coyoacán, D.F.

THE CLASS, THE PARTY, AND THE LEADERSHIP

WHY WAS THE SPANISH PROLETARIAT DEFEATED?

Leon Trotsky
1940

Drafted on the eve of his assassination, this unfinished work is Trotsky at the height of his intellectual powers. After a lifetime of experience leading and analyzing revolutions, his understanding of the dialectical interconnection between the class, the party, and its leadership was unparalleled. With the lessons from the tragic defeat of the Spanish Revolution as its backdrop, Trotsky takes up questions such as the "maturity" of the proletariat, and the crucial importance of having a farsighted revolutionary leadership forged and tempered in advance of revolutionary events. Despite its fragmentary nature, it deserves to be read and reread regularly. One cannot help but wonder what other priceless insights Trotsky would have passed along on this and other decisive topics had he not been murdered by a Stalinist agent in August 1940.

The extent to which the working class movement has been thrown backward may be gauged, not only by the condition of the mass organizations, but by ideological groupings and those theoretical inquiries in which so many groups are engaged. In Paris there is published a periodical *Que Faire* (*What Is to Be Done*), which for some reason considers itself Marxist, but in reality remains completely within the framework of the empiricism of the left bourgeois intellectuals and those isolated workers who have assimilated all the vices of the intellectuals.

Like all groups lacking a scientific foundation, without a program and without any tradition, this little periodical tried to hang on to the coat-tails of the POUM—which seemed to open the shortest avenue to the masses and to victory. But the result of these ties with the Spanish Revolution seems at first entirely unexpected: The periodical did not advance, but on the contrary, retrogressed. As a matter of fact, this is wholly in the nature of things. The contradictions between the petty bourgeoisie, conservatism, and the needs of the proletarian revolution have developed in the extreme. It is only natural that the defenders and interpreters of the policies of the POUM found themselves thrown far back both in political and theoretical fields.

The periodical *Que Faire* is in and of itself of no importance whatever. But it is of symptomatic interest. That is why we think it profitable to dwell upon this periodical's appraisal of the causes for the collapse of the Spanish revolution, inasmuch as this appraisal discloses very graphically the fundamental features now prevailing in the left flank of pseudo-Marxism.

Que Faire Explains

We begin with a verbatim quotation from a review of the pamphlet *Spain Betrayed* by Comrade Casanova:

> Why was the revolution crushed? Because, replies the author (Casanova), the Communist Party conducted a false policy which was unfortunately followed by the revolutionary masses. But why, in the devil's name, did the revolutionary masses who left their former leaders rally to the banner of the Communist Party? "Because there was no genuinely revolutionary party." We are presented with a pure tautology. A false policy of the masses; an immature party either manifests a certain condition of social forces (immaturity of the working class, lack of independence of the peasantry) which must be explained by proceeding from facts, presented among others by Casanova himself; or it is the product of the actions of certain malicious individuals or groups of individuals, actions which do not correspond to the efforts of "sincere individuals" alone capable of saving the revolution. After groping for the first and Marxist road, Casanova takes the second. We are ushered into the domain of pure demonology; the criminal responsible for the defeat is the chief Devil, Stalin, abetted by the anarchists and all the other little devils; the God of revolutionists unfortunately did not send a Lenin or a Trotsky to Spain as He did in Russia in 1917.

The conclusion then follows: "This is what comes of seeking at any cost to force the ossified orthodoxy of a chapel upon facts." This theoretical haughtiness is made all the more magnificent by the fact that it is hard to imagine how so great a number of banalities, vulgarisms, and mistakes, quite specifically of conservative philistine type, could be compressed into so few lines.

The author of the above quotation avoids giving any explanation for the defeat of the Spanish Revolution; he only indicates that profound explanations, like the "condition of social forces" are necessary. The evasion of any explanation is not accidental. These critics of Bolshevism are all theoretical cowards, for the simple reason that they have nothing solid under their feet. In order not to reveal their own bankruptcy they juggle facts and prowl around the opinions of others. They confine themselves to hints and half-thoughts as if they just haven't the time to delineate their full wisdom. As a matter of fact they possess no wisdom at all. Their haughtiness is lined with intellectual charlatanism.

Let us analyze step by step the hints and half-thoughts of our author. According to him, a false policy of the masses can be explained only as it "manifests a certain condition of social forces," namely, the immaturity of the working class and the lack of independence of the peasantry. Anyone searching for tautologies couldn't find in general a flatter one. A "false policy of the masses" is explained by the "immaturity" of the masses. But what is "immaturity" of the masses? Obviously, their predisposition to false policies. Just what the false policy consisted of, and who were its initiators—the masses or the leaders—that is passed over in silence by our author. By means of a tautology he unloads the responsibility on the masses. This classical trick of all traitors, deserters, and their attorneys is especially revolting in connection with the Spanish proletariat.

Sophistry of the betrayers

In July 1936—not to refer to an earlier period—the Spanish workers repelled the assault of the officers who had prepared their conspiracy under the protection of the People's Front. The masses improvised militias and created workers' committees, the strongholds of their future dictatorship. The leading organizations of the proletariat, on the other hand, helped the bourgeoisie to destroy these committees, to liquidate the assaults of the workers on private property, and to subordinate the workers' militias to the command of the bourgeoisie, with the POUM, moreover, participating in the government and assuming direct responsibility for this work of the counterrevolution.

What does "immaturity" of the proletariat signify in this case? Self-evidently only this, that despite the correct political line chosen by the masses, the latter were unable to smash the coalition of socialists, Stalinists, anarchists, and the POUM with the bourgeoisie. This piece of sophistry takes as its starting point a concept of some absolute maturity, i.e., a perfect condition of the masses in which they do not require a correct leadership, and, more than that, are capable of conquering against their own leadership. There is not and there cannot be such maturity.

But why should workers who show such correct revolutionary instinct and such superior fighting qualities submit to treacherous leadership? object our sages. Our answer is: There wasn't even a hint of mere subordination. The workers' line of march at all times cut a certain angle to the line of the leadership. And at the most critical moments this angle became 180 degrees. The leadership then helped directly or indirectly to subdue the workers by armed force.

In May 1937, the workers of Catalonia rose, not only without their own leadership, but against it. The anarchist leaders—pathetic and contemptible bourgeois masquerading cheaply as revolutionists—have repeated hundreds of times in their press that had the CNT wanted to take power and set up their dictatorship in May, they could have done so without any difficulty. This time the anarchist leaders speak the unadulterated truth. The POUM leadership actually dragged at the tail of the CNT, only they covered up their policy with a different phraseology. It was thanks to this and this alone that the bourgeoisie succeeded in crushing the May uprising of the "immature" proletariat.

One must understand exactly nothing in the sphere of the interrelationships between the class and the party, between the masses and the leaders, in order to repeat the hollow statement that the Spanish masses merely followed their leaders. The only thing that can be said is that the masses who sought at all times to blast their way to the correct road found it beyond their strength to produce in the very fire of battle a new leadership corresponding to the demands of the revolution. Before us is a profoundly dynamic process, with the various stages of the revolution shifting swiftly, with the leadership or various sections of the leadership quickly deserting to the side of the class enemy, and our sages engage in a purely static discussion: Why did the working class as a whole follow a bad leadership?

The dialectical approach

There is an ancient, evolutionary-liberal epigram: Every people gets the government it deserves. History, however, shows that one and the same people may in the course of a comparatively brief epoch get very different governments (Russia, Italy, Germany, Spain, etc.), and furthermore, that the order of these governments doesn't at all proceed in one and the same direction: from despotism to freedom as was imagined by the evolutionist liberals. The secret is this, that a people is comprised of hostile classes, and the classes themselves are comprised of different and in part antagonistic layers, which fall under different leadership. Furthermore, every people falls under the influence of other peoples who are likewise comprised of classes. Governments do not express the systematically growing "maturity" of a "people" but are the product of the struggle between different classes and the different layers within one and the same class, and, finally, the action of external forces—alliances, conflicts, wars, and so on. To this should be added that a government, once it has established itself, may endure much longer than the relationship of forces which produced it. It is precisely out of this historical contradiction that revolutions, *coups d'état*, counterrevolutions, etc. arise.

The very same dialectic approach is necessary in dealing with the question of the leadership of a class. Imitating the liberals, our sages tacitly accept the axiom that every class gets the leadership it deserves. In reality, leadership is not at all a mere "reflection" of a class or the product of its own free creativeness. A leadership is shaped in the process of clashes between the different classes or the friction between the different layers within a given class. Having once arisen, the leadership invariably rises above its class and thereby becomes predisposed to the pressure and influence of other classes. The proletariat may "tolerate" for a long time a leadership that has already suffered a complete inner degeneration but has not as yet had the opportunity to express this degeneration amid great events. A great historic shock is necessary to sharply reveal the contradiction between the leadership and the class. The mightiest historical shocks are wars and revolutions. Precisely for this reason the working class is often caught unawares by war and revolution. But even in cases where the old leadership has revealed its internal corruption, the class cannot improvise immediately a new leadership, especially if it has not inherited from the previous period strong revolutionary cadres capable of utilizing the collapse of the old leading party. The Marxist, i.e., dialectical, and not scholastic interpretation of the interrelationship between a class and its leadership does not leave a single stone unturned of our author's legalistic sophistry.

How the Russian workers matured

He conceives of the proletariat's maturity as something purely static. Yet, during a revolution, the consciousness of a class is the most dynamic process directly determining the course of the revolution. Was it possible in January 1917 or even in March, after the overthrow of tsarism, to give an answer to the question whether the Russian proletariat had sufficiently "matured" for the conquest of power in eight to nine months? The working class was at that time extremely heterogeneous socially and politically. During the years of the war it had been renewed by 30–40% from the ranks of the petty bourgeoisie, often reactionary, at the expense of backward peasants, at the expense of women and youth. The Bolshevik Party, in March 1917, was followed by an insignificant minority of the working class and furthermore, there was discord within the party itself. The overwhelming majority of the workers supported the Mensheviks and the "Socialists-Revolutionaries," i.e., conservative social-patriots. The situation was even less favorable with regard to the army and the peasantry. We must add to this: the general low level of culture in the country, the lack of political experience among the broadest layers of the proletariat, especially in the provinces, let alone the peasants and soldiers.

What was the "active" of Bolshevism? A clear and thoroughly thought-out revolutionary conception at the beginning of the revolution was held only by Lenin. The Russian cadres of the party were scattered and to a considerable degree bewildered. But the party had authority among the advanced workers. Lenin had great authority with the party cadres. Lenin's political conception corresponded to the actual development of the revolution and was reinformed by each new event. These elements of the "active" worked wonders in a revolutionary situation, that is, in conditions of bitter class struggle. The party quickly aligned its policy to correspond with Lenin's conception, to correspond, that is, with the actual course of the revolution. Thanks to this it met with firm support among tens of thousands of advanced workers. Within a few months, by basing itself upon the development of the revolution, the party was able to convince the majority of the workers of the correctness of its slogans.

This majority organized into soviets was able in its turn to attract the soldiers and peasants. How can this dynamic, dialectical process be exhausted by a formula of the maturity or immaturity of the proletariat? A colossal factor in the maturity of the Russian proletariat in February or March 1917 was Lenin. He did not fall from the skies. He personified the revolutionary tradition of the working class. For Lenin's slogans to find their way to the masses there had to exist cadres, even though numerically small at the beginning; there had to exist the confidence of the cadres in the leadership, a confidence based on the entire experience of the past. To cancel these elements from one's calculations is simply to ignore the living revolution, to substitute for it an abstraction, the "relationship of forces," because the development of the revolution precisely consists of this, that the relationship of forces keeps incessantly and rapidly changing under the impact of the changes in the consciousness of the proletariat, the attraction of backward layers to the advanced, the growing assurance of the class in its own strength. The vital mainspring in this process is the party, just as the vital mainspring in the mechanism of the party is its leadership. The role and the responsibility of the leadership in a revolutionary epoch is colossal.

Relativity of "maturity"

The October victory is a serious testimonial of the "maturity" of the proletariat. But this maturity is relative. A few years later, the very same proletariat permitted the revolution to be strangled by a bureaucracy which rose from its ranks. Victory is not at all the ripe fruit of the proletariat's "maturity." Victory is a strategic task. It is necessary to utilize the favorable conditions of a revolutionary crisis in order to mobilize the masses. Taking as a starting point the given level of their "maturity," it is necessary to propel them forward, teach them to understand that the enemy is by no means omnipotent, that it is torn asunder with contradictions, that behind the imposing façade, panic prevails. Had the Bolshevik Party failed to carry out this work, there couldn't even be talk of the victory of the proletarian revolution. The soviets would have been crushed by the counterrevolution and the little sages of all countries would have written articles and books on the keynote that only uprooted visionaries could dream in Russia of the dictatorship of the proletariat, so small numerically and so immature.

Auxiliary role of peasants

Equally abstract, pedantic, and false is the reference to the "lack of independence" of the peasantry. When and where did our sage ever observe in capitalist society a peasantry with an independent revolutionary program or a capacity for independent revolutionary initiative? The peasantry can play a very great role in the revolution, but only an auxiliary role.

In many instances the Spanish peasants acted boldly and fought courageously. But to rouse the entire mass of the peasantry, the proletariat had to set an example of a decisive uprising against the bourgeoisie and inspire the peasants with faith in the possibility of victory. In the meantime, the revolutionary initiative of the proletariat itself was paralyzed at every step by its own organizations.

The "immaturity" of the proletariat, the "lack of independence" of the peasantry, are neither final nor basic factors in historical events. Underlying the consciousness of the classes are the classes themselves, their numerical strength, their role in economic life. Underlying the classes is a specific system of production which is determined in its turn by the level of the development of productive forces. Why not then say that the defeat of the Spanish proletariat was determined by the low level of technology?

The role of personality

Our author substitutes mechanistic determinism for the dialectical conditioning of the historical process. Hence the cheap jibes about the role of individuals, good and bad. History is a process of the class struggle. But classes do not bring their full weight to bear automatically and simultaneously. In the process of struggle the classes create various organs which play an important and independent role and are subject to deformations. This also provides the basis for the role of personalities in history. There are, naturally, great objective causes which created the autocratic rule of Hitler. But only dull-witted pedants of "determinism" could deny today the enormous historic role of Hitler. The arrival of Lenin in Petrograd on April 3, 1917 turned the Bolshevik Party in time and enabled the party to lead the revolution to victory. Our sages might say that, had Lenin died abroad at the beginning of 1917, the October Revolution would have taken place "just the same." But that is not so. Lenin represented one of the living elements of the historical process. He personified the experience and the perspicacity of the most active section of the proletariat. His timely appearance on the arena of the revolution was necessary in order to mobilize the vanguard and provide it with an opportunity to rally the working class and the peasant masses. Political leadership in the crucial moments of historical turns can become just as decisive a factor as is the role of the chief command during the critical moments of war. History is not an automatic process. Otherwise, why leaders? why parties? why programs? why theoretical struggles?

Stalinism in Spain

"But why, in the devil's name," asks the author, as we have already heard, "did the revolutionary masses who left their former leaders rally to the banner of the Communist Party?" The question is falsely posed. It is not true that the revolutionary masses left all of their former leaders. The workers who were previously connected with specific organizations continued to cling to them, while they observed and checked. Workers in general do not easily break with the party that awakens them to conscious life. Moreover, the existence of mutual protection within the People's Front lulled them: Since everybody agreed, everything must be all right. The new and fresh masses naturally turned to the Comintern as the party which had accomplished the only victorious proletarian revolution, and which, it was hoped, was capable of assuring arms to Spain. Furthermore, the Comintern was the most zealous champion of the idea of the People's Front; this inspired confidence among the inexperienced layers of workers. Within the People's Front, the Comintern was the most zealous champion of the bourgeois character of the revolution; this inspired the confidence of the petty and in part the middle bourgeoisie. That is why the masses "rallied to the banner of the Communist Party."

Our author depicts the matter as if the proletariat were in a well-stocked shoe store, selecting a new pair of boots. Even this simple operation, as is well known, does not always prove successful. As regards new leadership, the choice is very limited. Only gradually, only on the basis of their own experience, through several stages, can the broad layers of the masses become convinced that a new leadership is firmer, more reliable, more loyal than the old. To be sure, during a revolution, i.e., when events move swiftly, a weak party can quickly grow into a mighty one, provided it lucidly understands the course of the revolution and possesses staunch

cadres that do not become intoxicated with phrases and are not ter-
rorized by persecution. But such a party must be available prior to the
revolution inasmuch as the process of educating the cadres requires a
considerable period of time and the revolution does not afford this time.

Treachery of the POUM

To the left of all the other parties in Spain stood the POUM, which undoubtedly embraced revolutionary proletarian elements not previously
firmly tied to anarchism. But it was precisely this party that played a fatal
role in the development of the Spanish Revolution. It could not become a
mass party because, in order to do so, it was first necessary to overthrow
the old parties, and it was possible to overthrow them only by an irreconcilable struggle, by a merciless exposure of their bourgeois character. Yet
the POUM, while criticizing the old parties, subordinated itself to them on
all fundamental questions. It participated in the "People's" election bloc;
entered the government which liquidated workers' committees; engaged
in a struggle to reconstitute this governmental coalition; capitulated time
and again to the anarchist leadership; conducted, in connection with
this, a false trade union policy; took a vacillating and nonrevolutionary
attitude toward the May 1937 uprising. From the standpoint of determinism in general it is possible, of course, to recognize that the policy
of the POUM was not accidental. Everything in this world has its cause.
However, the series of causes engendering the centrism of the POUM are
by no means a mere reflection of condition of the Spanish or Catalan proletariat. Two causalities moved toward each other at an angle and at a
certain moment they came into hostile conflict. It is possible, by taking
into account previous international experience, Moscow's influence, the
influence of a number of defeats, etc., to explain politically and psycho-
logically why the POUM unfolded as a centrist party. But this does not
alter its centrist character, nor does it alter the fact that a centrist party
invariably acts as a brake upon the revolution, must each time smash its
own head, and may bring about the collapse of the revolution. It does
not alter the fact that the Catalan masses were far more revolutionary
than the POUM, which in turn was more revolutionary than its leadership. In these conditions, to unload the responsibility for false policies
on the "immaturity" of the masses is to engage in sheer charlatanism,
frequently resorted to by political bankrupts.

Responsibility of leadership

The historical falsification consists in this, that the responsibility for the defeat of the Spanish masses is unloaded on the working masses and not those parties which paralyzed or simply crushed the revolutionary movement of the masses. The attorneys of the POUM simply deny the responsibility of the leaders, in order thus to escape shouldering their own responsibility. This impotent philosophy, which seeks to reconcile defeats as a necessary link in the chain of cosmic developments, is completely incapable of posing and refuses to pose the question of such concrete factors as programs, parties, and personalities that were the organizers of defeat. This philosophy of fatalism and prostration is diametrically opposed to Marxism as the theory of revolutionary action.

Civil war is a process wherein political tasks are solved by military means. Were the outcome of this war determined by the "condition of class forces," the war itself would not be necessary. War has its own organization, its own policies, its own methods, its own leadership, by which its fate is directly determined. Naturally, the "condition of class forces" supplies the foundation for all other political factors. But just as the foundation of a building does not reduce the importance of walls, windows, doors, and roofs, so the "condition of classes" does not invalidate the importance of parties, their strategy, their leadership. By dissolving the concrete in the abstract, our sages really halted midway. The most "profound" solution of the problem would have been to declare the defeat of the Spanish proletariat as due to the inadequate development of productive forces. Such a key is accessible to any fool.

By reducing to zero the significance of the party and of the leadership, these sages deny in general the possibility of revolutionary victory. Because there are not the least grounds for expecting conditions more favorable. Capitalism has ceased to advance, the proletariat does not grow numerically, on the contrary it is the army of unemployed that grows, which does not increase but reduces the fighting force of the proletariat and has a negative effect also upon its consciousness. There are similarly no grounds for believing that under the regime of capitalism the peasantry is capable of attaining a higher revolutionary consciousness. The conclusion from the analysis of our author is thus complete pessimism, a sliding away from revolutionary perspectives. It must be said—to do them justice—that they do not themselves understand what they say.

As a matter of fact, the demands they make upon the consciousness of the masses are utterly fantastic. The Spanish workers, as well as the Spanish peasants, gave the maximum of what these classes are able to give in a revolutionary situation. We have in mind precisely the class of millions and tens of millions.

Que Faire represents merely one of these little schools, or churches, or chapels who, frightened by the course of the class struggle and the onset of reaction, publish their little journals and their theoretical études in a corner, on the sidelines, away from the actual developments of revolutionary thought, let alone the movement of the masses.

Repression of Spanish Revolution

The Spanish proletariat fell the victim of a coalition composed of imperialists, Spanish republicans, socialists, anarchists, Stalinists, and on the left flank, the POUM. They all paralyzed the socialist revolution which the Spanish proletariat had actually begun to realize. It is not easy to dispose of the socialist revolution. No one has yet devised other methods than ruthless repressions, massacre of the vanguard, execution of the leaders, etc. The POUM, of course, did not want this. It wanted, on the one hand, to participate in the Republican government and to enter as a loyal peace-loving opposition into the general bloc of ruling parties; and on the other hand, to achieve peaceful comradely relations at a time when it was a question of implacable civil war. For this very reason the POUM fell victim to the contradictions of its own policy. The most consistent policy in the ruling bloc was pursued by the Stalinists. They were the fighting vanguard of the bourgeois-republican counterrevolution. They wanted to eliminate the need of fascism by proving to the Spanish and world bourgeoisie that they were themselves capable of strangling the proletarian revolution under the banner of "democracy." This was the gist of their policies. The bankrupts of the Spanish People's Front are today trying to unload the blame on the GPU. I trust that we cannot be suspected of leniency toward the crimes of the GPU. But we see clearly and we tell the workers that the GPU acted in this instance only as the most resolute detachment in the service of the People's Front. Therein was the strength of the GPU, therein was the historic role of Stalin. Only ignorant philistines can wave this aside with stupid little jokes about the Chief Devil.

These gentlemen do not even bother with the question of the social character of the revolution. Moscow's lackeys, for the benefit of England and France, proclaimed the Spanish Revolution as bourgeois. Upon this fraud were erected the perfidious policies of the People's Front, policies which would have been completely false even if the Spanish Revolution had really been bourgeois. But from the very beginning, the revolution expressed much more graphically the proletarian character than did the revolution of 1917 in Russia. In the leadership of the POUM gentlemen sit today who consider that the policy of Andrés Nin was too "leftist," that the really correct thing was to have remained the left flank of the People's Front. The real misfortune was that Nin, covering himself with the authority of Lenin and the October Revolution, could not make up his mind to break with the People's Front. Victor Serge, who is in a hurry to compromise himself by a frivolous attitude toward serious questions writes that Nin did not wish to submit to commands from Oslo or Coyoacán. Can a serious man really be capable of reducing to petty gossip the problem of the class content of a revolution? The sages of *Que Faire* have no answer whatever to this question. They do not understand the question itself. Of what significance, indeed, is the fact that the "immature" proletariat founded its own organs of power, seized enterprises, and sought to regulate production, while the POUM tried with all its might to keep from breaking with bourgeois anarchists, who, in an alliance with the bourgeois republicans and the no less bourgeois socialists and Stalinists, assaulted and strangled the proletarian revolution! Such "trifles" are obviously of interest only to representatives of "ossified orthodoxy." The sages of *Que Faire* possess, instead, a special apparatus which measures the maturity of the proletariat and the relationship of forces independently of all questions of revolutionary class strategy . . .

[end of manuscript]

DIALECTICAL MATERIALISM AND SCIENCE

Leon Trotsky
September 17, 1925

Trotsky delivered the following speech to the Mendeleev Congress in his capacity as chairman of the technical and scientific board of industry of the Soviet Union. Although it was already beginning to crystallize, Stalinism had not yet secured its death grip on the Russian Revolution, and the potential for the newly established property relations to revolutionize science seemed unlimited. By 1938, as Trotsky explains in his foreword to the English translation, the Stalinist bureaucracy had become a colossal fetter on the further progress of scientific inquiry—not to mention the world revolution. As we know today, the Stalinists eventually succeeded in strangling the revolution, and capitalism was restored in Russia, with terrible consequences for the population. Today, we live in a world in which the objective potential for socialism is incomparably greater than in 1925. In this context, Trotsky's revolutionary optimism and insights into the socialist transition between capitalism and communism are of tremendous interest and relevance.

Foreword to the English Translation
(April 18, 1938)

This speech was delivered in 1925, at a time when the author still firmly hoped that Soviet democracy would overcome the tendencies towards bureaucratism and create exceptionally favorable conditions for the development of scientific thought. Because of a combination of historical causes this hope has not yet materialized. On the contrary, the Soviet state in the intervening thirteen years has fallen victim to complete bureaucratic ossification and has assumed a totalitarian character equally baneful to the development of science and art. Through the cruel irony of history, genuine Marxism has now become the most proscribed of all doctrines in the Soviet Union. In the field of social science, shackled Soviet thought has not only failed to utter a single new word but, on the contrary, has sunk to the depths of pathetic scholasticism. The totalitarian regime likewise exercises a disastrous influence upon the development of the natural sciences. Nevertheless, the views developed in this speech retain their validity, in the section too, which deals with the interrelations between the social regime and scientific thought. However, they should be placed, not against the background of the present Soviet state, a product of degeneration and disintegration, but rather, taken in the light of that socialist state which will arise from the future victorious struggle of the international working class.

* * *

The continuity of cultural heritage

Your Congress convenes amid the celebrations of the 200th anniversary of the founding of the Academy of Sciences. The connection between your Congress and the Academy is made all the firmer by the fact that Russian chemistry occupies by no means the last place in the achievements that have brought fame to the Academy. Here it is perhaps proper to pose the question: What is the inner historical significance of the elaborate academic celebrations? They have a significance far beyond mere visits to museums, theaters, and banquets. How can we estimate this significance? Not merely by the fact that foreign scientists, kind enough to come here as our guests, have had the opportunity of ascertaining that the revolution, far from destroying scientific institutions, has on the contrary, developed them. This evidence acquired by the foreign scientists possesses a meaning of its own. But the significance of the academic celebrations is far greater and deeper. I would formulate it as follows: *The new state, a new society based on the laws of the October Revolution, takes possession triumphantly—before the eyes of the whole world—of the cultural heritage of the past.*

Since I have inadvertently referred to heritage, I must make clear the sense in which I use this term so as to avoid any possible misunderstandings. We would be guilty of disrespect to the future, dearer to all of us than the past, and we would be disrespectful of the past, which in many of its aspects merits profound respect, if we were to talk loosely about heritage. Not everything in the past is of value for the future. Furthermore, the development of human culture is not determined by simple concretion. There have been periods of organic growth as well as periods of rigorous criticism, sifting, and selection. It would be difficult to say which of these periods has proved more fruitful for the general development of culture. At all events, we are living in an epoch of sifting and selection.

Roman jurisprudence had, from the time of Justinian, established the law of inventorial inheritance. In contrast to pre-Justinian legislation, which established the right of an heir to accept inheritance provided only he likewise assumed responsibility for all obligations and debts, inventorial inheritance gave the inheritor a certain degree of choice. The revolutionary state, representing a new class, is a kind of inventorial inheritor in relation to the accumulated store of culture. Let me state frankly that not all of the 15,000 volumes published by the Academy during its two centuries of existence will enter into the inventory of socialism! There are two aspects of by no means equal merit to the scientific contributions of the past which are now ours and upon which we pride ourselves. Science as a whole has been directed toward acquiring knowledge of reality, research into the laws of evolution, and discovery of the properties and qualities of matter, in order to gain greater mastery over it. But knowledge did not develop within the four walls of a laboratory or a lecture hall. No, it remained a function of human society and reflected the structure of human society. For its needs, society requires knowledge of nature. But at the same time, society demands an affirmation of its right to be what it is; a justification of its particular institutions; first and foremost, the institutions of class domination, just as in the past it demanded the justification of serfdom, class privileges, monarchical prerogatives, national exceptionalism, etc. Socialist society accepts with utmost gratitude the heritage of the positive sciences, discarding, as is the right of inventorial choice, everything which is useless in acquiring knowledge of nature but only useful in justifying class inequality and all other kinds of historical untruth.

Every new social order appropriates the cultural heritage of the past not in its totality but only in accordance with its own structure. Thus, medieval society embodied in Christianity many elements of ancient philosophy, subordinating them, however, to the needs of the feudal regime and transforming them into scholasticism, the "handmaiden of theology." Similarly, bourgeois society inherited among other things from the Middle Ages, Christianity, but subjected it either to the Reformation, that is, revolt in the shape of Protestantism, or pacification in the shape of adaptation of Catholicism to the new regime. In any case, Christianity of the bourgeois epoch was brushed aside to the degree that the road had to be cleared for scientific research, at least, within those limits which were required for the development of the productive forces.

Socialist society, in its relation to scientific and cultural inheritance in general, holds to a far lesser degree an attitude of indifference, or passive acceptance. It can be said: The greater the trust of socialism in sciences devoted to the direct study of nature, all the greater is its critical distrust in approaching those sciences and pseudosciences which are linked closely to the structure of human society, its economic institutions, its state, laws, ethics, etc. Of course, these two spheres are not separated by an impenetrable wall. But at the same time, it is an indisputable fact that the heritage embodied in those sciences which deal not with human society but with "matter"—in natural sciences in the broad sense of the term, and consequently of course in chemistry—is of incomparably greater weight.

The need to know nature is imposed upon men by their need to subordinate nature to themselves. Any digressions in this sphere from objective relationships, which are determined by the properties of matter itself, are corrected by practical experience. This alone seriously guarantees the natural sciences, and chemical research, in particular, from intentional, unintentional, semi-deliberate distortions, misinterpretations, and falsifications. Social research primarily devoted its efforts toward justifying historically arisen society, so as to preserve it against the attacks of "destructive theories," etc. Herein is rooted the apologetic role of the official social sciences of bourgeois society; and this is the reason why their accomplishments are of little value.

So long as science as a whole remained a "handmaiden of theology," it could produce valuable results only surreptitiously. This was the case in the Middle Ages. It was during the bourgeois regime, as already pointed out, that the natural sciences gained the possibility of wide development.

But social science remained the servant of capitalism. This is also true, to a large extent, of psychology, which links the social and natural sciences; and philosophy, which systematizes the generalized conclusions of all sciences.

I said that *official* social science has produced little of value. This is best revealed by the inability of bourgeois science to foresee tomorrow. We have observed this in relation to the first imperialist World War and its consequences. We have seen it again in relation to the October Revolution. We now see it in the complete helplessness of official social science in the evaluation of the European situation, the interrelations with America and with the Soviet Union; in its inability to draw any conclusions regarding tomorrow. Yet the significance of science lies precisely in this: To know in order to foresee.

Natural science—and chemistry occupies a most important place in that field—indisputably constitutes the most valuable portion of our inheritance. Your Congress stands under the banner of Mendeleev who was and remains the pride of Russian science.

To know so that we may foresee and act

There is a difference in the degree of foresight and precision achieved in the various sciences. But it is through foresight—passive, in some instances as in astronomy, active, as in chemistry and chemical engineering—that science is able to verify itself and justify its social purpose. An individual scientist may not at all be concerned with the practical application of his research. The wider his scope, the bolder his flight, the greater his freedom from practical daily necessity in his mental operations, all the better. But science is not a function of individual scientists; it is a public function. The social evaluation of science, its historical evaluation is determined by its capacity to increase man's power and arm him with the power to foresee and master nature. Science is knowledge that endows us with power. When Leverrier, on the basis of the "eccentricities" in the orbit of Uranus, concluded that there must exist an unknown celestial body "disturbing" the movement of Uranus; when Leverrier on the basis of his purely mathematical calculations requested the German astronomer Galle to locate a body wandering without a passport in the skies at such and such an address; when Galle focused his telescope in that direction and discovered the planet called Neptune—at that moment the celestial mechanics of Newton celebrated a great victory.

This occurred in the autumn of 1846. In the year 1848, revolution swept like a whirlwind through Europe, demonstrating its "disturbing" influence on the movement of peoples and states. In the intervening period, between the discovery of Neptune and the revolution of 1848, two young scholars, Marx and Engels, wrote *The Communist Manifesto*, in which they not only predicted the inevitability of revolutionary events in the near future, but also analyzed in advance their component forces, the logic of their movement—up to the inevitable victory of the proletariat and the establishment of the dictatorship of the proletariat. It would not at all be superfluous to juxtapose this prognosis with the prophecies of the official social science of the Hohenzollerns, Romanovs, Louis Philippe, and others in 1848.

In 1869, Mendeleev, on the basis of his researches and reflection upon atomic weight, established his Periodic Law of the Elements. To the atomic weight, as a more stable criterion, Mendeleev linked a series of other properties and traits, arranged the elements in a definite order, and then through this order revealed the existence of a certain disorder, namely, the absence of certain elements. These unknown elements or chemical units, as Mendeleev once called them, should, in accordance with the logic of this "Law," occupy specific vacant places in that order. Here, with the authoritative gesture of a research worker confident in himself, Mendeleev knocked at one of nature's hitherto closed doors, and from within a voice answered: "Present!" Actually, three voices responded simultaneously, for in the places indicated by Mendeleev there were discovered three new elements, later called gallium, scandium, and germanium.

A marvellous triumph for thought, analytical and synthesizing! In his *Principles of Chemistry*, Mendeleev vividly characterizes scientific creative effort, comparing it with the projection of a bridge across a ravine: For this it is unnecessary to descend into the ravine and to fix supports at the bottom; it is only necessary to erect a foundation on one side and then project an accurately designed arc which will then find support on the opposite side. Similarly with scientific thought. It can base itself only on the granite foundation of experience, but its generalizations, like the arc of a bridge, can rise above the world of facts in order later, at another point calculated in advance, to meet the latter. At that moment of scientific thought when a generalization turns into prediction—and prediction is triumphantly verified through experience—at that moment, human thought is invariably supplied with its proudest and most justified satisfaction! Thus it was in chemistry with the discovery of new elements on the basis of the Periodic Law.

Mendeleev's prediction, which later produced a profound impression upon Friedrich Engels, was made in the year 1871, the year, that is, of the great tragedy of the Paris Commune in France. The attitude of our great chemist to this event can be gathered from his general hostility towards "Latinism," its violence and revolutions. Like all official thinkers of the ruling classes, not only in Russia and in Europe but throughout the world, Mendeleev did not ask himself: What is the real driving force behind the Paris Commune? He did not see that the new class growing from the womb of the old society was here exercising in its movement as "disturbing" an influence upon the orbit of the old society as the unknown planet did upon the orbit of Uranus. But a German exile, Karl Marx, did at that time analyze the causes and inner mechanics of the Paris Commune, and the rays of his scientific torch penetrated to the events of our own October and shed light upon them.

We have long found it unnecessary to resort to a more mysterious substance, called phlogiston, to explain chemical reactions. As a matter of fact, phlogiston served merely as a generalization for the ignorance of the alchemists. In the sphere of physiology, the time has long since passed when a need was felt for a special mystical substance, called the vital force, and which was the phlogiston of living matter. *In principle*, we now possess sufficient knowledge of physics and chemistry to explain physiological phenomena. In the sphere of the phenomena of consciousness, we are no longer in need of a substance labeled the soul, which in reactionary philosophy performs the role of the phlogiston of psychophysical phenomena. Psychology is for us, in the *final analysis*, reducible to physiology, and the latter—to chemistry, mechanics, and physics. This is far more viable than the theory of phlogiston in the sphere of social science, where this phlogiston appears in different costumes; now disguised as "historical mission," now disguised as changeless "national character," now as the disembodied idea of "progress," now as so-called "critical thought," and so on, *ad infinitum*. In all these cases, an attempt has been made to discover some supra-social substance to explain social phenomena. It is hardly necessary to repeat that these ideal substances are only ingenious disguises for sociological ignorance. Marxism rejected supra-historical essences, just as physiology has renounced the vital force, or chemistry, phlogiston.

The essence of Marxism consists in this, that it approaches society concretely, as a subject for objective research, and analyzes human history as one would a colossal laboratory record. Marxism appraises ideology as a subordinate integral element of the material social structure. Marxism examines the class structure of society as a historically conditioned form of the development of the productive forces; Marxism deduces from the productive forces of society the interrelations between human society and surrounding nature, and these, in turn, are determined at each historical stage by man's technology, his instruments and weapons, his capacities and methods for struggle with nature. Precisely this objective approach arms Marxism with the insuperable power of historical foresight.

Consider the history of Marxism, even if only on the national scale of Russia, and follow it not from the standpoint of your own political sympathies or antipathies but from the standpoint of Mendeleev's definition of science:

To know so that we may foresee and act. The initial period of the history of Marxism on Russian soil is the history of a struggle for correct socio-historical prognosis (foresight), as against the official governmental and official oppositional viewpoints. In the early 1880s, that is, at a time when official ideology existed as the trinity of absolutism, orthodoxy, and nationalism; liberalism daydreamed about a Zemstvo Assembly, i.e., a semi-constitutional monarchy, while the Narodniks combined feeble socialistic fantasies with economic reaction. At that time, Marxist thought predicted not only the inevitable and progressive work of capitalism, but also the appearance of the proletariat in an independent historical role— the proletariat taking hegemony in the struggle of the popular masses; the proletarian dictatorship leading the peasantry behind it.

There is no less a difference between the Marxist method of social analysis and the theories against which it fought than there is between Mendeleev's Periodic Law, with all its latest modifications on the one side, and the mumbo-jumbo of the alchemists on the other.

Natural science and Marxism

"The cause of chemical reaction lies in the physical and mechanical properties of compounds." This formula of Mendeleev is completely materialist in character. Chemistry, instead of resorting to some new supra-mechanical and supra-physical force to explain its phenomena, reduces chemical processes to the mechanical and physical properties of its compounds.

Biology and physiology stand in a similar relationship to chemistry. Scientific, that is, materialist physiology does not require a special supra-chemical vital force (as is the claim of Vitalists and neo-Vitalists) to explain phenomena in its field. Physiological processes are reducible in the last analysis to chemical ones, just as the latter—to mechanics and physics.

Psychology is similarly related to physiology. It is not for nothing that physiology is called the applied chemistry of living organisms. Just as there exists no special physiological force, so it is equally true that scientific, i.e., materialist psychology has no need of a mystic force—soul—to explain phenomena in its field, but finds them reducible in the final analysis to physiological phenomena. This is the school of the academician Pavlov; it views the so-called soul as a complex system of conditioned reflexes, completely rooted in the elementary physiological reflexes which in their turn find, through the potent stratum of chemistry, their root in the subsoil of mechanics and physics.

The same can be said of sociology also. To explain social phenomena it is not necessary to adduce some kind of eternal source, or to search for an origin in another world. Society is a product of the development of primary matter, like the earth's crust or the amoeba. In this manner, scientific thought with its methods cuts like a diamond drill through the complex phenomena of social ideology to the bedrock of matter, its component elements, its atoms, with their physical and mechanical properties.

Naturally, this does not mean to say that every phenomenon of chemistry can be reduced *directly* to mechanics; and even less so, that every social phenomenon is directly reducible to physiology and then—to laws of chemistry and mechanics. It may be said that this is the uppermost aim of science. But the method of gradual and continuous approach toward this aim is entirely different. Chemistry has its special approach to matter, its own methods of research, its own laws. If, without the knowledge that chemical reactions are reducible *in the final analysis* to mechanical properties of elementary particles of matter, there is not and cannot be a finished philosophy linking all phenomena into a single system, so, on the other hand, the mere knowledge that chemical phenomena are themselves rooted in mechanics and physics does not provide in itself the key to even one chemical reaction. Chemistry has *its own keys*. One can choose among them only from experience and generalization, through the chemical laboratory, chemical hypothesis, and chemical theory.

This applies to all sciences. Chemistry is a powerful pillar of physiology with which it is directly connected through the channels of organic and physiological chemistry. But chemistry is no substitute for physiology. Each science rests on the laws of other sciences only in the so-called *final instance*. But at the same time, the separation of the sciences from one another is determined precisely by the fact that each science covers a particular field of phenomena, i.e., a field of such complex combinations of elementary phenomena and laws as require a special approach, special research technique, special hypotheses and methods.

This idea seems so indisputable in relation to the sciences of mathematics and natural history that to harp on it would be like forcing an open door. It is otherwise with social science. Outstanding trained naturalists who in the field, say, of physiology would not proceed a step without taking into account rigidly tested experiments, verification, hypothetical generalization, latest verification, and so forth, approach social phenomena far more boldly, with the boldness of ignorance, as if tacitly acknowledging that in this extremely complex sphere of phenomena it is sufficient merely to have vague propensities, day-to-day observations, family traditions, and even a stock of current social prejudices.

Human society has not developed in accordance with a prearranged plan or system, but empirically, in the course of a long, complicated, and contradictory struggle of the human species for existence, and, later, for greater and greater mastery over nature itself. The ideology of human society took shape as a reflection of and an instrument in this process—belated, desultory, piecemeal—in the form, so to speak, of conditioned social reflexes which are in the final analysis reducible to the necessities of the struggle of collective man against nature. To arrive at judgments upon laws governing the development of human society on the basis of their ideological reflection, on the basis of so-called public opinion, etc., is almost equivalent to forming a judgment upon the anatomical and physiological structure of a lizard on the basis of its sensations as it lies basking in the sun or crawls out of a damp crevice. True enough, there is a very direct bond between the sensations of a lizard and the latter's organic structure. But this bond is a subject for research by means of objective methods.

There is, however, a tendency to become most subjective in judging the structure and laws that govern the development of human society in terms of the so-called consciousness of society, that is, its contradictory, disjointed, conservative, unverified ideology. Of course, one can become insulted and raise the objection that social ideology is, after all, at a higher elevation than the sensation of a lizard. It all depends on one's approach to the question. In my opinion, there is nothing paradoxical in the statement that from the sensations of a lizard one could, if it were possible to bring them into proper focus, draw much more direct conclusions concerning the structure and function of its organs than concerning the structure of society and its dynamics from such ideological reflections as, for example, religious creeds which once occupied and still continue to occupy so prominent a place in the life of human society; or from the contradictory and hypocritical codexes of official morality; or, finally, the idealistic philosophical conceptions, which, in order to explain complex organic processes occurring in man, seek to place responsibility upon a nebulous, subtle essence called the soul and endowed with the qualities of impenetrability and eternity.

Mendeleev's reaction to problems of social reorganization was one of hostility and even scorn. He maintained that from time immemorial nothing had yet come from the attempt. Mendeleev instead expected a happier future to arise through the positive sciences, and above all chemistry, which would reveal all of nature's secrets.

It is of interest to juxtapose this point of view to that of our remarkable physiologist Pavlov, who is of the opinion that wars and revolutions are something accidental, arising from people's ignorance, and who conjectures that only a profound knowledge of "human nature" will eliminate both wars and revolutions.

Darwin can be placed in the same category. This highly gifted biologist demonstrated how an accumulation of small *quantitative* variations produces an entirely new biologic "quality" and by that token he explained the origin of species. Without being aware of it, he thus applied the method of dialectic materialism to the sphere of organic life. Darwin, although unenlightened in philosophy, brilliantly applied Hegel's law of transition from quantity into quality. At the same time, we very often discover in this same Darwin, not to mention the Darwinians, utterly naïve and unscientific attempts at applying the conclusions of biology to society. To interpret competition as a "variety" of the biological struggle for existence is like seeing only mechanics in the physiology of mating.

In each of these cases we observe one and the same fundamental mistake: the methods and achievements of chemistry or physiology, in violation of all scientific boundaries, are transplanted into human society. A naturalist would hardly carry over without modification the laws governing the movement of atoms into the movement of molecules, which are governed by other laws. But many naturalists have an entirely different attitude upon the question of sociology. The historically conditioned structure of society is very often disregarded by them in favor of the anatomical structure of things, the physiological structure of reflexes, the biological struggle for existence. Of course, the life of human society, interlaced with material conditions, surrounded on all sides by chemical processes, itself represents, in the final analysis, a combination of chemical processes. On the other hand, society is constituted of human beings whose psychological mechanism is resolvable into a system of reflexes. But public life is neither a chemical nor a physiological process, but a social process, which is shaped according to its own laws, and these, in turn, are subject to an objective sociological analysis whose aims should be: to acquire the ability to foresee and to master the fate of society.

Mendeleev's philosophy

In his commentaries to the *Principles of Chemistry*, Mendeleev states:

> There are two basic or positive aims to the scientific study of objects: that of forecast and that of utility . . . The triumph of scientific forecasts would be of very little significance, if they did not in the end lead to direct and general usefulness. Scientific foresight, based on knowledge, endows human mastery with concepts by means of which it is possible to direct the substance of things into a desired channel.

And further Mendeleev adds cautiously:

> Religious and philosophical ideas have thrived and developed for many thousands of years, but those ideas which govern the exact sciences capable of forecasting have been regenerated for only a few centuries and have thus far encompassed only a limited sphere. Scarcely two hundred years have passed since chemistry became part of these sciences. Truly, there lies ahead of us a great deal both in respect to prediction and usefulness to be derived from these sciences.

These cautious, "insinuating" words are very noteworthy on the lips of Mendeleev. Their half-concealed meaning is clearly directed against religion and speculative philosophy. Mendeleev contrasts them to science. Religious ideas—he says in effect—have ruled for thousands of years and the benefits derived from these ideas are not very many; but you can see for yourselves what science has contributed in a short period of time and from this you can judge what its future benefits will be. This is the unquestionable meaning of the foregoing passage, included by Mendeleev in one of his commentaries, and printed in the finest type on page 405 of his *Principles of Chemistry*. Dmitri Ivanovich was a very cautious man and did not intend to quarrel with official public opinion!

Chemistry is a school of revolutionary thought—not because of the existence of a chemistry of explosives; explosives are far from always being revolutionary—but because chemistry is, above all, the science of the transmutation of elements. It is hostile to every kind of absolute or conservative thinking cast in immobile categories.

It is very instructive that Mendeleev, obviously under the pressure of conservative public opinion, defended the principle of stability and immutability in the great processes of chemical transformation. This great scientist insisted with remarkable stubbornness on the immutability of chemical elements and their non-transmutation into one another. He felt the need for firm pillars of support. He said:

> I am Dmitri Ivanovich, and you are Ivan Petrovich. Each of us possesses his own individuality even as the elements.

Mendeleev more than once scornfully denounced dialectics. By this he understood not the dialectic of Hegel or Marx but the superficial art of toying with ideas, half sophistry, half scholasticism. Scientific dialectic embraces general methods of thought which reflect the laws of development. One of these laws is the change of quantity into quality. Chemistry is thoroughly permeated with this law. Mendeleev's whole Periodic Law is built entirely on it, deducing qualitative differences in the elements from quantitative differences in atomic weights. Engels evaluated the discovery of new elements by Mendeleev precisely from this viewpoint. In his sketch, *The General Character of Dialectics as a Science* [in *Dialectics of Nature*], Engels wrote:

> Mendeleev showed that in a series of related elements arranged according to their atomic weights there are several gaps which indicated the existence of other hitherto undiscovered elements. He described in advance the general chemical properties of each of these unknown elements and foretold approximately their relative and atomic weights,

and their atomic place. Mendeleev, unconsciously applying Hegel's law of change of quantity into quality, accomplished a scientific feat which in its audaciousness can be placed alongside Leverrier's discovery of the yet unknown planet Neptune by computing its orbit.

The logic of the Periodic Law, although later modified, proved stronger than the conservative limits which its creator tried to place upon it. The kinship of elements and their mutual metamorphoses can be considered as proved empirically from the hour when, with the help of radioactive elements, it became possible to resolve the atom into its components. In Mendeleev's Periodic Law, in the chemistry of radioactive elements, the dialectic celebrates its own most outstanding victory!

Mendeleev did not have a finished philosophical system. Perhaps he lacked even a desire for one, because it would have brought him into inevitable conflict with his own conservative habits and sympathies.

A dualism upon basic questions of knowledge is to be observed in Mendeleev. Thus it would seem that he tended toward agnosticism, declaring that the "essence" of matter must forever remain beyond our cognition because it is "alien to our knowledge and spirit"(!). But almost immediately, he offers us a remarkable formula for knowledge, which at a single stroke brushes agnosticism aside. In the very same note, Mendeleev says:

> By accumulating gradually their knowledge of matter, men gain mastery over it, and to the degree in which they do so they make ever more precise predictions, verifiable factually, and *there is no way of seeing how there can be a limit to man's knowledge and mastery of matter.*

It is self-evident that if there are no limits to knowledge and mastery of matter, then there is no unknowable "essence." Knowledge which arms us with the ability to forecast all possible changes in matter, and endows us with the necessary power of producing these changes—such knowledge does in fact exhaust the essence of matter. The so-called unknowable "essence" is only a generalization of our inadequate knowledge about matter. It is a pseudonym for our ignorance. Dualistic demarcation of unknown matter from its known properties reminds me of the jocular definition of a gold ring as a hole surrounded by precious metal. It is obvious that if we gain knowledge of the precious metal of phenomena and are able to shape it, then we can remain completely indifferent to the "hole" of the substance; and we gladly make a present of it to the archaic philosophers and theologians.

Major miscalculations

Despite his verbal concessions to agnosticism—"unknowable essence"—Mendeleev is unconsciously a dialectical materialist in his methods and his higher achievements in the sphere of natural science, and especially, chemistry. But his materialism appears as though encased in a conservative shell, shielding its scientific thought from too sharp conflicts with official ideology. This does not imply that Mendeleev artificially created a conservative covering for his methods; he was himself sufficiently bound to the official ideology, and therefore undoubtedly felt an inner compulsion to blunt the razor edge of dialectical materialism.

It is otherwise in the sphere of sociological relationships: The warp of Mendeleev's social philosophy was conservative, but from time to time remarkable surmises, materialist in their essence and revolutionary in their tendency, are woven into this warp. But alongside these surmises there are miscalculations—and what miscalculations!

I shall confine myself to only two. Rejecting all plans for social reorganization as utopian and "Latinist," Mendeleev envisaged a better future only in connection with the development of scientific technology. But he had his own utopia. According to Mendeleev, better days would come when the governments of the major powers of the world realized the need of being strong and arrived at sufficient unanimity among themselves about the need of eliminating all wars, revolutions, and the utopian principles of all anarchists, communists, and other "mailed fists," incapable of understanding the progressive evolution occurring in all mankind. The dawn of this universal concord was already to be perceived in the Hague, Portsmouth, and Morocco Conferences. These instances represent major miscalculations on the part of a great man. History subjected Mendeleev's social utopia to a rigorous test. From the Hague and Portsmouth Conferences blossomed the Russo-Japanese war, the war in the Balkans, the great imperialist slaughter of nations, and a sharp decline in European economy; while from the Moroccan Conference, in particular, there arose the revolting carnage in Morocco which is now being completed under the flag of defense of European civilization. Mendeleev did not see the inner logic of social phenomena, or, more precisely, the inner dialectic of social processes, and was therefore unable to foresee the consequences of the Hague Conference. But, as we know, the significance of science lies, first and foremost, in foresight. If you turn to what the Marxists wrote about the Hague Conference in the days when it was arranged and convoked, then you will easily convince yourselves that the Marxists correctly foresaw the consequences. That is why, in the most critical moment of history, they proved to be armed with the "mailed fist." And there is really nothing lamentable in the fact that the historically rising class, armed with a correct theory of social knowledge and foresight, finally proved to be likewise armed with a fist sufficiently mailed to open a new epoch of human development.

Permit me to cite another miscalculation. Not long before his death, Mendeleev wrote:

> I especially fear for the quality of science and of all enlightenment, and general ethics under "State Socialism."

Were his fears well founded? Even today, the more farsighted students of Mendeleev have begun to see clearly the vast possibilities for the development of scientific and technico-scientific thought thanks to the fact that this thought is, so to speak, nationalized, emancipated from the internecine wars of private property, no longer required to lend itself to bribery of individual proprietors but intended to serve the economic development of the nation as a whole. The network of technico-scientific institutes now being established by the state is only a tiny and so-to-speak material symptom of the limitless possibilities that have been disclosed.

I do not cite these miscalculations in order to cast a slur on the great renown of Dmitri Ivanovich. History has passed its verdict on the main controversial issues, and there is no basis for resuming the dispute. But permit me to state that the major miscalculations of this great man contain an important lesson for students. From the field of chemistry itself there are no *direct* and *immediate* outlets to social perspectives. The objective method of social science is necessary. Marxism is such a method.

Whenever any Marxist attempted to transmute the theory of Marx into a universal master key and ignore all other spheres of learning, Vladimir Ilyich [Lenin] would rebuke him with the expressive phrase: *Komchvanstvo* ["Communist swagger"]. This would mean, in this particular case: Communism is not a substitute for chemistry. But the converse theorem is also true. An attempt to dismiss Marxism with the supposition that chemistry—or the natural sciences in general—is able to decide all questions is a peculiar *Khimchvanstvo* ["*Chemist* swagger"], which in point of theory is no less erroneous, and in point of fact no less pretentious than *Communist* swagger.

Great surmises

Mendeleev did not apply a scientific method to the study of society and its development. A very careful investigator who repeatedly checked himself before permitting his creative imagination to make a great leap forward in the sphere of generalization, Mendeleev remained an empiricist in socio-political problems, combining conjectures with an outlook inherited from the past. I need only say that the surmise was truly Mendeleevian, especially where it touched directly upon the scientific industrial interests of the great scientist.

The very gist of Mendeleev's philosophy might be defined as *technico-scientific optimism*. This optimism, coinciding with the line of development of capitalism, Mendeleev directed against the Narodniks, liberals, and radicals, against the followers of Tolstoy and, in general, against every kind of economic retrogression. Mendeleev believed in the victory of man over all of nature's forces. From this arises his hatred of Malthusianism. This is a remarkable trait in Mendeleev. It passes through all his writings, purely scientific, socio-publicistic, as well as his writings on questions of applied chemistry. Mendeleev greeted with pleasure the fact that the annual increase in Russia's population (1.5%) was higher than the average growth in the whole world. Computing that the population of the world would in 150–200 years reach 10 billion, Mendeleev saw no cause for any alarm. He wrote:

> Not only 10 billion but a population many times that size will find nourishment in this world, not only through the application of labor but also through the persistent inventiveness which governs knowledge. It is, in my opinion, sheer nonsense to fear lack of nourishment, provided the peaceful and active communion of the masses of the people is guaranteed.

Our great chemist and industrial optimist would have hardly listened with sympathy to the recent advice of Professor Keynes of England, who told us during the academic celebrations that we must busy ourselves with limiting the increase in population. Dmitri Ivanovich would have only repeated his old remark: "Or do the new Malthuses wish to arrest this growth? In my opinion, the more, the merrier." Mendeleev's sententious shrewdness very often expressed itself in such deliberately oversimplified formulas.

From   the   same   viewpoint—industrial   optimism—Mendeleev approached the great fetish of conservative idealism, the so-called *national* character. He wrote:

> Wherever agriculture in its primitive forms predominates, a nation is incapable of permanent regular and continuous labor but is able to work only fitfully and in a harvest-time manner. This reflects itself clearly in the customs in the sense that there is a lack of equanimity, calmness, and thriftiness; fidgetiness is to be observed in everything, a happy-go-lucky attitude prevails, along with it extravagance—there is either miserliness or squandering . . . Wherever, side-by-side with agriculture, factory industry has developed on a large scale, where one can see before one's eyes, in addition to sporadic agriculture, the regulated, continuous, uninterrupted labor in the factories, there obtains a correct appraisal of labor, and so on.

Of especial value in these lines is the outlook on national character, not as some primordial fixed element created for all time, but as a product of historical conditions and, more precisely, social forms of production. This is an indubitable, even if only a partial approach to the historical philosophy of Marxism.

In the development of industry Mendeleev sees the instrumentalities of national reeducation, the elaboration of a new, more balanced, more disciplined, and self-controlled national character. If we actually contrast the character of the peasant revolutionary movements with the movement of the proletariat, and especially the role of the proletariat in October and today, then the materialist prediction of Mendeleev will be illumined with sufficient clarity.

Our industrial optimist expressed himself with remarkable lucidity on the elimination of the contradictions between city and country, and every Communist will accept his formulation on this subject. Mendeleev wrote:

> Russian people have begun to migrate to cities in large numbers . . . My view is that it is sheer nonsense to fight against this development; this process will terminate only when the city, on the one side, will spread out to include more parks, gardens, etc., i.e., the aim in the cities will be not only to render life as healthy as possible for all but also to provide sufficient open spaces not only for children's playgrounds and for sport but for every form of recreation; and, on the other hand, in the villages and farms, etc., the non-urban population will so multiply as to require the building of many-storied houses; and there will arise the need for waterworks, street lighting, and other city comforts. In the course of time, all this will lead to the whole countryside (sufficiently densely

populated), becoming inhabited, with dwellings being separated by the so-to-speak kitchen gardens and orchards necessary for the production of foodstuffs, and with factories and plants for manufacturing and altering these products (*Towards an Understanding of Russia*, 1906).

Here, Mendeleev testifies convincingly in favor of the old thesis of socialism: the elimination of the contradiction between city and country. Mendeleev, however, does not here pose the question of changes in social forms of economy. He believes that capitalism will automatically lead to the levelling out of urban and rural conditions through the introduction of higher, more hygienic, and cultural forms of human habitation. Herein lies Mendeleev's mistake. It appears most clearly in the case of England, to which Mendeleev referred with such hope. Long before England could eliminate the contradictions between city and country, her economic development had already landed in a blind alley. Unemployment corrodes her economy. The leaders of English industry see the salvation of society in emigration, in forcing out the surplus population. Even the more "progressive" economist, Mr. Keynes, told us only the other day that the salvaging of English economy lies in Malthusianism! For England, too, the road of overcoming the contradictions between city and country leads through socialism.

There is another surmise made by our industrial optimist. In his last book, Mendeleev wrote:

> After the industrial epoch, there will probably follow in the future a most complex epoch, which, according to my view, would denote a facilitation, or *an extreme simplification of the methods of obtaining food, clothing, and shelter*. Established science should aim at this extreme simplification towards which it has already been partly directed in recent decades (*idem*).

These are remarkable words. Although Dmitri Ivanovich elsewhere makes reservations—against the realization, god forbid, of the utopia of socialists and communists—in these words he nevertheless outlines the technico-scientific perspectives of communism. A development of the productive forces that would lead us to attain extreme simplification of the methods of obtaining food, clothing, and shelter would also clearly lead us to reduce to a minimum the element of coercion in the social structure. With the elimination of the completely useless greediness from social relations, the forms of labor and distribution will assume a communist character. In the transition from socialism to communism, no revolution will be necessary, since the transition wholly depends upon the technical progress of society.

Utilitarian and "pure" science

Mendeleev's industrial optimism constantly directed his thought towards practical industrial questions and problems. In his purely theoretical works, we find his thought directed through the same channels to the problems of economy. There is a dissertation by Mendeleev devoted to the question of diluting alcohol with water, a question which is of economic significance even today. [An ironic reference to the resumption of the state sale of vodka] Mendeleev invented a smokeless powder for the needs of state defense. He occupied himself with a careful study of petroleum, and that, in two directions. One, purely theoretical—the origin of petroleum; and the other, its technico-industrial uses. Here we should always bear in mind Mendeleev's protest against using petroleum simply as a fuel: "Heating can be done with banknotes!" exclaimed our chemist. A confirmed protectionist, Mendeleev took leading part in elaborating tariff policies and wrote his Sensible Tariff Policy from which not a few valuable directives can be quoted even from the standpoint of socialist protectionism.

Problems of northern sea routes stirred his interest shortly before his death. He recommended to young investigators and navigators that they solve the problem of opening up the North Pole. He held that commercial routes must necessarily follow.

> Near that ice there is not a little gold and other minerals, our own America. I should be happy to die at the Pole, for there at least no one "putrefies."

These words have a very modern ring. When the old chemist reflected upon death, he thought about it from the standpoint of putrefaction and dreamt incidentally of dying in an atmosphere of eternal cold.

Mendeleev never tired of repeating that the goal of knowledge was "usefulness." In other words, he approached science from the standpoint of utilitarianism. At the same time, as we know, he insisted on the creative role of disinterested pursuit of knowledge. Why should anyone in particular seek for commercial routes by roundabout ways to reach the North Pole? Because reaching the Pole is a problem of disinterested research capable of arousing scientific research-sport passions. Is there not a contradiction between this and the affirmation that science's goal is usefulness? Not at all. Science is a function of society and not of an individual. From the socio-historic standpoint, science is utilitarian. But this does not at all mean that each scientist approaches problems of research from a utilitarian point of view. No! Most often scholars are motivated by their passion for knowledge, and the more significant a man's discovery, the less is he able, as a general rule, to foresee in advance its possible practical applications. Thus, the disinterested passion of a research worker does not contradict the utilitarian meaning of each science any more than the personal self-sacrifice of a revolutionary fighter contradicts the utilitarian aim of those class needs which he serves.

Mendeleev was able to combine perfectly his passion for knowledge for its own sake with incessant preoccupation about raising the technical power of mankind. That is why the two wings of this Congress—the representatives of theoretical and of applied branches of chemistry—stand with equal right under the banner of Mendeleev. We must educate the new generation of scientists in the spirit of this harmonious coordination of pure scientific research with industrial tasks. Mendeleev's faith in the unlimited possibilities for knowledge, prediction, and mastery of matter must become the scientific credo for the chemists of the socialist fatherland.

The German physiologist, Du Bois Reymond, once envisaged philosophic thought as departing from the scene of the class struggle and crying out: "*Ignorabimus*!" That is, "we shall never know, we shall never understand!" And scientific thought, linking its fate with the fate of the rising class, replies:

"You lie! The impenetrable does not exist for conscious thought! We will reach everything! We will master everything! We will rebuild everything!"

RADIO, SCIENCE, TECHNIQUE, AND SOCIETY

Leon Trotsky
March 1, 1926

In this speech, delivered at the First All-Union Congress of the Society of Friends of Radio, Trotsky again emphasizes the importance of studying dialectical materialism. His profound understanding of the dialectical interconnection between the socialist revolution and the march of scientific and intellectual progress, as well as his boundless revolutionary optimism are on full display. While some of the science and conclusions have been outpaced by more recent discoveries, Trotsky's prescient insights are astonishingly ahead of their time. This speech also raises many issues relevant to the transitional period between capitalism and communism, especially in a backwards country encircled by imperialism. By presenting an unalloyed picture of the backwardness from which Russia was starting and the need to catch up to the West, Trotsky inspired his listeners to fight for genuine socialism in the USSR and around the world. This was especially vital in the context of the growing conservatism of the Stalinist bureaucracy and the rise of the anti-Marxist concept of socialism in one country.

A new epoch of scientific and technical thought

Comrades, I have just come from the Turkmenistan jubilee celebrations. This sister republic of ours in Central Asia today commemorates the anniversary of its foundation. It might seem that the subject of Turkmenistan is remote from that of radio technique and from the Society of Friends of Radio, but in fact, there is a very close connection between them. Just because Turkmenistan is far, it ought to be near to the participants in this Congress. Given the immensity of our federative country, which includes Turkmenistan—a land covering five to six hundred thousand versts, bigger than Germany, bigger than France, bigger than any European State, a land where the population is scattered among oases, where there are no roads—given these conditions, radio communication might have been expressly invented for the benefit of Turkmenistan, to link it with us.

We are a backward country; the whole of our Union, including even the most advanced parts, is extremely backward from the technical standpoint, and at the same time we have no right to remain in this backward state, because we are building socialism, and socialism presupposes and demands a high level of technique. While constructing roads through the countryside, improving them and building bridges to carry them (and how terribly we need more such bridges!), we are obliged at the same time to catch up with the most advanced countries in the field of the latest scientific and technical achievements—among others, first and foremost, that of radio technique. The invention of the radiotelegraph and radiotelephone might have occurred especially to convince the bilious skeptics among us of the unlimited possibilities inherent in science and technique, to show that all the achievements that science has registered so far are only a brief introduction to what awaits us in the future.

Let us take the last twenty-five years—just a quarter of a century—and recall what conquests in the sphere of human technique have been accomplished before our eyes, the eyes of the older generation to which I belong. I remember—and probably I am not the only one among those present to do so, though the majority here are young people—the time when motorcars were still rarities. There was no talk, even, of the airplane at the end of the last century. In the whole world there were, I think, 5,000 motorcars, whereas now there are about 20 million, of which 18 million are in America alone—15 million light cars and three million trucks. The motorcar has before our eyes become a means of transport of first-class importance.

I can still recall the confused sounds and rustlings which I heard when I first listened to a phonograph. I was then in the first form at secondary school. Some enterprising man who was travelling around the cities of south Russia with a phonograph arrived in Odessa and demonstrated it to us. And now the gramophone, grandchild of the phonograph, is one of the most commonplace features of domestic life.

And aircraft? In 1902, that is, twenty-three years ago, the British man of letters, Wells—many of you will know his science fiction novels—published a book [*Anticipations*] in which he wrote, almost in so many words, that in his personal opinion—and he considered himself a bold and adventurous fantasist in technical matters—approximately in the middle of this present twentieth century, there would be not merely invented, but also to some degree perfected, a flying machine heavier than air that could be used for operations of war. This book was written in 1902. We know that aircraft played a definite part in the imperialist war—and there are still twenty-five years to go to mid-century!

And cinematography? That's also no small matter. Not so very long ago it didn't exist; many present will recall that time. Nowadays, however, it would be impossible to imagine our cultural life without the cinema.

All these innovations have come into our lives in the last quarter of a century, during which men have, in addition, accomplished also a few trifles such as imperialist wars, when cities and entire countries have been laid waste and millions of people exterminated. In the course of this quarter-century more than one revolution has taken place, though on a smaller scale than ours, in a whole series of countries. In twenty-five years, life has been invaded by the motorcar, the airplane, the gramophone, the cinema, radiotelegraphy, and radiotelephony. If you remember only the fact that, according to the hypothetical calculations of scholars, not less than 250,000 years were needed for man to pass from a simple hunter's way of life to stock breeding, this little fragment of time, twenty-five years, appears as a mere nothing. What does this fragment of time show us? That technique has entered a new phase, that its rate of development is getting continually faster and faster.

Liberal scholars—now they are no more—commonly used to depict the whole of the history of mankind as a continuous line of progress. This was wrong. The line of progress is curved, broken, zigzagging. Culture now advances, now declines. There was the culture of ancient Asia, there was the culture of antiquity, of Greece and Rome, then European culture began to develop, and now American culture is rising in skyscrapers. What has been retained from the cultures of the past? What has been accumulated as a result of historical progress? Technical process, methods of research. Scientific and technical thought, not without interruptions and failures, marches on. Even if you meditate on those far-off days when the sun will cease to shine and all forms of life die out upon the earth, nevertheless there is still plenty of time before us. I think that in the centuries immediately ahead of us, scientific and technical thought, in the hands of socialistically organized society, will advance without zigzags, breaks, or failures. It has matured to such an extent, it has become sufficiently independent and stands so firmly on its feet, that it will go forward in a planned and steady way, along with the growth of the productive forces with which it is linked in the closest degree.

A triumph of dialectical materialism

It is the task of science and technique to make matter subject to man, together with space and time, which are inseparable from matter. True, there are certain idealist books—not of a clerical character, but philosophical ones—wherein you can read that time and space are categories of our minds, that they result from the requirements of our thinking, and that nothing actually corresponds to them in reality. But it is difficult to agree with this view. If any idealist philosopher, instead of arriving in time to catch the 9:00 p.m. train, should turn up two minutes late, he would see the tail of the departing train and would be convinced by his own eyes that time and space are inseparable from material reality. The task is to diminish this space, to overcome it, to economize time, to prolong human life, to register past time, to raise life to a higher level, and enrich it. This is the reason for the struggle with space and time, at the basis of which lies the struggle to subject matter to man—matter, which constitutes the foundation not only of everything that really exists, but also of all imagination. Our struggle for scientific achievements is itself only a very complete system of reflexes, i.e., of phenomena of a physiological order, which have grown up on an anatomical basis, which in its turn has developed from the inorganic world, from chemistry and physics. Every science is an accumulation of knowledge, based on experience relating to matter, to its properties, of generalized understanding of how to subject this matter to the interests and needs of man.

The more science learns about matter, however, the more "unexpected" properties of matter it discovers, the more zealously does the decadent philosophical thought of the bourgeoisie try to use the new properties or manifestations of matter to show that matter is not matter. The progress of natural science in the mastering of matter is paralleled by a philosophical struggle against materialism. Certain philosophers and even some scientists have tried to utilize the phenomena of radioactivity for the purpose of struggle against materialism: There used to be atoms, elements, which were the basis of matter and of materialist thinking, but now this atom has come to pieces in our hands, has broken up into electrons, and at the very beginning of the popularity of the electronic theory, a struggle even flared up in our party around the question of whether the electrons testify for or against materialism. Whoever is interested in these questions will read with great profit Vladimir Ilyich's work on *Materialism and Empiriocriticism*. In fact, neither the "mysterious" phenomena of radioactivity nor the no less "mysterious" phenomena of wireless transmission of electromagnetic waves do the slightest damage to materialism.

The phenomena of radioactivity, which have led to the necessity of thinking of the atom as a complex system of still utterly "unimaginable" particles, can be directed against materialism only by a desperate specimen of a vulgar materialist who recognizes as matter only that which he can feel with his bare hands. But this is sensualism, not materialism. Both the molecule, the ultimate chemical particle, and the atom, the ultimate physical particle, are inaccessible to our sight and touch. But our organs of sense, though the instruments with which knowledge begins, are not at all, however, the last resort of knowledge. The human eye and the human ear are very primitive pieces of apparatus, inadequate to reach even the basic elements of physical and chemical phenomena. To the extent that in our thinking about reality we are guided merely by the everyday findings of our sense organs, it is hard for us to imagine that the atom is a complex system, that it has a nucleus, that around this nucleus electrons move, and that from this there result the phenomena of radioactivity. Our imagination in general accustoms itself only with difficulty to new conquests of cognition. When Copernicus, in the sixteenth century, discovered that it was not the sun that moved around the earth but the earth around the sun, this seemed fantastic, and conservative imagination still to this day finds it hard to adjust itself to this fact. We observe this in the case of illiterate people and in each fresh generation of schoolchildren. Yet we, people of some education, despite the fact that it appears to us, too, that the sun moves around the earth, nevertheless do not doubt that in reality things happen the other way round, for this is confirmed by extensive observation of astronomical phenomena. The human brain is a product of the development of matter, and at the same time is an instrument for the cognition of this matter; gradually it adjusts itself to its function, tries to overcome its limitations, creates ever new scientific methods, imagines ever more complex and exact instruments, checks its work again and yet again, step by step penetrates into previously unknown depths, changes our conception of matter, without, though, ever breaking away from this basis of all that exists.

Radioactivity, as we have already mentioned, in no way constitutes a threat to materialism, and it is at the same time a magnificent triumph of dialectics. Until recently, scientists supposed that there were in the world about ninety elements, which were beyond analysis and could not be transformed one into another; so to speak, a carpet for the universe woven from ninety threads of different qualities and colors. Such a notion contradicted materialist dialectics, which speaks of the unity of matter and, what is even more important, of the transformability of the elements of matter. Our great chemist, Mendeleev, to the end of his life was unwilling to reconcile himself to the idea that one element could be transformed into another; he firmly believed in the stability of these "individualities," although the phenomena of radioactivity were already known to him. But nowadays, no scientist believes in the unchangeability of the elements. Using the phenomena of radioactivity, chemists have succeeded in carrying out a direct "execution" of eight or nine elements and, along with this, the execution of the last remnants of metaphysics in materialism, for now the transformability of one chemical element into another has been proved experimentally. The phenomena of radioactivity have thus led to a supreme triumph of dialectical thought.

The phenomena of radio technique are based on wireless transmission of electromagnetic waves. Wireless does not at all mean nonmaterial transmission. Light does not come only from lamps but also from the sun, being also transmitted without the aid of wires. We are fully accustomed to the wireless transmission of light over quite respectable distances. We are greatly surprised, though, when we begin to transmit sound over a very much shorter distance, with the aid of those very same electromagnetic waves which underlie the phenomena of light. All these are phenomena of matter, material processes—waves and whirlwinds—in space and time. The new discoveries and their technical applications show only that matter is a great deal more heterogeneous and richer in potentialities than we had thought hitherto. But, as before, nothing is made out of nothing.

The most outstanding of our scientists say that science, and physics in particular, has in recent times arrived at a turning point. Not so very long ago, they say, we still approached matter, as it were, "phenomenally," i.e., from the angle of observing its manifestations, but now we are beginning to penetrate ever deeper into the very interior of matter, to learn its structure, and we shall soon be able to regulate it "from within." A good physicist would, of course, be able to talk about this better than I can. The phenomena of radioactivity are leading us to the problem of releasing intra-atomic energy. The atom contains within itself a mighty hidden energy, and the greatest task of physics consists in pumping out this energy, pulling out the cork, so that this hidden energy may burst forth in a fountain. Then the possibility will be opened up of replacing coal and oil by atomic energy, which will also become the basic motive power. This is not at all a hopeless task. And what prospects it opens before us! This alone gives us the right to declare that scientific and technical thought is approaching a great turning point, that the revolutionary epoch in the development of human society will be accompanied by a revolutionary epoch in the sphere of the cognition of matter and the mastering of it . . . Unbounded technical possibilities will open out before liberated mankind.

Radio, militarism, superstition

Perhaps, though, it is time to get closer to political and practical questions. What is the relation between radio technique and the social system? Is it socialist or capitalist? I raise the question because a few days ago the famous Italian, Marconi, said in Berlin that the transmission of pictures at a distance by means of Hertzian waves is a tremendous gift to pacifism, foretelling the speedy end of the militarist epoch. Why should this be? These ends of epochs have been proclaimed so often that the pacifists have got all ends and beginnings mixed up. The fact that we shall be able to see at a great distance is supposed to put an end to wars! Certainly, the invention of a means of transmitting a living image over a great distance is a very attractive task, for it is insulting to the optic nerve that the auditory one is at present, thanks to radio, in a privileged position in this respect. But to suppose that from this there must result the end of wars is merely absurd, and shows only that in the case of great men like Marconi, just as with the majority of people who are specialists in a particular field—even, one may say, with the majority of people in general—scientific thinking lays hold of the brain, to put the matter crudely, not as a whole, but only in small sectors. Just as inside the hull of a steamship, impenetrable partitions are placed so that in the event of an accident, the ship will not sink all at once, so also in man's consciousness there are numberless impenetrable partitions: in one sector, or even in a dozen sectors, you can find the most revolutionary scientific thinking, but beyond the partition lies philistinism of the highest degree. This is the great significance of Marxism, as thought which generalizes all human experience, that it helps to break down these internal partitions of consciousness through the integrity of its world outlook. But, to get closer to the matter in hand—why, precisely, if one can see one's enemy, must this result in the liquidation of war? In earlier times, whenever there was war, the adversaries saw each other face to face. That was how it was in Napoleon's day. Only the creation of long-distance weapons gradually pushed the adversaries further apart and led to a situation in which they were firing at unseen targets. And if the invisible becomes visible, this will only mean that the Hegelian triad has triumphed in this sphere as well—after the thesis and the antithesis has come the "synthesis" of mutual extermination.

I remember the time when men wrote that the development of aircraft would put an end to war, because it would draw the whole population into military operations, would bring to ruin the economic and cultural life of entire countries, etc. In fact, however, the invention of a flying machine heavier than air opened a new and crueler chapter in the history of militarism. There is no doubt that now, too, we are approaching the beginning of a still more frightful and bloody chapter. Technique and science have their own logic—the logic of the cognition of nature and the mastering of it in the interests of man. But technique and science develop, not in a vacuum, but in human society, which consists of classes. The ruling class, the possessing class, controls technique and through it controls nature. Technique in itself cannot be called either militaristic or pacifistic. In a society in which the ruling class is militaristic, technique is in the service of militarism.

It is considered unquestionable that technique and science undermine superstition. But the class character of society sets substantial limits here too. Take America. There, church sermons are broadcast by radio, which means that the radio is serving as a means of spreading prejudices. Such things don't happen here, I think—the Society of Friends of Radio watch over this, I hope? (*Laughter and applause*) Under the socialist system science and technique as a whole will undoubtedly be directed against religious prejudices, against superstition, which reflects the weakness of man before man or before nature. What, indeed, does a "voice from heaven" amount to when there is being broadcast all over the country a voice from the Polytechnical Museum! (*Laughter*)

We must not lag behind!

Victory over poverty and superstition is ensured to us, provided we go forward technically. We must not lag behind other countries. The first slogan which every friend of radio must fix in his mind is: don't lag behind! Yet we are extraordinarily backward in relation to the advanced capitalist countries; this backwardness is the main inheritance that we have received from the past. What are we to do? If, comrades, the situation were to be such that the capitalist countries continued to develop steadily and go forward, as before the war, then we should have to ask ourselves anxiously: shall we be able to catch up? And if we do not catch up, shall we not be crushed? To this we say: we cannot forget that scientific and technical thought in bourgeois society has attained its highest degree of development in that period when, economically, bourgeois society is getting more and more into a blind alley and is beginning to decay. European economy is not going forward. In the last fifteen years, Europe has become poorer, not richer. But its inventions and discoveries have been colossal. While ravaging Europe and devastating huge areas of the continent, the war at the same time gave a tremendous fillip to scientific and technical thought, which was suffocating in the clutches of decaying capitalism.

If, however, we take the material accumulations of technique, i.e., not that technique which exists in men's heads, but that which is embodied in machinery, factories, mills, railways, telegraphic, and telephone services, etc., then here, above all, it is plain that we are fearfully backward. It would be more correct to say that this backwardness would be fearful for us if we did not possess the immense advantage which consists in the Soviet organization of society, which makes possible a planned development of technique and science, while Europe is suffocating in its own contradictions. Our present backwardness in all spheres must not, however, be covered up, but must be measured with a severely objective yardstick, without losing heart but also without deceiving oneself for a single moment. How is a country transformed into a single economic and cultural whole? By means of communications: railways, steamships, postal services, the telegraph, and the telephone—and now radiotelegraphy and radiotelephone.

How do we stand in these fields? We are fearfully backward. In America, the railway network amounts to 405,000 kilometers, in Britain to nearly 40,000, in Germany to 54,000, but here to only 69,000 kilometers—and that with our vast distances! But it is much more instructive to compare the loads that are carried, in these countries and here, measuring them in ton-kilometers, i.e., taking as the unit one ton transported over one kilometer's distance. The USA last year carried 600 million ton-kilometers, we carried 48,500,000, Britain 30 million, Germany 69 million; i.e., the USA carried ten times as much as Germany, twenty times as much as Britain, and two or three times as much as the whole of Europe along with ourselves.

Let us take the postal service, one of the basic means of cultural communication. According to information provided by the Commissariat of Posts and Telegraphs, based on the latest figures, expenditure on postal communications in the USA last year amounted to a billion and a quarter rubles, which means 9 rubles 40 kopecks per head of population. In our country, postal expenditure comes to 75 million, which means 33 kopecks per head. There's a difference for you—between 9 rubles 40 kopecks, and 33 kopecks!

The figures for telegraph and telephone services are still more striking. The total length of telegraph wires in America is three million kilometers, in Britain half a million kilometers, and here 616,000 kilometers. But the length of telegraph wires is comparatively small in America because they have a lot of telephone wires—60 million kilometers of them, whereas in Britain there are only six million, and here only 311,000 kilometers. Let us neither mock at ourselves, comrades, nor take fright, but firmly keep these figures in mind; we must measure and compare, so as to catch up and surpass, at all costs! (*Applause*) The number of telephones—another good index of the level of culture—is in America 14 million, in Britain one million, and here 190,000. For every hundred persons in America there are thirteen telephones, in Britain two and a bit, and in our country one-tenth, or, in other words, in America the number of telephones in relation to the number of inhabitants is 130 times as great as here.

As regards radio, I do not know how much we spend per day on it—I think the Society of Friends of Radio should work this out—but in America they spend a million dollars, i.e., two million rubles a day on radio, which makes about 700 million a year.

These figures harshly reveal our backwardness. But they also reveal the importance that radio, as the cheapest form of communication, can and must have in our huge peasant country. We cannot seriously talk about socialism without having in mind the transformation of the country into a single whole, linked together by means of all kinds of communications. In order to introduce it we must first and foremost be able to talk to the most remote parts of the country, such as Turkmenistan. For Turkmenistan, with which I began my remarks today, produces cotton, and upon Turkmenistan's labors depends the work of the textile mills of the Moscow and Ivanovo-Voznesensk regions. For direct and immediate communication with all points in the country, one of the most important means is radio; that is, of course, if radio in our country is not to be a toy for the upper strata of the townspeople, who are established in more privileged conditions than others, but is to become an instrument of economic and cultural communication between town and country.

Town and country

Let us not forget that between town and country in the USSR there are monstrous contradictions, material and cultural, which as a whole we have inherited from capitalism. In that difficult period we went through when the town took refuge in the country and the country gave a *pood* of bread in exchange for an overcoat, some nails, or a guitar, the town looked quite pitiful in comparison with the comfortable countryside. But in proportion as the elementary foundations of our economy have been restored, in particular our industry, the tremendous technical and cultural advantages of the town over the country have reasserted themselves. We have done a great deal in the sphere of politics and law to mitigate and even out the contrasts between town and country. But in technique we have really not made a single big step forward so far. And we cannot build socialism with the countryside in this technically deprived condition and the peasantry culturally destitute. Developed socialism means above all technical and cultural levelling as between town and country, i.e., the dissolving of both town and country into homogeneous economic and cultural conditions. That is why the mere bringing closer together of town and country is a question of life and death for us.

While creating the industry and institutions of the town, capitalism held the country down and could not but do this—it could always obtain the necessary foodstuffs and raw materials not only from its own countryside but also from the backward lands across the ocean or from the colonies, produced by cheap peasant labor. The war and the postwar disturbances, the blockade and the danger that it might be repeated, and finally the instability of bourgeois society, have compelled the bourgeoisie to take a closer interest in the peasantry. Recently we have heard bourgeois and Social Democratic politicians more than once talk about the link with the peasantry. Briand, in his discussion with Comrade Rakovsky about the debts, laid emphasis on the needs of the small landholders, and in particular the French peasants. Otto Bauer, the Austrian "Left" Menshevik, in a recent speech spoke about the exceptional importance of the "link" with the countryside. Above all, our old acquaintance, Lloyd George—who, true, we have begun to forget a little—when he was still in circulation organized in Britain a special land league in the interests of the link with the peasantry. I don't know what form the link would take in British conditions, but on Lloyd George's tongue the word certainly sounds knavish enough. At all events, I would not recommend that he be elected patron of any rural district, nor an honorary member of the Society of Friends of Radio, for he would, without fail, put over some swindle or other. (*Applause*)

Whereas in Europe the revival of the question of the link with the countryside is, on the one hand, a parliamentary-political maneuver, and, on the other, a significant symptom of the tottering of the bourgeois regime, for us the problem of economic and cultural links with the countryside is a matter of life and death in the full sense of the word. The technical basis of this linkage must be electrification, and this is directly and immediately connected with the problem of the introduction of radio on a wide scale. In order to approach the fulfilment of the simplest and most urgent tasks it is necessary that all parts of the Soviet Union be able to talk to each other, that the country be able to listen to the town; as to its technically better-equipped and more cultured elder brother. Without the fulfillment of this task, the spread of radio will remain a plaything for the privileged circles of the townspeople.

It was stated in your report that in our country three-quarters of the rural population do not know what radio is, while the remaining quarter know it only through special demonstrations during festivals, etc. Our program must provide that every village, not only should know what radio is, but should have its own radio receiving station.

Where are we going?

The diagram attached to your report shows the distribution of members of your Society according to social class. Workers make up 20%—that's the small figure with the hammer; peasants 13%—the still smaller figure with the scythe; office workers 49%—the respectable figure carrying a briefcase; and then comes 18% of "others"—it's not stated who they are exactly, but there is a drawing of a gentleman in a bowler hat, with a cane and a white handkerchief in his breast pocket, evidently a Nepman. I don't suggest that these people with handkerchiefs should be driven out of the Society of Friends of Radio—but they ought to be surrounded and besieged more strongly, so that radio may be made cheaper for the people with hammers and scythes. (*Applause*) Still less am I inclined to think that the number of members with briefcases should be mechanically reduced. But it is necessary, though, that the two basic groups be increased, at all costs! (*Applause*) 20% workers—that's very few; 13% peasants—that's shamefully few. The number of people in bowler hats is nearly equal to the number of workers—18%—and exceeds the number of peasants, who make up only 13%! It is a flagrant breach of the Soviet constitution. It is necessary to take steps to ensure that in the next year or two, peasants become about 40%, workers 45%, office workers 10%, and what are called "others"—5%. That will be a normal proportion, fully in keeping with the spirit of the Soviet constitution.

The conquest of the village by radio is a task for the next few years, very closely connected with the task of eliminating illiteracy and electrifying the country, and to some extent a precondition for the fulfillment of these tasks. Each province should set out to conquer the countryside with a definite program of radio development. Place the map for a new war on the table! From each provincial center, first of all, every one of the larger villages should be conquered for radio. It is necessary that our illiterate and semiliterate village, even before it manages to master reading and writing as it ought, should be able to have access to culture through the radio, which is the most democratic medium of broadcasting information and knowledge. It is necessary that by means of the radio the peasant shall be able to feel himself a citizen of our Union, a citizen of the whole world.

Upon the peasantry depends to a large extent, not only the development of our own industry—that is more than clear—upon our peasantry and the growth of its economy there also depends, to a certain degree, the revolution in the countries of Europe. What worries the European workers—and that not by accident—in their struggle for power, what the Social Democrats utilize cleverly for their reactionary purposes, is the dependence of Europe's industry upon countries across the oceans as regards foodstuffs and raw materials. America provides grain and cotton, Egypt cotton, India sugarcane, the islands of the Malay Archipelago rubber, etc., etc. The danger is that an American blockade, say, might subject the industry of Europe, during the most difficult months and years of the proletarian revolution, to a famine of foodstuffs and raw materials.

In these conditions, an increased export of our Soviet grain and raw material of all kinds is a mighty revolutionary factor in relation to the countries of Europe. Our peasants must be made aware that every extra sheaf that they thresh and send abroad is so much additional weight in the scales of the revolutionary struggle of the European proletariat, for this sheaf reduces the dependence of Europe upon capitalist America. The Turkmen peasants who are raising cotton must be linked with the textile workers of Ivanovo-Voznesensk and Moscow, and also with the revolutionary proletariat of Europe. A network of radio receiving stations must be established in our country such as will make it possible for our peasants to live the life of the working people of Europe and the whole world, to participate in it from day to day. It is necessary that on that day when the workers of Europe take possession of the radio stations, when the proletariat of France take over the Eiffel Tower and announce from its summit in all the languages of Europe that they are the masters of France (*Applause*), that on that day and hour not only the workers of our cities and industries, but also the peasants of our remotest villages, may be able to reply to the call of the European workers—"Do you hear us?"—"We hear you, brothers, and we will help you!" (*Applause*) Siberia will help with fats, grain, and raw materials, the Kuban and the Don with grain and meat, Uzbekistan and Turkmenistan will contribute their cotton. This will show that our radio communications have brought nearer the transformation of Europe into a single economic organization. The development of a radiotelegraphic network is, among so many other things, a preparation for the moment when the people of Europe and Asia shall be united in a Soviet Union of Socialist Peoples. (*Applause*)

Lightning Source UK Ltd.
Milton Keynes UK
UKHW021546260821
389503UK00006B/47